C000125491

Egypt and the Struggle for Power in Sudan

For decades, the doctrine of the Unity of the Nile Valley united Egyptians of a variety of political and nationalist backgrounds. Many Egyptians regarded Sudan as an integral part of their homeland, and therefore battled to rid the entire Nile Valley of British imperialism and unite its inhabitants under the Egyptian crown. Here, Rami Ginat provides a vital and important revised account of the history of Egypt's colonialist struggle and their efforts to prove categorically that the Nile Valley constituted a single territorial unit. These were clustered around several dominant theoretical layers: history, geography, economy, culture, and ethnography. This book, for both Middle Eastern and African historians, uses a mixture of Arabic and English sources to critically examine the central stages in the historical development of Egypt's doctrine, concentrating on the defining decade (1943–1953) that first witnessed both the pinnacle of the doctrine's struggle and the subsequent shattering of a consensual nationalist dream.

RAMI GINAT is a professor of Middle Eastern politics and is heading the Department of Political Studies at Bar-Ilan University. He is a leading scholar in Egyptian history and Cold War politics in the Middle East, and has published many books and articles in these fields, including *A History of Egyptian Communism* (2011). His work pays careful attention to the mutual feedback between politics and ideas.

Egypt and the Struggle for Power in Sudan

From World War II to Nasserism

Rami Ginat

Bar-Ilan University, Israel

CAMBRIDGE
UNIVERSITY PRESS

CAMBRIDGE
UNIVERSITY PRESS

University Printing House, Cambridge CB2 8BS, United Kingdom

One Liberty Plaza, 20th Floor, New York, NY 10006, USA

477 Williamstown Road, Port Melbourne, VIC 3207, Australia

4843/24, 2nd Floor, Ansari Road, Daryaganj, Delhi – 110002, India

79 Anson Road, #06–04/06, Singapore 079906

Cambridge University Press is part of the University of Cambridge.

It furthers the University's mission by disseminating knowledge in the pursuit of education, learning, and research at the highest international levels of excellence.

www.cambridge.org
Information on this title: www.cambridge.org/9781107197930
DOI: 10.1017/9781108181952

First published 2017

Printed in the United Kingdom by Clays, St Ives plc

A catalogue record for this publication is available from the British Library.

Library of Congress Cataloging-in-Publication Data
Names: Ginat, Rami, author.
Title: Egypt and the struggle for power in Sudan : from World War II to Nasserism / Rami Ginat, Bar-Ilan University, Israel.
Description: Cambridge, United Kingdom : Cambridge University Press, 2018. | Includes bibliographical references and index.
Identifiers: LCCN 2017013415| ISBN 9781107197930 (hardback : alk. paper) | ISBN 9781316647929 (pbk. : alk. paper)
Subjects: LCSH: Egypt–Foreign relations–Sudan. | Sudan–Foreign relations–Egypt. | Sudan–Foreign public opinion, Egyptian. | World War, 1939-1945–Territorial questions–Egypt. | Imperialism. | Egypt–Politics and government–1882-1952. | Sudan–Politics and government–1899-1956.
Classification: LCC DT82.5.S8 G56 2018 | DDC 327.62062409/045–dc23 LC record available at https://lccn.loc.gov/2017013415

ISBN 978-1-107-19793-0 Hardback

For Lydia, Richard, and the staff of Pennyhooks Farm

Contents

Tables

Acknowledgments

Studying the modern history of the Nile valley, let alone the ways its peoples perceived it, requires a thorough study in Egypt – the "gift of the Nile" – and in many other archives and libraries scattered in several countries located on four continents. It is my pleasure to acknowledge the generosity and assistance extended to me throughout my research work by the personnel of the archives and libraries cited in the book's bibliography.

This prolonged study could not have been carried out without the generous research grants (390/08 and 1001/12) extended to me by the Israel Science Foundation (ISF), and I thank them for that. St. Cross College of the University of Oxford hosted me throughout my sabbatical year (2015–2016) during which I completed my book. I would like to thank the college and its staff for their kind hospitality, particularly my friend and colleague Stanley Ulijaszek who sponsored me there. I also would like to thank my friends and colleagues in the Department of Political Studies, Bar-Ilan University, for their thoughtfulness. Special thanks to Amikam Nachmani for his friendship and kindness.

I have profited significantly from the benevolence and assistance of many people, and it is a great pleasure to thank them for that. Special thanks to the late 'Abd al-Hamid 'Uthman who assisted me in the initial stages of my research work in Egypt. I was deeply saddened by his untimely death in early 2013. I also would like to acknowledge the assistance extended to me by my friend Ursula Wokoeck in the later stage of my study. Her remarks and comments were constructive and instructive. My friend Asaf Maliach was very helpful throughout, and Dima Course and Jesse Weinberg helped along the way. I also would like to include my friends and colleagues Israel Gershoni and Haggai Erlich of Tel-Aviv University, and Yehudit Ronen of my department for sharing their knowledge with me.

It has been a pleasure working with Maria Marsh and Cambridge University Press. Maria guided me patiently and diligently throughout the process of publication, and I thank her for that. I also thank the anonymous reviewers of my manuscript for their constructive and illuminating remarks and suggestions that helped bring this book to its present form.

While working on this book, my wife and I became involved along with Lydia Otter and Richard Hurford of Pennyhooks Farm in developing our vision of expanding their Autism Care Farm in Oxfordshire into a residential provision. Pennyhooks Farm has enabled young people with autism and complex needs to experience lives that are meaningful and purposeful. It has been a unique and fortunate experience for us to be part of such a vital project with people who exemplify the full meaning of altruism. I thank them wholeheartedly on behalf of my son Oliver, and this book is dedicated to them.

Introduction

For decades, the doctrine of the unity of the Nile valley united Egyptians of all political and nationalist stripes. Egyptians regarded Sudan as an integral part of their homeland, and as such, they battled to rid the entire Nile valley of British imperialism and subsequently unite its inhabitants under the Egyptian crown. This book provides a revised account of the history of that doctrine. It offers a critical examination of the central stages in the historical development of the issue, while concentrating on the defining decade (1943–1953) that witnessed two contradictory currents: the pinnacle of Egypt's struggle to advance its doctrine of the unity of the Nile valley, and the demise of that very doctrine and the subsequent shattering of a consensual nationalist dream.

Ever since Muhammad 'Ali's forces occupied Sudan in 1820–1821, Egyptians considered Sudan as an integral part of Egypt. The occupation of Sudan was derived from purely imperialistic considerations – political, strategic, and economic. Muhammad 'Ali, who arrived in Egypt in 1801 as a young Ottoman officer, managed cunningly and ruthlessly to be appointed Ottoman governor of the province of Egypt in 1805. After he consolidated his hegemony over Egypt, he decided to build up his own empire. The occupation of Sudan was part of his expansionist policy to establish regional hegemony. From that stage on, Egyptians regarded Sudan as "our historic fatherland" – an inseparable part of Egypt throughout history.[1]

Egypt's involvement in modern time – directly and indirectly – with Sudan and the Sudanese may be divided into several major historical phases: first, from its occupation until the rise of the Mahdi movement in the early 1880s; second, after a short period of Mahdi rule, Sudan was reconquered by Egyptian and British forces (1896–1898), and in January 1899 the two countries concluded the condominium treaty, establishing dual Anglo–Egyptian rule over Sudan – a British imperialist invention; and third, the condominium epoch (1899–1953) and the transitional period of Sudanese self-government (1953–1956), which led to independent Sudan.

1

The case of Sudan was quite unique: an internally divided country (north and south) that was ruled (1899–1956) by two foreign imperialist powers, one regional and the other global – Egypt and Britain. Formally, Egypt ruled Sudan on behalf of the Ottoman Empire until 1914. However, practically speaking, prior to British occupation (1882), Egypt was an autonomous entity with a separate army and independent foreign and domestic policies. Common wisdom suggests that colonialism "is a form of domination – the control by individuals or groups over the territory and/or behavior of other individuals or groups." It is also often seen as a form of economic exploitation and a "culture-change process."[2]

Why were Egyptians so determined to control Sudan? As this study shows there were several reasons. A central one was control over the Nile, Egypt's lifeline, which passes through Sudan. Controlling Sudan would make it easier to closely monitor the flow of the Nile water and safeguard its sources from neighboring countries. Economically, the utilization and exploitation of Sudan's natural resources and agrarian land were weighty considerations. Furthermore, Sudan could have accommodated substantial Egyptian emigration, especially among peasants, which could solve one of Egypt's most acute problems: its high population density. Moreover, Egyptian writers spoke of a cultural and civilizational mission, giving expression to fantasies of controlling and civilizing Sudan, especially the non-Arab and non-Muslim southern Sudan, where the population was diverse in ethnic and linguistic terms.

Nevertheless, neither Egyptian nor British rule over Sudan may be characterized as "settler colonialism," according to which "settlers in significant number migrate permanently to the colony from the colonizing power." Imperialism is a more suitable definition as it suggests that only "few, if any, permanent settlers from the imperial homeland migrate to the colony."[3] Egyptian emigration into Sudan was made impossible as Britain as the dominant partner in the condominium exercised full control over the influx of Egyptians into Sudan.

Anti-British sentiments in Egypt had grown constantly throughout the condominium period. The unity of the Nile valley was a national consensual issue uniting "territorialists and supra-Egyptianist spokesmen alike."[4] Nevertheless, their vantage points of a united Egyptian–Sudanese country differed. Whereas territorial nationalists emphasized the centrality of material factors, Islamic nationalists considered both Egypt and Sudan as an integral part of *al-Umma al-Islamiyya*.[5]

The Egyptian nationalist consensus, seeking unification of the Nile valley under the Egyptian crown, was shared by all political groups, with one exception: the Egyptian communists were the only group that viewed the Sudanese as equals, a people who should have their own right to self-determination and to shape their own future. The slogan of the mainstream ran: "the unity of the Nile valley: one Nile, one people, one king" [*wahdat wadi al-nil – Nil wahid – sha'b wahid – malik wahid*]. The communists promoted a very different slogan: "political and economic independence and a common struggle with the Sudanese people and its right to self-determination" [*al-istiqlal al-siyasi wa-al-iqtisadi wa-al-kifah al-mushtarak ma'a al-sha'b al-sudani wa-haqhu fi taqrir masirihi*].[6]

Was the unity of the Nile valley a manifestation of an "imagined community," to employ Benedict Anderson's concept on the development of national identity, or was it an "imaginary community," a product of the Egyptian colonialist vision? Anderson defines an "imagined community" as a group in which people living in the same administrative unit, usually a state, share similar life experiences, i.e., their daily lives are shaped by a similar economic, political, and social reality. Anderson's concept is based on the assumption that the majority of the people living within a territory share that collective identity.[7] By contrast, the reality molding daily life experience in Egypt and Sudan was rather diverse, and most people inhabiting Sudan did not share the Egyptian vision of a unified Nile valley under the Egyptian crown. An "imaginary community" can thus be depicted as an imposed identity by a dominant community/group of people on other groups of peoples inhabiting a disputed "common territory" who do not share or accept that identity, as was the case with Egypt seeking to expand its sovereignty over Sudan.

The troubled Anglo–Egyptian relations of the late nineteenth century through the late 1950s have been the subject of many studies. These studies have placed great emphasis on the various political, social, economic, and cultural issues related to the question of Sudan.[8] As these studies have shown, soon after the conclusion of World War II, successive Egyptian governments launched a large-scale campaign to promote Egypt's interests in Sudan – a campaign that the British attempted to thwart by any means necessary. The British exploited their substantial leverage as the dominant power in both Egypt and Sudan to reduce Egyptian influence in Sudan to the greatest extent possible. In addition, some studies have addressed the Anglo–Egyptian struggle over control of the Sudanese educational system.[9] They examine Britain's activity in the field of education and illustrate the way in which it developed, nurtured, and improved the Sudanese educational system to promote Sudanese national identity and encourage anti-Egyptian separatist tendencies.

Several studies, mostly in Arabic, have directly and indirectly dealt with the subject of the unity of the Nile valley. They may be divided into two main groups: those written by Egyptian academics and intellectuals before and after Sudan's independence, and those written by Sudanese thinkers mainly in the post-independence era. The two groups represent contradictory approaches vis-à-vis Egypt's claims for a united Nile valley. In general, Egyptian writers wrote favorably of the colonialist experience in Sudan; the blame for thwarting the prospect of a united Nile valley was placed mainly with Britain and to a certain extent with Sudanese territorial nationalists. These studies focused on the political and social aspects of the problematic triangle of Anglo–Egyptian–Sudanese relations.[10]

We can learn from these works that until the early 1950s, Egypt's demand to unite the Nile valley was supported by all successive governments including the new military regime during its first months in power. These governments categorically refused to come to terms with Britain on any agreement in which Sudan would be separated from Egypt. Britain, for its part, took every possible measure to split the two countries; it had its own reasons for, and interests in, such an outcome. Perhaps the most prominent work to describe and analyze in detail the political stages in Egypt's twofold struggle for independence and for the unity of the Nile valley is Muhammad 'Abd al-Hamid Ahmad Hannawi's *Ma'rakat al-jala' wa-wahdat wadi al-nil, 1945–1954* (Cairo, 1998). His study was based mostly on British and Egyptian archival material, official documents, and impressive secondary sources and interviews.

However, the methods, tactics, and arguments employed on both the diplomatic and the propaganda levels by Egyptian politicians and intellectuals to justify the call for unity and to persuade the international community to support its realization have not yet received attention in the literature. Moreover, the internal, at times stormy, political and public polemic discourse within Egypt still awaits thorough, systematic, and critical examination.

This book endeavors to address these issues. It describes and analyzes the intense Egyptian efforts to prove categorically that Egypt and Sudan constituted a single territorial unit. These efforts, as it demonstrates, were clustered around several dominant theoretical layers: history, geography, economy, culture, and ethnography. Furthermore, the book takes pains to explain the ideological, social, and political undercurrents that led to the dramatic shift in 1953 in the stance of Egypt's new military regime, which allowed the Sudanese people to exercise their right to self-determination, thus paving the way for the demise of the idea of the unity of the Nile valley.

Aims, Methods, and Approaches

This study has two objectives. The first is political: to demonstrate that the question of Sudan was in fact an integral part of Egypt's general foreign policy, formulated in the years immediately following World War II. The second is to survey and analyze the internal political and public debates on the unity of the Nile valley. The study utilizes an exceptional and valuable typology of interest groups in Egypt and provides important insights into the elements of both consensus and diversity in Egyptian national and nationalist thought at a crucial turning point in the development of Egyptian self-definition and self-awareness. The study is therefore composed of two interconnected tiers: politics and ideology.

For the first one, politics, while investigating the internal and external Egyptian political context, the study asks a number of basic questions:

1. Why was Britain determined to control Sudan, and why were members of Egypt's political elite equally determined to control it?
2. What place did Sudan hold in the context of other nationalist issues in Egypt?
3. Why did the 1952 regime change direction and open the door for a resolution of the Sudan issue? Why were the Free Officers more flexible than their predecessors?

With regard to foreign policy, the study describes and analyzes the factors that created the Anglo–Egyptian labyrinth that subsequently led to Egypt's decision to present its dispute with Britain to the United Nations Security Council in August 1947; Nuqrashi's appeal in August 1947 was rejected by a majority of members of the Security Council. The present book argues that the international diplomatic campaign for the unity of the Nile valley and for a full and speedy evacuation of British troops from Egypt and Sudan taught the Egyptians that their twofold demand was neither convincing nor acceptable to the vast majority of countries.

With regard to internal politics, Egypt's decision to renounce its claims regarding the unity of the Nile valley came only after the downfall of the monarchy. While Gabriel Warburg has shown that cracks appeared in the Egyptian consensus regarding the unity of the Nile valley as early as several weeks before the overthrow of King Faruq,[11] this book argues that the fissures in fact emerged much earlier, in the early 1940s, when the communists appeared to consolidate and present a divergent view regarding the unity of the Nile valley. Although they presented a dissident approach to the Sudan question, opposing the main nationalist current represented by the political establishment – the palace, the parliamentary parties, and extra-parliamentary nationalist and political groups – it was the communist approach that prevailed.

The Free Officers regime that took power in July 1952 made Egypt's liberation its first priority. The Free Officers realized that to gain international support for their demand of a British troop withdrawal from Egypt, they needed to make substantial concessions in Sudan. It would appear that they embraced some of the communist platform's principles on the Nile valley; one of these was the Sudanese right to self-determination. While displaying a rigid and uncompromising stance throughout the Anglo–Egyptian talks on the liberation of Egypt, insisting on a full and unconditional withdrawal of British troops from Egypt, they voiced their willingness to relinquish their demands in Sudan – a moderate, realpolitik stance that would pave the way to an Anglo–Egyptian agreement over Sudan in February 1953.

The second objective of this study – an ideological analysis focusing on the ways and means by which Egypt pursued its propaganda campaign for the unity of the Nile valley – has the following goals:

1. To emphasize the discursive statements and assumptions linking Sudan and Egypt in the latter's attempt at constructing a new, yet very significant, Egyptian anti-imperialist and nationalist narrative.
2. To explain the specific political, economic, and cultural interests that made this narrative so forceful and resilient.

As the Egyptian government was fully aware that the two major nationalist currents – territorial and supra-Egyptian nationalism (see the discussion that follows) – saw Sudan as an integral part of Egypt, it took pains to explain the geographical, ethnographical, cultural, and economic foundations on which the unity of Egypt and Sudan was supposedly built, using the works of leading theoreticians and experts in the study of the Nile valley, while presenting the expressions and forms in which that unity had manifested itself throughout history. Egypt, it was emphasized, was in a better position and was more anxious than Great Britain to prepare the Sudanese for "self-government," because the Egyptians and the Sudanese shared the same language, religion, and race, and both Sudan and Egypt depended on the Nile for their very existence.

In fact, this was no more than Egyptian lip service, devoid of any real political meaning. In a united Egyptian–Sudanese state, the Sudanese would enjoy no more than administrative autonomy; actual control would be left to Egypt. The present book offers a critical assessment of the assertions made by Egypt. It presents a balanced and thorough array of sources for arguments disputing these claims, and sheds light on the origins, relevance, and ramifications of these arguments vis-à-vis the Egyptian "cause." The book examines the reasons why these efforts ultimately failed, questioning whether this "failure" was a result of fallacies underpinning official Egyptian discourse or other factors. The book also examines why the Egyptians failed to base their case for unity on historical and cultural arguments, trying to ascertain the weakness of these arguments. Moreover, the book attempts to suggest alternative explanations as to why both Egypt and Britain failed to dictate the future of the Sudan.

During the period on which the book focuses, Egyptian nationalism was dominated by two major groups: those regarded as territorial nationalists, for whom the Nile constituted a chief feature of their identity and who had been determined to see Egypt and Sudan united since the early twentieth century, and those raising the idea of Pan-Arabism, including Sudan, in the late 1930s. The book explores the way in which the Free Officers regime gradually departed from both currents, taking on a new delineation of the collective identity – Egypt for the Egyptians, and the Sudanese right to self-determination. Only after the solution of the Sudanese dispute with Britain did the Free Officers consolidate their trans-territorial nationalist identity in the form of Pan-Arabism. It has been suggested that Pan-Arabism under Nasser, and particularly the initiation of the great project of the High Dam in Aswan, marked the end of the Nile in Egypt's nationalist identity; by closely scrutinizing Egypt's nationalist currents through the lens of the unity of the Nile valley, the present book provides a missing link in the intellectual history of Egypt in general and the place of the unity of the Nile valley in Egypt's nationalist identity in particular.

For the critical examination of the central stages in the historical development of the question of the unity of the Nile valley, 1943 serves as the starting point – a year that witnessed a significant change, as mentioned earlier, in Egypt's initial steps toward an independent foreign policy. The book concludes in 1953 – a year marking the demise of the idea of the unity of the Nile valley following the conclusion of the Anglo–Egyptian agreement, in which Egypt's newly established military regime agreed to renounce its claims to Sudan.[12] The year 1953 is of double significance for the present study: it marked the conclusion of the Anglo–Egyptian agreement as well as the abolition of political parties and the subsequent demise of a free press and the freedom of speech in Egypt. From 1953 on, Egypt's foreign policy transformed dramatically – but that period will not be addressed by this book, except for a few references.

The present book's analysis of the works and studies of Egyptian intellectuals focuses on two layers: "establishment intellectuals" acting within the framework of the regime and those acting independently in a variety of intellectual frameworks. Here the research draws a distinction between various ideological-political schools, representing a wide array of sociopolitical organizations. To this end, the book thoroughly and systematically analyzes daily newspapers, journals, and other forums expressing the prevailing beliefs of the various political factions. For instance, for left-wing groups, the analysis relies on Egyptian publications such as *al-Fajr al-Jadid*, *al-Damir*, *al-Jamahir*, *al-Majalla al-Jadida*, *Kifah al-Sha'b*, *Umdurman*, *Kifah al-Umma*, and *al-Bashir*.

The discussion of the ongoing debate among such right-wing groups as the Muslim Brothers and *Misr al-Fatat* (Young Egypt) directs us to such publications as *Wadi al-Nil*, *al-Nadhir*, *al-Ikhwan al-Muslimun*, *Misr al-Fatat*, and *al-Risala*. The analysis of the views and approaches presented by liberal intellectuals associated with political parties such as the Wafd and the Liberal Constitutionalists focuses on such publications as *al-Jihad*, *al-Misri*, *al-Balagh al-Usbu'i*, *al-Balagh*, *al-Siyasa al-Usbu'iyya*, *al-Siyasa*. Independent views and ideas were found in such publications as *al-Ahram*, *al-Musawwar*, *al-Hilal*, *al-Muqattam*, *Ruz al-Yusuf*, and *al-Asas*. The study argues that although almost all groups shared the belief that Egypt and Sudan constituted one entity, it is critically important to analyze the various arguments that they put forward; each came to the subject from a different perspective and approach.

Research has been carried out using historical methods, paying careful attention to the cross-feeding between political history and the history of ideas. The subject of the unity of the Nile valley was both a major staple of Egypt's foreign policy and an ideological issue with which many Egyptian intellectual circles were preoccupied. The study analyzes the Egyptian anti-imperialist and nationalist narrative of the unity of the Nile valley in terms of discourse and perspective. The complex issue of ideology vis-à-vis realpolitik is thoroughly examined, and the book provides an inquiry into whether the question of the unity of the Nile valley was first built around a cohesive ideology and then translated into political action, or vice versa. Did Egyptian intellectuals of all nationalist stripes, both inside and outside of the establishment, consolidate their attitudes regarding the future of Sudan as a result of the then-ongoing rivalry between the British and the Egyptian governments regarding hegemony over the region? Were their pronouncements and writings drafted as responses to the political and diplomatic context, as an attempt to shape that context, or perhaps as both? To clarify such issues this study utilizes methods and insights drawn from intellectual history and the history of ideas. These fields help to balance the internal/textualist approach and the external/contextualist approach, both of which are applied to this study.[13]

To investigate the nature of the interrelations between intelligentsia and regime, the book draws on the sociological models of Edward Shils

and S. N. Eisenstadt.[14] Here, the book considers whether the Egyptian
political elite encouraged "producer" intellectuals or "reproducer" intellectuals, as per our sociological paradigms. Parallel to this, the book
assesses the particular role played by those intellectuals acting within
the framework of the regime. The book examines the studies and writings
of such academic experts as Muhammad Shafiq Ghurbal, 'Abbas Mustafa 'Ammar, Ahmad Badawi, 'Abd al-Rahman Zaki, and Ibrahim Nashi
in soliciting their services to the ruling elite. It also examines works by
independent and politically oriented scholars such as 'Abd al-Rahman
al-Rafi'i, Sulayman Huzayyin, Rashid Al-Barawi (Rashed El-Barawy),
Muhammad Fu'ad Shukri, and others who were active at the time,
and closely scrutinizes works by post-revolutionary scholars, including
Yunan Labib Rizq, 'Abd al-'Azim Muhammad Ibrahim Ramadan, and
many others. The book also sheds light on the nature and patterns of
the intellectual activities of anti-governmental groups, both left and right
wing. The book examines the extent to which these intellectual activities
fell in line with the paradigm of the "dissident intellectual" suggested by
J. P. Nettl and Edgar Morin.[15] The book aims to determine whether a
direct connection existed between the modes of action employed by
them in advancing their suggested solution and their political thoughts
and theories regarding the future of Sudan. For the conceptualizations of
the role of intellectuals and the processes of framing narratives of contention in the broader field of social movement, the analysis also draws on
the works of scholars, such as Carl Boggs's *Social Movements and Political
Power* and Alberto Melucci's *Nomads of the Present.*[16]

The book offers a critical examination of the assertions made by
Egyptian historians and geographers that the unity of the Nile valley
was not a modern phenomenon but rather a deeply rooted historical
reality. For example, it investigates the validity and historical foundations
of the assertion that the ancient monuments of Egypt indicate that Egypt
had been closely united with Lower and Upper Nubia (Sudan) since the
earliest days of history and that the relations that continuously developed
between the northern and southern parts of the Nile valley had never
been interrupted. Is it true that Egypt and Sudan, as Salim Hasan stated,
"could never dispense with each other for the very strong reasons, which
bound them into one single unit, completely indivisible, even if their
inhabitants thought otherwise"?[17]

Egyptian geographers concentrated their arguments on the vital
importance of the Nile to the land through which it flows, particularly
Egypt. They proposed that Egypt should implement a tight net of
works and projects in Sudan to guarantee the required water supply.
The present study employs certain aspects of Karl Wittfogel's theory of

"hydraulic civilization," which focuses on the dependence of societies, mainly in historically underdeveloped areas (China, in particular), on the broad expansion of irrigation works. According to Wittfogel, extensive irrigation requires centralized coordination and direction by an authoritarian leadership – in his words, "a despotic ruler." Since both Egypt and Sudan were "hydraulic societies," it is quite obvious that Egyptian geographers granted the "leading role" to Egypt – "a colonialism that could exist between brothers," to borrow Eve Troutt Powell's phrase.[18]

While analyzing the ethnographic assertions made by Egyptian sociologists and anthropologists, my discussion draws on theories and definitions of ethnicity from the social sciences, such as Max Weber's definition of an ethnic group. According to Weber, an ethnic group is not a spontaneously developed community, or a group with specific geographical location, but "a group of people who believe they have ancestors in common from the past."[19] Weber's concept runs counter to arguments made by some Egyptian theoreticians, according to which geography and ethnography are interrelated in the Nile valley. The study discusses the historical rationale and theoretical foundations of these hegemonic and colonialist assertions.

The book draws upon a plethora of sources. Primary sources, studied in the original Arabic, consist of official documents, books, and essays, as well as articles by Egyptian academics, theoreticians, ideologues, journalists, politicians, and other intellectuals. These are used to elucidate the internal ideological discourse at each stage in the historical development of the question of the unity of the Nile valley. To describe and analyze the political context (i.e., the development of political events regarding the future of Sudan and Egypt's demand to form a unified state in the Nile valley), much of the source material is gleaned from archives in Egypt, Britain, India, the Netherlands, Russia, and the United States.

The fact that the Indian National Archives in Bombay and New Delhi are so rife with official Egyptian documents can be explained by the fact that since the conclusion of World War II, both India and Egypt had been embroiled in a struggle for national liberation against Britain; the existence of a common adversary provided the nations with a common ground for political cooperation, which would gradually give rise to solid, friendly relations. Egypt looked to India as a rising Asian power to help it gain international support in its dispute with Britain. As the Indian archives reveal, Jawaharlal Nehru, the Indian leader, took great interest in the events unfolding in Western Asia and Egypt.

The book also makes use of the archives of the International Institute of Social History (Amsterdam), whose rare collections of Egyptian left-wing primary sources, both political and theoretical, have proved to be invaluable to the research conducted for this book. The book also draws on secondary literature in various languages, including Arabic, French, Russian, Hebrew, and English. The discussion on both levels, political and intellectual, aims at shedding new light on Egypt's multifaceted struggle to win international support for its desire to unite the Nile valley under its hegemony.

Structure of the Book

The following discussion is divided into two parts comprising six chapters. Part I concentrates on the theoretical foundations of Egypt's claims regarding the unity of the Nile valley and is divided into two chapters (Chapters 1 and 2). These examine the Egyptian point of view, as expressed by academics, intellectuals, and ideologists representing a wide spectrum of political orientations, on why Egypt and Sudan constituted one continuous territorial entity along the Nile valley. Their arguments focused mainly on the historical, physical-geographical, ethnographical, cultural, and economic factors on which the unity of the Nile valley was thought to be based.

Part II (Chapters 3–6) examines the various stages in Egypt's struggle for power in Sudan, focusing on politics, diplomacy, and public discourse. Chapter 3 examines the main stages in the political and diplomatic development of the doctrine of the unity of the Nile valley from the early to late- 1940s. There was a broad national consensus in monarchial Egypt concerning Egypt's twofold nationalist paradigm: the liberation of the Nile valley from all vestiges of British imperialism and the unification of independent Egypt and Sudan under the Egyptian crown. Egypt launched a national and international campaign to advance its political goals. The public discourse on Egypt's rights to unite the Nile valley under the Egyptian crown intensified following the end of World War II and reached the international scene in summer 1947, when the Egyptian government yielded to public pressure and took its dispute with Britain to the UN Security Council. Egypt's efforts to win international support ended in a fiasco – the international community refused to endorse Egypt's demands, and even those few who supported Egypt were reluctant to support its demand to unite the Nile valley under the Egyptian crown.

Chapter 4 examines the power struggle over Sudan between British and Egyptian imperialisms. It depicts and analyzes the British long-term project of Sudanization, that is, the creation of a new reality whereby qualified and well-trained Sudanese would gradually take over governmental and administrative posts as part of their preparation for self-government. Such development, the British believed, would be followed by the emergence and development of a territorial-particularist Sudanese nationalism and the demise of unification trends. The Egyptian reaction to Sudanization is also dealt with, in both the political and the public spheres. The chapter also examines the struggle for hegemony over the Sudanese educational system between the two unequal masters of Sudan. It is divided into two main parts: the first focuses on the interplay between British educational policy and foreign policy in Sudan. It argues that the British developed and nurtured the education system mainly for the purpose of training a new generation of Sudanese intellectuals with particularist national consciousness and pro-British orientation. The second part reviews Egypt's educational policy in Sudan throughout the condominium period. It examines Egypt's response to the British educational policy in Sudan and its contribution to the development of Sudanese educational institutions, particularly in the post–World War II years.

Chapter 5 examines the radicalization of the Egyptian approach to the Sudan issue after the fiasco at the UN Security Council and more intensely in the period 1950–1952, when the Wafd seized the reins of government. The Anglo–Egyptian political labyrinth situated the relations between the two countries at their lowest ebb. The Free Officers revolution of July 1952 constituted a landmark for the future of Sudan. The study inquires why the new military regime relinquished Egypt's claim to Sudan.

Chapter 6 describes and analyzes the remarkably polar positions of left- and right-wing opposition movements toward the question of the unity of the Nile valley. More specifically, it concentrates on the movements of the Muslim Brothers and *Misr al-Fatat*, representing the far right, and the heterogeneous communist movement on the far left. The chapter demonstrates that the groups on the right were not only part of the broad national consensus, which called for the unification of the Nile valley under the Egyptian crown, but also constituted the most extreme position on this issue. The communist groups, in contrast, were the only political and social forces to go against the national consensus, staking out an unabashedly dissident position that called for the independence of the Nile valley from British colonial rule in Egypt, and from British and Egyptian rule in Sudan, granting self-determination to the Sudanese people. This unpopular approach was rejected out of hand by the establishment and by most of the political spectrum, yet shortly after the July 1952 revolution, the Free Officers adopted the foundations of the communist formula for the resolution of the Sudan issue, while denying its origin.

Notes

1 On Egypt under Muhammad 'Ali, see, for instance, Afaf Lutfi Sayyid-Marsot, *Egypt in the Reign of Muhammad Ali* (Cambridge: Cambridge University Press, 1994); Robert Tignor, *Egypt: A Short History* (Princeton, NJ: Princeton University Press, 2011), pp. 196–227; P. J. Vatikiotis, *The History of Modern Egypt from Muhammad Ali to Mubarak* (London: Weidenfeld and Nicolson, 1991), pp. 49–69; Arthur Goldschmidt Jr., *Modern Egypt, the Formation of a Nation State* (Boulder, CO: Westview Press, 2004), pp. 15–27.

2 Ronald J. Horvath, "A Definition of Colonialism," *Current Anthropology*, 13/1 (1972), p. 46.

3 Ibid., p. 50.

4 Israel Gershoni and James P. Jankowski, *Redefining Egyptian Nation, 1930–1945* (Cambridge: Cambridge University Press, 1995), pp. 110–111.

5 Ibid. On the rise to prominence of Egyptian territorial nationalism, see Israel Gershoni and James P. Jankowski, *Egypt, Islam and the Arabs* (Oxford: Oxford University Press, 1987).

6 This position was first formulated in the early 1940s; until that time, the communist position regarding Sudan had been in line with the nationalist consensus. On the communists' stand, see Rami Ginat, "Swimming Against the Nationalist Current," in Israel Gershoni and Meir Hatina (eds.), *Narrating the Nile* (Boulder, CO: Lynne Rienner Publishers, 2008), pp. 68–90. See also Chapter 6.

7 Benedict Anderson, *Imagined Communities: Reflections on the Origin and Spread of Nationalism* (London and New York: Verso, 2006).

8 'Abd al-Rahman al-Rafi'i, *Fi a'qab al-thawra al-misriyya – Thawrat 1919*, 3 vols. (Cairo: Dar al-Ma'arif, 1989); Rafi'i, *Misr wa-al-sudan fi awa'il 'ahd al-ihtilal* (Cairo: Sharikat Maktabat wa-Matba'at Mustafa al-Babi al-Halabi wa-Awladihi bi-Misr, 1942); John Marlowe, *A History of Modern Egypt and Anglo–Egyptian Relations, 1800–1956*, 2nd ed. (Hamden, CT: Archon Books, 1965); Eve Troutt Powell, *A Different Shade of Colonialism: Egypt, Great Britain, and the Mastery of the Sudan* (Berkeley: University of California Press, 2003); Troutt Powell, "Brothers along the Nile: Egyptian Concepts of Race and Ethnicity, 1895–1910," in Haggai Erlich and Israel Gershoni (eds.), *The Nile: Histories, Cultures, Myths* (Boulder, CO: Lynne Rienner, 2000), pp. 171–181; Afaf Lutfi Sayyid-Marsot, *Egypt and Cromer: A Study in Anglo–Egyptian Relations* (New York: Praeger, 1969); William Travis Hanes, *Imperial Diplomacy in the Era of Decolonization: The Sudan and Anglo–Egyptian Relations, 1945–1956* (Westport, CT: Greenwood Press, 1995); J. A. Hail, *Britain's Foreign Policy in Egypt and Sudan, 1947–1956* (Reading: Ithaca Press, 1996); Rashed El-Barawy, *Egypt, Britain and the Sudan* (Cairo: Renaissance Bookshop, 1952); L. A. Fabunmi, *The Sudan in Anglo–Egyptian Relations: A Case Study in Power Politics 1800–1956* (London: Longmans, 1960); Peter Woodward, *Condominium and Sudanese Nationalism* (London: Rex Collings, 1979); Abd El Fattah Ibrahim El-Sayed Baddour, *Sudanese–Egyptian Relations: A Chronological and Analytical Study* (The Hague: Nijhoff, 1960). On the economic aspects of Egypt's activities in Sudan and the causes for its failure to advance its plan to unite the Nile valley, see David E. Mills, *Dividing*

14   Introduction

the Nile: Egypt's Economic Nationalists in the Sudan 1918–1956 (Cairo: The American University in Cairo Press, 2014).

9 Mohamed Omer Beshir, *Educational Development in the Sudan, 1898–1956* (London: Oxford University Press, 1969); Salih Ahmad Nazli, *al-Dimuqratiyya wa-al-tarbiyya* (Cairo: Maktabat al-Anjlu al-Misriyya, 1979); Lilian Passmore Sanderson and Neville Sanderson, *Education, Religion and Politics in Southern Sudan 1899–1964* (London: Ithaca Press, 1981); Heather J. Sharkey, *Living with Colonialism: Nationalism and Culture in the Anglo-Egyptian Sudan* (Berkeley: University of California Press, 2003); Rami Ginat, "The Reopening of Gordon College: A Layer in the Anglo-Egyptian Struggle for Hegemony over the Building of the Sudanese Educational System, 1943–1946," in Ami Ayalon and David Wasserstein (eds.), *Madrasa: Education, State and Religion in the Middle East* (Tel-Aviv: Dayan Center, 2005), pp. 217–239 [Hebrew].

10 Isma'il Azhari, *Difa' 'an wahdat wadi al-nil* (Beirut: Matabi'al-Kashshaf, n. d.); Dirar Salih Dirar, *Hijrat al-qaba'il al-'arabiyya ila wadi al-nil misr wa-al-sudan* (Riyad: Maktabat al-Tawba, 1997); Muhammad 'Abd al-Hamid Ahmad Hannawi, *Ma'rakat al-jala' wa-wahdat wadi al-nil, 1945–1954* (Cairo: al-Hay'ah al-Misriyya al-'Amma lil-Kitab, 1998); Yunan Labib Rizq, *Qadiyat wahdat wadi al-nil bayna al-mu'ahada wa taghyir al-waqi' al-isti'mari, 1936–1946* (Cairo: Jami'at al-Duwal al-'Arabiyya, 1975); Muhammad Fu'ad Shukri, *Misr wa-al-sudan: ta'rikh wahdat wadi al-nil al-siyasiyya fi al-qarn al-tasi' 'ashar* (Cairo: Dar al-Ma'arif, 1963); Shukri, *al-Hukm al-misri fi al-sudan 1820–1885* (Cairo: Dar al-Fikr al-'Arabi, 1947); 'Umar Bashari Mahjub, *Ma'alim al-haraka al-wataniyya fi al-sudan* (Beirut: al-Maktaba al-Thaqafiya, 1996); Ahmad 'Abd al-Razzaq Sanhuri, *Qadiyat wadi al-nil, misr wa-al-sudan* (Cairo: al-Matba'a al-Amiriyya, 1949); 'Abdalla Husayn, *al-Sudan min al-ta'rikh al-qadim ila rihlat al-ba'tha al-misriyya*, 3 vols. (Cairo: al-Matba'a al-Rahmaniyya bi-Misr, 1935); Salah al-Din al-Shami, *al-Mawani al-sudaniyya: dirasa fi al-jughrafiyya al-tarikhiyya* (Cairo: Maktabat Misr, 1961); Dirar Salih Dirar, *Ta'rikh al-sudan al-hadith* (Beirut: Dar Maktabat al-Hayat, 1965); John Obert Voll, "Unity of the Nile Valley: Identity and Regional Integration," *Journal of African Studies*, 3/2 (Summer 1976), pp. 205–228.

11 Gabriel Warburg, *Islam, Nationalism and Communism in a Traditional Society: The Case of Sudan* (London: Frank Cass, 1978), pp. 75–76.

12 M. W. Daly, *Imperial Sudan: The Anglo–Egyptian Condominium 1934–1956* (Cambridge and New York: Cambridge University Press, 1991); P. M. Holt and M. W. Daly, *A History of the Sudan from the Coming of Islam to the Present Day*, 6th ed. (London and New York: Routledge, 2011); Gabriel Warburg, *Islam, Sectarianism and Politics in Sudan since the Mahdiyya* (London: Hurst & Co., 2003); P. M. Holt, *A Modern History of the Sudan* (London: Weidenfeld and Nicolson, 1961).

13 See, for instance, Quentin Skinner, "Meaning and Understanding in the History of Ideas," *History and Theory*, 8 (1969), pp. 3–53; John Higham, "Intellectual History and its Neighbors," *Journal of the History of Ideas*, 15 (1954), pp. 339–347; Higham, "American Intellectual History: A Critical Appraisal," *American Quarterly*, 13/2 (Summer 1961), pp. 219–233; Rush

Welter, "The History of Ideas in America: An Essay in Redefinition," in Robert Meredith (ed.), *American Studies: Essays on Theory and Methods* (Columbus, OH: Charles E. Merrill, 1968), pp. 236–253; Isaiah Berlin, *Against the Current: Essays in the History of Ideas* (London: Hogarth Press, 1979); Charles D. Smith, "The Intellectual and Modernization: Definitions and Reconsiderations, the Egyptian Experience," *Comparative Studies in Society and History*, 22 (1980), pp. 513–533; Israel Gershoni, "The Theory of Crisis and the Crisis in a Theory: Intellectual History in Twentieth-Century Middle Eastern Studies," in Israel Gershoni, Amy Singer, and Hakan Erdem (eds.), *Middle East Historiographies: Narrating the Twentieth Century* (Seattle, WA: University of Washington Press, 2006), pp. 131–182.

14 Edward Shils, "Intellectuals," in David L. Sills (ed.), *International Encyclopedia of the Social Sciences*, Vol. 7 (New York: Macmillan Company, 1968), pp. 399–415; S. N. Eisenstadt, "Intellectuals and Tradition," in Eisenstadt and S. R. Graubard (eds.), *Intellectuals and Tradition* (New York: Humanities Press, 1973), pp. 1–19.

15 J. P. Nettl, "Ideas, Intellectuals and Structures of Dissent," in Philip Rieff (ed.), *On Intellectuals: Theoretical Studies, Case Studies* (Garden City, NY: Doubleday, 1969), pp. 53–122.

16 Alberto Melucci, *Nomads of the Present: Social Movements and Individual Needs in Contemporary Society*, ed. by John Keane and Paul Mier (London: Hutchinson, 1989); Carl Boggs, *Social Movements and Political Power: Emerging Forms of Radicalism in the West* (Philadelphia: Temple University Press, 1986).

17 Salim Hasan, "5000 Years of Unity," in *Egypt Sudan* (Cairo: Government Press, 1947), pp. 14–17 (hereafter cited as Egypt Sudan).

18 Troutt Powell, "Brothers along the Nile," p. 173.

19 Weber is quoted from Khalil Abdalla El Madani, "On the Epistemology of Ethnicity – A Critical Review of the Theories on Ethnic Formation," in Sayyid H. Hurreiz and Elfatih A. Abdel Salam (eds.), *Ethnicity, Conflict and National Integration in the Sudan* (Khartoum: University of Khartoum Printing Press, 1989), pp. 3–4.

Part I

The Theoretical Foundations of Egypt's Claims for the Unity of the Nile Valley

1 Egyptian Perceptions of Sudan
Historical Narratives

The main battle in imperialism is over land, of course; but when it came to who owned the land, who had the right to settle and work on it, who kept it going, who won it back, and who now plans its future – these issues were reflected, contested, and even for a time decided in narrative.[1]

The historical perspective constituted a basic component in the narratives made by Egyptian historians, geographers, and protagonists of the unity of the Nile valley to justify why Egypt and Sudan were a single entity since ancient times. The chapter is divided into four asymmetric sections. The first and major one examines the pre-condominium period – from ancient to modern times. It focuses on the nineteenth-century history of colonized Sudan since it was conquered by Muhammad 'Ali, as seen through Egyptian lenses. A central argument repeats itself in these narratives – Sudan is part of Egypt by right of conquest. The second section focuses on the period between the two Anglo-Egyptian treaties of 1899 and 1936. Egyptian scholars and nationalists were united in their firm belief that British imperialism imposed these treaties on Egypt and dictated an artificial reality to divide the homeland of the peoples of the Nile valley. Methodologically, they relied, among other items, on relevant aspects of international law to prove that Sudan had never ceased to be part of Egypt. The third section reviews the controversial reception of the 1936 treaty and its aftermath.

The historical narratives are closely scrutinized, and special references are often made to the argumentative manner in which British diplomats and policymakers, at the time, perceived them. The chapter also discusses the works of Sudanese scholars who studied that period and presented perspectives divergent from those of their Egyptian counterparts. Sudanese scholars perceived both Egypt and Britain as two modes of imperialism.

Egypt and Sudan Prior to the Condominium

Egyptian historians and geographers argued that the unity of the Nile valley was not a new development of modern times but a deeply rooted historical reality. The ancient monuments of Egypt, revealed Professor Salim Hasan, showed us that Egypt, from the earliest days of history, was firmly united with Lower and Upper Nubia (Sudan). The continuously developing relations between the northern and southern parts of the Nile valley had never been interrupted. In fact, the two countries, Egypt and Sudan, stressed Hasan, "could never dispense with each other for the very strong reasons that bound them into one single unit, completely indivisible even if their inhabitants thought otherwise."[2]

"The monuments of Egypt have resisted the ravages of time for more than 5,000 years to give clear evidence of the close union between Egypt and the Sudan in former times," stated Egyptian protagonist academics. Already during the Pharaohs' time Egypt extended its authority over the entire southern part of the Nile valley. To prove the validity of their historical arguments the Egyptian protagonist academics relied on what they described as "recent archeological discoveries," which verified the fact that Egyptian civilization, culture, and religion flourished also in South Sudan. Even in the Ptolemaic and Roman eras the unity of the Nile valley was not interrupted.[3] Under the Ptolemies and Romans, Egyptian scholars observed the growth of mercantile activity, chronicling the expansion of Egyptian trade south- and eastward to the Red Sea coast. With the Romans, trade expanded further inland into the interior of Sudan. Following the Arab invasion of Egypt in 639 by Caliph 'Umar Ibn al-Khattab, Nubia was conquered by the Arabs in 651. The Arab–Islamic hegemony in Sudan was consolidated with a peace treaty and an annual tax that would last for 600 years. The Mamluks expanded their control into Nubia and extended their rule further into Sudan in the fourteenth century. This process continued under the Ottomans, who conquered Egypt in 1517 and then expanded their grip further into the southern Nile valley. The Ottoman presence remained unchanged until Muhammad 'Ali conquered Sudan in 1820, launching a new phase in the shared history of the Nile valley.[4] If Sudan was dominated by the Ottomans, why did Muhammad 'Ali's Egypt, which was itself an Ottoman province, have to reoccupy Sudan? This question remained unanswered.

Islamist theoreticians chose for obvious religious reasons to link the origins of Egypt's involvement in Sudan with the emergence of the Muslim empire. They argued that the buds of the Arab–Sudanese relations emerged immediately after Egypt was occupied by 'Amr Ibn al-'As, the "preeminent Muslim commander," in 641. Ibn al-'As, who ruled Egypt during the reign of 'Umar ibn al-Khattab, the second caliph, looked at Sudan with the idea to annex it. However, his efforts to implement his plan were doomed to fail: the difficult terrain hampered his advance. Moreover, the tough military battle with the Sudanese

fighters prevented 'Amr ibn al-'As from occupying the Sudanese hinter-
land, and he hardly succeeded in attaining his goals. The situation
changed only during the reign of 'Uthman ibn al-'Affan, the third caliph.
'Abd Allah ibn Sa'd Ibn Abi Sarh, Egypt's military ruler, was determined
to defeat the Christian kingdom of Makuria and its capital, Dongola,
after they kept violating the truce and refused to pay the *jizya* ("tribute" –
tax imposed on non-Muslim subjects). After bloody battles Dongola
(situated on the east bank of the Nile about 160 km southeast of
present-day Donqula) was occupied, and an Arab–Sudanese peace treaty
(*mu'ahada*) was concluded, under which the Sudanese were granted the
protection of the Muslim empire. Ever since, Sudan and Egypt have
constituted a single entity.[5]

The eminent Egyptian historian Muhammad Rif'at,[6] who was active
within the establishment, held a different view arguing that the Sudan
region was occupied for the first time by the Mamluk leader al-Zahir
Baibars al-Bunduqdari. According to Rif'at, as a result of Baibars's
military successes in the mid-thirteen century, the Christian population
of Nubia was subordinated to Muslim rule for the first time and forced to
pay the *jizya* tax.[7]

In the mid-1930s the three large volumes of 'Abdallah Husayn's study
were published. Husayn, a lawyer who worked at the time as an editor for
the daily newspaper *al-Ahram*, conducted his research during a stormy
period of Anglo–Egyptian relations, when the Egyptian political system
was polarized and torn to pieces following years of monarchial dictatorship. The study reviewed in detail the history of Sudan (politics, economy, education, agriculture, etc.) from ancient times until the early
1930s. Husayn observed that throughout history, the Nile valley in its
entirety constituted a single weave. For instance, under the Pharaohs, all
the Nile valley countries were linked, thus constituting a single entity.
Muhammad 'Ali's reign over Sudan and that of his successors were
glorified for contributing significantly to the country's development and
prosperity. Husayn held the British and French solely responsible for any
decline in Sudan and for all its sore evils, such as the Mahdi revolt
(1881–1885) and the ensuing famine. The Sudanese people benefited
from Egyptian rule, which took upon itself the difficult task of advancing
them in all walks of life.[8]

Egyptian liberal historians propagating within the establishment
framework focused their historical analysis on the late nineteenth
century – the era of Western imperialism – as their starting point. When
the tide of European expansion reached Egypt and Sudan in the 1870s,
declared Professor Muhammad Shafiq Ghurbal,[9] it was found that
the independence and unity of Egypt and Sudan were firmly built on

solid foundations. All attempts to sabotage this unity had failed for the following reasons:

The one Fatherland of the Sudanese and the Egyptian people rests on moral as well as material foundations. Its principle of cohesion is derived from old as well as modern factors. Its roots strike deep in the soil of the valley and are nurtured by one single source of life. They are as old as the Pharaonic Crown. They are animated by the spirit of Arabism and Islam. But the Fatherland is at the same time one of the major units of the modern world. It fully shares in the life, the problems, the tasks, the burdens and the hopes of today.[10]

Muhammad Fu'ad Shukri, Ghurbal's colleague at the history department, prepared in the mid-1940s numerous comprehensive studies, with the aim to prove the historical bond connecting Egypt and Sudan. His studies relied on an impressive scientific apparatus (extensive bibliography, many footnotes, appendixes, and maps), covering the period of Egyptian rule over Sudan from Muhammad 'Ali to the condominium treaty of 1899.[11] In his study *Misr wa-al-siyada 'ala al-sudan* (Egypt and the Sovereignty over Sudan) Shukri presented historical facts with the intention to prove Egypt's legitimate rights of sovereignty over both parts of the Nile valley. For Shukri it was clear: the two countries constituted "one political fabric under one crown," as was the case under Muhammad 'Ali and his successors. Shukri pointed out that he chose to use the term *siyada* in its legal implication (sovereignty) and not in its literal meaning, which is authority or mastery.[12]

Shukri remained persistent in his historical arguments and findings also after the separation of Egypt and Sudan in the republican era. For instance, in 1957, a year after Sudan became independent, he published a broader and more profound version of his earlier study *al-Hukm al-misri fi al-sudan 1820–1885* (1947). In his new book he reiterated previous arguments, particularly paying tribute to the altruistic nature of the Egyptian administration in Sudan and its contribution to Sudanese well-being and progress. He placed greater emphasis on the acceleration of the process of Sudanization, which led to the integration of qualified Sudanese in the administration – a process that culminated with Sudanese occupying most of the administrative posts. Egypt facilitated the foundations for Sudanese self-government, thus allowing the Sudanese to manage their own affairs. The study also examined the reasons for the failure of the Mahdi movement in exercising full sovereignty over the entire Sudan, between 1885 (the withdrawal of the Egyptian forces) and 1898 (the reconquest by British and Egyptian forces). He focused on its bungle in establishing a strong central regime, thus losing territories that constituted part of Sudan during the period of the Egyptian rule.[13]

Shukri revealed the effective structure of the Egyptian administration, which was already then based on Sudanization, that is, the integration of Sudanese in their country's governance. Shukri claimed that throughout the period, the Egyptian rulers regarded Egypt and Sudan as a single entity, in which all its inhabitants, with no exception, enjoyed equal rights. To demonstrate the fairness of Egyptian rule, Shukri drew on documents of the Egyptian ministry of finance clearly showing that large amounts of money were transferred from Cairo to Khartoum to cover the deficit of the Sudanese treasury. The history of Egyptian rule over Sudan was distorted by the British occupation, remonstrated Shukri. His study, he asserted, was aimed at restoring historical justice: Egypt acted in the most humanitarian manner to advance the Sudanese and their well-being. Shukri argued that since Sudan was occupied by Muhammad 'Ali's army, which acted on behalf of the Ottoman sultan – the sovereign of Sudan and Ethiopia since the sixteenth century – Sudan and Egypt were therefore one Ottoman province. With the consent of the sultan, the two countries were united politically. Shukri went further, stating that Egypt occupied Sudan following a request made by the Sudanese people to impose Egyptian rule in Sudan to eradicate the prevailing state of anarchy and to establish law, order, and security, which would lead to economic recovery.[14]

Rashed El-Barawy, an economics scholar and a moderate socialist, provided a different account concerning Muhammad 'Ali's decision to occupy Sudan. According to him, Muhammad 'Ali's goal was to discover the sources of the Nile and "to follow up the ancient traditions aiming at the unification of the Nile valley." His son Isma'il occupied most of Sudan and politically unified Egypt and the occupied Sudanese territories. He also established Khartoum as the new capital and introduced new methods of modern administration.[15]

From Shukri's account it follows that Sudan was already ruled by semi-independent Egypt in the early 1820s. Isma'il Kamil, Muhammad 'Ali's son, who led the military conquest, was appointed the first governor-general of Sudan in 1822. His appointment and that of his successors were made by the Egyptian rulers and not by the Ottoman sultan, which meant that the sovereignty over Sudan was Egyptian, still within the framework of Egypt's formal link with the Ottoman Empire.[16]

Other Egyptian proponents of the unity of the Nile valley expanded on the issue of sovereignty, stating that the international legal status of Sudan was determined by the Ottomans, formally the rulers of that region. The sultan issued an internationally recognized *firman* on 13 February 1841, empowering Muhammad 'Ali with the authority to rule the provinces of Nubia, Darfur, Kordofan, and Sennar. However, Muhammad 'Ali's rule over Sudan was not hereditary, unlike the case of Egypt, which was based on dynastic rule. The *firman* of 1866 accomplished the unity of the Nile valley, granting Khedive Isma'il hereditary rights over Egypt and Sudan, amalgamating both under his rule.[17]

By 1854, Shukri went on, it was clear that there was a need for major reform, be it financial, administrative, or in relation to slavery. Such reform was needed to empower the central government in Khartoum – a desired development, which could safeguard the political unification of Egypt and Sudan. At the same time, the Egyptian political elite was determined to develop and advance Sudan. For that reason the Egyptian ruler Sa'id Pasha (r. 1854–1863) nominated his brother Muhammad 'Abd al-Halim as governor-general of Sudan.[18]

Shukri, like other Egyptian scholars,[19] concentrated on the legal aspect of the status of both Egypt and Sudan. Methodologically, he relied on the *firmans* promulgated by the Ottoman sultan in the period 1863–1879. For instance, the *firman* of 22 January 1863 determined that Sudan would be recognized as a territory annexed to Egypt. The Ottomans authorized the inheritance of power in Egypt to male descendants of Muhammad 'Ali's family, who would hold the Ottoman title of Pasha. The Egyptian ruler and his successors would govern Sudan throughout their lives. On 27 May 1866, a new *firman* upgraded the dynastic rule – succession not only within Muhammad 'Ali's family, but rather from father to son. This would include Egypt and its annexed territories including Sudan. The *firman* of 8 June 1867 established Egypt as *khidiviya*, that is, the ruler was granted the highest honorary and political Ottoman title (khedive), equivalent to the British viceroy.

The khedive had the right to act independently, but Egypt was still formally part of the Ottoman Empire. In 1867, Egypt participated in the international monetary conference in Paris separately from the Ottoman Empire. However, the Porte was not always satisfied with decisions made by the khedive. For instance, the Ottoman central government disliked the appointment of the British Samuel Baker in April 1869 to governor-general of the new territory of Equatoria for four years, without its permission. It also disapproved of the visit of Isma'il (r. 1863–1879) to Europe, which it perceived as an Egyptian attempt to gain independence from the Ottoman Empire.[20] Isma'il acted untiringly to complete the political unity of the Nile valley by means of Ottoman *firmans* and agreements with countries linked with Sudanese and eastern African affairs such as Britain.

Egyptian scholars advocating for the unity of the Nile valley expanded on that issue. According to them, the Ottoman *firmans* accentuated the fusion of Sudan with Egypt, showing that the system of administration implemented in Sudan was "centralized and incorporated with that of Egypt." Therefore issues of finance and taxation related to the Sudanese provinces were redirected to the Ministry of Finance in Cairo, while military and defense issues were forwarded to the Ministry of War.[21]

As further proof of Egypt's expansion of its territory along the length of the Nile valley, Shukri's detailed account shows that by the mid-1870s Egypt managed to gain the following:

1. Extension of its sovereignty over eastern Sudan, the entire western Red Sea coast up to Bab al-Mandab, and the Somali countries (*bilad al-Sumal*) up to the Juba Estuary.
2. The occupation of the Darfur region in western Sudan.
3. A *firman* on 18 July 1875 certifying Egypt's sovereignty over Zila', which meant that the entire African Red Sea coast was under Egyptian sovereignty.
4. The occupation of the Sultanate of Harar (situated in present-day Ethiopia).
5. The occupation of the areas of the Upper Nile and al-Ghazal Lake.
6. The extension of Egypt's sovereignty on the eastern African coast from Guardafui to the Juba Estuary.[22]

Isma'il's expansionist policy, stated Shukri, was costly and led to war with Ethiopia over the control of the Red Sea and other vital territories. The dismissal of Khedive Isma'il in 1879 was to have an effect on Egypt's tough policies of preventing slave trade in Sudan and the establishment of law and order in many parts of the country. Tawfiq, Isma'il's son and successor, relied heavily on European powers to establish his position domestically. He nominated Muhammad Ra'uf in 1880 as governor-general of Sudan, instead of Charles Gordon (who resigned in 1879). Ra'uf, argued Shukri, acted aggressively and violently to stop the slave trade, similarly to Gordon earlier. Like Gordon he was assisted by foreigners, whom he appointed as local governors and supervisors to combat slave traders.[23]

'Abd al-Rahman al-Rafi'i, a renowned historian and politician (senior member of the National Party), argued that Egypt's failure to crush the Mahdi forces was caused by Britain. On the eve of the Mahdi revolt, he detailed, the number of Egyptian troops stationed on Sudanese soil was 32,610. The Egyptian army had the military capability to thwart the revolt, Rafi'i stated confidently, yet the fact that it failed to do so was utterly due to the unbearable British interference in Egyptian affairs. The British benefited from the historical coincidence that the Mahdi and the 'Urabi revolts occurred at the same time. The 'Urabi revolt (1881–1882) provided the British imperialists with a pretext to occupy Egypt, whereas they exploited the Mahdi uprising to separate Sudan from Egypt and then to take control of the country. True, they were not behind these uprisings, since each had its causes, yet the British controlled the developments to advance their interests. When the Mahdi revolt intensified and the Egyptian authorities in both Sudan (led by the governor-general 'Abd al-Qadir Hilmi Pasha) and Egypt were determined to crush the rebels by dispatching more troops to Sudan, the British ordered the weak Khedive Tawfiq to dismiss 'Abd al-Qadir and replace him by a weak governor-general ('Ala' al-Din). The latter lacked the capabilities of his predecessor and upon unequivocal "British advice" Egypt withdrew its army from Sudan. Prime Minister Sharif Pasha, who refused to follow the "advice," stressing that "if we leave the Sudan, the Sudan would not leave us," was forced to resign on 7 January 1884. His successor, Nubar Pasha, fulfilled the British "advice" and evacuated 11,000 Egyptian and European officials from Khartoum as well as 25,000 combatants of the Egyptian garrisons in Sudan. The evacuation, opined Rafi'i, was the hardest blow Egypt had experienced since the British occupation of 1882.[24]

Like al-Rafi'i, Shukri thought that the Egyptian army had no reason to withdraw from Sudan in the wake of the Mahdi uprising. It was not a result of flawed Egyptian management but rather "a war of slave merchants against a community of European functionaries." The political guidelines for Egyptian rule over Sudan, said Shukri, were formulated by Muhammad 'Ali, and were based on "the preservation of the unity of the Nile valley; the participation of Sudanese in the administration and the management of state affairs under the auspices of 'a fatherly government,' comprised of Egyptians and Sudanese." Under Egyptian rule, Sudan was opened to the world, which broadened its people's horizons. Thus the Sudanese people were better able to comprehend their geographic surroundings, having a better understanding of agricultural and agrarian issues as well as their natural resources. This remarkable development was facilitated by the recruitment of foreign scientists by the Egyptian authorities for the purpose of academic research on Sudan. On the basis of these scientific findings, Egypt could introduce major reforms in Sudan.[25]

The Arabization of Sudan was accomplished primarily through Egyptian efforts. However, there was little evidence showing major waves of Arab migrants coming to Sudan from other directions. There was evidence of minor migration waves of Arab tribes from the Arabian Peninsula making their way to northwestern or western Africa. For the Egyptian geographer Dr. 'Abbas 'Ammar (Fu'ad I University), it was Muhammed 'Ali who emerged as the figure that would lead Sudan toward the salvation from its flaws:

The salvation of the Sudan from chaos and anarchy was one of the main objectives of the Egyptian campaign in the early nineteenth century, a campaign which, for the first time in history, unified the Sudan from Wadi Halfa to the Equatorial Province; thus saving the Sudanese from the fate of almost all other African peoples, who have been suffering from European exploitation ever since the partition of the Dark Continent.[26]

Sudan remained united under Egyptian control until the Mahdi revolt of the early 1880s, after which Egypt was forced by the British government to evacuate the interior regions of Sudan.[27]

Professor (Maître) Mahmoud Kamel took pains to show that Egypt's claim to sovereignty over Sudan goes back to 3197 BC, when the Pharaohs of the First Dynasty ruled both Egypt and Nubia. Stressing historical continuity of Egyptian rule over Sudan, he argued that Egypt lost Sudan in the wake of the Mahdi uprising in 1885, as a result of British ill-advice followed by pressure that "compelled the Khedive to evacuate inexorably the southern province of Egypt." Kamel went on to say that Egypt would have continued to rule Sudan if it were not for British interference.[28]

The British Embassy replied, conversely, that if Egypt had not followed the British advice, it "would have suffered further reverses in the Sudan, thus leaving the way clear for the Mahdi's forces to penetrate north of Wadi Halfa and invade Egypt itself."[29] Moreover, the research department of the British Foreign Office prepared a study aiming to challenge allegations made by Egyptian scholars that Sudan was ruled continuously by Egypt from time immemorial.[30] Parts of the research relied on works written within the 'Abdin Project – a nearly two-and-a-half-decade project initiated by King Fu'ad (1922–1936), in which monarchist historians and foreign experts (archivists, philologists, and historians) were invited by the king to rewrite the history of Egypt.[31] This extensive royal historiographical project, as Di-Capua put it, was "to explain the modern Egyptian experience as part of a story of modernization and transition whose center was the dynasty itself."[32]

Defining the borders of the lower valley of the Nile as "the First Cataract to the South, the Mediterranean on the North, the Arabian and Libyan deserts to East and West," the study noted the area was known by the name the Black Land. The area between the First and Second Cataracts was known as Wawat, and the country to the south of the Second Cataract as Kush – nowadays known as Lower Nubia – a country where the people spoke both Arabic and Nubian languages. Around 3200 BC the Black Land area was occupied by "a Hamitic race related to the Berbers of North Africa and to the Gallas and Somalis. Tribal migrations brought about important modifications in the racial characteristics." At a later period, two new kingdoms evolved: in the north (the Delta) and in the south. The two were united and separated but were finally integrated under Menes the king of the south at about 3200 BC. His successors extended the borders after defeating the Nubians and reaching the boundaries of Upper Egypt (between Jabal al-Silsila and Aswan). The people of this area were of "Hamitic stock" and the "negroes of the south," settling in this area only several centuries later during the Third Dynasty.

In the period 2470–2270 BC, which marked the Sixth Dynasty, efforts were made by the northerners to subdue the regions south of the First Cataract, with Nubia being occupied for a short period. However, the last king of the Eleventh Dynasty (about 2000 BC) succeeded in expanding Egypt's rule to the Third Cataract (Dongola area). Egyptian rule continued through the period 2000–1780 BC. Under the Eighteenth Dynasty, Egyptian rule continued to expand, reaching as far as Napata (Jabal Barkal some 400 km north of Khartoum), but never beyond it. Northern Sudan was ruled and colonized by Egypt until 1090 BC. Nevertheless, the power of Egypt declined gradually under the Ramesside Pharaohs (1167–1090 BC), and consequently the people of the south gradually freed themselves of Egyptian domination. By 945 BC they established their own kingdom, with Napata as its capital. In 748 BC King Piye of Ethiopia conquered both the southern and the northern areas of the Nile valley, and Egypt was under Ethiopian control until the Assyrian invasion in 663 BC. In the period 332 BC–638 AD, the Ptolemaic–Roman era, Egypt managed to stretch its southern borders no farther than Qasr Ibrim (about 145 mi south of Shellal – a village south of Aswan). The Muslim Arab ruler 'Amr (640 AD) occupied areas in northern Sudan up to Dongola but without subduing Sudan. It was only Muhammad 'Ali's son Isma'il who occupied Sudan in its entirety in 1821 upon his father's order.[33]

Both British and Egyptian scholars agreed that Sudan was under Egyptian rule since it was fully occupied by Muhammad 'Ali's forces in the early 1820s. Nevertheless, Egyptian propagandists of the unity of the Nile valley continued throughout the 1940s vigorously to prove by all possible methods that Sudan was Egypt's domain throughout the nineteenth century. Their arguments focused on Samuel Baker's book *Ismailia*,[34] which provides a detailed account of his work in the service of Khedive Isma'il (1869–1873), for whom he participated in the task to suppress "the slave-hunters of Central Africa, and to annex the countries constituting the Nile Basin, with the object of opening those savage regions to legitimate commerce and establishing a permanent government."[35]

For Egyptian propagandists, Baker's book was proof that Sudan was ruled fairly by the Egyptian khedive and that the latter took pains to establish law and order in the Nile valley. They quoted Baker as saying (without reference to the source): "the European tourist in 1861 was able to travel alone throughout the vast regions of the Sudan with the same feeling of security as that of Londoners frequenting Hyde Park at sunset. The people of the Sudan are law abiding and courteous."[36] Nevertheless, neither 'Ammar nor any other propagandists provided any satisfactory explanation regarding the motives behind the Mahdi revolt and its essence. According to Baker, the situation in Sudan was disorderly and chaotic prior to the Mahdi revolt: "the entire country was leased out to piratical slave-hunters, under the name of traders, by the Khartoum government."[37] However, Baker had no doubts:

I am perfectly convinced that the Khedive was thoroughly sincere in his declared purpose of suppressing the slave-trade, not only as a humanitarian, but as an enlightened man of the world, who knew, from the example of the great Powers of Europe, that the time had arrived when civilization demanded the extinction of such horrors as were the necessary adjuncts of slave-hunting. The Khedive had thus determined to annex the Nile Basin, and establish his government, which would afford protection, and open an immense country to the advantages of commerce. This reform must be the death-blow to the so-called traders of Khartoum, who were positively the tenants of the governor-general of the Soudan.[38]

The khedive was sincere in his intention to suppress slavery and to establish order in the Nile valley. His decision to do so was unpopular and in direct opposition to public opinion. Overall, his efforts to establish his hegemony over Sudan were met with scant success. British diplomats concluded unequivocally that the Mahdi revolt was against misgovernment;[39] they somehow chose to ignore the religious aspects of the rebellion.

In his authoritative study *Historical Discord in the Nile*, Gabriel Warburg displayed considerable differences in the way Egyptian and Sudanese writers interpreted similar major events in the nineteenth century – the Turco–Egyptian rule of Sudan (1820–1885) and the Mahdi movement and rule (1881–1898). For the Egyptian masses as well as elites, that period constituted an integral part of their relationship with the Nile valley. They portrayed the Egyptian rule as civilizing and progressive. They maintained that the appearance of the Mahdi and the main reason for its revolt were due to the unpopular rule of those Christian European high functionaries, such as Charles Gordon (governor-general of Sudan 1873–1880), who were recruited by Khedive Isma'il.

Sudanese historians writing in the post-condominium years, when the politics of a unified Nile valley was no longer on the agenda, portrayed the Turco–Egyptian and British colonialist periods differently from their Egyptian counterparts. For instance, Mekki Shibeika presented aspects of the Turco–Egyptian rule over Sudan in the nineteenth century favorably. He nevertheless emphasized the centrality of the economic factors (slaves, gold, etc.) behind Muhammad 'Ali's decision to conquer Sudan, yet he was very critical of the state of Sudanese society at the time, which he viewed as "primitive and disjoined." For him the occupiers were the bearers of civilization. They gradually stopped the slave trade, modernized agricultural methods, made some progress in the development of education and justice, and opened Sudan to the external world. However, like British scholars, he blamed the Egyptian administration for "over taxation, corruption and other ills," similar to the situation in other Ottoman provinces.[40]

Hasan Ahmad Ibrahim, unlike Shibeika, was very critical of Egyptian historians who "have a paternalistic attitude toward the Sudan." Muhammad 'Ali and his successors did not take over Sudan to improve and develop Sudanese welfare, health, or education, but rather they did so to take slaves, gold, and other economic resources from Sudan. He pointed at the corrupt and inefficient administration and the extremely high taxes as the main reasons for Egypt's failure in Sudan in the nineteenth century.[41] Ibrahim al-Hardalu and Muhammad 'Umar Bashir (Mohamed Beshir) also focused on the corrupt, exploitative, and colonialist nature of the Turco–Egyptian rule. Like others, Beshir disputed Egyptian assertions characterizing Turco–Egyptian rule as a civilizing mission. The Egyptians, he revealed, "slaughtered all my relatives."[42] However, Beshir agreed that Turco–Egyptian rule laid the foundation of modern Sudan as it "had implied unity and order." Sudan was developed in the fields of education, agriculture and irrigation, foreign and internal trade, and communications.[43]

Egyptian and British writers disagreed on the issue of which of the two countries played a more significant role in the reoccupation of Sudan in the late nineteenth century. To demonstrate the indisputable nature of the unity of the Nile valley, Egyptian propagandists and politicians quoted selectively from Winston Churchill's *The River War* (1902). Indeed, Churchill admitted that Egypt ruled Sudan "from 1819 to 1883," yet he determined that its rule was

not kindly, wise, or beneficial. Its aim was to exploit, not to improve the local population. The miseries of the people were aggravated rather than lessened: but they were concealed ... Violence and plunder were more hideous, since they were cloaked with legality and armed with authority. The land was undeveloped and poor ... Scarcity was frequent. Famines were periodical ... Corrupt and incapable Governor-General succeeded each other at Khartoum with bewildering rapidly ... with hardly any exceptions, the Pashas were consistent in oppression ... The rule of Egypt was iniquitous: yet it preserved the magnificent appearance of Imperial dominion.[44]

The propagandists for the unity of the Nile valley could nevertheless find some comfort in Churchill's account of the Fashoda incident (1898), in which he clearly referred to the "re-establishment of Egyptian authority."[45] In September 1944, in the final stages of World War II, al-Ahram referred to the historical meaning of the Fashoda incident and concluded that the reconquest of Sudan was effectively in the name of Egypt alone. The 1899 condominium treaty should therefore have been considered null and void. The British played a minor part in the process of reconquering Sudan by providing Egypt with some logistic services. However, this was nothing compared to the massive military involvement of the British and American forces in the liberation of France.[46]

Countering British allegations that Egypt was forced to abandon Sudan following the take-over of Khartoum by the Mahdi's forces, Egyptian scholars argued that it was Britain, which had occupied Egypt since 1882, that ordered the Egyptian withdrawal. To support their argument, they relied on the British Consul-General Lord Cromer, who declared "any Egyptian minister who objected to that decision should relinquish his office."[47] Egyptian nationalists of the post–World War II period could safely rely on words of one of Egypt's nationalist father figures, Mustafa Kamil, who condemned the British occupation government in July 1895 for its harsh measures employed about a decade earlier, forcing Egypt to evacuate "the Sudan which we consider the spirit of our dear land, on which hangs the life of our country, and its death."[48] Egyptian experts declared, moreover, that the Egyptian government withdrew from Sudan in a tactical retreat, removing its troops to prevent a massacre at the hands of the Mahdi's forces. Even as Egyptian troops evacuated Sudan, the British still regarded Sudan as an Egyptian domain. This manifested itself in the Fashoda incident.[49] Even after the withdrawal of the Mahdi's forces, in the mind of the Egyptians, Sudan remained an integral part of Egypt.[50]

Following the end of World War II, the polemic in al-Ikhwan al-Muslimun over the question of whether the Sudanese people opted for unification intensified. For Muhammad Mahmud Jalal, a member of parliament, the answer was definitely positive. Drawing on historical research he challenged the common wisdom regarding the motives behind the Mahdi revolt. The uprising, he argued, manifested a desire for unification of the northern and southern zones of the Nile valley. It occurred in conjunction with the 'Urabi revolt in the north – both revolts were against the arbitrariness and extortion of a regime that they both wanted to topple.[51] Muhammad 'Ali and Isma'il laid the physical foundation for a single political Nile valley entity by building huge villages. Common history, language, hopes, and torments empowered and strengthened the north–south bonds.[52]

In 1925, shortly after the expulsion of the Egyptian military from Sudan, an Egyptian intellectual, who chose to remain anonymous, published in the US-based magazine *Current History* his account of "Egypt's Claim to the Sudan" with the stated intention of presenting the subject from "an objective and impartial" viewpoint. He divided the history of Sudan into three periods: first, from Muhammed 'Ali to the Mahdi revolt (1812–1881); second, from the Mahdi revolt to the withdrawal of British troops (1884); third, the reconquering of Sudan 1896–1899 until 1924.[53] The anonymous Egyptian writer argued that the incorporation of Sudan and Egypt began under Muhammed 'Ali in 1812. The military campaign led by his son Isma'il in 1821 succeeded in establishing Egyptian rule. Khedive Isma'il, who took power in 1863, strengthened the links between Egypt and Sudan. Isma'il, emphasized the anonymous writer, expanded the territory of Sudan, and his army conquered the entire Red Sea zone and extensively developed Sudan's infrastructure, constructing a railroad from Wadi Halfa to Khartoum, and building many roads. Isma'il also abolished slavery and established schools. Egypt was the first to occupy and develop Sudan, and all that country's achievements should be attributed to the Egyptians.[54]

When the Mahdi revolt began in 1881, "Egypt had in the Sudan an army of 40,490 soldiers, twelve military steamships on the Nile, 20,000 volunteers, and 30,000 officials." It was significant, stated the writer, that "the 'Urabi and the Mahdi revolutions started at the same time." In both cases, "the British were said to encourage" the uprising so that they could have an excuse to take control of the Nile valley in its entirety. In 1882, the Mahdi's forces defeated the Egyptian army commanded by Yusuf Pasha al-Salami. The military confrontation continued in various parts of Sudan until 1884. At that point the British government instructed the Egyptian government to withdraw. Sharif Pasha, the prime minister, was given two options: withdrawal or resignation. He opted for resignation, stating: "'We have no right to withdraw, because the Sudan belongs to Turkey [the Ottoman Empire], who gave it to us to take care of.' Nubar Pasha, an Armenian, who succeeded Sharif Pasha in 1884, ordered a year later the Egyptian army to withdraw."[55]

In his depiction of the Anglo–Egyptian reconquest of Sudan, the Egyptian writer took pains to prove that throughout the process the British referred to Egypt as the legal sovereign of Sudan. In 1896, he asserted, the Egyptian army, led by Lord Kitchener, took control of Dongola, and in 1898 it arrived at Fashoda. By 1899, after the victory of Omdurman, Sudan in its entirety was reoccupied. British politicians as well as journalists proclaimed that the reconquering of Sudan was undertaken for the purpose of restoring the khedive's rule over those provinces. When Britain risked a war with France by persisting on the retreat of Major Marchand from Fashoda (1898), Lord Kitchener contended throughout his subtle talks with Marchand that Fashoda was an Egyptian territory, and it was the Egyptian flag that was raised on the fort at Fashoda.[56]

Relying on diplomatic correspondence, the anonymous writer argued that Egypt, on its part, had never relinquished its legal rights to Sudan. In his letter to Lord Cromer on 9 October 1898, Boutros Ghali, the Egyptian foreign minister, wrote:

The Government of His Highness the Khedive, as you know, did not at any time relax its efforts to reconquer the Sudan, which is the vital source of Egypt's life. If the government withdrew its army temporarily, it was due only to circumstances of force majeure. The revolting Sudanese were never recognized by any country, and therefore the Sudan remained, according to the principles of international law, the property of Egypt. The Sudan was never a res nullius at any time between 1884 and 1898, and therefore could not be occupied or reconquered except by Egypt, who remained the owner and who throughout the whole period from 1884 to 1899 never relinquished [its] rights in this territory.[57]

Moreover, throughout the Fashoda crisis, Britain too, argued the anonymous Egyptian writer, was of the opinion that Sudan belonged to Egypt. He provided two documents to prove his argument. On 10 October 1898, Lord Cromer wrote to Lord Salisbury, the British prime minister, that "the negotiations are now proceeding with the French government to secure the title of Egypt to the territories abandoned by her during the Mahdist rebellion under the pressure of force majeure, to which ... His Excellency (Boutros Pasha) explicitly records Egypt has never renounced her rights." And on 12 October 1898, Lord Salisbury wrote to Sir Edmund Monson, the British ambassador to France, that in a conversation he had with the French ambassador to London on the state of the Upper Nile, "I generally insisted on the view that the Valley of the Nile had belonged and still belongs to Egypt, and that whatever impediment or diminution that title might have suffered through the conquest and occupation of the Mahdi had been removed by the victory of the Anglo-Egyptian army on 2 September."[58]

Egypt retained a considerable quantitative advantage over Britain in all facets. For instance, during the reoccupation of Sudan "the Egyptian army provided 25,000 men compared to 800 British men (a number gradually increased to 2,000). That is, the British army was never more than one-twelfth of the Egyptian army." Egypt paid two-thirds of the £2,400,000 costs of the military expenses. Egypt also took upon itself the lion's share of the maintenance of the military forces in Sudan. Since the reconquest, the military contingent in Sudan consisted of 10,000 Egyptian soldiers, who cost the Egyptian government £13,000,000, and merely 1,000 British soldiers, at an expense of no more than £2,000,000. As far as infrastructure developments in Sudan were concerned, the Egyptian taxpayer bore the entire costs of building railroads, public buildings, and telegraphs, as well as of the administration of Sudan, totaling £5,600,000. The anonymous author concluded that Sudan had never ceased to be an Egyptian territory.[59]

The British presented a different version of the developments since their occupation of Egypt in 1882 – an occupation that occurred "not in opposition to the Egyptian government, but in order to help that government" to maintain internal order and to protect "Egypt's territory from foreign aggression." Britain was represented in Egypt by its agent and consul-general Lord Cromer. The British recognized Egypt's special status as an autonomous country under Ottoman suzerainty, "but in matters of importance the advice of the British agent was given and was expected to be followed." The British reorganized the Egyptian army by entrusting it to British officers' command. The British agreed that Sudan had been part of Egyptian territory until it was lost in 1883 following the Mahdi revolt. However, the British did not mention that in December 1883, as noted above by the Egyptian authors, they gave the order for the Egyptian evacuation from Sudan. Indeed, from then on, the status of Sudan was to change. In 1896 the British considered it possible and desirable to recover Sudan, and a military operation led by General Kitchener was completed successfully in 1898 with the recapture of Sudan in its entirety. The British admitted that these operations were conducted jointly by the Egyptian and British armies and that the expense of the war was also shared between the two countries.[60]

A British report drew a distinction between the northern and southern parts of Sudan in relation to the Egyptian claims over Sudan. It accepted some of the Egyptian arguments, chiefly that the Egyptians and the population of northern Sudan had a common religion, language, and, to some extent, racial origins. Geographically, the Nile "with its vital water supply resources is shared alike" by both Sudanese and Egyptians. Moreover, historically, the Egyptian claims of continuous reign over Sudan since the early nineteenth century were accepted by the British: "Egypt, by her conquest of the Sudan in 1821 and by subsequent agreements with Great Britain in 1899 and 1936, has alike legal and moral claims to *share* in the administration of the northern Sudan, until the Sudanese themselves are sufficiently politically developed to rule themselves."[61]

The consensus became narrower, however, in the next sections of the report. Egypt, as its record showed, failed to contribute to the welfare of the Sudanese, or to prepare them for self-government. Egypt was unable to maintain peace and order within its own territory and therefore was "unfit to exercise sole control over the people of another country," the report asserted. It pointed out several reasons why Egypt could claim only a partial share in the administration of northern Sudan and definitely had no claim to share in the administration of the "pagan negro" population living in southern Sudan. First, historically, Egypt had an infamous record as far as slavery was concerned. It was General Gordon whose interference terminated a long period, during which Egyptians regarded Sudan principally as an area that it could tap for slaves to work in the Egyptian fields. Slavery was no longer legal in Egypt, but "the memory of the Egyptian slave trade still lives in the minds of Sudanese," stressed the British report. Second, economically, Egypt's record in Sudan throughout the period 1821–1885 showed that the Egyptians exploited Sudan by colonizing the fertile parts of that country. They treated the Sudanese harshly and with cruelty to please and enrich their Pashas – a behavior that "will not die from the minds of the generation which lived under Egyptian rule."[62]

The British report accepted the fact that Muhammad 'Ali's son Isma'il conquered northern Sudan in 1821, yet

it is equally certain that after the Egyptians had been driven out by the Mahdist rule, the Northern Sudan was only recovered to Egypt with the assistance of Great Britain. It was Kitchener and the River Columns of his Expeditionary Force, composed alike of British and Egyptian troops, that fought and won the battle of Omdurman in 1898 and thus inaugurated the regime of the present Sudan Government, authority for which is based on the Condominium Agreement.

The British record of achievements in Sudan over a period of 47 years (1899–1946) was impressive. Key figures such as Gordon, Kitchener, Stack, and Newbold exemplified humane, altruistic values and in some cases gave their lives in the service of Sudan and the Sudanese. One may nevertheless question that if the British were motivated by altruism in Sudan, then why would they stress that Sudan was a strategic asset for the empire: "Should Great Britain agree to the removal of British military forces from Egypt itself, the strategic importance of the Sudan as a site for the location of air bases and military forces within range of the vital to

Great Britain's Far East possessions, i.e., the Suez Canal, would become even more important than it is at the present time."[63]

Like other Egyptian scholars, Rafi'i disputed the British narrative of the gradual reconquering of the Sudan in the 1890s. According to him, the British used Egyptian troops and money to advance their plot to take over the Sudan for themselves.[64] The reconquering of Sudan, liberal Egyptian scholars argued, was the initiative of the sirdar (commander in chief) of the Egyptian Army, who arranged with Lord Cromer, British agent and consul-general to Egypt, the dispatch of an expeditionary force to reconquer Sudan in 1896. The vast majority of the military force comprised Egyptian troops, and the Egyptian treasury covered the costs of the mission. In other words, the reconquering of Sudan was an Egyptian venture, and the British played a negligible role in the battle-fields. Legally, in the years of evacuation (1885–1898), Sudan consti-tuted an integral part of Egypt, and moreover, after the Egyptian forces conquered it, Sudan became an inseparable part of Egypt, both from "the legal and factual viewpoints."[65]

Undoubtedly, Rafi'i as well as other Egyptian historians were inspired by Ahmad Lutfi al-Sayyid, the iconic Egyptian liberal nationalist, who had already argued in his newspaper *al-Jarida* in 1910 that "the Sudan is Egypt's by right of conquest."[66] He stated further that Egypt was the first nation to colonize Sudan, which he regarded as an integral part of Egypt:

She is part of Egypt, and her not being separated is vital to Egypt's life, due to her holding the source of the Nile and being her neighbor. We loathed giving her up, then she was reconquered, this time with the participation of the English ... colonizing [*isti'mar*] the Sudan is the right of Egyptians, and no one else, just as the subsidizing of the Sudan is the duty of Egyptians, and no one else. Egyptians look at Sudanese as brothers, as a part of their community, so it's their responsibility to look out for their brothers' welfare.[67]

Muddathir 'Abdel Rahim, a Sudanese historian, argues that the Anglo–Egyptian joint occupation of Sudan took place despite protests from the Ottoman sultan. On 27 March 1896, noted Rahim, the grand vizier telegraphed the khedive to remind him that the Egyptian military force constituted an integral part of the Ottoman army and that "the use of these troops –especially when directed against Muslims, as was the case with the Mahdists, depended absolutely and entirely on the will and permission of his Imperial Majesty. Such permission had neither been sought nor granted ... and the whole enterprise was not in the interest of Egypt."[68] In other words, the reoccupation of Sudan by the Anglo–Egyptian forces was a move prohibited by the Ottoman sultan, the formal suzerain of Sudan. His objection was not taken into consideration, by either Britain or Egypt, a state of affairs that reflected the weakness of the Ottoman Empire at the time.

The decision to reoccupy Sudan in 1896, stated 'Abdel Rahim, was directed by the British government following the Italian defeat by the forces of the Ethiopian Empire (the Adwa battle) in March 1896. British Prime Minister Lord Salisbury (1895–1902) explained in a letter to Cromer that this move "was inspired by a desire to help the Italian at Kasala [Eastern Sudan] and to prevent the Dervishes [the Mahdi forces] from winning a conspicuous success which might have far-reaching effects."[69] In other words, the reoccupation of Sudan was derived from European imperialist calculations rather than regional considerations. This occurred during the peak of the European imperialist expansionism known as the "colonial scramble for Africa." Indeed, Ethiopia was an exception until 1935–1936.

The Fashoda incident of September 1898 should therefore be viewed as part of the struggle for control of the Nile valley between France and Britain. However, to justify the legality of its military actions in the area, 'Abdel Rahim argues, the British force led by Kitchener hoisted the Egyptian flag (not the British), warning the French force that it had no right to hoist the French flag "in the domains of His Highness the Khedive."[70] That is, for imperialist manipulative purposes the British admitted that Egypt had the sovereignty over Sudan. As soon as their goal was achieved, they marginalized Egypt's role, relegating it to a secondary partner in Sudan. As we have seen, 'Abdel Rahim's account of the Fashoda incident supports the one presented by Egyptian historians. However, as we shall later see, his view of the foundations of the doctrine of the unity of the Nile valley was adverse and critical.

Egyptian scholars constantly refuted the actual validity of the condominium rule: the treaties of 19 January and 10 July 1899 were forcefully imposed by the British and were never approved by any Egyptian parliament, they emphasized. Moreover, Egypt's legal circumstances prevented it from concluding the treaties as Sudan was officially under Ottoman sovereignty, a status that was not relinquished until 5 November 1914, the day that Britain and France declared war on the Ottoman Empire. When the treaties were signed, Britain acknowledged the Ottoman suzerainty over Egypt. Therefore, the fact that the Ottoman government did not ratify the agreements made them invalid internationally.[71] El-Barawy went further, blaming Khedive Tawfiq for acting illegally by signing the treaties of 1899. Sudan, emphasized El-Barawy, was not reconquered but "restored to the lawful authority which had been temporarily suspended by the Mahdist rebellion." Britain, he argued, had no right to administer Sudan, as most casualties during the military operation against the Mahdi forces were Egyptians – military and civilians.[72]

Discussing the rationale behind the condominium treaty, the British emphasized their superior role. For the Egyptians, the objective of reconquering Sudan was to recover this territory for the khedive. The British did not belittle the fact that Egypt contributed its full share in the military and financial efforts required to recover Sudan, yet they argued that the British government through "British troops and money as well as a British commander-in-chief, had played a predominant part" in the battlefield and the subsequent victory. Moreover, to prevent future uprisings in Sudan similar to the Mahdi revolt, it was necessary to form a better government, in which the British would play a central role. Strategically, it was vital to defend the southern frontier of Egypt to protect British imperial interests. The condominium agreements of 1899 were the best solution at the time. They could satisfy Egyptian desires, at least on paper, by including Egypt as an equal partner, yet, at the same time, securing for themselves the position of governor-general, the highest administrative authority, who held "the whole powers of administration over the territory." The British asserted that successive governors-general "have established an administrative machine in the Sudan which seems admirably adapted for the country." The British argued that until the 1924 incident (the assassination of Governor-General Lee Stack) the condominium administration was conducted smoothly – the administrative posts in the civil service were "held almost exclusively by British subjects," yet numbers of Egyptians were "employed in the police and technical posts in the Sudan, and Egyptians as well as British forces were stationed there."[73] The British held the Egyptian government responsible for the assassination, which led to the removal of all Egyptian forces from Sudan.[74]

Soon after its conclusion, Egyptian liberal theoreticians asserted, the 1899 treaty was applied in a manner unfair to Egypt's rights – Britain unilaterally and systematically violated it. This assertion was supported by the African American historian Rayford Logan, who was also a pan-African activist. Writing in 1931 on Anglo–Egyptian Sudan, Logan stated that Egyptians were justifiably dissatisfied with the 1899 treaty because Britain had basically granted itself the dominant position in the partnership, whereas Egypt became the junior partner.[75] However, Logan was very critical of the immoral manner in which Egyptians ruled Sudan in the pre-condominium period – the exploitation of Sudanese and of Sudan's natural resources, and the Egyptian slave merchants, who made a fortune particularly during the reign of Muhammad 'Ali.[76]

Sudanese writers, as Warburg shows, took pride in the Mahdi, stressing that Muhammad 'Ali, who occupied Sudan, was looking for Sudanese slaves and gold and that his rule was oppressive and tyrannical. Warburg's general argument was that most Sudanese never supported the idea of the unity of the Nile valley and indeed opted for independence in the 1950s.[77]

From Protectorate to Limited Independence: The Legal Status of Sudan

Throughout the period under review here, Egyptian historians were preoccupied with the issue of the Nile valley after World War I, and more specifically, during the early 1920s – a time marked by a stormy struggle for independence. For instance, Da'ud Barakat's book *al-Sudan al-misri wa-matami' al-siyasa al-baritaniyya* was published in 1924. Barakat was determined to demonstrate that Sudan was an integral part of Egypt and that the latter "would not be able to survive politically and materially without the Sudan." Barakat focused his analysis on the significance of the Nile water flowing from Sudan and its indispensability for Egyptian agriculture. He sharply criticized the British policy toward Sudan, accusing Britain of employing malicious actions aimed at destroying the natural and historical unity of the Nile valley.[78]

Following the conclusion of the condominium treaty, the British disregarded Egypt as the co-administrator of Sudan and concluded foreign treaties on its behalf, remonstrated Egyptian liberal scholars. This process escalated following the outbreak of World War I. For the British, the Ottomans ceased to have any sovereign rights over Egypt after they entered the war on the side of the Central Powers. The British declared their own protectorate over Egypt on 18 December 1914, and this also applied to Sudan. The rise of Egyptian nationalism and the outbreak of the 1919 Revolution led to Britain's unilateral declaration of Egypt's independence in February 1922. For Egyptian scholars, the British abolition of their protectorate over Egypt included Sudan. Nevertheless, the British insisted on upholding the condominium treaty of 1899 in Sudan, ignoring their partnership with Egypt.[79]

The unity of the Nile valley could have been achieved in the period 1919–1924, stated Yunan Labib Rizq in a contemporary study. In his view that period witnessed a marked development in the prospects for Sudanese–Egyptian unification. A large number of Egyptian troops were stationed in Sudan and maintained close links with their "Sudanese brothers," and the two influenced each other. The Sudanese administration relied on "Egyptian expertise" in the process of rebuilding itself.

The fact that Egyptians occupied junior positions in the Sudanese administration was to have positive consequences – they intermingled with the Sudanese people and thus created the foundations for the emergence of a common Sudanese–Egyptian culture. Egyptian teachers played a central role in the development of the Sudanese educational system. In addition, Sudanese and Egyptians found themselves facing a common occupier – the British – in Egypt in the form of the protectorate regime, and in Sudan in the form of the condominium rule. Rizq somehow overlooked the fact that Egypt itself was a partner to the imposed condominium.

Rizq argued that the events of late 1924 were to have adverse effects on the progress made toward the unity of the Nile valley. The removal of the Egyptian troops from Sudan had twofold repercussions: the emerging nationalist movement in Sudan was eliminated, and the Wafd gradually relinquished its revolutionary zeal concerning the unity of the Nile valley, embracing instead a new approach of "mutual understanding," based on diplomatic dialogue with the British. The latter exploited the void created by the diminished Egyptian presence in Sudan to create a new "imperialist reality" in the period 1924–1936. Egypt thus lost its stronghold in Sudan and its proximity with Sudanese everyday life.[80] Likewise, Eve Troutt Powell argued that "by 1919 there was a well-established slogan that called for 'the unity of the Nile Valley.'" According to her, a wide spectrum of Egyptian nationalists saw a link between Egypt's irrepressible struggle for independence and its claim to mastery over Sudan.[81]

According to Egyptian scholars, the British adopted a policy designed to separate Sudan from Egypt, repeatedly and deliberately breaching the condominium treaty. Nevertheless, despite these breaches, the status of Sudan before the conclusion of the 1936 treaty was determined by the following points:

1. The Lausanne Treaty of 1923 mandated that the Ottomans withdraw any sovereign claims over Egypt and Sudan that they exercised prior to 5 November 1914.
2. Sudan continued to be an inextricable part of Egypt in terms of international law.
3. In constitutional and administrative terms, Sudan was separated from Egypt by virtue of the 1899 treaty.[82]

The British held a different view. Egypt and Sudan were under British occupation following the Ottoman Empire's entry into World War I as Britain's enemy. Consequently, the British government was "exercising a role of control in a territory nominally under the suzerainty of an enemy of the United Kingdom." The British declared Egypt their protectorate, and Ottoman suzerainty was terminated. During the Peace Conference after the war, the defeated powers recognized the British protectorate. In the Lausanne Treaty (1923), Turkey renounced its old suzerainty over Egypt as from November 1914, recognizing that "any question arising from the recognition of the State of Egypt should be settled in a manner to be determined later by the powers concerned."[83]

The Milner Committee was formed by the British government to investigate the causes of the uprising of March 1919. The committee began its activity in Egypt in December 1919 and submitted its conclusions to the British government in February 1921. Its findings included the recommendation to terminate the British protectorate in Egypt. 'Abd al-'Azim Ramadan argued that the committee avoided investigating the Sudan issue in order not to harm British interests there. The committee regarded it as a separate issue related to the 1899 treaty. Sudan, it was stated in Milner's report, was entirely different from Egypt as far as its characters, population composition, and political condition were concerned. The British renounced Egyptian efforts to prove that historically they held "ownership rights" over Sudan, as Ahmad Lutfi al-Sayyid, a member of the Egyptian delegation to the Paris Peace Conference (1919), put it. According to Sayyid, the British claimed that the 1899 treaty got legal validity after the conclusion of the Treaty of Sèvres (1920). They also asserted that the Sudanese comprised scattered and separated tribes, most of which were racially different from the Egyptians. Sudan for the Sudanese was the basic principle of the Milner Committee and the British, concluded Sayyid. The Wafd and its leader Sa'd Zaghlul, stated Ramadan, were of the opinion that the separation of the Sudan issue from the Anglo–Egyptian negotiations did not mean that they relinquished Egypt's right over Sudan. Egypt, they maintained, was strong enough to gain its full rights over Sudan, once it settled its dispute with Britain.[84]

Ramadan, who published his historical account in the post-condominium period, argued critically that the Egyptian national movement displayed growing interest in and concern for Sudan in the years after the war, which stemmed from the mounting imperial interests manifested by the British in that country at the time. Ramadan quoted the Indian leader Jawaharlal Nehru, who summarized the Anglo–Egyptian dispute over Sudan as follows: "when the issue of Egypt's independence came up [at the end of World War I], the British wanted to retain the Sudan for themselves. Egyptians on the other hand felt that their very existence was utterly dependent on controlling the Upper Nile sources in the Sudan. The clash of interests between the two countries was consequently inevitable."[85]

According to Ramadan, the clash of interests became clearly visible when talks on the termination of the British protectorate were opened in London in late 1921 between the Egyptian delegation, headed by Prime Minister 'Adli Yakan, and representatives of the British government. During the talks the British regarded the condominium as the legal status of Sudan, whereas Yakan spoke of participation in the administration, but stressed that the sovereignty over Sudan was solely Egyptian. Sudan, he said, was

an Egyptian land and there is no dispute that Egypt has the sovereign rights over the Sudan ... our main concern now is to redefine our rights in the Sudan in an open and frank manner ... Egypt's stand on the Sudan is not derived from its lust for power or from the pleasure of holding the reins of government, but rather we are driven by our interests in the Sudan and the need to protect them. The Nile is our first interest in the Sudan but not the only one. Also, the Sudanese and Egyptian militaries should merge and be subordinated to the Egyptian ruler; we are concerned with the immigration of Egyptians to the Sudan and the necessity to ease their lives as much as possible, including granting them full rights.[86]

British Prime Minister Lloyd George stated unequivocally Britain's interests in Sudan: "beyond our will to secure our transportation via the Sudan, we do not want to interfere with Sudanese affairs, [but] we do not want to waive our center in the Sudan like we did in Egypt." Utterly disregarding Yakan's position on Sudan, British Secretary of Foreign Affairs Lord Curzon formulated his government's requirements as follows: "Egypt undertakes to provide the Sudan government the same military assistance as in the past or alternatively to provide financial aid, the amount of which would be agreed upon by the two governments. All Egyptian forces in the Sudan would be subject to the authority of the Governor General. In return, Britain undertakes to guarantee that Egypt would be supplied with the right amount of Nile water."[87]

In 1947 'Abd al-Rahman al-Rafi'i presented his version of the Sudan problem. He argued that the declaration of independence made by King Fu'ad on 15 March 1922 was not received cheerfully by the peoples of the Nile valley. The Egyptian people saw no manifestations of independence, but the opposite: British occupation continued, martial law was still in force, and Sudan was practically cut off from Egypt.[88] Moreover, according to Muhammad Husayn Haykal, the eminent Egyptian intellectual and leader of the Liberal Constitutionalist (al-Ahrar al-Dusturiyyin) party, Prime Minister 'Abd al-Khaliq Tharwat (March 1922–November 1922), a member of Haykal's party, consulted his colleagues regarding the king's title. According to Haykal, the committee drafting Egypt's new constitution put forward two alternatives: either the constitution would state the title as "King of Egypt and Sudan," or it would apply to Egypt only. In the latter case, Sudan would require a separate constitutional law, yet Sudan would still be regarded as an integral part of Egypt. Tharwat was advised by his party to endorse the two versions. However, the British opposed the two versions, arguing that both contradicted their statement of 28 February 1922 regarding Sudan's status. The British position prevailed, and consequently Tharwat stepped down. When Faruq was declared king in 1936, following his father's death, his title remained King of Egypt.[89]

When the Lausanne Conference was convened in November 1922 to negotiate a peace treaty with Mustafa Kemal's Turkey, the Wafd sent a memorandum to Lord Curzon, the British foreign secretary, requesting that Sa'd Zaghlul, the exiled leader, be allowed to present, on behalf of the Egyptian people, the following national demands before the participating states:

1. Recognition of the full independence of the Nile valley (Egypt and Sudan).
2. Evacuation of British troops from the Nile valley in its entirety.
3. Preservation of the full neutrality of the Suez Canal.[90]

The Wafd took the liberty to speak on behalf of the Egyptian people, disregarding the unpopular government of Muhammad Tawfiq Nasim Pasha, the king's man. It made it clear that the presence of British troops in the Nile valley constituted a constant threat to the Suez Canal's neutrality and to the principle of equality between countries, as stated in the 1888 treaty (signed in Istanbul on 29 October 1888 relating to free navigation through the Suez Canal). The independence of Egypt, the Wafd concluded, was the best means for real preservation of the Suez Canal's neutrality. In this regard, Egypt's interest coincided with that of other countries.[91]

Muhammad Tawfiq Nasim's government (November 1922–March 1923) did nothing to advance the national demands. On the contrary, while finalizing the more controversial clauses of the new constitution, it acted vigorously to expand the powers of the king and surrendered to British ultimatums on the provisions related to Sudan. Sudan was omitted from Fu'ad's title. Instead of King of Egypt and Sudan, he was now King of Egypt only. In addition, the government agreed that the constitution would apply only to the Egyptian kingdom, but nevertheless added that Egypt's rights in Sudan should not be affected.[92]

The 1919 Revolution echoed positively in Sudan. Young, educated Sudanese were greatly influenced by the revolution, which also contributed to the rise of nationalist ideas among many of them. In 1920 the Union Association (*Jam'iyyat al-Ittihad*) was founded by a group of young Sudanese, who called for the full independence of Egypt and Sudan. The group took upon itself to prepare the Sudanese people for independence from British imperialist rule. In 1922 a brave Sudanese officer, Lieutenant 'Ali 'Abd al-Latif, launched a rebellion against the imperialist policy. He pronounced his nationalist principles, which were the following: Egypt and Sudan constituted a single and inseparable entity, and the British manipulations among Sudanese intended to sabotage the unity of the Nile valley; the British did so against the will of the Sudanese people; those Sudanese who declared loyalty to the British represented themselves only; and the British policy did not bring any benefit to the people of Sudan. The British reacted swiftly and aggressively. They persecuted the movement and arrested its leaders.

Sudanese people heaved a sigh of relief when the Egyptian nationalist leader Sa'd Zaghlul formed his government in 1924. The nationalist movement in Sudan expanded, and educated Sudanese hoped that the popular government would mark a new era, during which the goals of the people of the Nile valley would be realized. The facts that Zaghlul's government enjoyed popularity in Sudan and that the Sudanese people adhered to unity with Egypt and desired to see the withdrawal of the British from the Nile valley were angrily received by the British. The latter continued with their machinations to separate Sudan from Egypt. Their decisive contribution to the downfall of Zaghlul's government in November 1924 marked an important success in that direction.[93] For instance in April 1924 an exhibition of the British colonies took place in London. The Sudan government was presented there as one of the colonies; Egypt as a party to the condominium was neither asked for permission nor mentioned at all. Governor-General Lee Stack was told off by Sa'd Zaghlul in a letter of protest, but his actions were backed by London and Lord Allenby, the British high commissioner. Shortly afterward, the arrival in Cairo of a pro-unionist Sudanese delegation was prevented by the Sudan government. This led to a stormy debate in the Egyptian parliament on 23 June 1924, in which Rafi'i, now in his capacity as an MP, delivered an anti-British speech, saying:

Severe events are happening nowadays in the Sudan; two opposing Sudanese movements have emerged – the first, a natural movement, has emerged from within the Sudanese people, whereas the other is an artificial product of British imperialism. The natural movement ... includes open minded Sudanese, who wanted to visit Egypt in order to express their loyalty to Egypt and its king, but they were prevented [by the British] from doing so ... It is our duty to inform the world that the movement organized by the British is an artificial one ... we should announce to the world that our main concern is the prosperity and progress of the Sudan. History is our witness that we always assisted in the advancement of the Sudan. The British claim that for the sake of the Sudan's prosperity it is essential for them to maintain their sovereignty over that country, is false because the Egyptians were the ones to lay the railways line, to build palaces and buildings, to open schools; they dug ditches, built dams and bridges, strengthened the infrastructure and sacrificed their lives and properties for the sake of the Sudan's prosperity.[94]

Sa'd Zaghlul reassured parliament that his government would do its utmost to protect Egypt's rights in the Sudan. Yet, he soon discovered that his capabilities were quite limited. In November 1924, the British exploited the substantial opportunity created by the assassination of Lee Stack to get rid of Zaghlul's government, holding it responsible for the anti-British atmosphere that led to the murder.[95]

The 1936 Treaty – More of the Same

The conclusion of the Anglo–Egyptian treaty in August 1936 was adversely received in Sudan by all political stripes – unionists and separatists. Sudanese leaders were disappointed by the fact that the parties to the agreement disregarded them and the Sudanese interests. They were not consulted at any point in the prolonged negotiations discussing the future of their country.[96] The treaty was also adversely received by Egyptians of all political shades. The fact that Egypt failed to advance the unity of the Nile valley was particularly criticized. This consensual view clearly found expression in Rafi'i's work. As both historian and politician, who opposed the Wafd, he analyzed the clauses of the 1936 treaty in relation to Sudan in a very censorious manner. It was not a treaty between two independent countries, since one of them – Britain – was granted the right to keep its combat forces in the territory of its ally and to take control of the sea ports, airports, and routes of transportation in case of war or threat of war. He ridiculed clause 8, which stipulated that the presence of British forces in Egypt would not violate Egypt's sovereign rights over its territory. The treaty turned Sudan into an "English colony" guarded by Egyptian soldiers subordinated to the British governor-general of Sudan.

Rafi'i remonstrated that the incorporation of the 1899 treaty into the 1936 treaty was utterly wrong. The 1899 treaty was regarded by Egyptians as well as international jurists as null and void, since it was imposed by the stronger party. It cut off Sudan – "a vital and important part of the homeland." In contrast to what clause 11 of the 1936 treaty states, Egypt was left with no sovereign right over Sudan. The perpetuation of the 1899 treaty meant that the military and civil rule over Sudan remained in the hands of the governor-general, who was a British government appointee and could be dismissed only with its consent. He could enact laws and establish regulations as he wished. On the other hand, laws and decisions made by the Egyptian government did not apply to Sudan. Egypt, asserted Rafi'i, had never regarded Sudan as a foreign country but an inseparable part of the homeland – it had always considered Sudan as one of Egypt's regions. For instance, when the Egyptian parliament was opened on 26 December 1881 (before the British occupation), the government allocated seats for Sudanese delegates. On 25 March 1882 the election law was promulgated, and its clause 6 allocated seats to Sudanese proportionally to the size of population in each Sudanese election district.[97]

The 1936 treaty was utterly asymmetric – Britain had the advantage over Egypt in every possible aspect. The British controlled the Sudan government – there were more British cabinet members. The governor-general and his deputy as well as the heads of government departments and senior officials were all British. In fact Egypt had not a single member in the cabinet. Even the Egyptian inspector of irrigation affairs in Sudan was not allowed in, unless there were discussions related to Egyptian issues.[98]

Rafi'i did not agree with Egyptian politicians, who praised the 1936 treaty for reinstating Egyptian military presence in Sudan. As a matter of fact, he opined, the Egyptian army in Sudan would be subordinated directly to orders from the British governor-general and not the Egyptian government. The former would determine the required quantity of Egyptian soldiers to serve in Sudan, their place of service, the location of their military bases, etc. Its mission was to defend Sudan – a British colony according to the 1936 treaty. In this regard, the mission in Sudan could not be dissimilar to missions in other British colonies, such as Uganda (which was originally Egyptian), Kenya, or Tanzania. Britain needed the Egyptian army in Sudan to defend the borders from its imperialist rivals, such as Italy, which had conquered Ethiopia. Rafi'i belittled the Egyptian achievements that were pointed out by the treaty's signatories, including the removal of restrictions on Egyptian immigration to Sudan. Why would Egyptians rush to move from the northern part of the valley to its southern part? pondered Rafi'i. In fact, the northern, eastern, and western lands of the Delta were not heavily populated and were opened to migrants, reasoned Rafi'i.[99]

Ghurbal, who was politically closer to the Sa'dist Party (whose leaders Ahmad Mahir and Nuqrashi were members of the Wafd at the time of the conclusion), argued that the 1936 treaty was the lesser of two evils. At the time of the conclusion the Wafd government had no alternative but negotiation with the British. Ghurbal questioned Rafi'i's professional integrity, saying "only a naïve historian expects nations to live constantly in a stage of revolution, and only a naïve historian would regard a return to normal life as a setback and [political] corruption. The return of students to study, clerks to their office, and peasants, workers, and traders to their work ... is the natural thing ... [On the contrary], the trading-in of the principles and the norms of [these] politics is the true corruption."[100]

Unlike Rafi'i, Egyptian intellectuals within the establishment attempted to harness the treaty to the discourse on Egypt's campaign to unite the Nile valley under the Egyptian crown. An observation of the articles of the 1936 treaty regarding Sudan displayed that the unity between Egypt and Sudan was not to be infringed by the temporary administrative form of government.[101] The Egyptian scholars inferred that Egypt's position in Sudan remained intact, even after the conclusion of the 1936 treaty, and remained as it was before the Mahdi revolt of the early 1880s. From the international perspective, therefore, Sudan remained an integral part of Egypt.[102]

Following the conclusion of the 1936 treaty, Britain's position in Sudan was viewed by Egyptian intellectuals as an inherently problematic one. Egypt recognized the British right to share in the administration of Sudan, in line with the 1899 treaties, yet these treaties did not justify the presence of British forces in Sudan. The presence of these troops as an occupying force was therefore no different to the position of the troops stationed in Egypt. To the Egyptians, Sudan was not a foreign territory, but rather constituted an integral part of Egypt.[103]

The British response to those arguments was that "it is impossible to ignore situations of facts which have juridical consequences complementary to any written agreements, which indeed must be presumed to have taken these situations of fact for granted."[104] Indeed, disagreements between the Egyptians and the British were not only concerned with the political future of Sudan but even pertained to their interpretation of the historical facts related to colonial Sudan. For Egyptian scholars, history was viewed as scientific evidence, the most integral component to substantiating Egypt's sovereign rights over Sudan. As we shall see in the next chapter, Egyptian scholars relied also on other disciplines – geography, economics, and ethnography – to support and strengthen their arguments.

The Future of Sudan: Internal and External Perceptions – the Aftermath of the 1936 Treaty

The post–1936 treaty years witnessed the rise of new political forces that challenged the traditional nationalist parties in light of their failure to advance Egypt's twofold national goals – the liberation of Egypt and

Sudan, and the subsequent unification of the two countries under the Egyptian crown. As Yunan Labib Rizq put it, "the most important step taken by these new forces was to take the issue of the unity of the Nile valley away from the Anglo–Egyptian negotiating table and to transfer it to the hearts of the Egyptian masses, who called to revive unification by forming joint Sudanese–Egyptian political groups, thus forcing the traditional parties to adopt that change."[105] Following the conclusion of World War II with Britain's victory, Egyptians of all walks of life believed that their alliance with and loyalty to Britain should now lead to the realization of the twofold national goal. The desire to unite the Nile valley was stronger than ever before.

The bonds between the Sudanese and Egyptians had been tightening ever since the conclusion of the 1936 treaty, which allowed Egypt to reenter Sudan. More Egyptians visited Sudan to get to know Sudan and its people. The peak was Prime Minister 'Ali Mahir's trip to Sudan in 1940, the first official visit by an Egyptian prime minister. His visit was followed by visits of politicians and journalists, who upon their return wrote articles and delivered lectures on Sudan and disseminated the idea of the unity of the Nile valley. Mahir was accompanied by the ministers of defense and of infrastructure works. They traveled to Sudan's main cities (Khartoum, Umm Durman, Port Sudan, etc.) and met with Egyptian institutions and individuals that were engaged in irrigation, the military, clubs, and study centers. Mahir's visit was successful and left a good impression in Sudan. According to Rafi'i, it strengthened the bonds of unity between the northern and southern parts of the valley. At the same time, young Sudanese pursued their higher education at Egyptian universities, colleges, and educational institutions. They were influenced by the various Egyptian political currents and joined some of them. For instance, many of them were attracted to the newly emerged Egyptian left, as will be discussed later[106]. Educated Sudanese published weekly journals in Egypt, such as *New Sudan* by Ahmad Yusuf Hashim; *Sudan* by 'Ali al-Barir (1944); and *Umdurman* by Muhammad Amin Husayn (1945). 'Ali al-Barir, who was among the founders of the Sudanese Graduates' General Congress, even submitted his candidacy for the Egyptian parliament in late 1944.[107]

One may deem the "axiomatic arguments," voiced enthusiastically by Egyptian intellectuals and politicians, as to the desires of the Sudanese people to unite with Egypt, quite convincing. However, a more nuanced and complex picture regarding the Sudanese perception of the Egyptian paradigm of the unity of the Nile valley under the Egyptian crown was portrayed by Sheikh Ahmad 'Uthman al-Qadi, president of Arabic publications in the press and publicity section of the civil secretary's office in

Khartoum. Qadi was a notable Sudanese with close links to both the Egyptian political elite and the king as well as to the British. His record of meetings with key Egyptian figures following his six-month stay in Egypt in summer 1943 sheds refreshing light on the Sudan question from both Egyptian and Sudanese angles. On 2 June 1943, he met with the king, who received him "with affability." The king's main concern was the supply policy in Sudan during wartime. Qadi replied that the Sudan government was handling the situation successfully. The king, who had little sympathy for the Nahhas government, agreed with Qadi: "Yes, the British are a disciplined people who know how to organize, but our government here is 'zift' [rotten] in the matter of supply control. And everything is in a state of chaos."[108] Overall, concluded Qadi, the king spoke in a new and friendly spirit toward the British people despite his awkward relations with the British Embassy in Cairo that favored, at that stage, the Wafd government.[109]

Qadi also met several times with Prime Minister Mustafa al-Nahhas. Nahhas enquired as to the content of the memorandum issued by the Graduates' General Congress (*Mu'tamar al-Khirrijin al-'Amm*) [GGC] on 3 April 1942.[110] The memorandum focused on judicial and educational reforms, yet it also demanded that as soon as the war was over "the British and Egyptian Governments [issue] a joint declaration, granting the Sudan ... the right of self-determination ... as well as guarantees assuring the Sudanese the right of determining their natural rights with Egypt in a special agreement between the Egyptian and Sudanese nations."[111] The purpose and aims of the GGC memorandum were unclear to Egyptians. Egyptian nationalists, of all ranks and shades, perceived it as anti-Egyptian and a deviation from the national consensus, and they were convinced that the GGC was a British-sponsored movement representing separatist trends. Because of this perception the GGC was highly unpopular in Egypt at the time despite the lobbying efforts of its leaders.

Qadi countered the prevailing Egyptian belief that the Sudan government was behind the conception and formulation of the document, hoping to encourage the Sudanese to demand autonomy rather than the unity of the Nile valley. According to him, neither the British nor the Sudanese people (with the exception of the GGC members) had known anything about it and were taken by surprise by its content. What did the Sudanese people really want? Nahhas enquired. Qadi replied: "the real aim of Sudanese nationalism was a distinct Sudanese identity ... Egypt, the Sudan's elder sister, would [not] deny the Sudanese the right (which she herself exercised vis-à-vis Turkey) to develop their identity as a people which has its own national characteristics and way of life."[112] Although Nahhas was not satisfied by the content of Qadi's words, he appreciated his interlocutor's frank views: "We need to learn about events in the Sudan from someone like you who tells us the truth," the prime minister concluded their talks.[113]

Prince 'Umar Tusun (1872–1944), head of the Royal Agricultural Society and member of the Geographical Society, a scholar and a committed Egyptian nationalist, who was a champion of Egyptian–Sudanese unification, also participated in Qadi's meetings. Tusun expressed his love for the Sudanese and reiterated his adherence to the unity of the Nile valley. He stated, however, that anything contributing to the welfare of the Sudanese "gives me genuine pleasure, whether it comes from Egypt or any other quarter, and quite frankly, I do not think that our politicians and public men could do the Sudan such good in this direction, since they have not done it to their own country. I congratulate you on your present Government and wish you all progress."[114]

Qadi's deliberations and debates with a host of influential Egyptians undermined his assumption that the Sudanese were perceived by Egyptians as naïve victims rather than manipulators. The Sudanese at heart, he noted, preferred the British to the Egyptians but pretended the contrary to the Egyptians "mainly in order to obtain material benefits from Egypt."[115]

During his long stay in Egypt, Qadi also held meetings with Sudanese residing in Egypt. Their views of the present and future Egyptian–Sudanese relations were of utmost importance. Qadi classified these Sudanese into four types: merchants, students, small shopkeepers, and petty employees. He presented 'Ali al-Barir as representative of the merchants. He described him as "the most active politically and the most dangerous." Barir revealed to Qadi confidentially that he would not exchange the British for the Egyptians in Sudan. He was not seeking political benefits from the Egyptians but exploiting the existing situation for material expediency for Sudanese living in Egypt, including students. Qadi was not convinced of Barir's sincerity, and detested the manipulative game he claimed to be pursuing: "The political harm which results from his activities outweighs the value of any material gain he may succeed in obtaining ... I do not trust his motives ... [he] is an extremely vain self-centered individual."[116] Egyptians, noted Qadi, were not taken in by Barir's transparent games and disliked him. It would appear Qadi belittled Barir's position in Egypt.

Barir served since 1942 as the representative of the Omdurman GGC in Cairo. Ex officio he established his position among students and exercised full control over the Northern Sudan Union – one of the two principal Sudanese organizations in Cairo. The GGC cell in Cairo also included other key activists of liberal professions: Ahmad Ujail, Ahmad al-Sa'id, Ja'far 'Uthman (lawyers), Bashir al-Bakri (editor, the *Sudan Magazine*), and Muhammad al-Din Sabir (poet). This group of Sudanese, including Barir, was also on the editorial board of the *Sudan Magazine* – an advocate of the unity of the Nile valley under the Egyptian crown. For them Egyptian–Sudanese unification was the only future for Sudan. It is needless to point out that the group was anti-British.[117] Barir had access to the palace through his close relations with Husni, the king's private secretary. King Faruq knew about these relations and in fact encouraged them, to the resentment of the British officials in Egypt, who understood the king's move as political.[118] Eventually the king yielded to British pressure and instructed Husni to halt those meetings in the palace.[119]

As we shall later see, neither the king nor the government could control or check the growing public discontent with the obsequious way in which the "national question" was handled by the Egyptian establishment. For them, the establishment failed to strengthen the bonds with those Sudanese who looked at Egypt as their motherland. Indeed, the government would soon respond submissively to this public pressure. It is noteworthy, wrote *Ruz al-Yusuf*, that since the expulsion of the Egyptian military from Sudan in 1924, a large number of pro-unionist Sudanese moved to Egypt to help their Egyptian compatriots to advance the anti-British struggle for liberation. The Sudanese activists founded clubs and associations, among them the Sudanese Club, which Barir was elected to chair. The club cooperated closely with Egyptian nationalist figures that were active politically.[120]

Qadi was also very critical of the Sudanese students, whom he described as "a dangerous element." They acquired habits and ways of thought "which are alien to the Sudanese national character." He concluded that on their return to Sudan, they would become "very disruptive of indigenous morals and social forms." He predicted that a large number of returning students would cause a social calamity, thus harming the future of their country's development.[121] To avoid this, Qadi suggested that the Sudan government should monitor and look after the needs and requirements of these students by placing an official representative in Cairo rather than leaving this important task at the hands of "self-appointed commercial consuls like 'Ali al-Barir." He also recommended that instead of allowing Sudanese students to attend Egyptian secondary schools in Egypt, the Sudan government should divert them to Egyptian schools in Sudan. Such a move would lessen the Egyptian influence upon these students, who would remain in a Sudanese environment.[122]

Qadi's analysis of the question of Sudanese–Egyptian relations went counter to the doctrine of the unity of the Nile valley. While he conceded that religion, language, neighborhood, and other ties did exist between Egypt and Sudan since ancient times, he stressed that these ties had never been strong enough to unite the two countries politically. Historically, political union was imposed on Sudan following Muhammad 'Ali's conquests in the early nineteenth century. Moreover, some parts of Sudan were not part of this union. For instance, the Sultanate of Darfur remained an independent entity. The Mahdist uprising put an end to the union until the formation of the British–Egyptian condominium following the reoccupation of Sudan by the two countries at the end of the nineteenth century.

Qadi did not deny Egyptian financial assistance to Sudan since 1899, yet he made it clear that Sudan owed nothing to Egypt as far as its general development was concerned. Sudan might benefit, to some extent, from economic, cultural, and other modes of cooperation with Egypt, but such relations should be maintained only after the Sudan question was settled, and he ruled out any form of political unity with Egypt. In case Britain decided to evacuate Sudan, Qadi preferred Sudanese self-rule despite the political anarchy (as a result of "ignorance and tribal divisions") this might incur, rather than be united with Egypt "and swamped by Egyptian influence."[123]

Another prominent Sudanese figure, who represented the anti-unionist trend, was Ibrahim Ahmad, president of the Graduates' General Congress (1942, 1944) and a key mover behind the 1942 memorandum.[124] In early 1944, shortly after his reelection as president of the GGC, he revealed in a conversation with E. S. Atiyha (the public relations officer in the civil secretary's office, Khartoum) his views on the future of Sudan and the unity with Egypt. Ahmad accurately portrayed the prevailing political trends in Sudan concerning the future of that country, stressing that there was no clear homogenous opinion but many conflicting desires and views. Sudan, he opined, was not ready yet for independence and needed more guidance and training before self-government was granted. He preferred the British to the Egyptians as Sudan's mentor and trainer in preparation for self-rule. The British were described as good administrators, and Ahmad believed that they should stay in Sudan for a considerable time until the Sudanese were well-prepared. However, Ahmad did not want to see the withdrawal of Egypt and the dissolution of the condominium at that stage because as much as he

admired the British as administrators and desired their help, he did not trust them sufficiently to be willing to place the Sudan entirely at their mercy.

The Sudan was a small and weak country and if Great Britain obtained exclusive control over it, the Sudanese would have no safeguards against exploitation. The Egyptians were very bad administrators, their morals were corrupt and the Sudan could not benefit directly from their presence, but their partnership in the Condominium constituted a check on the British ... this check was very beneficial to the Sudan. Besides, the Sudanese had many things in common with the Egyptians and it was to their advantage to maintain friendly mutual relations with Egypt.[125]

Ahmad believed that a pro-British stand would naturally turn Egypt into a neighboring enemy – an undesirable possibility for Sudan. The Sudanese could benefit most if the present state of affairs continued: Egypt's share would remain nominal, whereas the real control and administration remained in British hands. Under these circumstances, the Sudanese could get more and better training in governing themselves, and when they felt ready to take the reins of government, they would decide about the nature of their relations with both Britain and Egypt. Ahmad was fully aware of Egypt's hegemonic demand over Sudan and believed that the only effective way to counter it was to set up a separate Sudanese nationality by law. Such a law would clarify to the Egyptians that the Sudanese were not Egyptians and moreover did not wish to become Egyptians. The Sudanese regarded themselves "as a separate nation and wished to develop as such." He rejected Egypt's present demands for more political and administrative posts in the Sudan government.[126]

Likewise, Sudanese historian Muddathir 'Abdel Rahim maintained that the tenets of the doctrine of the unity of the Nile valley as presented in the writings of its Egyptian protagonists before and after the conclusion of the 1936 treaty were lacking authoritative foundations. Referring to the strongest component of that doctrine, the historical, he criticized:

Unnecessary and unwarranted exaggerations about the nature and extent of historical contacts between Egypt and the Sudan from the earliest times to the present day had a similarly weakening effect on Egypt's position and her advocacy of the Unity of the Nile Valley. As a result even legitimate Egyptian interests in the Sudan suffered – not only as a consequence of Egypt's weakened moral standing in the country but also by arousing the suspicion and hostility of large sections of the Sudanese.[127]

In sum, as this chapter shows, there was a tremendous gulf between the narratives of Egyptian scholars and politicians and their Sudanese counterparts. The next chapter will discuss other tenets of the doctrine of the unity of the Nile valley as presented by Egyptian advocates for Egyptian–Sudanese unification.

Notes

1 Edward W. Said, *Culture and Imperialism* (London: Wingate Books, 1994), p. xiii.
2 Salim Hasan, "5000 Years of Unity," in *Egypt Sudan*. The book was prepared by the Egyptian government and distributed by the Egyptian consulate in Bombay. Among the scholars who contributed to this research project were Ibrahim Noshi and Ahmad Badawi, both of the History Department of Fu'ad I University; M. Shafik Ghorbal, Professor of History and Dean of the Faculty of Arts, Fu'ad I University; Lt. Col. Abdel Rahman Zaki, Director of Egyptian Military Museum; and Salim Hasan, Senior Lecturer at the Geography Department of Fu'ad I University (that is the way their names are spelled in the book; hereafter cited as Egyptian scholars). The book was attached to Letter No. S.131/15566-A-I, from Sir Ivon Taunton, Chief Secretary to the Government of Bombay, Political and Services Department, Bombay Castle, to the Secretary to the Government of India, Department of External Affairs and Commonwealth Relations, 12 August 1947, File No. F6/43 – AWT/47, National Archives of India, New Delhi (cited as NAI).
3 See a pamphlet issued by the Egyptian government entitled *The Egyptian Question 1882–1951*, attached to Letter from British Embassy, Washington, 5 December 1951, FO953/1115, PG11637/102.
4 Rami Ginat, "Egypt's Efforts to Unite the Nile Valley: Diplomacy and Propaganda, 1945–1947," *Middle Eastern Studies*, 43/2 (2007), p. 206; *Egypt Sudan*, p. 33; Abbas 'Ammar, "The Transformation of Egypt and the Sudan into a Muslim Arabic Speaking Country," in *Egyptian Kingdom, Presidency of Council of Ministers (ed.), The Unity of the Nile Valley, Its Geographical Bases and Its Manifestations in History* (Cairo: Government Press, 1947), pp. 58–60 (hereafter cited as *The Unity of the Nile Valley*), attached to Letter No. 562/47 (6-3-10Pt:II) from Consul-General for Egypt, Bombay, to the Secretary of the Government of India, Department of External Affairs and Commonwealth Relations, New Delhi, 18 June 1947, File No. F.23(13) – AWT/47, NAI. See also Egyptian Government, Committee of Experts, *Status of the Sudan* (Cairo: Government Press, 1947), pp. 2–3. It is noteworthy that the experts' names were not mentioned.
5 Ibrahim al-Mubarak, "Mu'ahada 'arabiyya sudaniyya," *al-Risala*, No. 633, 30 August 1945, pp. 900–901. Holt presents a different account. According to him, the Muslim army failed to occupy Dongola, and its forces withdrew following the conclusion of "a treaty which established for some six hundred years trading relations and *modus vivendi* between Muslim Egypt and Christian Nubia." Holt, *A Modern History of the Sudan*, p. 16.
6 Muhammad Rif'at was an influential historian who was active within the academia and in the late 1930s served in the ministry of education under different governments – "a cautious official who knew fairly well how to find his way around opposing political parties," according to Di-Capua. See Yoav Di-Capua, *Gatekeepers of the Arab Past: Historian and History Writing in Twentieth-Century Egypt* (Berkeley: University of California Press, 2009), pp. 175, 189.

7 Muhammad Rif'at and Muhammad Ahmad Hasuna, *Ma'alim ta'rikh al-'usur al-wusta* (Cairo: Dar al-Ma'arif, 1947), pp. 157–158.

8 'Abdallah Husayn, *al-Sudan min al-ta'rikh al-qadim 'ila' rihlat al-ba'tha al-misriyya*, 3 vols. (Cairo: al-Matba'a al-Rahmaniyya bi-Misr, 1935).

9 He took his BA and MA studies in distinguished British academic institutions. In 1928 he joined the Faculty of Arts at Fu'ad I University and later became Professor of History and Dean (1938–1940) of that faculty. In the 1940s he was appointed as undersecretary of state in the ministry of education. Politically, he then got closer to the pro-monarchic Sa'dist and the Liberal Constitutionalist parties. See more on Ghurbal and his intellectual activity in Di-Capua, *Gatekeepers of the Arab Past*, pp. 186–218. Ghurbal and Muhammad Rif'at cooperated in a joint effort to Egyptianize history writing. Di-Capua described Ghurbal as "a staunch supporter of elitism as a cultural and political mission," which went counter to the Wafd's approach of advocating "the universal availability of education." Ibid., p. 209.

10 M. Shafiq Ghurbal, "The Building-up of a Single Egyptian–Sudanese Fatherland in the 19th Century," in *The Unity of the Nile Valley*, p. 61.

11 Muhammad Fu'ad Shukri, *Misr wa-al-siyada 'ala al-sudan: al-wad' al-ta'rikhi lil-mas'ala* (Cairo: Dar al-Fikr al-'Arabi, 1946); Shukri, *al-Hukm al-misri fi al-sudan 1820–1885* (Cairo: Dar al-Fikr al-'Arabi, 1947). The appendixes section is designed to prove that Muhammad 'Ali and his successors sought to advance the Sudanese on "the route of progress and culture." For a broader and more profound version of *al-Hukm al-misri fi al-sudan*, see his *Misr wa-al-sudan: Ta'rikh wahdat wadi al-nil al-siyasiyya fi al-qarn al-tasi' 'ashir*, 3rd ed. (Cairo: Dar al-Ma'arif bi-Misr, 1963). In contrast, Holt argues that one of Muhammad 'Ali's goals in occupying "the Nilotic Sudan" was to "control a principal channel of the slave-trade." The creation of a submissive slave-army "trained in the European manner and personally loyal to him" could serve well his long-term imperialistic plans. See Holt, *A Modern History of the Sudan*, pp. 36–37.

12 Shukri, *Misr wa-al-siyada*.

13 Shukri, *Misr wa-al-sudan: Ta'rikh wahdat wadi al-nil*, pp. 7–8.

14 Ibid., pp. 7–9.

15 El-Barawy, *Egypt, Britain and the Sudan*, p. 4.

16 Shukri, *Misr wa-al-sudan: Ta'rikh wahdat wadi al-nil*, pp. 7–9. For a detailed account of the occupation of the Sudan, see Makki Shibika, *Ta'rikh shu'ub wadi al-nil* (Beirut: Dar al-Thaqafa, 1965), pp. 309–341. See also Holt, *A Modern History of the Sudan*, pp. 35–48.

17 *Egypt Sudan*, p. 34; Egyptian Government, Committee of Experts, *Status of the Sudan*, pp. 3–4; Hay'at al-Mustasharin, *Qadiyyat al-sudan* (Cairo: al-Matba'a al-Amiriyya, 1947), pp. 2–5. See also the French version of the booklet in Presidence du Conseil des Ministers, Comite des Experts, *La Cause du Soudan* (Cairo: Imprimerie Nationale, 1947).

18 Shukri, *Misr wa-al-sudan: Ta'rikh wahdat wadi al-nil*, pp. 72–73.

19 See, for instance, *Egypt Sudan*, p. 34; Committee of Experts, *Status of the Sudan*, pp. 3–4; Hay'at al-Mustasharin, *Qadiyyat al-sudan*, pp. 2–5.

20 Shukri, *Misr wa-al-sudan: Ta'rikh wahdat wadi al-nil*, pp. 92–94.

21 *Egypt Sudan*, p. 35.
22 Ibid., pp. 98, 124. See also 'Abd al-Rahman al-Rafi'i, *Misr wa-al-sudan fi awa'il 'ahd al-ihtilal* (Cairo: Sharikat Maktabat wa-Matba'at Mustafa al-Babi al-Halabi wa-Awladihi bi-Misr, 1942), pp. 93–94.
23 Shukri, *Misr wa-al-sudan: Ta'rikh wahdat wadi al-nil*, pp. 255–257; al-Rafi'i, *Misr wa-al-sudan fi awa'il 'ahd al-ihtilal*, p. 96.
24 Ibid., pp. 97–108, 124–130; El-Barawy, *Egypt, Britain and the Sudan*, p. 5.
25 Shukri, *al-Hukm al-misri*.
26 'Abbas 'Ammar, "The Transformation of Egypt and the Sudan into a Muslim Arabic Speaking Country," in *The Unity of the Nile Valley*, p. 60. On the Arabness of the Nile valley, see also Ahmad Ramzi, "'Urubat mamlakat wadi al-nil," *al-'Alam al-'Arabi*, 10 March 1948, pp. 35–27; Sulayman Huzayyin, "Rawabit al-tabi'a wa-al-ta'rikh fi wadi al-nil," *al-Katib al-Misri*, 6:21 (June 1947), pp. 228–242.
27 "The Unity of Egypt and the Sudan: the Legal Aspect of the Case," in *Egypt Sudan*, p. 33. See also Egyptian Government, Committee of Experts, *Status of the Sudan*, pp. 2–3; Muhammad Rif'at, "Misr wa-al-sudan," *al-Katib al-Misri*, 6:21 (June 1947), pp. 22–23.
28 Mahmoud Kamel, "Documented Study on the Unity of the Nile Valley," *La Bourse Egyptienne*, 6 September 1948, in Robertson Files, SA 524/2/5. See also Rif'at, "Misr wa-al-sudan," p. 24.
29 See the British Embassy reply in Robertson Files, SA 524/2/5.
30 A study entitled *Egyptian Penetration of the Sudan during the Pharaonic Period*, by the Foreign Office Research Department, 31 August 1951, FO371/90153, JE1052/40.
31 See a detailed account on the project and the participants in Di-Capua, *Gatekeepers of the Arab Past*, pp. 91–140. See also Israel Gershoni and James P. Jankowski, *Egypt, Islam and the Arabs* (Oxford: Oxford University Press, 1987), p. 144. The study refers to *Precis de l'Histoire d'Egypte*, Vol. 1, published in Cairo in 1932 as part of the 'Abdin Project.
32 Di-Capua, *Gatekeepers of the Arab Past*, p. 92.
33 A study entitled *Egyptian Penetration of the Sudan during the Pharaonic Period*. On Egypt and pre-1821 Sudan, see also Robert O. Collins and Robert L. Tignor, *Egypt and the Sudan* (Englewood Cliffs, NJ: Prentice-Hall, 1967), pp. 40–49. The periodization and dates are not always similar, but the argument is not dissimilar, that is, Sudan in its post-1821 boundaries was not ruled by Egypt throughout history and even in those northern parts of Sudan that were ruled by Egypt there was no continuous control. See also John O. Voll and Sarah P. Voll, *The Sudan: Unity and Diversity in a Multicultural State* (Boulder, CO: Westview Press, 1985), pp. 28–35.
34 See a copy of Samuel Baker's *Ismailia* (1874) at www.gutenberg.org/cache/epub/3607/pg3607.html (accessed 6 September 2013).
35 Quoted from Baker's preface to his book, at ibid.
36 Baker is quoted in Egyptian Government, Committee of Experts, *Status of the Sudan*, p. 4. See also 'Umar Tusun, *Misr wa-al-sudan* (al-Iskandariyya: Matba'at al-'Adl, n.d.), p. 5.
37 Baker, *Ismailia*, chapter V.

38 Ibid.
39 Robertson Files, SA 524/2/5, p. 341.
40 Gabriel Warburg, *Historical Discord in the Nile Valley* (Evanston, IL: Northwestern University Press, 1992), pp. 37–39
41 Ibid., pp. 39–40.
42 See Robert O. Collins's book review of Warburg's *Historical Discord*, in *The International History Review*, 16:4 (November 1994), p. 800.
43 Warburg, *Historical Discord*, pp. 40–41.
44 Winston Churchill, *The River War: An Historical Account of the Reconquest of the Soudan* (London: Longmans, Green and Co., 1902), chapter 1 ("The Rebellion of the Mahdi"), at www.gutenberg.org/files/4943/4943-h/4943-h.htm (accessed 6 September 2013).
45 Ibid., chapter 17.
46 *al-Ahram*, 12 September 1944.
47 *Egypt Sudan*, pp. 36–37; Hay'at al-Mustasharin, *Qadiyyat al-sudan*, p. 13
48 Troutt Powell, *A Different Shade of Colonialism*, p. 156.
49 On the Fashoda Incident see below.
50 Hay'at al-Mustasharin, *Qadiyyat al-sudan*, p. 16.
51 Muhammad Mahmud Jalal, "al-Sudan," *al-Ikhwan al-Muslimun*, 4 October 1945, pp. 8–10.
52 [anonymous] Anwar, "Likay la nansa," *al-Ikhwan al-Muslimun*, 14 December 1946, p. 8.
53 [anonymous] An Egyptian publicist, "Egypt's Claim to the Sudan," *Current History*, 21:5 (1925), pp. 721–727.
54 Ibid.
55 Ibid.
56 Ibid.
57 Ibid.
58 Lord Salisbury to Sir Monson, 12 October 1998, CAB/37/48/75, quoted from [anonymous] An Egyptian publicist, "Egypt's Claim to the Sudan."
59 [anonymous] An Egyptian publicist, "Egypt's Claim to the Sudan."
60 "Memorandum on Anglo–Egyptian Relations for the Information of his Majesty's Representatives Abroad," 9 May 1947, J 2128/12/16, SA521/5/5. Abbas Mekki, a Sudanese scholar, disputes allegations made by Egyptian protagonists of the unity of the Nile valley that the British government forced Egypt to evacuate Sudan for imperialist and expansionist reasons. Such charges, he professed, could not be proven. Moreover, a decade before the British occupation of Egypt, they took pains to persuade the Egyptians to evacuate Sudan – at a time the British had "no strategic or interests in the Sudan." See Mekki Abbas, *The Sudan Question: The Dispute over the Anglo-Egyptian Condominium 1884–1951* (London: Faber and Faber, 1952), pp. 37–39.
61 Report by the Foreign Office, London, "Note on the Political Future of the Anglo–Egyptian Sudan vis-à-vis the Impending Negotiations between Great Britain and Egypt," 27 February 1946, SA521/3/39.
62 Ibid., SA521/3/40–41. Lord Cromer depicted the Turco–Egyptian rule in Sudan as "the worst form of misgovernment." See Warburg, *Historical Discord*, p. 16.

58   Egypt's Claims for the Unity of the Nile Valley

63 Ibid., SA521/3/41–42.
64 Rafi'i, *Misr wa-al-sudan fi awa'il 'ahd al-ihtilal*, pp. 159, 174–175.
65 Ginat, "Egypt's Efforts," p. 208; "The Unity of Egypt and the Sudan: The Legal Aspect of the Case," p. 38.
66 Lutfi al-Sayyid is quoted from Eve Troutt Powell, "Brothers along the Nile: Egyptian Concepts of Race and Ethnicity, 1895–1910," in Erlich and Gershoni (eds.), *The Nile: Histories, Cultures, Myths*, p. 178.
67 Quoted from Troutt Powell, *A Different Shade of Colonialism*, p. 165.
68 Muddathir 'Abdel Rahim, *Imperialism and Nationalism in the Sudan* (Khartoum: Khartoum University Press, 1986), p. 26.
69 Ibid., p. 24.
70 Ibid., p. 27.
71 "The Unity of Egypt and the Sudan: The Legal Aspect of the Case," p. 38. See also Presidence du Conseil des Ministres, *Note sur les pouvoirs du gouvernement Egyptien en matière législative au Soudan* (Cairo: Imprimerie Nationale, 1947).
72 El-Barawy, *Egypt, Britain and the Sudan*, pp. 10–11.
73 "Memorandum on Anglo–Egyptian Relations," p. 8.
74 On the repercussions of the assassination on Britain's policy toward the Nile valley see a detailed account in Jayne Gifford, "Extracting the Best Deal for Britain: The Assassination of Sir Lee Stack in November 1924 and the Revision of Britain's Nile Valley Policy," *Canadian Journal of History*, 48:1, pp. 87–114.
75 Rayford Whittingham Logan, "The Anglo–Egyptian Sudan: A Problem in International Relations," *The Journal of Negro History*, 16:4 (1931), p. 372.
76 Ibid., pp. 373–377.
77 Warburg, *Historical Discord*, pp. 42–55.
78 Da'ud Barakat, *al-Sudan al-misri wa-matami' al-siyasa al-baritaniyya* (Cairo: al-Matba'a al-Salafiyya bi-Misr, 1924).
79 "The Unity of Egypt and the Sudan: The Legal Aspect of the Case," p. 44. See also Rafi'i, *Fi a'qab al-thawra al-misriyya – Thawrat 1919*, Vol. 2, p. 91; El-Barawy, *Egypt, Britain and the Sudan*, pp. 6–7; Fred H. Lawson, "Reassessing Egypt's Foreign Policy during the 1920s and 1930s," in Arthur Goldschmidt, Amy J. Johnson, and Barak A. Salmoni (eds.), *Re-Envisioning Egypt 1919–1952* (Cairo: The American University in Cairo Press, 2005), p. 60.
80 Rizq, *Qadiyyat wahdat wadi al-nil*, pp. 6–9. See also Afaf Lutfi al-Sayyid-Marsot, *Egypt's Liberal Experiment: 1922–1936* (Berkeley: University of California Press, 1977), p. 82; Muhammad Ibrahim al-Jaziri, *Athar al-za'im sa'd zaghlul and wizarat al-sha'b* (Cairo: Maktabat Madbuli, 1991), p. 55.
81 Troutt Powell, *A Different Shade of Colonialism*, p. 7.
82 "The Unity of Egypt and the Sudan: The Legal Aspect of the Case," p. 44.
83 "Memorandum on Anglo–Egyptian Relations," pp. 8–10.
84 'Abd al-'Azim Muhammad Ibrahim Ramadan, *Tatawwur al-haraka al-wataniyya fi misr min 1918 ila 1936* (Cairo: Maktabat al-Madbuli, 1983), pp. 282–283.
85 Ibid., p. 431.

86 Ibid., p. 433.
87 For details on Yakan's talks in London, see ibid., pp. 433–434.
88 Rafi'i, *Fi a'qab al-thawra al-misriyya – Thawrat 1919*, Vol. 1, p. 81.
89 Muhammad Husayn Haykal, *Mudhakkirat fi al-siyasa al-misriyya* (Cairo: Dar al-Ma'arif, 1990), part 1, pp. 130–131, 335. See also al-Rafi'i, *Fi a'qab al-thawra al-misriyya – Thawrat 1919*, Vol. 3, p. 15.
90 Rafi'i, *Fi a'qab al-thawra al-misriyya – Thawrat 1919*, Vol. 1, pp. 108–110.
91 Ibid., pp. 108–111.
92 Ibid., pp. 118–119.
93 Ibid., pp. 204–206.
94 Ibid., pp. 212–213. On the exhibition in London, see also Ramadan, *Tatawwur al-haraka al-wataniyya fi misr min 1918 ila 1936*, p. 435.
95 Rafi'i, *Fi a'qab al-thawra al-misriyya – Thawrat 1919*, Vol. 1, pp. 213–216.
96 El-Barawy, *Egypt, Britain and the Sudan*, p. 8.
97 Rafi'i, *Fi a'qab al-thawra al-misriyya – Thawrat 1919*, Vol. 3, pp. 30–32; El-Barawy, *Egypt, Britain and the Sudan*, pp. 7–8.
98 Rafi'i, *Fi a'qab al-thawra al-misriyya – Thawrat 1919*, Vol. 3, pp. 34–35.
99 Ibid., pp. 36–37.
100 Ghurbal is quoted from Di-Capua, *Gatekeepers of the Arab Past*, p. 225. On the polemic between Rafi'i and Ghurbal, see more in ibid., pp. 224–226.
101 "The Unity of Egypt and the Sudan: The Legal Aspect of the Case," pp. 45–46. For the full text of the agreement and its annexes, see Muhammad Khalil, *The Arab States and the Arab League: A Documentary Record* (Beirut: Khayats, 1962), pp. 697–718.
102 *Egypt Sudan*, p. 47. On the analysis of the 1899 treaty, see Hay'at al-Mustasharin, *Qadiyyat al-sudan*, pp. 16–34.
103 *Egypt Sudan*, pp. 47–48; Hay'at al-Mustasharin, *Qadiyyat al-sudan*, pp. 38–47.
104 See Foreign Office Minute, by A. McD, 29 April 1947, FO141/1179, 364/6/47.
105 Rizq, *Qadiyyat wahdat wadi al-nil*, p. 13.
106 This subject is discussed in Chapter 6.
107 Ibid., pp. 13–15; al-Rafi'i, *Fi a'qab al-thawra al-misriyya – Thawrat 1919*, Vol. 3, p. 82. On 'Ali Mahir's visit see also Holt, *A Modern History of the Sudan*, pp. 141–142. See al-Barir's biography in al-Mu'tasim Ahmad al-Hajj, *Mu'jam Shakhsiyyat Mu'tamar al-Khirrijin* (Umm Durman: Markaz Muhammad 'Umar Bashir lil-Dirasat al-Sudaniyya, 2009), pp. 266–267. See the biographies of Ahmad Yusuf Hashim and Muhammad Amin Husayn in ibid., pp. 103–105, 307–309. On the Sudanese press in the first decades of the condominium rule, see Mahjub Muhammad Salih, *al-Sihafa al-sudaniyya fi nisf qarn 1903–1953*, Vol. 1 (Khartoum: Jami'at al-Khartum, 1971); Hasanain 'Abd al-Qadir, *Ta'rikh al-sihafa fi al-sudan 1899–1919*, Vol. 1 (Cairo: Dar al-Nahda al-'Arabiyya, 1967).
108 Note by Sheikh Ahmad 'Uthman al-Qadi on his stay in Egypt from 1 May 1943 to 12 October 1943 attached to Letter SA/52-A.1. from Sudan Agency, Cairo, to Sir Walter Smart, British Embassy, Cairo, 8 February 1944, FO141/939, 31/9/44.

60   Egypt's Claims for the Unity of the Nile Valley

109 Ibid.

110 The Graduates' General Congress was established in 1938 and it "gave rise
to political parties and functioned as the precursor to the National Assem-
bly." Sharkey, *Living with Colonialism*, p. 54. See also a detailed account in
Warburg, *Islam, Sectarianism and Politics*, pp. 110–128; Ahmad Khayr, *Kifah
Jil: ta'rikh harakat al-Khirrijin wa-tatawwuriha fi al-Sudan* (Khartoum: al-
Dar al-Sudaniyya lil-kutub, 2002).

111 Quoted from Robert O. Collins, *A History of Modern Sudan* (Cambridge:
Cambridge University Press, 2008), pp. 50–51. See also Warburg, *Islam,
Sectarianism and Politics*, pp. 117–118.

112 Note by Sheikh Ahmad 'Uthman al-Qadi.

113 Ibid.

114 Ibid. Indeed, Prince 'Umar Tusun argued that Egypt and Sudan were
an inseparable entity since Sudan was an integral part of Egypt (*juz' la
yatajaza'u*), and vice versa, since the dawn of history. See Tusun, *Misr
wa-al-sudan*, pp. 3–7.

115 Note by Sheikh Ahmad 'Uthman al-Qadi.

116 Ibid. Already in the late 1930s, Barir was depicted as a "trader active in
Egyptian–Sudanese commerce." See Mills, *Dividing the Nile*, pp. 86–87.

117 Memorandum No. SA/36-C-1/59 by the Sudan Agency, Cairo, 17 January
1945, FO141/1013, 41/9/45.

118 See minute by Sir W. Smart, 17 January 1945, Foreign Office, London,
FO141/1013, 41/10/45.

119 See a record of conversation between Amir Pasha and Killearn, Cairo,
20 January 1945, FO141/1013, 41/13/45.

120 "al-Sudan ... fi misr!," *Ruz al-Yusuf*, No. 998 (July 30, 1947), p. 2.

121 Note by Sheikh Ahmad 'Uthman al-Qadi.

122 Ibid.

123 Ibid.

124 See Ibrahim Ahmad's biography in al-Hajj, *Mu'jam Shakhsiyyat Mu'tamar
al-Khirrijin*, pp. 43–45.

125 Extracts from a conversation between Ibrahim Ahmad and E. S. Atiyha,
7 January 1944, attached to Letter SA/52-A.1. from Sudan Agency, Cairo,
to Sir Walter Smart, British Embassy, Cairo, 8 February 1944, FO141/939,
31/9/44. See also FO371/41363.

126 Extracts from a conversation between Ibrahim Ahmad and E. S. Atiyha,
7 January 1944.

127 'Abdel Rahim, *Imperialism and Nationalism in the Sudan*, p. 265.

2   The Unity of the Nile Valley
Geographical, Economic, and Ethnographical Perspectives

This chapter reviews the assertions made by Egyptian scholars, writers, and politicians to prove the material and physical solidity of the Egyptian–Sudanese unity. The chapter is divided into four sections examining the geographical, the economic, and the ethnographical and cultural factors on which the inseparable kingdom of the Nile valley was thought to be based. Although the main purpose of this chapter is to present and analyze the central Egyptian assertions made to substantiate Egypt's fundamental natural rights over Sudan, it nevertheless presents also unconventional viewpoints, such as communist and Marxist ideas that enriched the socioeconomic historical discussion in Egypt in the 1920s, as well as references to right-wing radical contentions. In addition, British viewpoints and counterclaims contesting the factual foundations of Egyptian assertions are reviewed.

The Geographical Foundation of the Unity

Nowhere in the world do people depend for their very existence on a river, as the people of the Nile basin depend on the Nile; and no country in the world is so indebted for the fertility of its soil to a river, as Egypt and the Sudan are indebted to the river Nile. Egypt and the Sudan both owe their life and existence to this great river.[1]

In his depiction of the symbiotic relationship between the Nile River and its inhabitants, Dr. 'Abbas 'Ammar of the Geography Department at Fu'ad I University provided an introspective observation of the vitality and indispensability of the Nile to the life of both Egyptians and Sudanese. He concentrated on the geographical roots of the unity, emphasizing the vitality of the Nile to the existence of its inhabitants. He placed greater importance on the lack of geographic obstacles between the north and south of the valley, thus allowing the diffuse movement of people and goods throughout without having to adapt to the surroundings. Furthermore, it was hard to detect along the Nile valley any significant change in climate, but rather gradual transitions:

It is noteworthy that nature has reaffirmed the unity of the northern and southern regions of the Valley, by the evident uniformity and interrelation of natural phenomena in both sections. The topography is almost identical while the climate and flora present such a normal gradation as to render the change almost imperceptible between Egypt and the Sudan. Moreover, there were never any natural, insurmountable barriers, even in ancient times, when even the slightest would have proved an obstacle to intercommunication.[2]

Rashed El-Barawy followed suit, stressing that there were no natural boundaries to separate the northern and southern parts of the Nile valley. The Nile was the main route of communications and thus played a significant part in the establishment of common economic interests and in the sharing of material resources. El-Barawy, however, divided Sudan geographically into three main climatic areas:[3]

1. The northern part was mainly desert apart from the Nile valley.
2. The central part teemed with meadows and farm lands.
3. The southern part was rich with forests.

Egyptian geographers such as Sulayman Huzayyin asserted that there was "perfect harmony between the water, the soil, and human life and work." Huzayyin outlined the natural geographical boundaries: "Egypt to the north and the Sudan to the south organically connected by the Nile valley and delimited by the deserts surrounding the valley in the east and the west."[4]

Egyptian geographers argued that a quick look at the map would display territorial continuity between Egypt and Sudan. The two existed on the "bounty of a single life-giving blood-stream – the Nile!" They pointed at the fact that the Nile was one of the greatest rivers of the world, comparing it with the Mississippi and the Amazon Rivers. More than 80 percent of the Nile was located in Egyptian and Sudanese territory: "the immense basin of the Nile – the Sudan alone, with an area of 1 million square miles, is larger than the whole of the United States east of the Mississippi – is but a single unit. Each of its two great parts – Egypt and the Sudan – is indissolubly bound with the other." Egypt, they concluded, could not exist without Sudan and vice versa.[5]

While studying the history of relations between the Nile valley and other parts of the world, 'Ammar argued, it is safe to state that communications were made possible principally through the natural course of the river. He attributed it partly to the fact that geographical conditions – forests in the south and mountains in the east – made communication via any other route very difficult.[6] Also, one should look back to ancient history when Egypt had developed a civilization before any other country in Africa. Furthermore, Egypt's unique geostrategic location on the Mediterranean made it the key to the ancient world and a linchpin between various countries that wished to develop commercial and cultural relations. Britain was blamed for the decline in Nile trade by diverting trade toward the Red Sea ports. It was part of the British plot to undermine relations between Egypt and Sudan and to cut off the strong bonds created by nature. Moreover, the British aimed at diverting trade away from Egypt, toward their own channels.[7]

'Ammar and other Egyptian theoreticians concluded that the existing borders between Egypt and Sudan were artificial, the result of agreements imposed by force. According to Egyptian intellectuals the boundaries between Egypt and Sudan were fluid, lacking any geographical frontiers.[8] In the same vein, the seminal Egyptian intellectual Husayn Haykal, then president of the Egyptian Senate, propagated this argument viewing the Nile River as the thread that fused Egypt and Sudan together under the Egyptian crown.[9]

Within the Egyptian discourse on the natural geographic boundaries of the Nile valley, Islamist intellectuals attacked both the Egyptian government and particularly British imperialism for neglecting the welfare and infrastructure development of Nubia – a desert region, a quarter of which was in Egypt from Aswan southward and the rest in Sudan, in an area reaching Khartoum.[10] 'Abd al-Hafiz Abu al-Sa'ud, an eminent publicist in *al-Risala*, condemned the helplessness of Egyptian politicians in their failure to look after the essential needs of Nubia. Nubia became a godforsaken area, a place for exiled Egyptian clerks. There was nothing new or significant for the traveler to observe in Nubia.[11] After directing his scathing indictment against the Egyptian government, Abu al-Sa'ud linked the notoriously bad reputation of the Nubia region with the British interest to separate the two parts of the Nile valley – Egypt and Sudan. The sleaziness, neglect, and desolateness of Nubia were used by Britain as a pretext for separation.[12]

Egyptian geographers took pains to prove that the Nile was Egyptian in terms of its international legal status and recognition. 'Ammar spelled it out clearly, stressing that British writers unanimously agreed on "the legitimacy of Egypt's claims to these waters and its necessity to obtain full guarantees to exercise these rights."[13] He referred to Lord Cromer, who saw the Nile as "Egypt's river." Cromer was quoted by 'Ammar as saying that "the Black Country was a viaduct which carries life-giving silt to the fertile Delta."[14]

Further corroboration of Ammar's argument may be found in the sphere of control over the supply of Nile water. Most of the studies examining the best ways to utilize and improve the distribution of Nile water for irrigation were conducted by the British. Some minor projects were undertaken prior to World War I. A branch of the Egyptian Irrigation Service was established in Sudan in 1904, headed by the British C. Dupuis. In 1904 Sir William Garstin, undersecretary of state at the Sudan ministry of public works, recommended the investigation of various projects. The main goal was to increase Egypt's water supply in the summer and to secure that Sudan would have similar benefits. Garstin, a civil engineer by profession, proposed the following: regulation of and storage in Lakes Victoria and Albert; improvements in the Sudd region; reduction of the great wastage of water there; storage on the Blue Nile and on the Atbara River. The works in Lakes Victoria and Albert and the Sudd region were designed to benefit the irrigation of Egypt, whereas the latter works were intended to develop the irrigation schemes in Sudan.[15] At that stage Garstin opined that "the control of the flow of the Nile should remain always and absolutely in the hands of one authority, and that this authority should be the Egyptian Ministry of Public Works."[16]

The British dominated the organizational management of the Nile water until 1922. In 1920 Sir Murdoch Macdonald, an irrigation adviser, issued a comprehensive report entitled *Nile Control*. The report estimated the water needs of Egypt and Sudan. According to his assessment Egypt would need 50,000 million cubic meters annually, whereas Sudan only 6,000 million.[17] However, in 1921 Macdonald resigned, and his post remained vacant. In 1922 the British government proclaimed unilaterally Egypt's independence with certain reservations – not including irrigation, to the resentment of British officials in both Egypt and Sudan. If the status of Sudan remained the same, they pondered, why were the irrigation projects of the Upper Nile not included among the reservations? They wanted to see Macdonald's post reassigned to a British functionary. Indeed, the proclamation of independence "put an end to the High Commissioner's powers of general direction of irrigation projects, whilst at the same time the Egyptian irrigation Service was left without anyone to give the high level technical direction needed for the planning and execution of a chain of major engineering works strung out over 3,000 miles or so of the Nile."[18]

The British doubted the capability of Egyptian experts to fill the void created by the upgrading of Egypt's political status and the resignation of experienced British functionaries. On 7 May 1929, Lord George Lloyd, the British high commissioner, and Muhammad Mahmud, the Egyptian prime minister, reached an agreement on the use of the Nile water based on a report prepared by British experts. The agreement provided for "working arrangements agreed upon between the technical authorities responsible for the control of water distribution ... [the agreement] is the basis of the allocation and sharing of waters between the Sudan and

Egypt, and endorses the proposals of the Nile Commission report, which were prepared 'with the object of devising a practical working arrangement which would respect the needs of established irrigation, while permitting such programme of extension as might be feasible under present conditions and those of the near future, without at the same time compromising in any way the possibilities of the more distant future.'" Development projects were to be undertaken in the Sennar Reservoir and the Gezira Scheme; the Jabel al-Awliya' Reservoir; and the Nag Hammadi Barrage.[19]

The British did not want to see a situation whereby Egypt would exercise full control over the Nile water and determine issues related to water allocation. Indeed, Egypt regarded Sudan as an integral part of its territorial sovereignty and reiterated its argument about the vital importance of the Nile to the lands through which it flows, particularly Egypt. Egyptian geographers predicted a substantial increase in the Egyptian population, which necessitated studying "the vital problem of increasing the cultivated areas and completing the reclamation of land still capable of being brought under irrigation in both the Delta and Upper Egypt."[20] If Egypt was to safeguard its required annual water supply in the near future, the geographers recommended the expansion of a series of public works projects in Sudan. Such views partly fit Karl Wittfogel's theory that hydraulic management causes "internal pressures for a structured bureaucratic organization under centralized control and forced people into unequality: 'those who control the hydraulic network are uniquely prepared to wield supreme power.' As systems grew, leadership was required to build new canals, maintain existing ones, and ensure efficient distribution of water."[21] Wittfogel maintained that extensive irrigation required centralized coordination and direction.[22]

Egypt and Sudan were "hydraulic societies," and Egypt as the master of the Nile valley, predetermined Egyptian geographers, should occupy the leading role in controlling and maintaining the water regime along the Nile. This colonialist stand and supremacist approach employed by Egyptian geographers acting within the establishment framework was a precise reflection of the prevailing national consensus on the Sudan issue. In contrast, the British took every possible step to thwart Egypt's scheme for the unity of the Nile valley under the Egyptian crown that would turn it into a "powerful hydraulic empire," to employ Wittfogel's term. The British goal was to create a situation whereby the Sudan would not be dependent on Egyptian goodwill as far as water issues – irrigation and planning – were concerned.[23]

In their extensive effort to justify Egypt's quest for hegemony over the Nile's irrigation systems, Egyptian geographers also relied on work done by the British engineer Sir William Garstin. He was involved with the implementation of the treaty of 1902 between Britain and Ethiopian Emperor Menelik. It was stipulated in the treaty that Ethiopia would undertake not to "construct or allow to be constructed any works across the Blue Nile, Lake Tana or the Soobat ... which would arrest the flow of waters into the Nile except with the agreement of the governments of Britain and Anglo–Egyptian Sudan." Consequently, Garstin supervised the activity of an engineering and survey expedition in Lake Tana in 1902. The conclusion was that "it would make an excellent reservoir."[24] In a comprehensive study, titled *A Guide to the Upper-Nile Sources*, published on 21 March 1904, Garstin maintained that the Sudanese irrigation department should be under Egyptian control and that the Egyptian office of public works should supervise it. The allocation of the Nile water should be under the control of a single apparatus. Egypt alone should bear the expenses of the irrigation department, and Sudan would be exempted of any cost because it had no control over the irrigation works.[25]

Egyptian protagonists of the unity of the Nile valley concluded that in the early phases of the condominium rule, British engineers as well as policymakers recognized the unity of the Nile valley.[26]

Although the agreement of May 1929 safeguarded Egypt's vital interests and placed it in a hegemonic position regarding the Nile water regime, and Prime Minister Muhammad Mahmud could congratulate himself for such an achievement, the opposition parties, particularly the Wafd, voiced criticism. The party's newspaper *al-Balagh* published on 18 May a critical article concerning the water agreement. The prime minister, it was stated, who acted as a dictator, dissolved parliament so that there would be no debate among the people's representatives on his policies.[27] The Wafd's criticism of the non-democratic nature of Mahmud's government may be based on solid ground, yet the agreement was favorable for Egypt; moreover, it improved Anglo–Egyptian relations at least for the next few years.

Prime Minister Mahmud responded to the opposition critics, arguing that the agreement was in Egypt's favor:

I, as an Egyptian, believe that the agreement on the waters of the Nile fully and completely safeguards Egypt's rights. Had I had the slightest fear that this agreement would deprive Egypt of any right she has hitherto enjoyed, or prejudice any just claim she may make in future, I would not have signed it. I have consulted engineers of the highest standing, technically and otherwise, and I am convinced that the agreement embodies the Egyptian point of view in regard to the waters of the Nile.[28]

The Wafd's opposition to the 1929 agreement received tail wind from Britain's rival – the USSR. Indeed, the Sudan question attracted the attention of the newly emerging Soviet power already in the early 1920s. In 1919 the International Communist Organization (Comintern) was formed to advance the global social revolution – the Nile valley was not excluded. By 1922 the Comintern favored the unification of Egypt and Sudan because the latter "was a continuation of and supplement to Egypt and therefore should politically be a part of the latter."[29] The Comintern closely monitored the political crisis within Egypt following the downfall of the Wafd in mid-1928 and the formation of the Mahmud government. British imperialism was held responsible for the decision of Mahmud's government on 19 July to dissolve parliament and to abrogate the constitutional rights for three years.

The Comintern experts reasoned that these measures were taken due to the resistance of parliament, dominated by the Wafd, to Britain's grand irrigation project. According to the British plan, the course of the Nile would be regulated from its very sources. The British planned to construct a reservoir in Jabal al-Awliya', situated on Sudanese territory, that would hold some 10,000 million cubic meters of water. The reservoir, it was explained, would give the British the possibility to reduce the water supply to Egypt and to enlarge the area of cotton plantations in Sudan. To discredit the Wafd and to win public support, Mahmud's government propagated among the fellahin that the project would serve their interests, providing them with more water and extending the area of cultivated land.[30] The Comintern justified the Wafd's stand against the project and its proposal to raise the Aswan Dam, instead. Such a move, the Soviet experts asserted, would provide a smaller increase in the water supply, but had the advantage of being on Egyptian territory. Thus the Egyptians would not be dependent on British goodwill, reasoned these experts. In its campaign to advance the project, noted critically the Comintern experts, Mahmud's government based its support for the option of Jabal al-Awliya' on the conclusions of the International Technical Commission (consisting of three members: a British, an American, and a Swiss). After "a hasty investigation," the commission found that raising the Aswan Dam "must be rejected because the proposed projects are all unsuitable."[31]

Mahmud, stated the Comintern, made it clear that his government would regard "agitation against its irrigation plans as high treason." According to the Comintern Britain was also displeased with the ongoing debate in parliament throughout 1928 on the need to limit the privileges of foreign subjects based on the Capitulation arrangements.

The Comintern discussed in detail the Wafd's campaign to restore democracy and parliamentary life in the country.[32]

Contrary to the negative assessments of the Comintern and the Egyptian Communist Party at the time, a critical review, in retrospect, of the 1929 treaty by independent scholars supports Mahmud's satisfaction with its results. Egypt, argued Mwangi Kimenyi and John Mukum, was granted "virtually unlimited control over the Nile – Egypt claimed the entire timely flow of the river – and actually limited the ability of Sudan to access the waters of the Nile." The 1929 treaty, they emphasized, gave Egypt two crucial vantage points: first, it had the right to "monitor Nile-related activities by upstream riparian states to make certain that they did not negatively affect availability of water to Egypt's agricultural projects"; second, Egypt was allowed to "veto any construction projects by other riparians considered harmful" to its interests in the Nile. The agreement allocated Egypt 48 billion cubic meters per year out of the estimated total of 84 billion, whereas Sudan was given only 4 billion cubic meters; the remaining 32 billion were left for "possible allocation between the upstream riparian states."[33]

Rafi'i, who was a member of the opposition party al-Hizb al-Watani, presented an ambiguous approach with regard to the agreement. On the one hand, he depicted its benefits for Egypt, which were the following:

1. The inspector general of the Egyptian department of irrigation in Sudan or his assistants would be allowed to cooperate with the engineer of the Sennar Dam so that the Egyptian government would be able to verify that the water distribution was done in line with the agreement.
2. All irrigation actions along the Nile should be subject to Egyptian consent. In any case, Egypt's water quota and interests would not be harmed.
3. The Egyptian government would be granted the required assistance to undertake hydrological studies of Sudan's Nile.
4. Should the Egyptian government decide to perform operations on the Nile and its tributaries in the Sudan area or to increase the water quota in Egypt's favor, it should first and foremost come to terms with the local authorities. However, the inspection, management, and protection of such operations would be carried out by the Egyptian government only.
5. The British government recognized Egypt's natural and historical rights to the Nile water and deemed the safeguard of these rights a major principle of its policy.[34]

On the other hand, like *al-Balagh* before, Rafi'i disputed Mahmud's right to sign such an agreement after he abolished the constitution and therefore had no authority to represent the nation as a negotiator with other governments, "let alone when it is related to key issues such as the unity between Egypt and the Sudan." This agreement, Rafi'i went on, established, as a matter of fact, the general principle of the British policy: an economic separation between Egypt and Sudan. For Egypt, he stated, Egypt's and Sudan's economies were inseparable. Like Ammar before, Rafi'i believed that the management of irrigation activities along the Nile in both Egypt and Sudan should continue to be governed by the Egyptian ministry of public works. Following the assassination of Lee Stack in 1924, the British exploited the situation to introduce changes into the policy regarding the Nile water. Among other changes, the management of the irrigation in Sudan was removed from the responsibility of the Egyptian minister of public works, by the establishment of a separate Sudanese office to deal with the matter. The British also took over the management of the Sennar Dam and the Jazira irrigation in Sudan.[35]

After Egypt abrogated in 1951 unilaterally the 1936 treaty with Britain, it launched an international campaign to justify its move as well as the vitality of the Nile as the sole life spring for both parts of the Nile valley – Egypt and Sudan. A pamphlet, entitled *The Egyptian Question 1882–1951*, distributed in the United States by the Egyptian embassy in December 1951, emphasized that whoever controlled the water of the Upper Nile could easily control Egypt. Britain, it was stressed, was currently the dominant power in Sudan, and Egypt's existence therefore depended on its goodwill. Egypt's dependence on the Nile for its economic well-being had not lessened since the Pharaonic times. Agricultural production relied on an elaborate system of irrigation, utilizing the water of the river, a practice that had been refined through the centuries. The Egyptian government argued that should "the course of the Nile be diverted or damage occur to the dams and reservoirs built by the Egyptians along the 4,100 mile long river, Egypt would be drought-ridden or ravaged by floods. The Nile flows through Sudanese territory for more than 2,100 miles, from the heart of Africa to the present southern Egyptian border."[36] Britain took pains to legalize its occupation of both Egypt and Sudan by compelling the former to sign the 1899 agreements. Under the pretext of a joint Anglo–Egyptian administration in Sudan, the British tried to effect a physical separation of Sudan from Egypt by establishing its southern border along the 22nd parallel. As an occupied country, Egypt could not object to the British terms or the legality of the agreements. Consequently, the fate of the whole Nile valley was, indeed, in British hands.[37]

Irrigation, Agrarian, and Labor Concerns:
A Marxist Viewpoint

As we have seen, the geographical factor featured prominently in Egypt's efforts to unite the Nile valley under its hegemony. The British refuted Egypt's assertions and opted to separate Sudan from Egypt. An instructive and fascinating external Marxist viewpoint is provided by Comintern experts who studied the geographical aspects of the Nile valley in the 1920s. At the time, the Egyptian Communist Party (ECP) was a member of the Comintern and provided the latter with factual data about the social, economic, and political situation in Egypt and Sudan. As the Egyptian branch of the Comintern, the ECP was totally bound to its patronage including ideological and operative directions.[38]

Comintern theoreticians analyzed the data and prepared extensive reports and guidelines for action for the Egyptian communists. These theoreticians also viewed the British and Egyptian struggle over Sudan from the perspective of water control. Special emphasis was given to the geopolitical aspect of that rivalry. They determined that the two main goals pursued by the British in Sudan were political. For one, they wanted to secure an overland communication line between South Africa, India, and the Far East "without having to go via the Suez Canal. Secondly, controlling the Sudan guaranteed control over the Nile – a strategic advantage that could leave Egypt helpless by cutting the Upper and Lower Nile off from its tributaries which are controlled by the Sudan."[39]

British imperialism was the Soviets' main target at the time. In line with the Marxist doctrine, the Comintern could not ignore the economic factor. British imperialism regarded Sudan as an extensive agrarian reservoir that could supply its markets with raw cotton (even better than Egypt), minerals, and agricultural products, and "as a promising market for the disposal of British manufactures, as a sphere for capital investment and the construction of irrigation works, railroads etc."[40] As long as Sudan, a "colony of a colony," to employ the Soviet phrase, was controlled by British capitalists, Egypt would be in danger and

the millions of peasants and workers under the constant menace of death and starvation ... As long as the Sudan serves as a connecting link between the two parts of the British Empire, the cutting off of the latter from the Suez Canal will only render difficult but not destroy the vital direct connection between the "nape" and the "backbone," the home country and the colonies. The deprivation of the Sudan would also interfere with Britain's grand plan, the political part of which has already been realized, of uniting with a steel chain of railroads, the whole of the East and South Africa with the Near East from Cape Town to Cairo and Bagdad.[41]

At that stage both the ECP and the Comintern accepted the prevailing Egyptian geographic paradigm of the unity of the Nile valley, that is, Sudan constitutes the southern flank of Egypt. Sudan, it was noted, was a natural continuation of and supplement to Egypt and should therefore be a political part of the latter. It should belong to Egypt because "the working classes of revolutionary Egypt" would be able to support reliably the toilers of Sudan "as the weaker, defenseless and the as yet quite un-awakened class." A geographically united Egypt–Sudan could become economically successful, if the British allowed the development of the coal, which Sudan was blessed with, and let the countries of the Nile valley develop their cotton industry independently. Economically, the Comintern and the ECP perceived Egypt and Sudan as Siamese twins that could not be separated. Moreover, they wanted to see British imperialism away from the Nile valley, and they wanted the two countries to go through a social revolutionary process, which would subsequently link them with international communism.[42]

Comintern theoreticians emphasized that there was no logical correl-ation between the size of the populations of Egypt and Sudan and the size of the territory held by each one of them – the latter suffered from underpopulation, whereas the former from overpopulation. Conse-quently, Egypt was unable to feed its inhabitants, even if the land were divided more equally. The Comintern appreciated that a mass Egyptian emigration to Sudan would solve many of the problems. The Egyptians could help their Sudanese compatriots in developing their agriculture and industry. However, reasoned the Comintern, such a move would not serve the interests of British imperialism and the Egyptian bourgeoisie and landlords because "the emigration of workers from Egypt would reduce the reserve army of labor in Egypt" – affecting the exploiters, who benefited from the present situation.[43]

By late 1924 the Comintern continued to argue that Sudan was more significant for the British for its geographical advantages rather than its economic importance. "Together with the former German possession of East Africa, the Sudan forms the connecting link between the South African Union and India. The position of the Sudan at the entrance to the Red Sea is also of importance. The railways cover a distance of 2,400 kilometers and the telegraph lines 7,000." The possession of Sudan, asserted the Comintern, was a "life and death question" for Egypt, because the fertility of Egypt completely depended on the regulation of the overflow of the Nile, whose upper course was placed in Sudan.[44]

The Comintern consistently emphasized the class division in Egypt, which was based on blatant grievances – a tiny group of wealthy landlords possessed the greatest part of the agricultural land. The Comintern's analysts asserted that the Egyptian class division manifested itself politic-ally. They argued that the small group of big landowners, who gained from the British investment in Egypt, and the big merchants, who had British connections, were the strongest supporters of British imperial-ism.[45] The ECP was instructed to cooperate in the anti-imperialist struggle with "petty-bourgeois groups, and particularly the students, who have a strong nationalist tradition, as well as with the foreign (non-British) population that includes numerous small shopkeepers etc. in the large towns." The ideological foundation for such cooperation should be "a struggle against a common enemy," which was the enemy of both Egypt and Sudan.[46]

The Comintern thoroughly studied Egypt's agrarian issues, and lots of research was done on this subject in the late 1920s. The land issue was related in Egypt with the water problem, and because the British con-trolled the water sources in Sudan, Sudan became the core of the Anglo–Egyptian dispute. The ECP was required to cooperate with the Sudanese popular classes, who were enslaved like the Egyptian people by common enemies: British imperialism and the Egyptian bourgeoisie. The latter wished to unite Egypt and Sudan in pursuit of its own economic and political interests. The ECP should emphasize the right of the two peoples to independence, which could be achieved only if they con-ducted a joint struggle against imperialism.[47] That is, at that stage the Comintern drew a distinction between the Egyptian bourgeoisie, who wished to unite the Nile valley for economic exploitation of both the Egyptian and the Sudanese working classes, and the progressive forces led by the communists, who wished to liberate the Nile valley from the yoke of domestic bourgeoisie and feudalists, who allied themselves with British imperialism. As we shall see, the Marxist theoreticians analyzed convincingly Egypt's social and economic clefts and asymmetric polarity, yet they failed to see the anti-imperialist sentiments and desires of all Egyptians across the entire political spectrum, who sought the liberation of the Nile valley in its entirety and subsequently its unification under the Egyptian crown. In this regard, there was no difference between the upper and the lower classes.

Why Was Unification Economically Inevitable?

Economic concerns were another vital component in the unity of the Nile valley paradigm. Egyptians of all political stripes referred to it in their writings. For instance, 'Abd al-Rahman al-Rafi'i advocated enthu-siastically that the Egyptian authorities should turn Egypt and Sudan into a single economic unit. The unity of the Nile valley was not only based on geographic or political factors, but also on an economic foundation essential for both Egypt and Sudan. The first pillar of economic unification was the exchange trade between the two countries, which was small because of inappropriate routes of transportation and little interest shown by the government and economic institutions. Rafi'i explained, furthermore, that the main reason for the low volume of the exchange trade was due to obstacles placed by the imperialist administration in Sudan, that is, the Sudan government.[48]

The British imperialist policy, blamed Rafi'i, did everything possible to sabotage economic unification by placing obstructions along traffic arteries and preventing access to railroads that could ease transportation of merchandises between the two countries. It founded Port Sudan to divert Sudanese goods, thus creating independent Sudanese waterways. Up to 1948 the Egyptian government avoided, due to imperialist pressure, extending the railways from Egypt to Sudan despite the fact that the distance between the very end of the Egyptian railways in Aswan and the northern starting point of the Sudanese railways did not exceed 300 ki. Moreover, the ships traveling on the Nile from Aswan and the Halfa valley belonged to the imperialist administration despite the fact that they traveled along undisputed Egyptian territory. The separation of the customs mechanism weakened the barter between the two countries, and Egyptian goods were rejected (in contravention of clause 7 of the January 1899 treaty), whereas foreign goods were treated favorably.[49]

When World War II broke out, argued Rafi'i, the Sudan government imposed restrictions on the export of Sudanese crops to Egypt and thus harmed the interests of the two countries. It granted an export franchise to a British company that purchased these crops cheaply and sold them for double price in Egypt. The economic unification between Egypt and Sudan required the extension of the railways between them, the establishment of a single customs mechanism, free barter, and the removal of restrictions imposed by Britain, which prevented such imperative trade. It was only on 19 April 1946 that the Egyptian authorities convened the "first economic conference" in Egypt to discuss comprehensively the economic relations between Egypt and Sudan. Although politically Rafi'i opposed Sidqi's government, he pointed at several essential decisions that were made and could help realize economic unification:

1. The unity of the Nile valley after British evacuation, enabling direction of the national economy (*al-iqtisad al-qawmi*) in the two parts of the valley.
2. Free commercial relations and the removal of all existing customs restrictions and barriers.

3. The amalgamation of Egyptian and Sudanese customs on the basis of the exchange of goods and currency, while safeguarding the purchasing power of the Sudanese inhabitants to consume Egyptian products in the Sudan markets.

4. Stimulation of the Sudanese agriculture by sharing Egyptian knowledge, experience, labor force, and money. The two countries should establish Egyptian–Sudanese agricultural firms that would take upon themselves to improve land and prepare it for sowing. Egypt and Sudan complemented each other and could not allow themselves to disregard each other.

5. Coordination of the two countries' production policies in a way that would produce products essential to each other. Also, new industries should be developed in Sudan to elevate the standard of living of the Sudanese people.

6. The building of roads and other infrastructures to improve transportation between the two parts of the valley, including airlines to connect between Sudanese and Egyptian cities, thus shortening the travel time for businesspeople and other passengers.

7. The establishment of Egyptian banks and financial institutions in Sudan to assist a variety of Sudanese developing projects.

8. Encouraging the exchange of scientific delegations to discuss the development of education, industry, and commerce.[50]

The interrelation between economy and migration in the Nile valley was one of the main subjects to be discussed during the inter-Arab engineers' conference held at Fu'ad I University in Cairo in 1946.[51] The key message was that the Nile valley was indivisible and its people should stick to it even if it meant great sacrifices for the next generations. Jawdat al-Sayyid, the secretary of the standing committee, ridiculed the British assertion that Egypt desired to rule Sudan to enslave its people. The British promised the Sudanese no less than heaven, yet they solely saw Sudan in terms of their strategic imperial interests. The British policymakers should study thoroughly the present state of Egypt's society, especially the miserable standard of living of the vast majority of its population – the fellahin. Egypt was the most crowded place in the world; "it is more suitable for dogs to live in such density," asserted exaggeratedly Sayyid.[52]

Sayyid portrayed a gloomy picture of the welfare conditions in Cairo: one of the largest cities in the world, with a high poverty rate, poor nutrition, and poor health services. The only way to solve these problems, he proposed, was to allow emigration to Sudan. Sudan was the safety valve for rescuing Egyptians from poverty. However, against this logic, Britain was constantly preventing "our natural right" to immigrate to Sudan, which shares with us the Nile, language, geography, and religion. The Sudanese were lacking man power to cultivate their huge agricultural areas, and therefore Egyptian immigration was essential. Sayyid refuted the British paradigm that Sudan's sovereignty could not be handed over without Sudanese consent. Egypt, stressed Sayyid, did not seek sovereignty over Sudan, but the amalgamation of the two countries into one state. The Sudanese living in Egypt and Egyptians living in Sudan, he spelled out, would have the same rights and duties, and one government and king. Full cooperation and integration of the peoples of the Nile valley were the guarantee for prosperity and growth. Britain had not yet shown any gratitude to its Egyptian ally, "who supported her to beat her enemies" during the war.[53]

The liberal newspaper *Ruz al-Yusuf* blamed the British Sudan government for placing obstacles to sabotage Egypt's efforts to develop and advance the infrastructures linking the northern and southern parts of the Nile valley as an essential means for the development of economic ties between Egypt and Sudan. The British and their yes-men in Sudan, asserted *Ruz al-Yusuf*, with their policy of separation, took pains to weaken commercial ties by establishing alternative trade routes for Sudan, such as ports along the Red Sea. They created their own monopoly on waterborne commerce along the Nile by prohibiting Egyptian vessels from sailing southward.[54] In his attempts to break the British blockade, wrote *Ruz al-Yusuf*, Prime Minister Nuqrashi instructed the transportation ministry to plan the extension of the Egyptian railways to connect it to the Sudanese ones. The technical schemes that were prepared offered solutions to geographical and natural obstructions, but the Sudan government set political obstacles. *Ruz al-Yusuf* remonstrated that the 1899 treaty stipulated that the Sudan government would not have the authority to object to such projects, especially when the Egyptian government would pay the costs. Legally, the Sudan government was to be under the supervision and inspection of the Egyptian government, and therefore it had no right to object to the railways project.[55]

The British were sabotaging the unity of the Nile valley, wrote *al-Balagh*, because British imperialism was driven by multifaceted interests, including the economic imperialism of one strong nation exploiting other weaker nations. By being the dominant power in the Nile valley, the British controlled and exploited ruthlessly all the natural resources and means of production of the people of that region. They laid their hands on the cotton that was the valley's main crop and delivered it to their motherland, where they utilized it in their large and modern textile industry, which was lacking enough raw materials – cotton – to produce an enormous amount of various apparels for local and international markets. The textile industry constituted a significant component of the British economy, and millions of Britons benefited from it. Thus it was clear why Britain refused to evacuate the Nile valley.[56]

In late 1951 the Egyptian government blamed the British for the lack of agricultural and subsequent economic development and prosperity in Sudan. It must be noted, it was stated in an official Egyptian pamphlet, that Sudan was sparsely populated, while Egypt was overpopulated. "Should the present obstacles preventing the economic cooperation between the two sections of the Nile Valley be removed, the Egyptian farmer, whose ingenuity and frugality are world-renowned, would be able to obviate in a considerable degree the existing deficiency in farming experience in the Sudan."[57]

In the very early 1950s, the Egyptian government announced its ambitious economic plans for the Nile valley. The goal was clear: only Egypt could advance the economic welfare of Sudan, because the economies of Egypt and Sudan complemented each other. Since both were largely based on agriculture and utterly dependent on the planned use of the Nile water and on water storage during the flood season, the two countries, it was emphasized, shared a common interest – the reclamation of desert land – and therefore

a perennial system of irrigation in Egypt intensified the necessity for construction projects to regulate the flow of the Nile. Some such projects exist today; others must be envisaged for the future. The Merowe Dam at the fourth Cataract outside the present boundaries of Egypt is now under construction by the Egyptian government, and is expected to be finished next year, 1952. It will cost Egypt $60,000,000. Both the Sudan and Egypt will benefit greatly by it. An agreement concerning Owens Reservoir at Owens Falls in Uganda is already signed. Uganda, the Sudan and Egypt will all benefit greatly by it, Uganda by generated electricity, and the Nile Valley by the water. New dams and new reservoirs will be as beneficial to the Sudan as to other parts of Egypt.[58]

A fair distribution of Nile water is the common interest of all the peoples in the Nile valley. To demonstrate the indispensability of the Nile water to Egypt, Egyptian officials relied on statements made by British functionaries such as Sir Scott Moncrieff (1855–1924), the famous British engineer, who stated that a hostile power on the Upper Nile could "at will either parch or inundate Egypt." Similar words were uttered by British Admiral Sir Reginald Portal (1894–1983), who said that "he who holds the Upper Nile, could dispose of Egypt as he likes and even destroy her." For the Egyptian government the unity of the Nile valley was far from being a slogan for propaganda purposes; it was rather "Nature's own behest."[59]

The Egyptian stand on Sudan, as presented so far, may fall in line with what Hans Morgenthau defined as three systems of imperialism: first, military imperialism that aims at gaining military occupation – indeed, Egypt occupied Sudan twice militarily in the nineteenth century (the second time by a joint occupation with British imperialism); second, economic imperialism, in which one strong nation exploits other weaker nations – this was indeed the Egyptian long-term goal as described above; and third, cultural imperialism, which aims at the replacement of one culture by another.[60] Edward Said agreed that the "main battle in imperialism is over land," yet he also emphasized the strong bonds between culture and imperialism – "the power to narrate, or block other narratives from forming and emerging."[61] Elements of cultural imperialism are clearly discernible in the following discussion. However, Egyptian imperialist aspirations in Sudan were mainly political and economic; as Benjamin Cohen put it, "any relationship of effective domination or control, political or economic, direct or indirect, of one nation over another."[62]

The Ethnographic Bases

For Egyptian intellectuals, their analysis of the unity of the Nile valley did not only encompass historical and material factors, but also placed great emphasis on the ethnographic links between Egyptians and Sudanese. Unlike the eminent German sociologist Max Weber, who maintained that an ethnic group is not "a spontaneously developed community, or a group with specific geographical location, but a group of people who believe they have ancestors in common from the past,"[63] Egyptian scholars conversely argued that geography and ethnography were inextricably linked in the Nile valley. The geographic homogeneity of the Nile valley, comprising mainly vast flat lands, facilitated the rapid diffusion and constant intermingling of the peoples along the Nile throughout the centuries:

The first waves which invaded and settled in most of the parts of the Nile Valley consisted of shepherds whose movements were unhindered by natural obstacles. This was also the case of the last Muslim invaders who arrived in Egypt with the Arab conquerors and later moved southward and finally reached the Sudan, where favorable pastoral conditions existed not different from those prevailing in the Arab peninsula from which the new invaders' ancestors originally came. That some of these pastoral elements have definitely settled along the banks of the Nile and adopted sedentary agricultural life, does not alter the fact that they do not differ from other neighboring groups who have continued to pursue their pastoral and nomadic life. This is but the natural outcome of the evolution and trend towards a more civilized life.[64]

Egyptian scholars argued that as time elapsed, the ethnographic composition of the Nile valley began to visibly change, as different groups dispersed to both the north and the south:

Whether we study the colour of the skin, the shape of the nose, or the hair formation, this fact will remain valid, as it is impossible to find a brusque and unexpected change in any of these characteristics while crossing from one area to another. Consequently the demarcation line that is drawn by certain writers between what they call Negroid Africa and Caucasian Africa ... and dividing the Sudan into two, the Caucasian North and the Negroid South, must not be given an exaggerated scientific importance but it must be looked at as an attempt to simplify matters for public minds.[65]

The Egyptian scholars argued that British motivations in Sudan were exploitative, built to undermine the unity of the Nile valley by playing up the racial and ethnic divisions as a divisive factor.[66] They argued that by utilizing ethnographic analysis, based on the following principles, they could disprove the British view on the racial division of the peoples of the Nile valley:

1. Racial unity does not mean either complete uniformity of morphological characteristics or thorough fusion of physical peculiarities. Purity of race is a myth, with no basis in biology or in human history.
2. The racial boundaries indicated on ethnographic maps are hypothetical and general. Racial regions overlap each other, and there are transitional zones of mixed elements and heterogeneous populations.
3. The term *race* is absolutely misused by politicians, who are more concerned with cultural than with morphological facts. Nationalists, everywhere, have always been under the influence of linguistic and historical considerations.
4. The existence of ethnic minorities, peculiar in their cultural and physical characteristics – within particular nationalities – is a well-known fact to students of political geography.[67]

In their efforts to unearth the racial origins of the Egyptians and Sudanese, the Egyptian scholars focused their argument on the fact that the "purity of race" was groundless. In actuality, their starting point for much of the ethnographic analysis of the Egyptian and Sudanese peoples centered on their perceived shared origins as members of the Hamitic race. Ironically, while the scholars sought to dismiss the concept of the "purity of race," they ended up adopting it as a central trope of their argument on the unity of the Nile valley. They claimed that scientific factors showed that "Hamitic elements," whose ancestry was rooted in southwest Arabia or somewhere near the Persian Gulf, migrated in

various historical stages. The Egyptian scholars contended that the
Sudanese people shared a common ancestry with their Egyptian brethren
since ancient times, proven, they noted, by the archeological and anthropological discoveries made by a Nubian expedition.[68]

However, in their analysis of Sudanese ethnography, they drew a
distinction between northern and southern Sudan, undermining their
previous contention of the shared Hamitic origins of both Egyptians
and Sudanese. According to their analysis, southern Sudan's close
proximity to the habitat of black Africans in central and western Africa,
as well as the lack of geographical obstacles, could not prevent the
migration of black Africans into Sudan. These were pertinent factors
that made the Hamitic characteristics less influential in certain parts of
the country, especially in the south, far less prominent compared to
Nubia and Egypt.[69]

For the Egyptian scholars, an additional unifying factor contributed to
the perceived bonds between Egyptians and Sudanese: the shared Arabic
language and Islamic culture. The Arab invasion of Sudan and the
eventual control of all of Sudan by the thirteen century established the
cultural hegemony of the Arab–Islamic culture, with Arabic becoming
the lingua franca, and Islam becoming the religion of the people.[70] This
influence was underscored by the Egyptian nationalist Mustafa Kamil,
who noted the close ties between the Sudanese and Islam, stating that
"the Muslims of the Sudan are very rigid and fanatical; they would never
and will never accept that any but Muslims rule them."[71]

For Sulayman Huzayyin, it was clear that ancient Egyptian cultural
and social influences had reached the south and left their marks there – in
an area here its inhabitants, unlike northern Egyptians, were not exposed
to constant struggles and external innovations. The social mechanisms of
the southerners, therefore, remained intact, and ancient customs and
traditions continued to thrive. There was plenty of evidence to support
the existence of close relations between Egypt and the upper part of
the Nile (northern Sudan) in ancient times, as, for example, from the
period of the "Eastern Hamitic people," who settled in the remote areas
between the Upper and the Lower Nile, and the Pharaonic period, when
Hamitic and Semitic dynasties intermingled in the northern valley
and from there moved south. Also, elements of material culture, which
characterized the north, seeped gradually to the south, such as agricultural practices, animal husbandry, and pastures. The northern influence
also manifested itself in nurturing cultural and spiritual ties, which struck
roots in the south. These interactions were not one-sided – Egyptian
ancient and modern music was influenced by southern folklore, which
had its Hamitic origins. Moreover, parts of the Upper Nile tribes were

still using musical instruments similar to those used in Pharaonic Egypt. In addition, some Pharaonic religious rituals, such as sun worship, burial customs, and mummification, expanded southward, reaching the equator and the Congo basin. The Nile, along which a unique culture had developed, was a wonderful river that linked the pre-historical and the present epochs. The social structure and spiritual heritage of the population inhabiting the northern part of the valley were most similar to those of the southern population.[72]

Huzayyin found it easier to spot closer historical bonds between northern Sudan and Egypt. This could be explained, he asserted, by the fact that the offspring of the ancient Hamitic people still inhabited the eastern desert in Sudan and part of the eastern desert in Egypt, and blood and family relations between the populations of both areas could be detected. Ethnic and cultural Egyptian influences featured prominently in central and northern Sudan due to the constant settlement of Egyptians in these places throughout history. A monolithic Nile culture uniting south and north had become a reality. A social and political unity followed suit without southern or northern hegemony, argued Huzayyin.[73]

With the advent of Islam, Huzayyin continued, a new era opened in the cultural and ethnic relations between Egypt and Sudan. Only few Arabs immigrated from the Hijaz and the Arabian Peninsula to Sudan via the Red Sea. A large number of Arab tribes arrived first in the Sinai Peninsula via land and from there headed to Egypt and continued along the Nile up to northern Sudan. Their flow southward began only in the twelfth century and intensified during the fourteenth century. The waves of Arab migrants were to affect the ethnic composition of Sudan. They moreover spread Islam, its language, and its culture among Sudanese. This was another important factor to unite Egypt and Sudan, but nevertheless not the main one – the "Hamitic blood" had already preceded it. Things went wrong under the Mamluks, when Sudan found itself in a state of chaos, with tribes dispersed in all directions, and without a central government to link all parts of the country and unite them culturally and ideologically. This state of affairs continued until Muhammad 'Ali breathed new life into the Nile valley by uniting its two parts. The process of the Nile valley's awakening was interrupted by the appearance of British imperialism in the late nineteenth century.[74]

Huzayyin's analysis of the "Arabization" of Sudan was supported by Egyptian scholars active within the establishment. They, too, noted that the Arabization had not disposed with the ancient Hamitic influence, even in the provinces most influenced by Arabs. Although the Hamitic people were the basic ethnic element, common to all the peoples of the valley, the Semites, the Egyptian scholars pointed out, had in fact contributed more to the ethnic makeup of the land of the Nile.[75] They even went further, suggesting that the Hamites and the Semites were of one racial stem, differing but little in morphological characteristics. The Arabization of Sudan was mostly felt in the Arabic language and the Islamic faith. It had been proven that the process of Arabization in Sudan was achieved peacefully, through intermarriage and union, a policy followed by Muslims all over the world.[76]

Ruz al-Yusuf stated confidently that there was a consensus among the Arab Muslim inhabitants of the Nile valley that their lofty manners and customs distinguished them from other peoples. The Egyptian, Sudanese, and Bedouin fellahin were similar in their character, trait, nature, dignity, revenge, courage, energy, and sharp wit. They also had similar Islamic religious, mourning, marriage, and other ceremonies. The ancient Egyptian and Pharaonic influences found expressions in these ceremonies experienced by those Sudanese and Bedouins, who lived along the banks of the Nile – the magnificent river – the master of the ancient Egyptians that still dominated indirectly the life of anyone who lived in its proximity.[77]

Successive waves of Egyptian migrants penetrated Sudan, and no color bar prevented the integration of the peoples of the Nile valley, concluded the Egyptian scholars. This tendency, they clarified, was reinforced by the spread of Egyptian culture and the fact that Arabic became the common language spoken by the inhabitants of the Nile valley.[78]

These Egyptian assertions were disputed by Mekki 'Abbas, a Sudanese intellectual who graduated from the Gordon Memorial College (1931) and worked in the Education Department of the Sudan government in the pre-independence years (until 1946). 'Abbas predicated categorically that Sudan was dissimilar to Egypt as far as the physical and social environment was concerned. The dissimilarities between the two countries were attributable to geographical and ethnic obstacles. The majority of the Sudanese Arabs, he argued, were detached from Egypt until the condominium period since only then did the means of communication develop. Moreover, the Egyptian and the Sudanese "Arabs" were different in their ethnic origins. The Egyptian Arab "is a blend of ancient Egyptian, Caucasian, Arab, Turk, Georgian, Albanian and many other elements," which settled and integrated within Egyptian society throughout history. The Sudanese Arab, on the other hand, "is a blend of Arab, negro, and some Caucasian elements." Relying on *The Future of Culture in Egypt* (1938) by the eminent Egyptian intellectual Taha Husayn, 'Abbas argued that Egyptians were closer to the "Mediterranean types than to the Arabs of the Peninsula, whereas the ordinary Sudanese is nearer to the African."[79]

Sudanese historian 'Abdel Rahim concluded that it was not difficult to pinpoint "holes" in the Egyptian doctrine of the unity of the Nile valley in both its juridical tenet and its Sudanese–Egyptian components of "fraternal and cultural links." As for the latter, the presentation of Sudanese and Egyptians "from the Equator to the Delta, as one and same people, ethnically as well as culturally" was lacking an authoritative foundation and indeed was ridiculed by British commentators and spokespeople.[80]

The ethnographic foundation of the unity of the Nile valley as presented mainly by Egyptian scholars is the weakest layer in the con-struction of unification. Racial issues as well as the ethnic origins of the Sudanese people, particularly the southerners, are very much disputable. These complex issues are beyond the scope of this study. Nevertheless, more authoritative studies that dealt with such issues comprehensively presented a different picture of the multifaceted components of the Sudanese peoples. For instance, Stephanie Beswick concluded that "the theme of long-distance migrations, either because of bad weather conditions such as drought, or raids, wars and devastations, has predom-inated in Southern Sudanese history for centuries. Hence, the majority of South Sudanese today are not indigenous to the region but rather arrived only within the last two to four centuries."[81] In fact, there were nearly 600 ethnic groups, who spoke more than 400 languages and dialects, as Mohamed Fadlalla stated.[82] It is noteworthy that prior to the partition, approximately 40 percent of the Sudanese population was Arab, most of whom lived in the north.[83] The division of Sudan into two separate independent states in July 2011 after years of bloodshed was just a natural development. Imperial Sudan was an artificial creation – a prod-uct of both British and Egyptian imperialisms. To quote Sharkey, "The Sudan after 1898 was something of a legal anomaly: a de jure territory of two countries, Great Britain and Egypt. Its unusual situation derived from a nineteenth-century bout of colonialism which preceded the British arrival."[84]

Notes

1 'Abbas 'Ammar, "The Physical, Ethnographical, Cultural and Economic Bases of the Unity," in *The Unity of the Nile Valley*, p. 9.
2 Ibid., pp. 10–11. On the analysis and theory of the Egyptian geographer Sulayman Huzayyin regarding the process in which the Nile valley was created, see Israel Gershoni, "Geographers and Nationalism in Egypt: Huzayyin and the Unity of the Nile Valley, 1945–1948," in Erlich and Gershoni (eds.), *The Nile*, pp. 205–206.
3 El-Barawy, *Egypt, Britain and the Sudan*, p. 3. On the employment of geography as a tool of imperial propaganda, see a broader study focusing

on European imperialism in the period 1820–1940 in Morag Bell, Robin Butlin, and Michael Heffernan (eds.), *Geography and Imperialism, 1820–1840* (Manchester: Manchester University Press, 1995).

4 Gershoni, "Geographers and Nationalism in Egypt," p. 201.

5 See a pamphlet issued by the Egyptian government entitled *The Egyptian Question 1882–1951*, attached to Letter from British Embassy, Washington, 5 December 1951, FO953/1115, PG11637/102.

6 'Ammar, "The Physical," p. 11. Ginat, "Egypt's Efforts," p. 210.

7 "The Unity of the Nile Valley," in *Egypt Sudan*, pp. 68–69.

8 Ibid., p. 69.

9 Husayn Haykal, "No Basic Reason for Disagreement on the Sudan," in *Egypt Sudan*, p. 13. Fu'ad Shukri held a similar view, adding that the unity was based on natural foundations: geographic, ethnographic, cultural, economic, but, above all, historic ties from ancient times. See Shukri, *Misr wa-al-sudan: ta'rikh wahdat wadi al-nil*, p. 7.

10 Later on, Lake Nasser came to cover large parts of its territory.

11 'Abd al-Hafiz Abu al-Sa'ud, "Isba' al-injliz fi al-nuba," *al-Risala*, No. 788, 9 August 1948, p. 894.

12 Ibid., p. 895

13 'Ammar, "The Physical," p. 28.

14 Ibid., pp. 28–29. 'Ammar referred also to Lord Kitchener's declaration made during the Anglo–French dispute over Fashoda in 1898. "The Arab States and Egypt's Right in the Question of the Unity of the Nile Valley," in *Egypt Sudan*, pp. 52–53. See more on the Fashoda incident in Chapter 1.

15 R. M. MacGregor, "The Upper Nile Irrigation Projects," 10 December 1945, FO141/1100, J4314/643/16; a memorandum on use of the Nile waters by W. N. Allan, Director of Irrigation, Wad Medani, May 1945, Sudan, FO141/ 1100, 164/29/46.

16 Ibid.

17 Ibid.

18 R. M. MacGregor, "The Upper Nile Irrigation Projects," p. 4.

19 A memorandum on use of the Nile waters by W. N. Allan. See also 'Abd al-Rahman al-Rafi'i, *Fi a'qab al-thawra al-misriyya – Thawrat 1919*, Vol. 2, p. 92.

20 'Ammar, "The Physical," p. 11.

21 Tushaar Shah, *Taming the Anarchy: Groundwater Governance in South Asia* (Washington DC: Resources for the Future, 2009), p. 78.

22 On Karl Wittfogel's theory of hydraulic management and hydraulic societies, see his *Oriental Despotism: A Critical Study of Total Power* (Oxford: Oxford University Press, 1957). More specifically, for an illuminating analysis on the Nile valley, see John Waterbury, *Hydropolitics of the Nile Valley* (New York: Syracuse University Press, 1979).

23 R. M. MacGregor, "The Upper Nile Irrigation Projects"; Muhammad Rif'at, "Misr wa-al-sudan," *al-Katib al-Misri*, 6/21 (June 1947), p. 30.

24 Richard Snailham, "Europeans on the Blue Nile," *The Anglo-Ethiopian Society* (1992), at www.anglo-ethiopian.org/publications/articles.php?type=O&refer ence=publications/occasionalpapers/papers/europeansbluenile.php (accessed 15 January 2016).

25 "Misr wa-al-sudan qutr wahid," *al-Balagh*, 16 June 1951, p. 2.

26 Ibid.

27 Quoted from "The Nile Waters Agreement," *Foreign Affairs* (October 1929), at www.foreignaffairs.com/articles/69025/pierre-crabites/the-nile-waters-agreement (accessed 26 September 2013).

28 Quoted from ibid.

29 Rami Ginat, *A History of Egyptian Communism: Jews and Their Compatriots in Quest of Revolution* (Boulder, CO: Lynne Rienner, 2011), p. 305.

30 See Internal Comintern Document No. EH/JS/Russian 3639/12, on the situation in Egypt, 22 February 1929, Russian Governmental Archive of Social-Political History (hereafter RGASPI), Fond 495, OP 85, D. 76, L. 43–47.

31 See ibid.

32 See ibid.

33 Mwangi S. Kimenyi and John Mukum Mkabu, "Turbulence in the Nile: Toward a consensual and sustainable allocation of the Nile River waters," The Brookings Institution (August 2010), at www.brookings.edu/~/media/research/files/reports/2010/8/nile%20river%20basin%20kimenyi/08_nile_river_basin_kimenyi.pdf (accessed 26 September 2013). The two also maintained that the 1959 agreement between Sudan and Egypt also favored Egypt's interests. Like the 1929 treaty, "the 1959 agreement purported to bound upstream riparian states despite the fact that these states were neither signatories nor participants in the compacting of the agreement. As in 1929, Egypt was assigned the bulk of the Nile waters – Egypt increased its allotment to 55.5 billion cubic meters per year, while Sudan's share was raised to 18.5 billion cubic meters per year. That allocation left only 10 billion cubic meters unallocated, primarily to account for seepage and evaporation." Ibid. See also Arthur Okoth-Owiro, "The Nile Treaty, State Succession and International Treaty Commitments: A Case Study of the Nile Water Treaties," *Occasional Papers, East Africa*, Konrad Adenauer Foundation, Nairobi, Kenia, 2004, at www.kas.de/wf/doc/kas_6306-544-1-30.pdf (accessed 26 September 2013).

34 Rafi'i, *Fi a'qab al-thawra al-misriyya*, Vol. 2, pp. 92–94.

35 Ibid., pp. 91–95.

36 See a pamphlet issued by the Egyptian government entitled *The Egyptian Question 1882–1951*.

37 Ibid.

38 On the ECP and the Comintern in the 1920s, see Ginat, *A History*, pp. 55–186.

39 "The Sudan," supplementary Theses, 22 November 1922, RGASPI, Fond 495, OP85, D6, L57–59.

40 Ibid.

41 Ibid.

42 Ibid. For the ECP's stand on the Sudan issue, see "Misr wa-al-shuyu'iyya," *al-Ahram* (Cairo), 14 February 1924; 'Asim Disuqi, "al-Mashru' al-watani wa-al-ijtima'i fi barnamaj al-hizb al-shuyu'iy al-misri fi al-'ishriniyyat wa-al-thalathiniyyat," *Qadaya Fikriyya*, July 1996, pp. 38–45. See a program of action of the ECP in Document 3148/6/2.4.32, 11 February 1932, RGASPI, Fond 495, OP 85, D 93, L186.

43 "The Sudan," supplementary Theses.

44 Information Report No. 137, "The Sudan Question," 19 September 1924, RGASPI, Fond 495, OP 85, D37, L119–121.

45 See the Comintern's sociopolitical reports on Egypt, 1929, RGASPI, Fond 495, OP 85, D 76, L 65–71.

46 Ibid.

47 Ibid.; an internal Comintern report on the goals of the ECP (possibly written by one of the Egyptian comrades in Moscow), 8 June 1929, RGASPI, Fond 495, OP 85, D 79, L 7–15.

48 Rafi'i, *Fi a'qab al-thawra al-misriyya*, Vol. 2, pp. 330–331.

49 Ibid., p. 331.

50 Ibid., pp. 332–333.

51 al-Sayyid Jawdat, "Wadi al-nil la yatajaza'u," *al-Ahram*, 27 October 1946, p. 5.

52 Ibid.

53 Ibid.

54 "al-Nuqrashi basha ya'muru bi-madd al-sikak al-hadidiyya hata al-sudan," *Ruz al-Yusuf*, No. 978, 12 March 1947, p. 2.

55 Ibid. See also "al-Tijara bayna misr wa-al-sudan," *al-Muqattam*, 25 May 1950, p. 3.

56 Hamid al-Qasbi, "al-Dhahab al-abyad – bughyat al-injliz min al-sudan," *al-Balagh*, 23 June 1951, p. 3.

57 See a pamphlet issued by the Egyptian government entitled *The Egyptian Question 1882–1951*.

58 Ibid.

59 Ibid.

60 Hans J. Morgenthau, *Politics among Nations*, Vol. 1 (Tel-Aviv: Yachdav, 1968), pp. 72–79 [in Hebrew].

61 Said, *Culture and Imperialism*, p. xiii.

62 Benjamin J. Cohen, *The Question of Imperialism: The Political Economy of Dominance and Dependence* (New York: Basic Books, 1973), p. 61.

63 El Madani, "On the Epistemology of Ethnicity," pp. 3–4.

64 "Ethnographic Elements," in *Egypt Sudan*, p. 74, quoted in Ginat, "Egypt's Efforts," p. 211.

65 Ibid., p. 212. See also Sulayman Huzayyin, "Rabitat al-jins wa-al-thaqafa fi wadi al-nil," *al-Katib al-Misri*, 6:21 (June 1947), pp. 228–231.

66 "Ethnographic Elements," in *Egypt Sudan*, p. 74.

67 Quoted from *The Unity of the Nile Valley*, p. 12. See also Ginat, "Egypt's Efforts," p. 212.

68 *Egypt Sudan*, p. 74; *The Unity of the Nile Valley*, p. 13. The date and composition of the mission were not mentioned.

69 *Egypt Sudan*, pp. 74–75; *The Unity of the Nile Valley*, pp. 13–14. Ginat, "Egypt's Efforts," p. 213. The Egyptian scholars based their account of the Hamitic issue on the works of C. G. Seligman, whom they called "the greatest British authority on the ethnography of the Nile land." Some of his works included "Some Aspects of the Hamitic Problem in the Anglo-Egyptian Sudan," *The Journal of the Royal Anthropological Institute of Great Britain and Ireland*, 43 (1913), pp. 593–705; *Races of Africa* (London: Home University

Library, 1939); C. G. Seligman and B. Z. Seligman, *Pagan Tribes of the Nilotic Sudan* (London: George Routledge and Sons, 1932). Seligman's theory and the concept of "race" were decades later criticized by scholars such as W. E. B. Du Bois, who argued that race was an invention – a social construction (p. 72). Race is an active and deliberate consciousness – there is no biological principle to it in Du Bois's conceptualization. Du Bois also argued that the question of racial definition was political. For more on his studies, see Maghan Keita, *Race and the Writing of History Riddling the Sphinx* (Oxford and New York: Oxford University Press, 2000), pp. 72–74, 80.

70 *Egypt Sudan*, p. 75; *The Unity of the Nile Valley*, pp. 14–15.

71 Mustafa Kamil is quoted from Troutt Powell, "Brothers along the Nile," p. 174.

72 Huzayyin, "Rabitat al-jins wa-al-thaqafa," pp. 233–236.

73 Ibid., pp. 236–237.

74 Ibid., pp. 239–241.

75 *The Unity of the Nile Valley*, p. 15.

76 Ibid., p. 16. Egyptian scholars relied on the works of A. H. MacMichael. In the early 1920s he published his monumental study *A History of the Arabs in the Sudan and some Account of the People who preceded them and of the Tribes Inhabiting Darfur*, 2 vols. (Cambridge: The University Press Publication, 1922).

77 "al-Fara'inah yaskununa al-sudan," *Ruz al-Yusuf*, No. 984, 24 April 1947, p. 7.

78 See a pamphlet issued by the Egyptian government entitled *The Egyptian Question 1882–1951*.

79 'Abbas, *The Sudan Question*, pp. 13–14.

80 'Abdel Rahim, *Imperialism and Nationalism in the Sudan*, p. 265.

81 Stephanie Beswick, *Sudan's Blood Memory: The Legacy of War, Ethnicity and Slavery in South Sudan* (Rochester, NY: University of Rochester Press, 2004), p. 187. See also Sayed Hamid A. Hurreiz and Elfatih A. Abdel Salam (eds.), *Ethnicity, Conflict and National Integration in the Sudan* (Khartoum: Institute of Asian and African Studies, University of Khartoum, 1989).

82 Mohamed H. Fadlalla, *Short History of Sudan* (Lincoln, NE: iUniverse, 2004), p. 65. See also Didar Fawzy-Rossano, *Le Soudan en question* (Paris: LA Table Ronde, 2002), pp. 57–60

83 Voll and Voll, *The Sudan: Unity and Diversity*, pp. 7–10.

84 Sharkey, *Living with Colonialism*, p. 4.

Part II

The Struggle for Sudan
Politics, Diplomacy, and Public Discourse

3 The Sudan Question
The Egyptian Transition from Wartime Lethargy to Postwar Overtures and Deeds

The conclusion of World War I ended Egypt's formal links with the Ottoman Empire. The British protectorate over Egypt, declared shortly after the outbreak of World War I, was short lived, as Britain unilaterally granted the Egyptians their independence in February 1922, transforming the country into a constitutional monarchy. The Egyptian political scene was consolidated into a triangle of political forces: the king, the parliament and political parties (notably the Wafd), and the British. The privileges the king was granted by the constitution of 1923, coupled with the cynical and self-interested methods of divide and rule employed by the British, were a pattern for the castration of Egyptian constitutionalism and parliamentarism in the interwar period. The Wafd, the people's party, won parliamentary elections with comfortable majorities, yet it was not given its legitimate right to rule, and the governments it formed since 1924 were short-lived following interferences by both the king and the British. In the late 1930s, the party faced a major split with the formation of the Sa'dist Party, which soon became its chief political rival. The Sa'dist Party, mainly under Nuqrashi's premierships (1945–1946, 1946–1948), was to play an important role in advancing the Sudan question in the postwar years (1945–1949). The debacle of Isma'il Sidqi, the unpopular and anti-democratic prime minister (February 1946–December 1946), to get political approval for a draft treaty he concluded as a replacement to the 1936 treaty with the British left his successor, Nuqrashi Pasha, not much room for maneuver with the British. There was a bipartisan consensus against the treaty and enormous public pressure to halt negotiations with Britain and to transfer the Anglo–Egyptian dispute to the international arena.

The political changes that swept Egypt in the 1930s had an indelible impact on the Egyptian political discourse on the unity of the Nile valley. New forces in the Egyptian body politic challenged the traditional narrative on the issue of the unity of the Nile valley, placing the issue at the forefront of the public discourse. Furthermore, the gradual decline in Britain's international standing in the postwar years (following the appearance of the two new superpowers – the United States and the USSR) was to weaken its hegemonic position within Egypt. The post–World War II years witnessed a growing influence of the hitherto weakest side of the triangle of forces – the legislative and the executive authorities, parliament and government. Indeed, the latter 1940s and the early 1950s saw the internationalization of the Anglo–Egyptian dispute, as the following chapters show. However, as far as the Sudan issue was concerned, it would appear that Britain's stranglehold remained intact.

The British succeeded in advancing their long-term goal of leading Sudan toward self-government and separation from Egypt. Indeed, since the late 1930s the British had increased their efforts to develop the foundation for Sudanese self-government. Britain's strategy was based on a long-term plan to thwart public and intellectual sentiment in Sudan toward political unification with Egypt. To achieve this goal, Britain enforced the policy of Sudanization of the bureaucracy and the political class, which eventually led to the genesis for self-government and Sudanese nationalism. Thus, in the 1940s, the Sudanese political class evolved along two particular lines: one that sought to achieve Sudan's full political and economic independence, represented by the independent *Umma* Party, affiliated with followers of the Mahdi and his son, Sayyid 'Abd-al-Rahman al-Mahdi, leader of al-Ansar (Sufi order). The *Umma* aimed to achieve Sudanese independence through practical and pragmatic cooperation with the British. The second line, which advocated for political unification under the Egyptian crown, was led by the unionist Ashiqqa' Party, closely linked to the Khatmiyya Sufi order, led by Sayyid 'Ali al-Mirghani.[1]

This chapter depicts and analyzes the major political and diplomatic steps taken by Egyptian governments to advance the doctrine of the unity of the Nile valley. It also measures and assesses the impact that the passionate public discourse had on policymakers in the period 1939–1947. This period is divided into two segments: the "quiet years" of wartime, during which the Sudan question was relegated to a secondary place; and the immediate postwar "stormy years," which witnessed the radicalization of the national question from within. Public pressure on policymakers to transfer the Anglo–Egyptian dispute to the international arena yielded fruit, yet the results were not satisfactory.

The War Years and the Gradual Awakening of the Sudan Question

With the outbreak of World War II, 'Abd al-Rahman 'Azzam, then Minister of Religious Affairs in 'Ali Mahir's cabinet (1939–1940), a nationalist figure, who was also in King Faruq's inner circle, met with Sir Charles H. Bateman, a senior British officer (Counsellor, 1938–1940) in Cairo – according to 'Azzam, the second-in-command (*al-rajul al-thani*) at the British embassy. 'Azzam opposed a declaration of war against Germany without appropriate British compensation at the end of the war. In their talks 'Azzam presented Egypt's conditions for joining Britain in its war against Germany: a willingness to fully evacuate all of Egypt's territories as well as the acceptance of Egypt's claims to the unity of the Nile valley under its rule. Britain refused 'Azzam's conditions.[2] In the period 1939–1944, the largest and most popular nationalist party, the Wafd, in opposition and in government, held a neutral approach – it refused to declare war against Germany and called upon Britain to evacuate the Nile valley at the end of the war and to recognize Egypt's sovereignty in the northern and southern regions of the valley.[3]

Under the Wafd government (1942–1944), the Sudan question was at first not a central issue on its agenda. Externally, the threat from the Axis powers occupied Egypt's attention until late 1942, and the effects of the war raised many internal challenges as well. The German defeat and retreat in November 1942 marked a turning point in the battle for Egypt, and the Wafd government felt more confident to formulate a new foreign policy.[4]

Several significant actions taken by that government made their mark on Egypt's postwar foreign policy. These actions were made possible as the Anglo–Egyptian treaty of 1936 granted Egypt a wider scope to manage its foreign affairs than before. For instance, in March 1943, it initiated the process that subsequently led to the formation of the Arab League (1945), in which Egypt held the predominant position. In August 1943, Egypt established diplomatic relations with the Soviet Union, a rising world power, relations it hoped to exploit in its struggle for complete national liberation. At the same time, Egypt launched an extensive public relations campaign to advance its national interests in Sudan – a move that was anathema to the British. They responded vigorously, acting through the Sudan government, which was controlled by British officials, including the governor-general, with the intention to minimize Egypt's influence over Sudan.[5] Britain showed particular interest in the field of education, developing and nurturing the Sudanese educational system. The goal was to develop and sharpen Sudanese collective identity and to encourage anti-Egyptian separatist trends. Britain aimed at separating Sudan from Egypt.[6]

By late 1943, Douglas Newbold, the civil secretary of Sudan, opined that with the conclusion of the war Egypt and Britain would be heading toward another crisis over Sudan. The Egyptians believed that the Sudan government under the protection of the 1936 treaty had encouraged a separatist Sudanese movement unfavorable to Egypt's interests. Therefore, Egypt should act swiftly and effectively in order not to lose Sudan. Newbold argued that the Sudanese independent self-consciousness had been enhanced following their experience in World War II, during which they contributed men and material to the British war effort. Their political status should be elevated after the war. Neither the continuance of the condominium nor Egypt's idea of the unity of the Nile valley was to reign supreme any longer. Britain must be prepared to thwart Egypt's expansionist plans and ideas as expressed by its foremost leaders that "the Sudanese and Egyptians are the sons of one nation having equal rights and obligations."[7]

Lord Killearn, the British ambassador to Cairo, agreed with Newbold that before Egypt would put forward its claims in Sudan, Britain should offer the Sudanese

a more hopeful prospect than Egypt can do ... We should endeavour to associate the Sudanese more and more in the administration of the Sudan and at the same time to endeavour to promote Anglo-Sudanese economic development. If in this way numerous educated elements are absorbed into administrative and economic jobs and they see that they are making a good thing out of the British connection, there is less chance that the "yellow carrot" of the Egyptians will prove much of an attraction [to the Sudanese].[8]

Killearn, however, doubted Newbold's assessment that the Wafd government had a definite political plan toward Sudan. He surmised that under the then existing circumstances, the Wafd government would not confront the British over Sudan because "they are afraid of offending us at a moment when their continuance in office depends entirely on our support."[9]

Killearn was right. The Wafd government did not put the Sudan issue on the front burner. It became a central issue mainly after the war. The Nahhas cabinet trod a fine line in its handling of the Sudan issue vis-à-vis the British authorities. For instance, on 1 January 1944, Nahhas sent a memorandum to the governor-general of Sudan summing up the meeting on 11 November 1943, in which the Nahhas cabinet accused the governor-general of violating sections of the 1936 treaty relating to the joint Anglo–Egyptian administration of Sudan. The memorandum presented the cabinet's demand that the Sudan government rectify these violations. Nahhas called upon the Sudan government to allow the restoration of the public Friday sermons, which had been suspended during the Anglo–Egyptian crisis following the assassination of Sirdar Sir Lee Stack in 1924. He also demanded to facilitate the improvement of the Islamic educational system in Sudan. According to Nahhas, some of the administrative changes and actions carried out by the Sudan government made him believe that it intended to divide Sudan into two entities – a northern and a southern one. People from the north were prevented from entering the southern zone and vice versa: "You appointed an advisory Council to the Northern division. At the same time you have given extensive authority in administrative and legal matters to the Tribal Chiefs [of the south] ... keeping the Southern division isolated to be a pasture land for the Christian Missionary societies." Nahhas warned that this might provoke tension between Muslims and other religious groups inhabiting the Nile valley. He also remonstrated that the Sudan government discriminated against Egyptians in admission to available administrative posts. He stressed that all the recent moves were taken without consulting the Egyptian government as stipulated in the 1936 treaty.[10] It is noteworthy that Nahhas failed to mention in any section of his detailed account Egypt's unequivocal national demand for the unity of the Nile valley under the Egyptian crown.

About three months later, Hubert J. Huddleston, the governor-general (1940–1947), replied to Nahhas's memorandum. His detailed refutation of Egypt's claims and arguments give an indication of the nature of the postwar escalation of the Anglo–Egyptian dispute over the Sudan question. Huddleston reiterated his commitment to the faithful implementation of the 1899 and 1936 treaties with Egypt.[11] As far as the restoration of the public Friday sermons were concerned, Huddleston stated that it was not within the governor-general's prerogative to issue an official order determining the prayers of Muslims in their mosques. He denied that any concrete measures had been taken by the Sudan government to divide Sudan into northern and southern parts. The existing division of Sudan was a result of the "natural, historic and tribal composition of the country. The six northern provinces are predominantly Arab in origin and culture, and the two southern provinces are inhabited by people akin racially to the tribes of central Africa and largely Pagan."[12] Representatives of the southern provinces were not included in the advisory council because they had not yet reached the required level of development for membership. Huddleston did not rule out the possibility that when they were developed enough, the advisory council would be open to them. There were Christian missionary societies in southern Sudan already before the formation of the condominium, and they were first admitted there by the Egyptian government. The Sudan government followed suit, and these humanitarian missionaries continued voluntarily with their devoted efforts to improve the education and health "of the primitive tribes of Upper Nile and Equatoria Provinces." Neither Egyptian nor northern Sudanese travelers were prohibited from visiting the southern provinces or vice versa. Egyptians living in Sudan did not face discrimination under any circumstances. Great emphasis was placed by the education department on the teaching of Arabic in Sudan's schools because "Arabic is the sole vehicle of instruction" in all government schools, and efforts were constantly made to raise the Arabic standard of the schools in Sudan. The same applied to the improvement of the level of education and the teaching of Islam in religious schools. Islamic leaders in Sudan were very satisfied with the Sudan government's efforts to meet with their religious requirements. The most respected of them were utterly against the involvement of religious institutions in politics and civil disorder.[13]

Another controversial issue to cast a shadow on the strained relations between Killearn and Nahhas was the decision made in late 1944 by both the Sudanese 'Ali al-Barir and the Egyptian authorities to allow the former to present his candidacy for a seat in the elections to the Egyptian chamber of deputies. This move provoked an angry response by the British embassy in Cairo. The British were fuming because Barir presented himself in his electoral posters, which appeared in Cairo, as a Sudanese and a candidate of Sudan in the Egyptian parliament, and the Egyptian officials accepted his candidature as such. In a letter to Nahhas, Killearn declared this to be a violation of the Anglo–Egyptian treaty of 1936, according to which "the question of sovereignty over the Sudan was reserved." Barir was ineligible to present his candidacy, remonstrated Killearn, and warned Nahhas that should his government continue to endorse Barir's candidature, it would have a severe effect on Anglo–Egyptian relations. Nahhas was left with little choice but to withdraw Barir's candidature.[14] This development showed that the devastating effect of the Abdeen Palace incident of 1942 had not faded away and that the British ambassador continued to bully and manipulate the Egyptian political scene to his government's own ends.

The submission and helplessness of the Egyptian government were received angrily by Sudanese and Egyptian students, who took to the streets of Cairo. The anti-British sentiment, noted a British report, was more bitter than had been experienced for many years. The focus of the demonstrations was the Sudan question, and in Giza alone more than a thousand students demonstrated, chanting slogans such as "down with England and Imperialism." The intervention of the Egyptian police prevented the demonstrators from getting to the British embassy and dispersed the demonstrations forcefully. British officials in Cairo held the Wafd accountable for this anti-British wave by organizing and subsidizing the demonstrations. Killearn, who wanted to remind King Faruq who the true supreme authority in Egypt was, warned the latter that "his countrymen were playing with fire" and that he would not tolerate such actions. The king "must see that the agitation was at once stopped," Killearn warned.[15] Killearn was wrong. The question of Sudan was no longer a monopoly of the king and the Egyptian government. The Egyptian public, represented by youth, students, workers, and ex-parliamentary forces from right and left, took the issue to the streets, stressing that they would not tolerate submission to the British.[16]

Months before the end of World War II, Lord Killearn felt confident enough to declare that the British interests in Sudan were guaranteed. He nevertheless predicted in August 1944 that Anglo–Egyptian relations would face great challenges in the immediate postwar period. The focus of the dispute would be the Egyptian claims to Sudan and the demand for British evacuation of Egypt:

We are working in closest collaboration with the Wafd who were formerly the focus of agitation, but who now depend largely on us for their continued holding of power ... there is undoubtedly a considerable volume of discussion in the Egyptian press and among Egyptians of the more politically minded classes about the claims which Egypt should put forward at the end of the war. The two claims most consistently made are those for the total evacuation of Egypt by foreign troops and for the increased Egyptian control over the Sudan.

Lord Killearn had no doubts that Britain would prevail in that dispute: "We shall have to resist both of these claims and I do not doubt we will do so successfully."[17]

Indeed, the British policy toward Sudan was based on the following principles:

1. To maintain its predominant influence in Sudan, a strategically important area, by establishing its exclusive political and administrative control; at the same time, to promote and develop Sudanese self-government, which "in itself will militate against Egyptian re-entry into the Sudan."
2. To maintain the present state of affairs of the condominium and reject any Egyptian demands to modify the Anglo–Egyptian treaties to create favorable conditions for Egyptian penetration.
3. To drive a wedge between Egyptians and Sudanese by championing Sudanese self-government and enhancing their separate national identity, so that in the long term, they would favor Britain over Egypt as their senior partner: "We do not want Egyptian influence competing with ours in the Sudan."[18]

Britain, however, appeared to employ the stick-and-carrot method vis-à-vis Egypt as one British Foreign Office official put it. Britain, he noted, should not break the rules of the game with Egypt and should avoid provoking or confronting its interests in Sudan: "we should help the Egyptian government to maintain the condominium façade by consulting them and keeping them informed in formal questions, and we should be most careful to avoid giving the impression that we intend to use our position in the Sudan to the detriment of Egypt." If Egypt took extreme actions to jeopardize British interests, Britain could use the Nile water as a stick "with which to beat the Egyptians" by threatening to withhold it – a vital matter as far as Egypt was concerned.[19] Killearn suggested that such a decisive sanction would be "a sovereign act by His Majesty's Government of a less drastic nature than a resort to war."[20]

The accession of the Sa'dist government led by Ahmad Mahir (October 1944–February 1945) did not yet move the Sudan question to the forefront of Anglo–Egyptian relations. However, at the end of World War II Egypt witnessed growing anti-British radicalization led by Egyptian ex-parliamentary groups both right and left as well as the Wafd, now in opposition. A strategy of street politics maneuvered and orchestrated by these groups was to influence the evolution of Anglo–Egyptian relations. The GGC cell in Cairo participated in this anti-British street campaign. The *Sudan Magazine* (first issued in June 1944) became a vehicle through which the Sudan question was presented to the Egyptians. The first issues were dedicated to the historical links between Egypt and Sudan. The magazine criticized the Sudan government for training the Sudanese for self-government and for employing divide-and-rule tactics designed to cut off Sudan from Egypt. Egyptians were urged to bring the Sudan question to the fore of the political debate. The magazine had a circulation of 2,000 copies, which were sold out completely shortly after their publication, which meant that it attracted educated Egyptians.[21]

The Sudan Question Moves to the Fore (1945–1946)

On 23 September 1945, the Egyptian government approved the statement made by the political advisory committee,[22] according to which Egypt should revise the 1936 treaty with the aim of gaining full sovereignty over the Nile valley, based on the concept of the unity of the Nile valley, after British evacuation.[23] Indeed, in December 1945, Nuqrashi Pasha's government (February 1945–February 1946) approached Britain with a request to revise the 1936 treaty. His decision to do so was accompanied by an upsurge in protests and public disgruntlement led by a wide spectrum of oppositional groups, particularly his main rival, the Wafd. The Sudan question featured prominently in the anti-government campaign. The brunt of the criticism was directed at the 1936 treaty – the mother of all sins – and at its poor implementation. Although the treaty stipulated that Sudan would be administered jointly and equally by the two parties to the condominium, in fact Britain exploited its advantage as the senior and more powerful partner to grant the British governor-general of Sudan absolute authority and power to rule Sudan in line with the dictates from London.

As was noted, the paradigm of the unity of the Nile valley reigned supreme in public opinion in monarchial Egypt. The vast majority of the Egyptian political spectrum was determined to see a full unity between Egypt and Sudan, with a willingness to grant the Sudanese some kind of self-government under the Egyptian crown. There was a consensus among Egyptians that the true goal of the British was to undermine and sabotage the Egyptian nationalist doctrine of unification. The Egyptians were not wrong. Britain did want to prepare the Sudanese people for self-government, as a first stage, leading eventually to full independence and alliance with Britain. The Egyptian desire to revise the 1936 treaty was intended to achieve both British evacuation from the Nile valley in its entirety and unification of Egypt and Sudan.[24] It is noteworthy that the issue of treaty revision had already been raised in the early stages of World War II, when Egypt made similar demands: British evacuation from the Nile valley and the unification of the Nile valley under the Egyptian crown. The British viewed these demands as unrealistic: "Egypt could not defend itself or the Suez Canal, and the Sudan was evolving into an independent state and must be left free to work out its own destiny." Moreover, the British made it clear that revision was not a one-way process and that it would also entail British demands for modifications.[25]

In the immediate postwar period, Egypt witnessed an active, at times heated, public debate, encompassing the wall-to-wall political spectrum, on the national question, with special emphasis on the future of Sudan. The national consensus was well summed up by Muhammad Husayn Haykal, a seminal and renowned intellectual associated with the Liberal Constitutionalist Party. On 4 January 1946, he wrote in the independent newspaper *al-Ahram:*

Egypt – its government and people – expected in the course of the six-year war that the end of that war would constitute the opening of a fair Anglo–Egyptian relationship. The expectations were that the shackles imposed on Egypt's independence and sovereignty by the 1936 treaty would be removed. All Egyptian parties were unanimous that the preliminary action in this direction was the full evacuation of British forces from Egyptian land ... [thus] realizing the hopes of the inhabitants of the Nile valley – the unity of the Nile valley.[26]

The Wafd, the main opposition party, critically received the content of Nuqrashi's appeal and the British reply to it. It noted the fact that Sudan was hardly mentioned except for a vague reference that in the future

Egypt would safeguard "the interests and hopes of the Sudanese." Why did Nuqrashi not spell out clearly and resolutely our uncompromising demand with regard to the unity of the Nile valley? the Wafd asked. The British intention was to separate Sudan from Egypt. The Sudanese interests and hopes would be realized only when Egypt and Sudan become one nation: "our rights – their rights, our duties – their duties." The government should stand firmly behind this most important nationalist demand – "one of our most hallowed rights" – in any future talks with the British. The achievement of the unity of the valley would entail hard work, and the nation should be prepared for a jihad.[27]

The request was also severely criticized by the Muslim Brothers. Past circumstances had already shown that the 1936 treaty could not constitute a basis for correct and equal relations between the two countries, asserted *al-Ikhwan al-Muslimun*. On the contrary, past experience taught that the abolition of the treaty was inevitable. The abolition of the League of Nations and Egypt's acceptance of the United Nations Charter emptied the treaty of its international legal content. The government failed to present firmly its national demands: full British evacuation of the Nile valley in its entirety and the unification of Egypt and Sudan. The government spoke weakly of the Sudanese's rights as though they were a separate entity – "the Sudanese demands and aspirations" – instead of clearly and soundly stating that the Egyptian and Sudanese demands were one – "full evacuation and complete unification."[28]

Egypt's request for the revision of the 1936 treaty was made to the newly elected Labour government (1945–1951) led by Clement Attlee, who defeated Winston Churchill in the 1945 elections. Attlee and Foreign Secretary Ernest Bevin emphasized that Britain's change in government would not lead to a revision in its foreign policy outlook. However, in practice, the Labour government comprehended the decline in Britain's position internationally following the conclusion of World War II and the subsequent appearance of two new global superpowers – the United States and the Soviet Union.[29] As far as Egypt and Sudan were concerned, Attlee wanted to preserve Britain's main interests in the Nile valley.

These interests centered on political, strategic, and economic concerns: the Egyptian Suez Canal was the chief sea route to India – the jewel in the crown until 1947. The rise in tensions between the West and the Soviet Union, leading to the outbreak of the Cold War, underscored the strategic importance of the Middle East. Prime Minister Attlee and American President Harry S. Truman saw the Middle East and the eastern Mediterranean as an important strategic zone in the fight against the ascendant Soviet Union and worried about the potential for Soviet control over any of the region's countries. The most important of the Middle Eastern states, from the Western viewpoint, was Egypt, an integral part of the allied defense effort in both world wars. Geographically separated from Europe, Egypt's position placed it as an integral component of the Western defense framework, with the ability to house and transport troops with its strategic position along the Suez Canal. Special emphasis was placed on safeguarding Western oil interest in the region.[30] Economically, Britain intended to continue to exploit its substantial advantages as the dominant power in the Nile valley to import cheap cotton – Egypt's main export product – for its textile industry, and to market profitably its final textile products to Middle Eastern countries, Egypt included.[31]

Observing the Egyptian political landscape with an upsurge of opposition to the 1936 treaty, the Attlee government was aware that the status quo would be untenable with the Egyptian government. As a result, the Attlee government was willing to enter discussions with the Egyptians for a revision of the treaty. The British reply was coolly and critically received among Egyptian oppositional circles. The British continued with their strategy of procrastinations and evasions, declared the Muslim Brothers. The British ignored the new international circumstances that nullified the foundations of the 1936 treaty. They referred to Sudan as though it was a separate issue, thus drawing an artificial distinction between the Sudanese and Egyptian cases. The Muslim Brothers held both the Egyptian and the British governments accountable for this appalling state of affairs – the former displayed a frail position, whereas the latter continued to renounce the national rights of the inhabitants of the Nile valley. The Muslim Brothers called the nation (*al-umma*) to prepare itself for a continuous and aggressive jihad.[32]

At the beginning of 1946, before the Anglo–Egyptian negotiations began, Sudanese and Egyptian officials held unofficial talks aimed at consolidating a unified position on the unity of the Nile valley. However, there remained differences between the Sudanese and the Egyptian positions. The Sudanese were nominally in favor of a union with Egypt, but also asked for guarantees for eventual self-determination. The Egyptians refuted this position, asserting, that the British would use this fissure in the forthcoming talks as a means to spoil the negotiations, a tactic that the British eventually used.[33] The official negotiations between Egypt and Britain commenced in April 1946. With the arrival of the British delegation one month later, led by Lord Stansgate, a draft treaty was produced with both Egypt and Britain agreeing "that the primary object of their administration in the Sudan is the preparation of the Sudan for self-government."[34] As soon as the objective for self-government was obtained, "the Sudanese people shall be free to decide their future relations with the High Contracting Parties ... In the meantime ... the Sudan shall continue to be governed by the terms of the agreements of 19th January and 10th July 1899."[35] Both the British and the Egyptians had fundamentally different ideas of how Sudanese self-government would look. The British saw Sudanese self-government as the next step on Sudan's eventual road to independence, while the Egyptians regarded it as a temporary measure that would eventually lead to the unification of Sudan with Egypt under the Egyptian crown. After extended negotiations, an agreement between the British and the Egyptians was reached over a new treaty defining Anglo–Egyptian military cooperation and underlining the status of Sudan. Britain agreed to recognize Egyptian independence, authorizing a full-scale evacuation of Egypt within three years.

The Egyptians were forced to pay a considerable toll: first, they agreed to a new framework for Anglo–Egyptian military relations, replacing the military clauses of the 1936 treaty, whereby Egypt and Britain would take joint military action in the event of a military attack on Egypt or of Britain becoming involved in a wider conflagration.[36] Second, they would help to usher Sudan toward self-government through the larger framework of the unity of the Nile valley under the Egyptian crown. Yet, in the negotiations with the British, Sidqi was forced to relinquish much of the Egyptian position regarding Sudan and the unity of the Nile valley. The Egyptians were forced to accept the 1899 condominium agreement with the British and that there could be no change in the Egyptian relationship with Sudan without prior consultation with the Sudanese. By doing this, Sidqi effectively waived Egypt's claim for the unity of the Nile valley.[37]

On his return to Egypt following the negotiations, Sidqi paid lip service to the Egyptian press, claiming that it had been "decided to achieve unity between Egypt and the Sudan under the Egyptian crown." While the British had acknowledged the Egyptian claim over Sudan, Sidqi intentionally obfuscated the fine print in the agreement including the language on "self-government," "future status of the Sudan," or "the right of the Sudanese to choose their own future status."[38] Sidqi's position was met with opposition from across the Egyptian political spectrum, as it soon became evident that Egyptian independence would mean relinquishing claims on the unity of the Nile valley, with Sidqi's public statements contradicting the terms of his agreement with Bevin and the British negotiators.[39] The British recognition of the Egyptian claim over Sudan was purely symbolic, as the British spelled out, maintaining the claim for the Sudanese right to self-determination.[40] This created an inherently paradoxical situation whereby the British wanted to preserve the mirage of Egyptian sovereignty over Sudan so that it could be removed, while the Egyptians sought to give the Sudanese self-government so that their sovereignty over Sudan would no longer be symbolic.[41]

Yunan Labib Rizq and ʿAbd al-Rahman Rafiʿi argued that Sidqi's statement, according to which he brought Sudan to Egypt, had an adverse effect in Sudan. It caused resentment within Sudan, which was followed by much dissatisfaction. Consequently, anti-unionist groups held violent demonstrations in Khartoum. These demonstrations were tacitly supported by the Sudan government.[42] Indeed, it would appear the people of Sudan had their own view. Following the opening of the Anglo–Egyptian talks on the revision of the treaty of 1936, there was a Sudanese attempt to establish a unified front of all political parties to present their stand on the question of the future of Sudan.

The Egyptian Debate on the Visit of the Sudanese Delegation

A Sudanese delegation that arrived in early April 1946 in Cairo to represent the Sudanese political parties in the opening Anglo–Egyptian negotiations issued a statement on 7 April expressing its belief that the Egyptian government would support their demands because the two countries were struggling for independence from imperialism.[43] The delegation was entrusted to present the following demands,[44] upon which all the Sudanese agreed:

1. Britain and Egypt should issue a joint statement in which they recognize the establishment of a democratic Sudanese government, which would be free to enter into union with Egypt.
2. The Sudanese government would, however, be the one to decide the type of unity with Egypt.
3. The content of a future alliance with Britain would be utterly dependent on the type of the Sudanese–Egyptian union.[45]

The British withdrawal from the Nile valley was to be total – political, military, and economic – achieved through the unity of the Sudanese and Egyptian peoples in the Nile valley, and against a separate political solution for the respective polities. Only after a complete British evacuation would the Egyptians and the Sudanese agree on the "internal organization of the Nile valley." The Sudanese made it clear that any future political unification with Egypt would be based on the precondition of a full and complete withdrawal of Egyptian and British forces from their land, and the subsequent formation of an independent and democratic Sudan. The delegation made it clear that a Sudanese precondition for any future unity with Egypt was a complete evacuation of both British and Egyptian armies from Sudan, and subsequently the formation of an independent and democratic Sudan.[46]

On 7 April, Isma'il al-Azhari, in his capacity as head of the Sudanese delegation for negotiations, submitted a memorandum "on behalf of the Sudanese nation" to the British prime minister, demanding to participate in the Anglo–Egyptian negotiations, as the representative of the Sudanese delegation ("chosen by all bodies, parties, and sects of the Sudanese nation"). The Sudanese nation, noted al-Azhari, relied "on the natural right of man to live his own life and to be governed in the way he wishes and to determine his future ... neither the British nor the Egyptian governments can legitimately deny the realization of this right to the Sudanese."[47]

It is noteworthy that the Egyptian government refused to recognize the Sudanese delegation as the sole representative of the Sudanese people. The Egyptian government, it was stressed, would represent the views and interests of all Sudanese parties and would consult the Sudanese before introducing any modification in the status of Sudan. Indeed, *al-Ahram* reported that disagreements on vital issues such as the unity of the Nile valley occurred within the Sudanese delegation, after representatives of the *Umma* Party refused to endorse the above-mentioned statement, particularly its clause dealing with the unity of the Nile valley. The *Umma* Party, opined *al-Ahram*, supported Sudanese independence and an alliance with Britain, contrary to the *Ashiqqa'* Party, led by Isma'il al-Azhari, who headed the delegation. The latter was the chief Sudanese advocate of the unity of the Nile valley.[48]

The presence of the Sudanese delegation and its demands generated a polemic within and between Egyptian political currents and organizations from left to right.[49] The independent *Ruz al-Yusuf* took a firm stand vis-à-vis the issue of the Nile valley. Its editor, Ikhsan 'Abd al-Quddus, called upon the Sudanese delegation and the Egyptian negotiators to stop burying their heads in the sand as an ostrich. The British took over Sudan: they fully controlled its government and ignored the condominium arrangements by not nominating Egyptians to high posts as required. Egyptians were prevented from entering Sudan by British official guards and thus could not propagate the urgent need for the unity of the Nile valley – the lifeline of both Sudanese and Egyptians. There was an Egyptian consensus that the only solution for Sudan was the unity of the Nile valley. The British had spread deceitful promises that they would advance welfare all over Sudan, and Sudanese, for their part, interpreted welfare as independence.

For Egyptians welfare meant the establishment of a strong and solid state comprising Sudanese and Egyptians.[50]

Former Army General and Minister of War Salih Harb Pasha, now in his capacity as president of the Muslim Youth Associations, took a particularly sharp line vis-à-vis the Sudan question. The ongoing Anglo–Egyptian negotiation was the last chance for Egyptians to prove to the Sudanese that only Egypt could defend their welfare. Any postponement of the Sudan question would mean a catastrophe not only for Egypt and Sudan, but for the whole Nile valley. Egypt, declared Harb, should unite with the Sudanese in demanding British evacuation from the Nile valley in its entirety.[51]

An anti-unionist campaign conducted by the *Umma* Party and separatists in Sudan appeared to constrain Azhari's ability to maneuver in Cairo. The Sudanese paper *al-Nil* declared that "the unity of the Nile valley is an idea that Egyptians would deprive Sudanese from participating in." The newspaper *al-Umma* remonstrated that "our Egyptian brothers believe in their national demands but deny ours ... The Sudan is not owned by anyone other than the Sudanese." Sudan should pursue independence, concluded *al-Umma*.[52] Indeed, substantial disagreements between the *Umma* Party and the Sudanese delegation in Cairo led to the latter's decision to send away *al-Umma's* representatives, who refused to introduce any changes to the Sudanese demands stated on 7 April.[53] The pro-Wafdist paper *al-Balagh* accused the British of creating the *Umma* Party to sabotage the unity of the Nile valley. It regarded that party as a tool in the hands of imperialism.[54]

In Cairo the Wafd held a warm reception for the Sudanese delegation, and its head, Isma'il al-Azhari, was welcomed as the champion of the unity of the Nile valley. In a patronizing speech in honor of the delegation, Mustafa al-Nahhas delivered his party's credo on the issue of unity. Stressing historical continuity Nahhas Pasha referred to Sa'd Zaghlul, the legendary Wafdist nationalist hero, who stated that Egypt was struggling for the independence of Egypt and Sudan as a single entity. Zaghlul condemned the British imperialist attempts to separate the two parts of the valley, telling them: "under no circumstances could the British amputate what God intends to preserve."[55]

While in office, the Wafd governments took pains to strengthen the cultural and economic relations between the northern and southern parts of the valley. The Wafd's standpoint on the present and future of Sudan, stressed Nahhas, was that Egypt and Sudan

are one nation, our rights are their rights and our duties are their duties. We are one nation that was united by God's hand on the banks of this splendid valley.

The Nile valley is the life spring of the citizens of Egypt and the Sudan. History bonded between us from time immemorial. We are linked by race, language, religion, customs and traditions. Our natural right is to live in our valley free and independent without foreign interference in our affairs ... our natural right to self-determination was endorsed by the allies in two world wars.

Nahhas warned the Sudanese that lack of unification would enable the British to advance their imperialist plans: first, to claim that Sudan was not ready to exercise its full sovereignty over its territory, and second, to use its weakness to establish military bases in strategic locations and thus to preserve its rule and subsequently to suspend Sudan's independence.[56]

Nahhas's speech was condemned by Prime Minister Isma'il Sidqi. The Egyptian government, he declared, made no concession on Sudan, and the Anglo–Egyptian negotiations were progressing satisfactorily. Nahhas should stick to the facts, and if he was not familiar with them he should wait until the end of the talks.[57]

Beyond the exchange of words of courtesy between the Sudanese delegation and its Egyptian hosts, there was apparently a widening gulf between the way Egyptians and pro-unionist Sudanese understood the concept of the unity of the Nile valley. Wahid Ra'fat, the royal advisor to the Egyptian prime minister, pointed out the key disagreements in an article he published in *al-Ahram*. Egyptians, he reasoned, demanded an inclusive unity (*wahda*) based on the following components: one nation, one government, one parliament, and one crown. The Sudanese unionists on their part wished for a different form of future political link – a federation (*ittihad*) under one crown. The structure and content of such political framework, stressed Ra'fat, were not yet spelled out by the Sudanese. Do they wish for a symbolic amalgamation with a common king, yet with meaningless cooperation similar to what existed between Britain and Hanover (1814–1837) when each party managed its internal and foreign affairs independently, or a real union, in the framework of which the two countries would maintain close links on many issues, would have one head of state, and would have a united army, joint diplomatic and consular representation, and unity in financial affairs, customs, and trade, as was the case with Sweden and Norway (1814–1905) and Austria and Hungary (1867–1918)? Alternatively, do they wish to follow the U.S. or Swiss federative structures?[58]

According to Ra'fat, the last model was feasible only when the federation comprised many regions/states, unlike the case of the Nile valley, which consisted of two regions – the north and the south, Egypt and Sudan. Symbolic union, he ruled, could not exist because it was impossible to disregard the geographic and economic links beyond the ties of religion, language, customs, and sentiments between the two parts of the valley. Egyptians and most Sudanese desired to see a form of real unification such as the Austro–Hungarian model. They understood that nowadays there was no place for small independent countries; forms of substantial political unifications were inevitable, remarked Ra'fat. Those anti-unionist Sudanese should receive assurances that Egypt had no superior, hegemonic, or Machiavellian intentions in relation to Sudan. Egypt did not want to swallow Sudan after the British withdrawal – on the contrary, Egyptians shared similar nationalist sentiments with their Sudanese brothers. Unity would be based on full equality with no partiality between Sudanese and Egyptians. It was senseless to say that Sudan was under Egyptian imperialism or vice versa. Unity should not disarrange the division between the northern and southern parts of the Nile valley in terms of administrative, local, and regional systems. "Our southern brothers should trust us as much as we trust them ... We should coordinate our efforts and unite our demands," concluded Ra'fat. He opined that to advance the independence of the Nile valley, both Egypt and Sudan should come to terms regarding an agreeable mode of unification – a united Egyptian–Sudanese front would weaken the British demands over the Nile valley.[59]

Al-Siyasa made an appeal to the Egyptian press to avoid publishing articles stressing disagreements between Egyptians and Sudanese. Only "one point of view common to both" should be presented. Egyptians should welcome attempts by their Sudanese brothers to establish close relations, and should refrain from employing patronizing attitudes toward these Sudanese.[60]

Two articles published in *al-Balagh* on 6 and 7 April reiterated the prevailing Egyptian belief that Sudan and Egypt were inseparable. The occupation of Sudan by Muhammad 'Ali and Egypt's consequent administration of Sudan were never meant to be a mode of colonialism but rather an interest in the affairs of Sudan in the same manner as in the affairs of Egypt, "because the Sudan is but a part of the Egyptian territories. The Egyptian extension to the Sudan was a natural and geographical necessity, as well as a necessity to safeguard Egypt from encroachments."[61] Any separation between Sudan and Egypt, declared 'Abd al-Majid Naf'i, a Wafdist lawyer, would mean "cutting off the Nile and separating the soul from the body. Egypt without the Nile would become an absolute desert." Since the assassination of Lee Stack in 1924, the British no longer recognized the Nile as an Egyptian river, but rather turned it into a Sudanese heritage, "a drink fit for the colonizers only."[62]

After a prolonged waiting period, the Sudanese delegation met on 11 May with Sidqi and the Egyptian delegates to the negotiations with

Britain. In their meeting the Sudanese reiterated their April demands stressing that they share with Egypt a common desire to see the full British evacuation of the Nile valley, its unification under the Egyptian crown, and the formation of a united military and a joint foreign policy. However, the Sudanese would manage their internal affairs by means of a democratically elected government. Sidqi remarked that the issue of the Nile valley was inseparable and that Egypt did not relinquish its commitment to the unity of the Nile valley after its liberation. The Sudanese delegation, anxious that Sidqi would strike a deal with Britain that would lead to British evacuation of Egypt but not Sudan, was relieved following Sidqi's words.[63] However, several weeks later, Azhari sent a letter to Sidqi on behalf of the Sudanese people calling on him to stop the talks with the British because the latter were not willing to evacuate the Nile valley, and the Sudanese delegation felt that the negotiations were doomed to fail and thus would strengthen the British imperialist goals. Egypt, urged Azhari, should halt talks at once and declare the abrogation of the 1936 treaty. In addition, it should bring its dispute with Britain to the UN Security Council and demand its unconditional liberation and subsequently its unification under the Egyptian crown.[64]

On 23 September, Azhari sent a document to the Egyptian negotiating team summing up the Sudanese delegation's stand on the unity of the Nile valley and the future of Sudan. First, it called for immediate British evacuation and the exercise of Egyptian–Sudanese sovereignty over the Nile valley. Second, the State of the Nile Valley should be established under the Egyptian crown – a politically united state with a unified army under the command of "his Excellency the King of the Nile Valley." The king would then order the formation of a Sudanese government that would deal democratically with Sudanese affairs and would be subordinated to the king's authority. A joint Egyptian–Sudanese committee would coordinate and monitor issues related to the northern and southern regions – foreign policy, security of borders, etc. In addition, a representative council would be formed in Sudan to monitor the executive and legislative authorities.[65]

For Azhari and the Sudanese delegation there was only one party to be held accountable for the fiasco of the Anglo–Egyptian talks – imperialist Britain.[66]

The Aftermath of the Bevin–Sidqi Talks

The draft treaty was adversely received from within Sidqi's government, and from the opposition, including the Wafd, all of whom opposed its ratification.[67] In addition, students, workers, and left-wing political activists, who acted within the National Committee of Students and Workers, took to the streets expressing their opposition to the Sidqi government's handling of the negotiations. Upon Sidqi's return from London, the executive committee of the students issued a statement saying that "the reasons for which we launched our jihad are still valid; the negotiations should be based on an official British proclamation that recognizes our natural rights to a full [British] evacuation of the Nile valley and its unification [under the Egyptian crown]. The jihad and the blood we sacrificed were not intended to topple [Sidqi's] government but to achieve our rights in the Nile valley."[68]

A more painful blow to Sidqi came from within his own negotiating team composed of key political figures such as 'Ali Mahir, Husain Sirri, and 'Abd al-Fattah Yahya (all three, former prime ministers), as well as renowned politicians representing various political currents, including Makram 'Ubayd, Ahmad Lutfi al-Sayyid, 'Ali al-Shamsi, and Sharif Sabri. These seven refused to endorse the Bevin–Sidqi draft and published a position paper in al-Ahram setting out their reservations. They were particularly concerned about the apparent abandonment of what they perceived as a national consensus – British evacuation and the unity of the Nile valley under the Egyptian crown. According to the seven, the draft agreement turned the concept of unity from an actual aspiration to an abstract concept, as it gave the Sudanese the right to determine their political future after a transitional period, during which the 1899 agreement would remain intact as well as some other clauses of the 1936 treaty (11, 14, and 16). The draft agreement reinforced the status quo and, possibly worse than that, could lead to the separation of Egypt and Sudan and thus shatter the Egyptian dream of the unity of the Nile valley. In other words, these distinguished Egyptian politicians trusted neither the British nor the Sudanese nationalists. For them "the desire to realize the unity of the Nile valley holds no expansionist or imperialist intention, but rather a wish to fulfill the aspiration of the people who live in the Nile valley to a unity engendered by economic, historic, geographic, and spiritual bonds. [We see] no contradiction between the Egyptian and the Sudanese aspirations to apply self-government in the Sudan; on the contrary, such thing may reinforce [the unity]."[69]

Responding to the seven dissenters, Sidqi defended the draft treaty and argued that it protected Egypt's interests and set a practical formula for the future of Sudan, which would pave the way to the unity of the Nile valley under the Egyptian crown. How and when this formula would be materialized remained sketchy.[70]

The Sudanese political scene remained divided between those who endorsed Azhari's pro-unionist approach and those, particularly the

Umma Party, who wished to be freed of both British and Egyptian rule. The latter severely condemned Sidqi's October statement, noting his success "in bringing the Sudan to Egypt" and that "it has definitely been decided to achieve unity between Egypt and the Sudan under the Egyptian crown." Before the British made any reference to Sidqi's statement, the *Umma* Party declared that it would not participate in the British plan to advance the Sudanization (*Mashru' al-Sawdana*) of the administration, unless the British provided assurances that the Sudanization plan was intended to prepare the Sudanese for full independence. The 1898 condominium treaty was bad enough, but they regarded Sidqi's statement as even worse, since they deemed the former "as the end of our independence, whereas the latter meant our permanent enslavement."[71] The *Umma* Party made its view clear to both British and Egyptians: it condemned the transference of Sudanese sovereignty to Egypt and its subordination to the Egyptian crown. Sudan's freedom, it was said, should not be sacrificed on the altar of British interests. The party would take all necessary measures to realize Sudan's independence from both British and Egyptian imperialism.[72] Needless to say, the Sudanese unionists welcomed Sidqi's statement, while the anti-unionists took comfort from the British rejection of Sidqi's statement. The saga continued.

On 30 December *Sudan Star* published an interview with 'Abdulla Khalil, secretary of the *Umma* Party, who had returned from a working visit to London, during which he held talks with British government officials. According to him, the Anglo–Egyptian disagreements on the future of Sudan as they emerged from the extended talks persuaded him to abandon the idea of the immediate abrogation of the condominium. Instead, he believed that the Sudanese should begin at once with the formulation of a constitution, which would lead to the formation of a Sudanese government. When that government felt confident enough and prepared to take over the administration of Sudan, the Anglo–Egyptian condominium would become irrelevant and thus be abolished. The British government, he revealed, endorsed this line of action, and therefore the *Umma* Party decided to cooperate closely with the Sudan government headed by a British official.[73]

The Sudan protocol led to differing interpretations from both Sidqi and Bevin. Bevin articulated in a speech at the House of Commons on 27 January 1947 why Britain had not signed the treaty, arguing that the Egyptian government went to great lengths to "construe one phrase of the protocol on the Sudan as meaning that they could rely on the support of His Majesty's Government to deny the Sudanese complete freedom of choice when the time came for them to choose their future status."[74] Bevin noted that if the Egyptians agreed to it, he would be willing to guarantee Egypt that its interests in Sudan would be safeguarded, particularly its interests in the water of the Nile. Bevin was prepared to sign the treaty of mutual assistance and the evacuation protocol, and by doing so realize "one of Egypt's most eager aspirations," and to re-discuss the Sudan question in a conference with the participation of Egypt, Britain, and the Sudanese.[75]

The disagreement between Sidqi and Bevin over the Sudan protocol and the rising pressure of public opinion led to the fall of Sidqi's government in December 1946.[76]

Egypt's Quest for International Support: Hopes and Expectations

Shortly after the formation of Nuqrashi's second government (December 1946–December 1948), the Egyptian parliament issued a joint statement of all political parties saying:

When we argue for the unity of Egypt and the Sudan under the Egyptian crown, we always express the wish of the inhabitants of this valley ... under no circumstances will we spare any effort in leading the Sudan toward autonomy ... we do not want to dominate [the Sudan] ... therefore there is no place to perceive us as imperialists. We want an extended unity that is bound to the [Egyptian] crown and the Nile.[77]

A series of statements made by the British governor-general of Sudan during December 1946 were explicit in spelling out his intention to advance what he described as the Sudanese people's aspiration to exercise their right of independence and full sovereignty over their country. He reiterated the British government's understanding of Egyptian sovereignty over Sudan as "symbolic," stressing that only the Sudanese themselves would determine their future and as far as his government was concerned, it would do anything possible to pave their road to independence.[78]

In response, Nuqrashi asked the British government to state clearly its policy toward the future of the Nile valley: separation or unity. Sudan was vital for Egypt as the source of its water, and on the other hand Egypt's importance for Sudan was unquestionable. For Nuqrashi, the answer to the question of what the Sudanese people yearned for as far as their future relations with Egypt were concerned was pretty simple: unification with Egypt under the Egyptian crown.[79]

On 27 January 1947, Nuqrashi announced to the Egyptian parliament that negotiations with Britain had failed and that it was the intention of his government to place the issue before the UN Security Council.[80]

A week earlier, on 19 January, the anniversary of the signing of the 1899 treaty was declared by all political parties in Egypt as a general day of mourning. Entertainment venues were shut down, and people wore black ribbons. The nation was united for one day in its desire to see the end of British imperialism in the Nile valley – a historic day in the annals of the national movement (*al-haraka al-qawmiyya*), declared 'Abd al-Rahman al-Rafi'i.[81] The Nuqrashi government decided to refer the Egyptian case to the UN Security Council in face of public pressure and progressive opposition forces that, according to the British security services in Egypt, were well aware that this move was not enough and "great vigilance is still required to prevent a new sell-out to British imperialism."[82] Indeed, public pressure on the Egyptian government to bring its dispute with Britain before the Security Council bore fruit; Nuqrashi went ahead with it.

Pressure on Nuqrashi came from the entire political spectrum. The Islamic groups represented by *al-Risala* encouraged Nuqrashi not to be afraid of launching an anti-imperialist battle even if it meant sacrificing martyrs to secure the unity of the Nile valley and British evacuation. Mahmud Shakir (1909–1997), a senior writer in *al-Risala* and a renowned Egyptian thinker, who presented the orthodox Islamic line, described the Sudanese–Egyptian question as the crux of the Arab problem. He criticized the prevailing tendency among senior Egyptian policymakers to draw a distinction between Sudan and Egypt to advance Egypt's national goals. In his view, this approach was the result of British manipulation. To separate the issues of Egypt and Sudan, even for tactical calculations, would only be perceived as a sign of weakness. If Great Britain or the United States were one political and geographic entity, would they agree to give up Wales and Scotland, in the case of Britain, or the southern part of North America, in the case of the United States? Drawing on these two countries' models of annexation, Shakir opined that Egypt should do the same in Sudan, even forcefully if necessary, because with its water sources, Sudan was the life spring of Egypt. Ancient civilizations that developed in Sudan moved gradually northward because of the harshness of the Sudanese sun, feeling secure enough that they could continue to rely on the Sudanese water sources – some remnants of these civilizations still exist in contemporary Egypt.

For Shakir, Sudan was "the master of this valley and it has the prerogative to name the unified state after its name." He called Sudan "the treasure" for its water, "natural resources, the animals living there and basically everything there ... Egypt is the Sudan and there is no Egypt without the Sudan ... our duty is to die for the Sudan because the Sudan is our life and we are an integral part of it ... We do not want sovereignty over the Sudan because the Sudan is our master and we want Egypt to remain strong and alive under Sudanese protection." For Shakir there was only one entity that had an obvious interest to cut Sudan from Egypt – Britain. It wanted to preserve its hegemony in Sudan with all its vital resources, thus weakening Egypt and controlling its chief lifeline. "Egypt is the true power behind the people of the Sudan and the Sudan is the true life of Egypt. If the two were separated, they would both die out in between the fangs of the wild animal [Britain]," declared Shakir.[83]

Shakir was very critical of Egypt's politicians, whom he held responsible for the current miserable state of the Sudanese–Egyptian question. These politicians were motivated only by personal interests and lusts, showing no interest in their homeland's rights. He regarded the Bevin–Sidqi draft treaty as illegitimate since the vast majority of the people were against it, and neither the government nor the parliament had the moral right to implement it. Shakir saw no benefit in reviving the Anglo–Egyptian negotiations. For him the only solution to the problem was jihad.[84] The debates within the UN Security Council focused only on issues related to world peace to prevent future wars. By referring the Egyptian–Sudanese issue to the Security Council the people of the Nile valley would admit that their case was within the realm of a "state of war." That would mean a declaration of war against Britain, and therefore every Egyptian and every Sudanese should be on guard to seal the breaches along the borders and to block penetration attempts of the British enemy. Egyptian and Sudanese politicians must unite and fight together as though they were in a battlefield against their common enemy and drop their personal rivalries – the need to defend the homeland was sacred.[85] They should seek support in Russia, in the United States, and among other Security Council members. Lobbying activities should include other Eastern issues such as the Palestine problem and the Indian issue – all caused by Britain to sow division.[86]

Muhammad Husayn Haykal held a slightly different view regarding an appeal to the Security Council. He referred to the solution of the Sudanese question employing the term supranational unity (wahda qawmiyya) rather than using the prevailing territorial nationalist term wahda wataniyya. In other words, Haykal referred to Egypt and Sudan as two separate entities that should be united for the sake of both of them. It was natural, reasoned Haykal patronizingly, that when Sudan would reach the stage of self-government, its people would be the ones to choose the form of regime they wanted "within the framework of unity with Egypt under the Egyptian crown." An Egyptian–Sudanese agreement on unification, he stated, would lead to the disappearance of those advocating separatism. Haykal opined that there was no need for Egypt, at that stage, to bring the national question before the UN. The supra-national unity could be realized without taking such a step – and all it required was a strong will of both Egyptians and Sudanese to go ahead with it.[87] Referring to Haykal's argument that there was no point in resorting to the UN Security Council Muhammad Mandur of the Waf-dist left wing stated that Haykal was "paving the way for his [party] to seize the reins of power at the expense of the welfare of Egypt."[88]

The Sudanese national movement remained divided between the unionists and separatists in its stand vis-à-vis an Egyptian appeal to the UN. Thus, for instance, 'Abdulla Khalil of the *Umma* Party declared that the debate in the Security Council would be a positive step on Sudan's road to independence because the Security Council perceived the Sudanese as "a people under a protectorate – the Sudan has defined geographic borders and is recognized as a [separate] entity and therefore the Egyptians cannot demand rights of domination over the Sudan."[89] The Sudanese paper *al-Ra'i al-'Amm* disputed Egypt's argument of continual control over Sudan since the Ottoman Empire relinquished its imperialist rule in both Egypt and Sudan in the Lausanne Treaty (1923). The newspaper outlined its own narrative of the events in the pre-condominium era – a historical narrative that did not always corres-pond with the facts. The condominium treaty of 1899, it was noted, came after a defining period in Sudan's history, in which the country experienced the taste of independence under the Mahdi movement, which had formed a national state after it succeeded in defeating and expelling the Ottomans, who ruled Sudan. It was the Ottoman Empire, not Egypt, that ruled Sudan prior to the Mahdi revolt. The Egyptian appeal to the Security Council could be more effective and acceptable if the Egyptians would demand British evacuation from both Egypt and Sudan and the independence of the two countries. Britain would then have no excuse to remain in Sudan.[90] Isma'il al-Azhari, on the other hand, wholeheartedly supported Nuqrashi's plan to appeal to the UN and to advance the unity of the Nile valley after British evacuation.[91]

Nuqrashi issued a statement on 3 March 1947 discussing the nature of the Anglo–Egyptian dispute over Sudan and informing the public of Egypt's plans to bring the dispute to the UN Security Council. The talks with Britain had reached an impasse, he asserted, because Egypt was unable to reach an agreement on two paramount issues: first, its demand for the withdrawal of British troops from its territory; and second, its wish to maintain the union with Sudan, self-government for the Sudanese people, "and restoration to Egypt of its rights in the administration of the Sudan in order to further the preparation of the Sudanese for self-government."[92] Nuqrashi took a considerable amount of latitude in airing the Egyptian position, claiming to speak on behalf of all Sudanese and crafting the narrative that most were in favor of a union under Egyptian control, with British policies pushing the Sudanese away from their Egyptian brethren. Nuqrashi asserted that the reason for the inability of the Sudanese to rule themselves was because Egypt was deprived of its right to administer Sudan, since the Sudanese were of the same origin, spoke the same language, and practiced the same faith, and their livelihoods were determined by the same source, the Nile. With the negotiations with the British at a standstill, Egypt had no other option but to bring its case to the UN Security Council.[93] It is noteworthy that Mustafa al-Nahhas, the Wafd leader, expressed words in a similar vein in an interview he gave to *Journal de Genève*. Sudan and Egypt, he stressed, were inseparable because Sudan constituted an integral part of the homeland. As far as social welfare services were concerned, Sudanese districts were treated similarly and equally with Egyptian districts. Those few in Sudan who called for disengagement from Egypt were manipulated by the British administration in Sudan.[94]

Nuqrashi's assertion was met with a stinging British rebuke, with both Sir Ronald Campbell, the British ambassador to Cairo, and Prime Minister Attlee declaring it was "full of both false and tendentious statements."[95] Britain, Attlee argued in the House of Commons on 11 March, agreed to the Bevin–Sidqi draft treaty, which authorized the wholesale evacuation of British troops from Egypt by 1949. Yet the main stumbling block concerned Egypt's relationship with Sudan, as the Egyptians would not support the Sudanese people's freedom to determine their future without accepting the principal of the unity of the Nile valley. The British rejected Nuqrashi's assertions of "inciting the Sudanese to secede from Egypt." Furthermore, Attlee debunked Nuqrashi's argument that the Sudanese and the Egyptians were of the same race, language, and religion, noting "that the Sudanese comprise many races and types, Nilotic, Hamitic, and Negro, besides Arabs. Furthermore, out of approximately 7 million Sudanese, more than 2.5 million are not Muslims or Arabic speaking."[96]

After a considerable delay, Nuqrashi, realizing the hardened nature of the British position and under attack from the political opposition, was forced to go to the UN Security Council, dispatching a letter on 8 July setting out Egypt's demands. These were centered on two main principals: the evacuation of British troops from Egypt and Sudan, and the abrogation of the current administrative regime in Sudan, based on articles 35 and 37 of the UN Charter.[97] The unjustifiable occupation of Egypt in 1882, which was followed by the occupation of the "southern part of the Nile valley, the Sudan," Nuqrashi remonstrated, created a situation whereby the British first imposed upon Egypt in 1899 the joint administration of Sudan and later their assumption of exclusive authority therein. The British employed a policy designed to cut off Sudan from Egypt, "discrediting Egypt and the Egyptians; creating discord between them and the Sudanese and dissensions among the Sudanese themselves; instigating and encouraging artificial separatist movements." For Nuqrashi the British motives were utterly clear: to impair the unity of the Nile valley, despite the fact that this unity was urged "by the common interest and aspiration of its people."[98]

The Wafd opposition remained unconvinced that the Nuqrashi government was qualified to speak on Egypt's behalf. Wafdists asserted that Nuqrashi's letter to the UN showed the weakness of Egypt's negotiating position "since it does not mention unity of the Nile valley under the Egyptian crown, which is a principal demand on which [the whole] nation is agreed."[99] The Wafd did not stop at criticizing the government, but dispatched its own appeal to the UN on the same day. It questioned the legitimacy of the Nuqrashi government to represent "the people of the Nile valley," the vast majority of whom stood firmly behind the Wafd. Nuqrashi's dictatorial government represented a minority segment of "reactionary and feudalist interest groups," and its policies were utterly disapproved by the people of the Nile valley. The people demanded the full evacuation of the Nile valley and the recognition by the Security Council that "the Sudan and Egypt constitute one homeland united by history, temperament, blood, language, religion, and customs – a single homeland [based on equality] without rulers and ruled – all the citizens serve their single homeland." Nuqrashi, submissively, demanded only the termination of the current administrative system in Sudan, knowing that "the issue of the Sudan in relation to Egypt is a matter of life or death." The Wafd urged the Security Council to disregard Nuqrashi's appeal and rather endorse the Wafd's demands as presented in its appeal.[100]

Nuqrashi left Egypt on 21 July 1947, heading to the United States to present Egypt's case to the UN Security Council. On 5, 11, and 13 August he further elaborated on his statement of 8 July, declaring that the treaty of 1936 "was an obsolete instrument, which could no longer function as a basis for Anglo–Egyptian relations, which should now be determined by international law and the Charter of the United Nations." On the issue of Sudan, Nuqrashi asserted the following:

The unity of the Nile valley was an undisputable fact, recognized even by Mr. Churchill in his book *The River War*. The present line dividing the Sudan from Egypt along the 22nd parallel, as devised by the British, was purely artificial.

The economic unity, based on agricultural, industrial and commercial interests, was further enhanced by both countries' dependence on the Nile water. The process of Egyptian penetration in the Sudan was accomplished by peaceful and natural means on the basis of a common language and culture. Under the rule of Muhammad Ali, Egypt and the Sudan had become subject to one central authority and formed a political unit, confirmed by the sultan's *firmans* granted after 1840, which duly received international recognition. This political unit constituted a barrier to European expansion. During and after the so-called "reconquest" of the Sudan, the British, whenever faced with the pretensions of any other European power, invariably put forward the rights of Egypt to the whole of the Nile valley, as for instance, in the case of the Fashoda incident.[101]

Relying on the historical aspect of the Nile valley, Nuqrashi stated that Egypt's sovereignty over Sudan was not hindered by the 1899 agreements with Britain, "although, by applying the designation of Condominium to it, the British had essayed to prove that they had a share in this sovereignty." The British, he argued, utilized the murder of Lee Stack to eliminate the Anglo–Egyptian joint administration on their terms. Britain, he charged, ruled Sudan with a heavy hand, removing Egyptians from the Sudanese civil service and educational institutions, and pushing out those Sudanese who favored closer relations with Egypt. Britain also cracked down on the freedom of the press, stunting the development of Sudanese civil society.

Nuqrashi argued that Egypt "resolved to regard the relations between the Egyptians and the Sudanese as an internal domestic affair, concerning which they would brook no interference."[102]

For Nuqrashi the 1936 treaty could no longer be regarded as the basis for Anglo–Egyptian relations. The international reality after World War II created a new situation whereby international disputes between countries were determined by international law and the UN Charter. The Security Council should take into account the fact that times had changed since the British imposed upon Egypt unilateral declarations and bilateral treaties: "between the 1936 Treaty and the [UN] Charter, we have chosen the Charter," stated Nuqrashi.[103]

The British ambassador to the UN, Alexander Cadogan, picked up the gauntlet. He ridiculed Nuqrashi's allegations regarding the validity of the 1936 treaty in light of the world order after 1945 and the UN Charter. Cadogan fought back, portraying Egypt's actions in Sudan as imperialistic expansion. The conquests of Sudan by Muhammad 'Ali, contended Cadogan, had not been undertaken by peaceful means: "Egypt herself had indulged in imperialistic expansion in that country [the Sudan]." There was not a single historical or any other compelling basis to support Egypt's claims that Egypt and Sudan constituted a united entity:

The political unity of the Nile Valley was a myth, and if such a doctrine were pursued to its logical conclusion Ethiopia, Uganda, and the Belgian Congo would have to be included in such a political unit, since the Nile derived most of its waters from these countries ... the present frontier between Egypt and the Sudan, described [by Nuqrashi] as a British invention, had in fact existed since the year 661 B.C. The only ties which bind the Northern Sudanese, who are of mixed Arab and negroid origin, with Egypt, are those of language and religion, which is equally true of many other peoples who once formed part of the Ottoman Empire.[104]

Cadogan continued in his effort to refute Egypt's arguments regarding its historical right to Sudan. Egypt, he asserted, failed to abort the Mahdi's rebellion because it had neither the economic nor the military resources. Moreover, Nuqrashi belittled, intentionally, the most significant role played by the British in the reoccupation of Sudan, claimed Cadogan. He quoted relevant comparative data on the war contribution of Egyptian and British forces, including the number of casualties on both sides. The condominium form of administration was not imposed on Egypt by the British but was approved by the Ottomans, the then sovereign power. Sudan, noted Cadogan, was administered as a territory entirely separated from Egypt, "proof of which can be found in the judgments of two Egyptian courts of law."

For Cadogan, the national desire of the educated Sudanese was quite clear: they were united by a wish for early self-government. However, he opined acceptably, they differed only as to whether "it should take the form of a self-governing dominion under the Egyptian Crown or complete independence." However, as far as the national desires of the masses in Sudan were concerned, Cadogan appeared to be confident enough in his answer: they were not "anxious for any change and were most certainly not desirous of union with Egypt."[105]

Nuqrashi's diplomatic offensive, trying to convince the member states of the Security Council, was not successful, gaining support from only three states – Syria, the Soviet Union, and Poland. The two eastern bloc states were nevertheless lukewarm in their support for the Egyptian claims over Sudan. Conversely, the Syrian envoy was a vociferous backer of Egypt's claim, demanding the immediate British evacuation of the entire Nile valley.[106] The Chinese delegation was sympathetic to the Egyptian claims over Sudan, but still supported the continuation of negotiations between Britain and Egypt, noting that Egypt's stake in Sudan was "second to the Sudanese people's right of self-determination." The delegates from Australia, Belgium, Brazil, Colombia, and France were in favor of the continuation of negotiations to resolve the impasse, proposing to keep the Security Council informed of their progress. However, although there were several resolutions presented by Security Council members, the impasse was not resolved, and none of the resolutions was adopted.[107] While the Security Council stated that the Anglo–Egyptian dispute would remain on its agenda, it eventually became of secondary importance, fading to the background, as yet another fraught chapter in Anglo–Egyptian relations.[108]

The International Dimension: Modes and Means of Propaganda Activities

Despite its failure in the Security Council, Egypt did get international support and sympathy from other countries before, during, and after the deliberations in the Security Council. It managed successfully to receive a pledge of support from Arab states for its demands even after it officially requested Britain to renegotiate the 1936 treaty.[109] On 23 March 1947, during a meeting of the Arab League in Cairo, the Arab states unanimously affirmed their support of Egypt's demands to unify the Nile valley under the Egyptian crown.[110] The Arab states expressed concern over the deadlock and the subsequent interruption of the Anglo–Egyptian dialogue. They warned that the prevailing friendship between them and Britain would be adversely affected should the latter continue with its refusal to respond positively to Egypt's national demands.[111]

Before that statement was made, right-wing Egyptian circles firmly called on Arab states not to consider any mediating initiatives such as the one allegedly proposed by the governments of Syria and Lebanon. The Anglo–Egyptian dispute should be dealt with only in the Security Council – the approach of negotiating with the British had exhausted itself and led to the present dead end. Mahmud Muhammad Shakir warned the governments of Syria and Lebanon not to fall into the trap of British imperialism. Britain portrayed itself as the champion of the Sudanese right to self-determination, pushing for Sudanese self-government. This was a deceptive tactic aimed at misleading the international community. The goal was clear: to separate Sudan from Egypt and to establish British hegemony there as they did in Palestine, where "the British were turning a blind eye to Jewish terrorism." They deceptively supported Jewish immigration to Palestine, where the British had planned to establish a Jewish state in the heart of the Arab homelands surrounding Palestine. Egypt and Sudan were struggling to gain international support for their just demands, and every Arab and Eastern state should place its means of communication at the disposal of the jihad efforts made by Egypt and Sudan.[112]

The issue of the Arabization of Sudan found expression in a reference made in an article published by *al-Risala* to a statement made by the revered Syrian religious adjudicator Sheikh 'Ali Tantawi. Egypt, asserted Tantawi, "is our [the Arab states'] older sister, Egypt's problem is ours, Egypt's [Nile] valley is ours, Egypt's enemy is our enemy; if we abandon Egypt, we abandon our country, and if we do not stand by her, we betray our nation."[113] Only a united Arab front would lead to an Arab victory over British imperialism, added Mahmud Muhammad Shakir. He declared that the Arab language was spoken in all Arab countries, in which the vast majority of their inhabitants were Muslims, and therefore they constituted a single front stretching from east to west.[114] Shakir praised the Arabs and their abilities, asserting that if the Arabs were united and believed in the righteousness of their way then no one would have dared to anger them. The Arabs wanted to see their countries free and independent from foreign domination – only Arab unity would help to gain that goal. All Arab states' problems were inseparable, including the Sudan and the Palestine problems. Arab men should take an example from their ancient forefathers, who did not hesitate to wield their sword bravely, trusting and believing that God would help them to defeat their enemies.[115]

While Egypt's position among the Arab states was secure, it was necessary to expand its international base of support to the newly independent countries of postcolonial Asia.[116] India featured prominently among these countries, and the two main political groups prior to the partition of India, the Indian National Congress (led by Jawaharlal Nehru) and the All-India Muslim League (led by Muhammed Ali Jinnah, later the founder of independent Pakistan in August 1947), were both receptive to Egypt's desire to unify the Nile valley under the Egyptian crown. Jinnah stated in a letter to the secretariat of the Arab League in late April 1947 that the Indian Muslims "stand on Egypt's side in its struggle to ensure the [British] evacuation of the Nile Valley, its unification, and the realization of Egypt's hopes and aspirations."[117] The Egyptians went to great lengths to persuade the Indians to support the validity of the Egyptian claim over Sudan, sending significant academic material written by scholars and experts on the natural links between Egypt and Sudan.[118]

The anti-imperialist struggle against British domination, which both Egypt and India shared, led to a rapprochement between the two countries. India's support for the Arabs during the UN debates on the partition of Palestine and its support for the Egyptian appeal to the Security Council of August 1947 placed India as a champion of the Arab cause.[119] A manifestation of the Indo–Egyptian entente was seen when the Egyptian government led by Mustafa al-Nahhas unilaterally abrogated the 1936 treaty on 8 October 1951. India then supported the Egyptian claims for full sovereignty over the Suez Canal, yet Nehru was more discerning over Egyptian claims over Sudan, initially supporting the Sudanese right to determine their political fate, yet, at the same time, recognizing King Faruq as King of Egypt and Sudan.[120]

Egypt also sought the support of Soviet bloc countries, particularly the Soviet Union. Since the establishment of diplomatic relations between the two countries, the Soviet Union expressed its firm support for Egypt's struggle for national liberation. In late 1922, the Comintern accepted Egypt's demand for sovereignty over Sudan. Sudan, it was noted, was a natural continuation of and supplement to Egypt and should therefore be a political part of the latter.[121] However, in the immediate post-1945 years, the Soviet Union took a different stand on the Sudan question, as appeared during the deliberations in the Security Council in August 1947–September 1947. Before Nuqrashi presented his demands, his delegation endeavored to win Soviet sympathy, saying that Egypt would adhere to a neutralist policy in the interbloc conflict. Egypt also promised to side with the Soviet Union whenever necessary. Nevertheless, the Soviet press, like many opposition parties in Egypt, criticized Nuqrashi's performance, which was designed "to reduce opposition influence from the Wafd and to prepare the ground for an American loan." Despite this criticism, the Soviet Union and its Polish satellite were the only countries to support Egypt's demands for national liberation, yet both expressed reservations concerning Egypt's claims for sovereignty over Sudan. Andrei Gromyko, the Soviet delegate to the UN Security Council, said in a speech on August 20:

The USSR understands and sympathizes with these national aspirations on the part of Egypt and its people towards an independent existence on the basis of sovereign equality with other states and peoples ... Egypt's request for the immediate withdrawal of all United Kingdom troops from the territory of Egypt and the Sudan is well founded ... [yet] we do not know what the Sudanese want and what they are striving for. Without accurate information as to the aims of the Sudanese people, it is difficult for the Security Council to take any decision on this question.[122]

The United States held an ambivalent position concerning the solution for the Anglo–Egyptian dispute. The Egyptian delegation's efforts to portray its country as being anti-communist because communism was completely contrary to Islam – thus hoping to win US and Western empathy – were futile. The US delegation to the Security Council believed that the prolongation of the Anglo–Egyptian dispute was bad for Western interests in Egypt and the Arab world. However, it maintained that an immediate evacuation of British troops from Egypt would create a void that might be filled by a hostile power, possibly the Soviet Union. The solution it therefore offered was more of the same: the resumption of bilateral negotiations between the two countries to achieve a satisfactory settlement for both countries.[123] Neither Egypt nor Britain appeared to be pleased with the US stand. To quote a British report: "during the debates the UK delegation did not receive the support it might well have expected from the State Department, nor was the attitude of the United States delegate beyond reproach."[124]

However, Egypt did not give up and continued in the very early 1950s with its efforts to win US support. The Egyptians supposed, correctly, that the US government could put pressure on its British ally to alter its position vis-à-vis the Nile valley. For that reason Egypt also conducted an anti-British campaign within the United States, described by the British embassy in Washington as "tremendously active and expensive." One of the methods employed by the Egyptians was the distribution of pamphlets depicting the British as an imperialist and occupying power that did not respect the rights of the peoples of the Nile valley to national liberation. Egypt demanded freedom and independence on the basis of justice and right as a sovereign state. It did so not just for itself but for Sudan too – "for the millions of people of the same blood, the same religion, and the same interests, who inhabit the Valley of the Nile." The British refused to evacuate their troops from Egyptian soil "as they have done for the last 69 years."[125] Egypt was willing to allow the Sudanese to choose their own future, unhindered and untrammeled. To support this argument, the Egyptian propagandists referred to a bill, promulgated by the Egyptian parliament on 15 October 1951, providing for a special independent Sudanese government and parliament, united with the Egyptian government – a move that was welcomed by the Sudanese delegation, the party representing the majority of Sudanese.[126]

The British embassy in Washington expressed concern over the extent of harm this public campaign caused to British interests in America. It therefore suggested taking "not an anti-Egyptian line, but a rather righteous line, showing that we have a constructive policy in the interests of the free world and that we do not wish to waste time in self-destructive mutual abuse."[127]

The British concerns over the US attitude toward their dispute with Egypt were not without foundations. The Egyptian efforts to win US support met with success. In late 1951 Anthony Eden, the British Foreign Secretary, noticed that his government "continued to be urged by the United States Government to recognize King Farouk as King of the Sudan."[128] According to Voll, Cold War strategic and political considerations were behind the US government's decision to support the Egyptian nationalist doctrine, hoping that such a move "could allow the maintenance of British troops in Egyptian bases as part of broader regional defense arrangements."[129] However, shortly after the downfall of the Egyptian monarchy, the US government ceased to support the unity of the Nile valley as the new military regime abandoned that doctrine. It nevertheless took pains to settle the Anglo–Egyptian dispute, not always in a satisfactory manner from Britain's point of view.

Notes

1 Collins, *A History of Modern Sudan*, pp. 46–53; Holt and Daly, *A History of the*, pp. 100–101; Woodward, *Condominium and Sudanese Nationalism*, pp. 13–49; Warburg, *Islam, Sectarianism and Politics*, pp. 104–128; Iris Seri-Hersch, "Towards Social Progress and Post-Imperial Modernity? Colonial Politics of Iiteracy in the Anglo-Egyptian Sudan, 1946–1956," *History of Education*, 40:3 (2011), p. 342.

2 Jamil 'Arif 'Abd al-Rahman 'Azzam, *Safahat min al-mudhakkirat al-sirriyya li-awwal amin 'amm lil-jami'a al-'arabiyya* (Cairo: al-Maktab al-Misri al-Hadith, 1977), p. 255.

3 'Abd al-Rahman al-Rafi'i, *Fi a'qab al-thawra al-misriyya – Thawrat 1919*, Vol. 3 (Cairo: Dar al-Ma'arif, 1989), chapters 5–7. See also Muhammad Ibrahim 'Abd al-'Azim Ramadan, *Misr wa al-harb al-'alamiyya al-thaniyya: Ma'rakat tajnibu misr wa-yalat al-harb* (Cairo: al-Hay'a al-Misriyya al-'Amma lil-Kitab, 1998).

4 Sania Sharawi Lanfranchi, *Casting off the Veil: The Life of Huda Shaarawi, Egypt's First Feminist* (London: I.B. Tauris, 2015), pp. 255–256; Laura S. Etheredge (ed.), *Middle East Region in Transition, Egypt* (New York: Britannica Educational Publishing, 2011), p. 153.

5 On Egypt and the formation of the Arab League, see Yehoshua Porath, *In Search of Arab Unity, 1930–1945* (London: Frank Cass, 1986), chapter 5; Gershoni and Jankowski, *Redefining the Egyptian Nation*, pp. 192–211. On the establishment of diplomatic relations with the Soviet Union and Egypt's foreign policy at the time, see Rami Ginat, "British Concoction or Bilateral Decision? Revisiting the Genesis of Soviet–Egyptian Diplomatic Relations," *International Journal of Middle Eastern Studies*, 31 (1999); Eran Lerman, "A Revolution Prefigured: Foreign Policy Orientations in the Postwar Years," in Shimon Shamir (ed.), *Egypt from Monarchy to Republic* (Boulder, CO: Westview Press, 1995), pp. 283–308. Many studies have dealt with the complex relations between Britain and Egypt from the late nineteenth century until the mid-1950s, as well as the political, social, economic, and cultural developments in Sudan under the Anglo–Egyptian condominium. See, for instance, al-Rafi'i, *Misr wa-al-sudan*; 'Abd al-'Azim Muhammad Ibrahim Ramadan, *Tatawwur al-haraka al-wataniyya fi misr min sanat 1937 ila sana*

1948, 2 vols. (Beirut: al-Watan al-'Arabi, 1973); Azhari, *Difa' 'an wahdat wadi al-nil*; Hannawi, *Ma'rakat al-jala' wa-wahdat wadi al-nil*; Sayyid-Marsot, *Egypt and Cromer*; Hail, *Britain's Foreign Policy*; Hanes, *Imperial Diplomacy*; Daly, *Imperial Sudan*; Fabunmi, *The Sudan in Anglo-Egyptian Relations*; Holt, *A Modern History of the Sudan*; Sharkey, *Living with Colonialism*; Troutt Powell, *A Different Shade of Colonialism*. The last two studies deal with the Anglo–Egyptian colonialist dilemma: the first from a nationalist Sudanese perspective, and the second from the viewpoint of the Egyptian nationalist movement that, on the one hand, struggled to liberate Egypt from British colonialism and, on the other hand, conducted a twofold struggle: to expel Britain from the Nile valley and to perpetuate Egypt's colonial position in Sudan.

6 The subject of education and the Anglo–Egyptian rivalry over the development of the Sudanese educational system is to be discussed separately in Chapter 4.

7 Letter No. CS/SCR/97.H.6 from Douglas Newbold, the Civil Secretary of Sudan, to Foreign Office, 24 November 1943, FO141/905, 840/69/43.

8 Letter from Lord Killearn, Cairo, to Sir Alexander Cadogan, Foreign Office, London, 27 December 1943, FO141/905, 840/69/43.

9 Ibid.

10 Nahhas's memorandum is attached to Letter SA/48-A-7 from Sudan Agency, Cairo, 6 January 1944, FO141/939, 31/2/44. See it also in FO371/41363.

11 Letter No. E. 97.H.1. from Huddleston, Khartoum, to Nahhas Pasha, Cairo, attached to Dispatch 48 from Huddleston, Khartoum, to Killearn, British Embassy, Cairo, 22 March 1944, FO141/939, 31/14/44.

12 Ibid.

13 Ibid.

14 Letter WAS/JJ from Killearn, Cairo, to Nahhas Pasha, 22 December 1944, FO141/939, 31/69/44. See also a record of conversation between Nahhas Pasha and Hasan Rif'at Pasha, Cairo, 21 December 1944, FO141/939, 31/69/44. It is noteworthy that Nahhas Pasha ended his term in office on 10 October 1944. It is therefore quite probable that the correspondence was recorded several weeks after his departure. According to Yunan Labib Rizq, Prime Minister Ahmad Mahir (10 October 1944 to 24 February 1945) dealt with this issue shortly after he took office. See Rizq, *Qadiyyat wahdat wadi al-nil*, pp. 194–197; al-Hajj, *Mu'jam Shakhsiyyat Mu'tamar al-Khirrijin*, p. 266.

15 Dispatch 2701 from Killearn, British Ambassador, Cairo, 23 December 1944, FO141/939, 31/72/44.

16 Rizq, *Qadiyyat wahdat wadi al-nil*, pp. 198–205.

17 Telegram 162(S) from Lord Killearn, British Ambassador, Cairo, 29 August 1944, FO141/987, 910/3/46.

18 See minutes of Foreign Office officials, 8 January 1945, 18 January 1945, 21 January 1945, and 22 January 1945, in FO141/939, 31/76/44.

19 Ibid.

20 Letter No. 41 from Killearn, Cairo, to Huddleston, Khartoum, 7 February 1945, FO141/1013, 41/22/45.

21 Memorandum No. SA/36-C-1/59 by the Sudan Agency, Cairo, 17 January 1945, FO141/1013, 41/9/45.

22 A committee comprising leaders of political parties and independent politicians that was founded by former Prime Minister Ahmad Mahir to advise him on important national issues. See Rafi'i, *Fi a'qab al-thawra al-misriyya – Thawrat 1919*, Vol. 3, p. 186.

23 Ibid.

24 On Anglo–Egyptian relations before and during these years, and the dispute over Sudan, see Hanes, *Imperial Diplomacy*, pp. 1–43. See also Hail, *Britain's Foreign Policy*, pp. 1–19.

25 Stefanie Katharine Wichhart, "Intervention: Britain, Egypt and Iraq during World War II" (PhD Dissertation, University of Texas at Austin, 2007), pp. 375–376.

26 Muhammad Husayn Haykal, "Misr wa-matalibuha al-qawmiyya," *al-Ahram*, 4 January 1946.

27 "Bayan min al-wafd al-misri ila al-umma al-misriyya al-karima," *al-Ahram*, 3 February 1946, pp. 3–4. The pro-Wadfist paper *al-Balagh* was very critical of Nuqrashi. See "Bayan khatir min al-wafd al-misri ila al-umma al-misriyya al-karima," *al-Balagh*, 3 February 1946. A critical view of Nuqrashi's "conciliatory approach" toward the British government was also expressed by the independent newspaper *Ruz al-Yusuf*; see "Akhbar sariha – Misr wa-al-sudan," *Ruz al-Yusuf*, No. 908 (7 November 1945), p. 5.

28 "Bayan min al-ikhwan al-muslimina ila sha'b wadi al-nil," *al-Ikhwan al-Muslimun*, 9 February 1946, pp. 3–5.

29 Ginat, "Egypt's Efforts," pp. 195–196. See also Adrian Budd, "Nation and Empire: Labour's Foreign Policy 1945–51," *International Socialism*, 62 (Spring 1994), at http://pubs.socialistreviewindex.org.uk/isj62/budd .htm; T. Cliff and D. Gluckstein, *The Labour Party: A Marxist History* (London: Bookmarks, 1988), p. 240; J. Saville, *The Politics of Continuity: British Foreign Policy and the Labour Government 1945–51* (London: Verso, 1993), p. 136.

30 An intelligence report entitled *The Current Situation in Egypt*, 16 October 1947, President's Secretary's Files, File Subject: Central Intelligence Reports, ORE 1947, No. 54, Box 254, Harry S. Truman Library, Independence, Missouri. On the Anglo–American attempts to review and coordinate their policies in the Middle East in late 1947, see Rami Ginat, *The Soviet Union and Egypt, 1945–1955* (London: Frank Cass, 1993), pp. 94–97.

31 Elie Kedourie, "The Transition from a British to an American Era in the Middle East," in Haim Shaked and Itamar Rabinovich (eds.), *The Middle East and the United States* (New Brunswick and London: Transactions Books, 1980), pp. 3–4; Albert Hourani, *A History of the Arab Peoples* (Cambridge, MA: Harvard University Press, 1991), p. 320.

32 "Bayan min al-ikhwan al-muslimina ila sha'b wadi al-nil," *al-Ikhwan al-Muslimun*, 9 February 1946, pp. 3–5; 12 March 1946, pp. 3–5.

33 Daly, *Imperial Sudan*, pp. 222–225.

34 Note No. 95, "The Egyptian Case before the Security Council," February 1948, FO407/226, J4644/12/16.

35 A copy of the draft treaty is attached to Letter No. 3455/46 from Secretary of State for India, External Affairs Department, to the Government of India, 21 May 1946, External Affairs Department, 1946, File No. 8 (5) – M.E./46, National Archives of India, New Delhi (hereafter: NAI). See also Muhammad Khalil, *The Arab States and the Arab League: A Documentary Record* (Beirut: Khayats, 1962), pp. 718–721.

36 Khalil, *The Arab States*, pp. 718–721.

37 P. J. Vatikiotis, *The History of Modern Egypt* (London: Weidenfeld and Nicolson, 1991), p. 363.

38 See Bevin's statement in the House of Common, 27 January 1947, FO371/90152, JE1052/11. See also Letter No. 18 from Secretary of State, India Office, London, to Government of India (External Affairs Department), 31 October 1946, File No. 8 (5) – M.E./46, NAI. See also Hanes, *Imperial Diplomacy*, pp. 75–81.

39 On the draft agreement and the opposition to it, see Tariq al-Bishri, *al-Haraka al-siyasiyya fi misr, 1945–1952* (Cairo: Al-Hay'a al-'Amma lil-Kitab, 1972), pp. 136–138; Haggai Erlich, *Students and University in 20th Century Egyptian Politics* (London: Frank Cass, 1989), pp. 159–161.

40 Letter No. 12 from Secretary of State, India Office, London, to Government of India (External Affairs Department), 31 October 1946, File No. 8 (5) – M.E./46, NAI. See also Note No. 95 in FO407/226, p. 86.

41 Letter No. 18, File No. 8 (5) – M.E./46, INA.

42 Rizq, *Qadiyyat wahdat wadi al-nil*, p. 17; al-Rafi'i, *Fi a'qab al-thawra al-misriyya – Thawrat 1919*, Vol. 3, pp. 219–220. Huddleston and the Sudan government were criticized by the Foreign Office for not persuading "Sudanese leaders of the very real advantages of the Sudan protocol" for the future of their country. See Telegram 52 from Foreign Office to Governor-General, Khartoum, 5 November 1946, Sud/46/10, FO800/505.

43 "Kifah mushtarak dida 'adu mushtarak," *al-Fajr al-Jadid*, 1 May 1946. On the Sudanese delegation, see also "Wafd al-sudan fi misr," *al-Ahram*, 28 March 1946. The goals and assignments of the Sudanese delegation, as stated above, were clarified by Isma'il al-Azhari, who headed the delegation. See "al-Wafd al-sudani – Bayan 'an muhimmat al-wafd wa-ahdafihi," *al-Ahram*, 7 April 1946, pp. 2, 5.

44 Quoted from Ginat, "Egypt's Efforts," p. 198.

45 According to al-Hajj, 'Ali al-Barir played a central role in unifying all Sudanese parties behind the statement. See al-Hajj, *Mu'jam shakhsiyyat mu'tamar al-khirrijin*, p. 266.

46 Ibid. See also "Kifah mushtarak."

47 See the full text (in Arabic) of Isma'il al-Azhari's memorandum to the British Prime Minister in FO141/1096, 122/93/46.

48 "Mas'alat al-sudan," *al-Ahram*, 14 April 1946, pp. 3, 6; "al-Wafd al-sudani wa-ta'dil khutatihi," *al-Ahram*, 1 May 1946, p. 4. On disagreements among members of the united Sudanese mission, between those who supported the unity of the Nile valley and those who opposed it, see Gabriel Warburg, *Islam, Nationalism and Communism*, pp. 69–72.

49 See a broader discussion in Chapter 6.

50 Ihsan 'Abd al-Quddus, "Lahum al-sudan wa-lana al-kalam," *Ruz al-Yusuf*, No. 929 (4 April 1946).

51 *Al-Wafd al-Misri*, 6 April 1946.

52 "al-Wafd al-sudani – Muhimmatuhu wa-ahdafuhu," *al-Ahram*, 10 April 1946.

53 "al-Wafd al-sudani – Qararuhu bi-anna hizb al-umma ghayr mumaththil fihi," *al-Ahram*, 5 May 1946.

54 "'Udwan injlizi jadid 'ala wahdat misr wa-al-sudan," *al-Balagh*, 3 November 1946.

55 "al-Wafd al-sudani – fi al-nadi al-sa'di – khutba lil-nahhas – ahdaf al-wafd al-sudani," *al-Ahram*, 11 April 1946, pp. 3–4. See also *al-Misri*, 8 April 1946.

56 "al-Wafd al-sudani – fi al-nadi al-sa'di – khutba lil-nahhas – ahdaf al-wafd al-sudani," *al-Ahram*, 11 April 1946, pp. 3–4.

57 "Bayan ra'is al-hukuma 'an al-mufawadat wa-mas'alat al-sudan," *al-Ahram*, 9 May 1946; "Bayan li-ra'is al-wuzara' 'an al-mufawadat wa-mas'alat al-sudan," *al-Muqattam*, 9 May 1946, p. 3.

58 Wahid Ra'fat, "Misr wa-al-sudan – Yajib an yattafiqa abna' wadi al-nil fima baynahum awalan," *al-Ahram*, 21 April 1946, pp. 3, 5.

59 Ibid.

60 *Al-Siyasa*, 7 April 1946.

61 *Al-Balagh*, 6 April 1946.

62 *Al-Balagh*, 7 April 1946.

63 "Min wafd al-sudan ila sha'b wadi al-nil," *al-Ahram*, 3 June 1946, p. 3.

64 "Wafd al-sudan yatlubu bi-qat' al-mufawadat," *al-Ahram*, 1 July 1946.

65 "al-Wafd al-sudani yutalibu bi-insha' dawlat wadi al-nil," *al-Balagh*, 23 September 1946.

66 "Ihtijaj al-sudaniyyina 'ala al-muqtarahat al-baritaniyya," *al-Ahram*, 23 September 1946.

67 Even before the conclusion of the draft treaty, left- and right-wing oppositional groups vehemently called to terminate the 1936 treaty and demanded the unconditional withdrawal of British imperialism from the Nile valley in its entirety. *Misr al-Fatat* and the Muslim Brothers had already expressed their disappointment with the results of the negotiation a few months before its conclusion. See "Min hizb misr al-fatat," *al-Ahram*, 24 September 1946; Salih 'Ashmawi, "Mawqif hasim fi ta'rikh al-da'wah," *al-Ikhwan al-Muslimun*, 25 August 1946, p. 3. The anti-British, venomous tone manifested itself in communist periodicals throughout 1945 and 1946. See, for instance, Taha Sa'd 'Uthman, "al-Amana al-qawmiyya," *al-Damir*, No. 272, 3 October 1945, p. 1; Sa'id Khiyyal, "Ila majlis al-amn," *al-Fajr al-Jadid*, No. 19, 30 January 1946, p. 11; "al-'Alaqat al-misriyya al-baritaniyya," *al-Fajr al-Jadid*, No. 26, 20 March 1946, p. 7; Sa'id Khiyyal, "Qadiyyatuna wa-majlis al-amn," *al-Fajr al-Jadid*, No. 27, 27 March 1946, p. 8

68 al-Bishri, *al-Haraka al-siyasiyya*, p. 100. On the activity of the National Committee of Students and Workers, see also Joel Beinin and Zackary Lockman, *Workers on the Nile: Nationalism, Communism, Islam, and the Egyptian Working Class, 1882–1954* (Princeton, NJ: Princeton University Press, 1987), pp. 335–344; Muhammad Yusuf al-Jindi, "21 Fibrayir: dawr bariz

lil-shuyu'iyyun al-misriyyin fi al-haraka al-wataniyya al-misriyya," *Qadaya Fikriyya*, July 1992, pp. 236–241.

69 "Bayan sab'ah min a'da' hay'at al-mufawada," *al-Ahram*, 26 November 1946, p. 3.

70 For Sidqi's reply to the seven members of the negotiating team, see "Bayan min ra'is al-wuzara' raddan 'ala bayan al-mu'aridina min hay'at al-mufawa-dat," *al-Ahram*, 28 November 1946, p. 3.

71 "Ra'i al-sudan fi al-mawqif," *al-Ahram*, 29 October 1946, p. 5.

72 Ibid.

73 "Ta'awun al-infisaliyyina ma'a hukumat al-sudan," *al-Ahram*, 1 January 1947.

74 Note No. 61, "Reply to Nokrashi's Statement," Telegram 554 from Attlee, British Prime Minister, to Campbell, Cairo, 11 March 1947, FO407/226, J1190/12/16.

75 Statement made by Ernest Bevin, the Secretary of State for Foreign Affairs, to the House of Common, 27 January 1947, FO371/90152, JE1052/11.

76 See Note No. 95, FO407/226. For further information on the Bevin–Sidqi talks and their outcome, see Michael Doran, *Pan-Arabism before Nasser* (New York and Oxford: Oxford University Press, 1999), pp. 10–11, 41–43; Hanes, *Imperial Diplomacy*, pp. 75–108.

77 "Majlis al-nuwwab bi-jami' ahzabihi yu'ayidu al-hukuma," *al-Ahram*, 1 January 1947, p. 3.

78 "Tasrihat jadida li-hakim al-sudan," *al-Ahram*, 30 December 1946.

79 "Majlis al-nuwwab."

80 See Ginat, Egypt's Efforts, p. 199. See also Note No. 95, FO407/226. Muhammad Husayn Haykal, *Mudhakkirat fi al-siyasa al-misriyya* (Cairo: Dar al-Ma'arif, 1990), part 3, p. 58.

81 al-Rafi'i, *Fi a'qab al-thawra al-misriyya – Thawrat 1919*, Vol. 3, p. 225.

82 See Letter DS(E) 20/2/3 from R. M. Shields, British Security Services Representative, Cairo, to G. J. Jenkuns, Cairo, 26 August 1947, FO141/1158, 66/79/47.

83 Mahmud Muhammad Shakir, "Misr hiya al-sudan," *al-Risala*, No. 708, 27 January 1947, pp. 104–106; Shakir, "La tudabiru ayyuha al-rijal," *al-Risala*, No. 712, 24 February 1947, pp. 318–320.

84 Ibid., p. 318.

85 Ibid., p. 319.

86 Ibid., pp. 319–320. For similar views, see *al-Muqattam*, the conservative and pro-monarchial paper, "Qadiyyat wadi al-nil fi hay'at al-umam al-muttahida," *al-Muqattam*, 16 April 1947, p. 1.

87 "Haykal basha yatahaddath 'an al-sudan," *al-Ahram*, 3 January 1947, p. 3.

88 *Sawt al-Umma*, 22 March 1947.

89 "al-Nuqrashi pasha yaqulu anna mu'ahadat 36 ghayr qa'ima," *al-Ahram*, 28 January 1947, p. 2.

90 "al-Mawqif fi al-sudan – Matlab al-jala' 'an misr wa-al-sudan – ra'i jarida sudaniyya fihi," *al-Ahram*, 28 February 1947, p. 6.

91 "Hadith ra'is wafd al-sudan ma'a al-ahram raddan 'ala bayan hukumat al-sudan," *al-Ahram*, 6 March 1947, p. 2.

92 Note No. 59, "Breakdown of Negotiations: Statement by Nokrashi," Telegram 557 from Sir Ronald Campbell, Cairo, to Bevin, FO, 3 March 1947, FO407/226, J1019/12/16; "Bayan li-ra'is al-hukuma wa-ta'qib li-sidqi pasha," al-Ahram, 4 March 1947, p. 2.

93 Note No. 59, FO407/226. See also the content of Nuqrashi's speech on 18 May 1947, in "al-Nuqrashi basha yaruddu 'ala al-mistar bifin," al-Ahram, 19 May 1947, p. 2; El-Barawy, Egypt, Britain and the Sudan, p. 14.

94 "Mustafa al-nahhas basha yatahaddatu," al-Ahram, 2 June 1947, p. 3.

95 Note No. 60, "Reply to Nukrashi's Statement," Telegram 569 from Campbell to Attlee, 4 March 1947, FO407/226, J1043/12/16. See also al-Bishri, al-Haraka al-siyasiyya, p. 138.

96 Note No. 61, "Reply to Nokrashi's Statement," Telegram 569. See also Haykal, Mudhakkirat, pp. 78–79.

97 For a copy of the letter, see Note No. 95, FO407/226, J7828/24/16.

98 Ibid.

99 Note No. 25, "Egypt and the United Nations," Telegram 1573 from Campbell to Bevin, 16 July 1947, FO371/407/226, J333/12/16.

100 "Barqiyyat ra'is al-wafd al-misri ila ra'is majlis al-amn wa-hay'at al-umam al-muttahida," al-Ahram, 20 July 1947, p. 2.

101 For the content of Nuqrashi's speeches, see Note No. 95, FO407/226, J7828/24/16; "Khutbat al-nuqrashi pasha," al-Ahram, 12 August 1947, pp. 1–3. Ginat, "Egypt's Efforts," p. 200. On the historical context, see Muhammad Mahmud Jalal, "al-Sudan," al-Ikhwan al-Muslimun, 4 October 1945, pp. 8–10.

102 Note No. 95, FO407/226, J7828/24/16; Ginat, "Egypt's Efforts," p. 201; Haykal, Mudhakkirat, p. 84.

103 Note No. 95, FO407/226, J7828/24/16.

104 Ibid. For the full content of his speech, see "Radd al-sir alixandir kadujan 'ala al-nuqrashi pasha," al-Ahram, 12 August 1947, p. 3.

105 Note No. 95, FO407/226, J7828/24/16.

106 On the prolonged discussions and debates in the Security Council and the stances taken by the member states, see Note No. 95, FO407/226, J7828/24/16.

107 Ginat, "Egypt's Efforts," p. 201.

108 Ibid.

109 The Arab support was already fully expressed at the Arab summit, held at Inshas on 28 May 1946–29 May 1946, and at the extraordinary session of the League's Council held at Bloudan,8 June 1946–12 June 1946.

110 Egypt Sudan p. 4; "Majlis al-jami'a al-'arabiyya yu'ayyidu misr ta'yidan mutlaqan," al-Ahram, 24 March 1947, p. 2.

111 Ibid. On the position of the Arab states, see Haykal, Mudhakkirat, pp. 66–68.

112 Mahmud Muhammad Shakir, "Innahu jihad la siyasa!," al-Risala, No. 714, 10 March 1947, pp. 271–273. See also Shakir, "al-Khiyana al-'uthma ...!" al-Risala, No. 714, 24 March 1947, pp. 327–330.

113 Gha'ib Tu'mah Farman, "Ya ikhwanina fi wadi al-nil!" *al-Risala*, No. 717, 31 March 1947, pp. 366–367.

114 Mahmud Muhammad Shakir, "Hadhihi biladuna," *al-Risala*, No. 732, 14 July 1947, pp. 777–779.

115 Mahmud Muhammad Shakir, "Sha'b wahid, wa-qadiyya wahida!" *al-Risala*, No. 730, 30 June 1947, pp. 722–725.

116 On the character of this propaganda activity and the way it was conducted, see Letter No. 562/47 (6-3-10Pt:II) from the Consul General for Egypt, Bombay, to the Secretary of the Government of India, Department of External Affairs and Commonwealth Relations, New Delhi, 18 June 1947; Letter No. D.3332-ME/47 from Department of External Affairs and Commonwealth Relations, to the Consul General for Egypt, Bombay, 2 July 1947; Letter DY.3875 –MR/47 from Tarlok Singh, Private Secretary to Pandit Jawaharlal Nehru, to the Consul General for Egypt, Bombay, 4 August 1947, File NO. F.23(13) – AWT/47, NAI.

117 "al-Jala' al-shamil wa-wahdat al-wadi," *al-Ahram*, 27 April 1947, p. 2.

118 See Letter DY.3875 – MR/47.

119 On India's policy toward the Arabs in the late 1940s, see Rami Ginat, "India and the Palestine Question: The Emergence of the Asio-Arab Bloc and India's Quest for Hegemony in the Post-Colonial Third World," *Middle Eastern Studies*, 40/6 (November 2004), pp. 187–216.

120 Nehru made his remarks at two press conferences held in New Delhi on 3 October 1951 and 24 July 1952, and in a note he sent his Foreign Secretary, New Delhi, 3 August 1952. For the texts, see *Selected Works of Jawaharlal Nehru*, 2nd Series, Vol. 17 and Vol. 19 (New Delhi: Nehru Memorial Museum & Library, Teen Mutri House), pp. 541–546, 637–641. By June 1952, in addition to Arab and Muslim states (such as Lebanon, Jordan, Libya, Indonesia, and Afghanistan), other states recognized Faruq's new title, among them Greece, Italy, and Belgium. See "I'tiraf al-yunan wa-italiya bi-laqab jalalat malik misr wa-al-sudan," *al-Balagh*, 25 June 1952, p. 1. See also Telegram 3 from FO to Holy See, 12 January 1952, FO371/97051, JE1903/3; Telegram 23 from FO to Lisbon, 16 January 1952, ibid.

121 "The Sudan," supplementary Theses, 22 November 1922, RGASPI, fond 495, OP85, D6, L57–59.

122 Quoted from Ginat, *The Soviet Union and Egypt*, p. 75.

123 Ibid., pp. 75–76. See also John Voll, "US Policy toward the Unity of the Nile Valley, 1945–1952," in Gershoni and Hatina (eds.), *Narrating the Nile*, p. 96–97.

124 Ginat, "Egypt's Efforts," p. 201; Ginat, *The Soviet Union and Egypt*, pp. 74–77; Note No. 95, FO407/226, J7828/24/16.

125 See a pamphlet issued by the Egyptian government entitled *The Egyptian Question 1882–1951*, attached to Letter from British Embassy, Washington, 5 December 1951, FO953/1115, PG11637/102.

126 Ibid.

127 Letter from British Embassy, Washington, 5 December 1951, FO953/1115, PG11637/102.

128 Quoted from Voll, "US Policy toward the Unity," p. 93.

129 Ibid.

4 Between Two Modes of Imperialism
Education, Nationalism, and the Struggle for Power
in Sudan

This chapter scans postwar policies employed by the two masters of Sudan as part of their struggle to establish their long-term hegemony over that country. More specifically, it keeps track of the long-standing British project of Sudanization, that is, the creation of a new situation whereby qualified and well-trained Sudanese would gradually take over governmental and administrative posts as part of their preparation for self-rule. The British desired to pave the way for the emergence and development of a territorial-particularist Sudanese nationalism, hoping it would subsequently lead to the demise of pro-unionist Sudanese orientations. As we shall see, the Egyptians responded angrily to Sudanization. Their countermeasures encompassed both the political and the public spheres.

Considerable emphasis is placed on the tactics and strategies employed by Britain and Egypt in their struggle to develop, shape, and determine the Sudanese educational system. First, the chapter scrutinizes the interplay between British educational and foreign policies in Sudan. A robust educational system could serve the purpose of training a new generation of Sudanese intellectuals with a particularist national consciousness and pro-British orientation. Second, the chapter shows that the Egyptian response to the British educational policy took the form of corrective measures and initiatives aimed at minimizing the damage for their unification plan. Like the British, Egyptian policymakers and protagonists of the unity of the Nile valley were well-aware of the vitality and significance of hegemony over Sudanese education as a major factor in determining the future of Sudan. Egyptians, however, learned the hard way that they were playing in an unfair game – the British, through their proxy Sudan government, had the advantage of enjoying much more room for maneuver.

Sudanization and Its Effects on the Doctrine of the Unity of the Nile Valley

The reoccupation of Sudan (1896–1898) by a joint Anglo–Egyptian military force paved the way for the conclusion of the condominium agreement on 19 January 1899. The formation of the condominium was a product of the colonialist machinations of the Earl of Cromer (Evelyn Baring), Britain's agent and consul general in Egypt (1883–1907) and, practically speaking, Egypt's mighty ruler. It was a "deliberate ambiguity," as Cromer phrased it. According to him, it was necessary

to invent some method by which the Soudan should be, at one and the same time, Egyptian to such an extent as to satisfy equitable and political exigencies, and yet sufficiently British to prevent the administration of the country from being hampered by the international burr which necessarily hung on the skirts of Egyptian political existence. It was manifest that these conflicting requirements could not be satisfied without the creation of some hybrid form of government, hitherto unknown to international jurisprudence.[1]

However, Cromer made it clear that it was Britain's intention, right from the beginning, to see to it that Sudan would be governed by "a partnership of two, of which England was the predominant member." The sovereign rights of Britain and Egypt over Sudan, determined Cromer, were based on "the right of conquest."[2]

The purpose of the condominium, reasoned Peter Woodward, was to avert unnecessary complications in Egypt by the full British annexation of reoccupied Sudanese territories, which were controlled by Egypt previously: Britain's rights by way of conquest and reconquest of former provinces of Egypt. Egypt regained its rights in Sudan but under restrictive conditions and as the weaker partner in the dual rule. The condominium regime was very much effective from Britain's point of view until the British unilateral declaration of Egypt's independence in February 1922.[3] This independence was nevertheless closely monitored and limited, enabling Britain continuous domination of its imperial interests in the region – military bases and communications including full control of the Suez Canal area and Egypt's borders and security concerns; indirect control of Egypt's foreign policy and relations with other countries as well as its economy; and, with regard to Sudan, the preservation of Britain's hegemonic position in the unequal condominium arrangement.

As we have seen, the Anglo–Egyptian treaty of August 1936 granted Egypt a relatively high degree of sovereignty, while protecting Britain's major interests in Egypt and Sudan. Although it recognized Egypt's rights to play a more active role in Sudan, the condominium agreement of 1899 remained in effect and continued to preserve Britain's superiority in Sudan until its abolition following the declaration of Sudan's independence in 1956.

To sabotage the doctrine of the unity of the Nile valley under the Egyptian crown advanced by Egypt and its Sudanese supporters, the

British embarked in the latter part of the 1940s on their official program of Sudanization (*al-sawdana*). The scheme was intended to create a new reality whereby qualified and well-trained Sudanese would gradually take over governmental and administrative posts as part of their preparation for self-rule. The British hoped this would accelerate the development of Sudanese nationalism and promote a separatist orientation.

In her illuminating and instructive study, *Living with Colonialism*, Heather Sharkey argues that while Sudanization indeed became official policy in the 1940s and 1950s, as "a term for a bureaucratic process, it can describe the entire colonial period."[4] She divides the process of Sudanization into several phases. The first phase, which she terms "the rise of a Sudanese bureaucracy,"[5] extended from the formation of the condominium regime in 1898 until the 1919 uprising. Gordon College, opened in 1902, became the cradle for a small administrative class intended to occupy mid-level government posts.

The period 1919–1924 witnessed growing strife in Anglo–Egyptian relations, which led to the removal of educated Egyptians from Sudan's administration and their replacement by hundreds of Gordon College graduates. This process was reinforced following the Sudanese uprising of 1924 and the assassination in Cairo of Sir Lee Stack, Sudan's governor-general. Egyptians in Sudan were blamed for being the source of anti-British agitation, and Egyptian troops as well as many school-teachers and civil servants were expelled to Egypt. Many Gordon College graduates fell out of favor by expressing anti-British sentiments, leading the British to foster an alliance with members of the more traditional Sudanese elite such as *umdas, shaykhs,* and *nazirs* as part of the intro-duction of the system of indirect rule applied in other British colonies in Africa.[6]

The period 1924–1935 marked the third phase, according to Sharkey. The "Southern Policy" of the early 1930s sought to separate the south of Sudan from the north administratively and culturally "in order to minimize the southward spread of Islam and of 'subversive' . . . ideas." British officials now favored southern Sudanese graduates of Christian missionary schools and southern chiefs for administrative posts at the expense of northern Sudanese graduates of Gordon College, who had filled these posts until then, fueling frustration and discontent among them. Nevertheless, the British desire to minimize Egyptian influence in Sudan as much as possible by preventing Egyptians from filling the posts that Egypt should man as an equal partner in the administration of Sudan resulted in the Sudanization of these posts. In addition, graduates of the Kitchener School of Medicine, which opened in 1924, as well as other talented Gordon College graduates, who were sent to the American University of Beirut to pursue advanced studies, were appointed to positions hitherto held by non-Sudanese.[7] It is noteworthy that until 1924, many of the physicians in Sudan were Egyptians and Syrians.[8]

The fourth phase, 1935–1938, saw a slow but steady increase in the Sudanization of the administration. The appointment of Sir Stewart Symes as governor-general was a positive step in this direction. His policy of decentralization, which meant "provincial self-government," contributed to the creation of more responsible jobs for Sudanese, coming now not only at the expense of Egyptians and Lebanese but also of junior British officials.[9]

Egyptian historian Yunan Labib Rizq argues that twelve years after the unilateral British removal of Egyptian military and civil officials from Sudan, the 1936 treaty reinstated the pre-1924 status quo as far as Egypt's presence in Sudan was concerned. Nevertheless, the 1936 treaty stipulated that British and Egyptian troops were "to be placed for the defense of the Sudan at the disposal of the Governor-General of the Sudan in addition to Sudanese troops." That is, the governor-general still had the authority to select his recruits based on "merit alone." Moreover, the Egyptian troops were under his command.[10] In addition, the inspector general of the Egyptian Irrigation Service, who was invited to attend the council, was also subordinated professionally to the governor-general, like other Egyptian officials. Although Egyptians were now allowed to immigrate to Sudan, and the Egyptian presence there increased following the 1936 treaty, the term of service of Egyptian officials and military personnel assigned to Sudan was short, and its length was determined by the Sudan government. In such a short period of time they could not develop close bonds with their Sudanese neighbors or intermingle culturally. For the British the goal was clear: Sudanization of as many posts as possible in all administrative fields and in the military. Rizq accuses the British-controlled Sudan government of discrimination against Egyptians, aimed at diminishing their influence, to undermine the project of the unity of the Nile valley.[11]

The final phase (1938–1956), according to Sharkey, witnessed the rise of Sudanese nationalism with a demand for self-rule. This process was followed by a declared British policy of Sudanization intended to prepare the Sudanese for self-government. The term *Sudanization* entered the vocabulary of the Sudan government in 1944 when Douglas Newbold, the civil secretary, "suggested a plan to province governors for 'dilution' of British administrative posts – a plan which he described as 'Sudanization.'"[12]

Rizq supports Sharkey's analysis with statistics. According to him, there was a marked increase in the number of Sudanese officials in the period 1920–1944. In 1920 they constituted 36.8 percent of the total throughout Sudan, whereas in 1944 they already constituted 82.8 percent (5,684 officials). As of 1924, the Sudan government began to send Gordon College graduates to study at the American University of Beirut, and those who returned upon graduation constituted the top brass of the new Sudanese intelligentsia. One such person was the notable Isma'il al-Azhari, a firm supporter of the unification with Egypt until 1953. He, nevertheless, would be the one to lead his country to full independence.[13]

Sharkey's division is convincing and accepted. The following chapter text evaluates and analyzes the impact of Sudanization upon the Egyptian doctrine of the unity of the Nile valley. The starting point of our discussion is 1944, when Newbold coined the term *Sudanization*. Egypt, for obvious reasons, rejected Newbold's line of argument. *Al-Ahram* responded to this plan, saying that Article 11 of the 1936 treaty stipulated that Britain and Egypt should work for the welfare of the Sudanese. Why, asked the daily, should this be interpreted as educating them toward self-government? Egyptians wanted to see the Sudanese gaining full independence along with Egypt and to share together the same rights within one kingdom.[14]

A report by the governor-general on the administration of Sudan for the year 1943 pointed out that the treaties of 1899 and 1936 with Egypt clearly stated that the aims of the Sudan government were to work for the welfare of the Sudanese. The report stressed that the Sudan government comprehended and perceived its role as the mentor of the Sudanese people in preparing them for local self-government. Shortly after the conclusion of World War II, the Sudan government took concrete steps in this direction by setting up municipal, town, and rural district councils in addition to the other, already existing local administrations led by tribal leaders. Moreover, it had already established provincial councils and an advisory council for northern Sudan (1944–1948) intending to include as many Sudanese as possible in the country's administration. In August 1943 the North Sudan Advisory Council Ordinance was enacted "in order to constitute more permanent machinery both for consultation between the central government and the Sudanese and for explanation of policy." The ordinance was intended to "meet the growing need for some form of constitutional association between the Sudanese and the central government, which is the logical outcome of the policy adopted some twenty years ago of associating the Sudanese with government in the sphere of local government."[15] That line of argument was negatively received in Egypt.

The mainstream press pondered sarcastically: why did the advisory council refer only to northern Sudan? What about the southern part of that country? *al-Ahram* enquired.[16] The rise of the new Sudanese intelligentsia and the nationalist movement went against Egypt's doctrine of the unity of the Nile valley. The Sudanization and the gradual decolonization of Sudan brought Anglo–Egyptian relations to their lowest ebb.

Although Sudanization had become Britain's declared policy, there were certain disagreements between the British embassy in Cairo and the Sudan government with regard to its pace and content. There was, nevertheless, a consensus among the two, that Sudan should be separated from Egypt. On 26 March 1946, in a letter to the Foreign Office and the Sudan government, British Ambassador to Cairo Sir Ronald Campbell urged the latter to speed up the pace of Sudanization. He noted that uncertainty among the Sudanese as to the future status of their country could be manipulated by the Egyptians to advance their unification plans. Campbell was convinced that "the only effective way of countering the present Egyptian political offensive in the Sudan is to give the Sudanese effective assurances on the question of the future administration of their country." It was not enough to say that "our policy is to bring them to the point of self-administration in order that they may choose their own future, or merely that the process of Sudanization will be speeded up. What they want to know is when that self-administration will be realized." Campbell therefore strongly recommended that the Sudan government should immediately, and independently of treaty negotiations in Cairo, proceed to draw up a detailed plan of Sudanization in consultation with the Sudanese. He stressed that it would be for the Sudan government to decide "how such consultation should be effected, whether regionally by District Commissioners through committees of local representatives or centrally by the Government through representatives of the political parties, or through both these channels ... it would be necessary to present the Sudanese delegates with specific proposals ... the announcement of what is intended should be made forthwith – if possible in the course of the next two or three weeks."[17]

A Foreign Office memorandum also noted that Sudanese public opinion was not content with the pace of Sudanization and moreover displeased with the uncertainty created by the British and the Sudan government with regard to the future of Sudan. The Egyptians were taking advantage of this situation, disseminating propaganda in a bid to win Sudanese trust. The Egyptians were particularly active in the field of education, promising "in addition to the amenities of their own secondary school in Khartoum, attractive terms for Sudanese to come to school and university in Egypt."[18]

The governor-general of Sudan, Hubert Huddleston (October 1940–April 1947), was not enthusiastic to implement Campbell's ideas, some of which he deemed unrealistic. On 6 April, he replied that the Sudan government had never promoted Sudanese officials and bureaucrats on the basis of considerations other than efficiency, although it often had "strained the word efficiency to its extreme limit" because "we wanted to help on Sudanization, not for political reasons." This policy, opined Huddleston, had not always been viewed favorably by British officials. Intensified Sudanization would harm the achievements the Sudan government had gained to that point. It was generally agreed that everyone in Sudan preferred "a passably efficient Home Government to a highly efficient one imposed from outside," he argued. For that reason, the Sudan government was trying to advance the development of local authorities. "If we create Sudanese Bureaucracy," as Campbell suggested, "we shall substitute an Alien Government for a Home one, and a not very efficient one at that." Huddleston opined that the Sudan government should foster the formation of local councils to protect the uneducated masses from being exploited by the small educated class. He expressed concern that if for political reasons Britain would establish "an 'alien' Sudanese bureaucracy I have little doubt that local authorities will rapidly wither and die and the small man will never become a free man."[19] Nevertheless, on 17 April 1946 Huddleston assured the advisory council that "the Sudanese will soon be governing their own country."[20]

The Sudanese delegation that arrived in Cairo in early April 1946 did not hide its desire, according to British officials, to see complete independence of Sudan and the Sudanization of all government posts and to decide for themselves, as a self-governing body, the future relationship between Sudan, Egypt, and Britain. The delegation was clear in its intention to secure an agreement that the Sudanization of all government posts "shall be effected in the shortest possible period." Practically speaking, the delegation demanded to be consulted regarding the progress of Sudanization of all government posts, with the British in the position of advisers and not as their masters.[21] It is noteworthy that the Egyptian historian 'Abd al-Rahman al-Rafi'i argued the opposite. That is, the Sudanese delegation arrived in Egypt to advance its policy of unification with Egypt. The delegation, he noted, raised the banner of anti-British imperialism and Sudanese–Egyptian unification.[22] Both the British and Rafi'i portrayed an inaccurate picture. As we noted above, the delegation favored some sort of union with Egypt after an independent Sudanese government was established, and only that government would decide the type and nature of the union.

On 22 April 1946, the Sudan government announced the formation of an administration conference to recommend "the next steps in associating the Sudanese more closely with the administration of the country."[23]

About a year later, on 31 March 1947, the conference submitted its report. It recommended "the creation of a legislative assembly to represent the whole of Sudan." The report called to replace the advisory council with an executive council with 50 percent Sudanese representation. The report also stated that the Sudanese would not be granted self-rule "unless they have previously been trained in the art of government and this in turn can be learnt only through the assumption of responsibility. This responsibility, at any given time, should be sufficiently great to extend fully the capacity of the Sudanese to shoulder it successfully, in this way their training will proceed at the greatest possible rate."[24]

The Egyptian government spotted many faults in the recommendations, one of which related to the composition of the legislative assembly. Ten out of its seventy members were to be appointed by the governor-general, and the rest were to be elected. However, the way they were to be elected was more of a nomination than a proper election – the southern representatives were to be appointed by the provincial governors. Therefore, the legislative assembly was not properly representative and would contain civil servants. The proposed system overlooked the vital issue of constitutional freedom. The Sudanese, it was stated, were on "the threshold of a social and political awakening. It is essential that the regime under which they live should ensure for them respect of personal freedom, freedom of opinion, freedom of faith, freedom of meeting, freedom of the press and all other freedoms without which they cannot live as free men and cannot feel secure ... These freedoms have to be regulated by law." In addition, too much power was given in the proposed system to the governor-general, who could approve or disapprove legislation. The Sudanese representatives in the legislative assembly enjoyed limited power, which was not sufficient to self-govern Sudan. They were to function as a consultative body rather than a proper legislature. The Egyptians argued that the British took upon themselves an exclusive role in training the Sudanese in self-government, leaving Egypt, the other party of the condominium, completely out of the game. Out of thirty members of the conference, twenty-five were government officials – British or British proxies – with no Egyptians at all. Prominent Sudanese political parties, including the representative of the educated class – the Graduates' General Congress – were also not included. The Egyptian government refused to endorse the conference's recommendations, and so did members of the Sudanese delegation in Cairo.[25]

The Egyptian government asserted that the issue of including Sudanese in the central government had already been under its consideration. Egypt wanted to see the Sudanese people capable of governing themselves. The Sudanese should not lose any opportunity of having the maximum share of government responsibility accorded to them. The Egyptian government deemed it its duty "to accept participation, for the time being, in drawing up a regime which would pave the way to self-government," provided that this regime was free from the said defects. It firmly believed that the delay in settling the Anglo–Egyptian dispute should not cause any delay in advancing the Sudanese on the path to self-government. The Egyptian government could not approve the recommendations made by the administration conference unless they were modified to meet Egypt's conditions.[26]

The governor-general of Sudan replied in a firm but fair manner to the Egyptian government's comments. The Sudan government agreed with the Egyptian government that the Sudanese should be given greater responsibility. But the extent of responsibility should be inextricably linked with their objective capabilities to undertake such responsibility without imperiling good government. The governor-general, however, opined that the fears of the Egyptian government that the legislative assembly would be no more than a consultative body were groundless. It would be the statutory legal body "to which all the legislation will have to be presented and which will have power to debate, pass, amend, or reject it," stated the governor-general. The legislative assembly, he went further, would have the power to question any acts or policy of the government and to pass resolutions thereon. The governor-general could not "divest himself of the basic powers which he exercises under the 1899 Agreement" so long as the present regime was in effect. The 1899 agreement empowered the governor-general to make laws and thereafter to notify the British and Egyptian governments of these laws. To introduce into the new ordinance a provision for the prior submission of all legislation, as the Egyptian government suggested, would therefore be at variance with the existing constitution. "Until Sudanese of sufficient administrative experience have emerged, it is necessary for the good government of the country to retain seats on the Executive Council for senior members of the administration, but it is hoped that before long Sudanese ministers will be appointed, and that the Executive Council will gradually evolve into a Council of Ministers."[27]

As part of the Sudan government's attempts to realize the recommendations of the administration conference, the Juba Conference was convened on 12 June 1947–13 June 1947. The conference addressed the issue of proper representation of the south in the future legislative assembly. A record of the proceedings, which was later published, stated that if Sudan was to become self-governing and self-dependent it should not be divided up into small, weak units. The sooner southern and northern Sudanese came together and worked together, the sooner they would begin to coalesce and cooperate in the advancement of their country. This would subsequently speed up unification. The British attitude and policy toward the south, as was already formulated in 1945, was reiterated: "It is only [through] economic and educational development that these peoples can be equipped to stand up for themselves in the future, whether their lot be eventually cast with Northern Sudan or with East Africa, or partly with each." It was argued that since 1945 the south witnessed both economic and educational development, and it became clearer that the south "by its history and by accidents of geography, river transport and so on, must turn more to the North rather than to Uganda or the Congo." The Sudan government, it was emphasized, should take into account the fact that the southern Sudanese were "distinctly African and Negroid, but that geography and economics combine ... to render them inextricably bound for future development to the Middle East and Arabs of the Northern Sudan and therefore to ensure that they shall be by educational and economic developments equipped to take their places in the future as socially and economically the equals of their partners of the Northern Sudan in the Sudan of the future."[28] Daly criticized the way in which the "Southern Policy" was revised. In his view it involved "elements of dishonesty and naivety, bordering on self-delusion."[29] British administrators in the south opposed the new plan of bringing the southerners under the control of Khartoum and warned of the "disaster inherent in such forced centralization."[30] As future events were to demonstrate disaster did happen.

The Egyptian press, as expected, condemned the Sudanization project pursued by the Sudan government and the British. The independent *al-Ahram*, which represented the Egyptian consensus, hinged its arguments on the statement issued on 22 September 1946 by the Sudanese National Front, to which also the Graduates' General Congress and other political groups represented by the Sudanese delegation in Cairo belonged. The National Front rejected what it described as "British insistence" on continuing the condominium in Sudan. The Sudanese called for a three-stage plan: termination of the condominium, full withdrawal of the British from the Nile valley, and subsequent unification of the valley. The Sudanization project was a British deception designed to preserve the status quo. The Sudanese people should stand behind the delegation and support its demands for the formation of a democratic Sudanese government within the framework of the unity of the Nile valley.[31]

Harsh criticism of British operations in Sudan was expressed by Salih 'Ashmawi, Hasan al-Banna's deputy. The British declared impudently that they were a democratic nation, the champions of freedom and democracy, yet the truth was the opposite; wherever they established colonies, their record was one of abject and bloody subjugation. In Sudan they had aggressively and illegally expelled the Egyptians in 1924, for the purpose of separating Sudan from Egypt and annexing it to their empire. The condominium treaty remained empty and effectively inoperative – the Egyptian officials were sent packing, and Egyptians were not allowed to enter Sudan. The British imposed obstacles on trade between the two parts of the valley, and moreover, until recently there was no telephone line between Egypt and Sudan. Even the conclusion of the 1936 treaty did not alter the situation. The appointment of an Egyptian economic expert in Khartoum was mere window dressing. The expert soon realized that his position was a British pretense, and after a short while he returned to Egypt. The British even split the only remaining prestigious Egyptian spiritual position, which bonded Egypt and Sudan – the supreme justice (*qadi al-qudat*). The British strategy was clear: divide and rule to effect full separation. The British had taken pains to persuade the Sudanese that their separation from Egypt would lead to full independence. Sudanese were now offered jobs from which until recently they were barred. The British plan of granting Sudanese separate citizenship was part and parcel of the Sudanization process. There was no freedom of opinion and speech in Sudan, and any opposition to British objectives was harshly repressed. Britain ruled Sudan in a tyrannical manner no different than Mussolini or Hitler. The Muslim Brothers expected the world to show strong opposition to the British dictatorship in Sudan.[32]

Huddleston, the governor-general of Sudan, was regarded in Egypt as the architect of Sudanization and the driving force behind the British plot to sabotage the unity of the Nile valley under the Egyptian crown. When it was announced on 15 March that he would end his term of office, many in Egypt heaved a sigh of relief. Academics and politicians believed that the Egyptian government should seize the opportunity and appoint an Egyptian or Sudanese as governor-general. Sayyid Sabri, an Egyptian jurist, maintained that since Nuqrashi's government decided to transfer its dispute with Britain to the United Nations and declared that the 1899 and 1936 treaties were no longer valid because they did not correspond with the UN Charter, Egypt should appoint an Egyptian as governor-general. The appointment of a British governor-general would continue Huddleston's policy of destroying the unity of the peoples of the valley. Moreover, even the treaty of 1899 did not stipulate that Britain's nominee for that post must be British.[33] Hanafi Mahmud Jum'a, a lawyer and senior member of the Nationalist Party, espoused a similar view.[34] Ibrahim Shukri, the deputy chairman of *Misr al-Fatat*, went further, sending a telegram to the palace in which he demanded to pass the following message to the king: "Egypt is waiting today for a notable royal decree appointing an Egyptian or Sudanese to the post of governor general of the Sudan."[35] In addition, *Ruz al-Yusuf* devoted much attention to the appointment of the new governor-general.

The king and his government, however, did not yield to the pressure to nominate an Egyptian or Sudanese as governor-general. On 17 March 1947, the king issued a royal decree appointing the British Robert Howe as Huddleston's successor. The British project of Sudanization was gathering momentum.[36]

On 18 May, a few months before Egypt referred its dispute with Britain to the Security Council, Nuqrashi accused Britain of implementing a policy in Sudan designed to separate Sudan from Egypt. The unification of the Nile valley was the deep desire of the people of the valley. Under such unity, the Sudanese people would be able to manage their affairs independently as they wished. The British had no right to station troops in either Sudan or Egypt.[37]

Official correspondence between King Faruq and Syrian President Shukri al-Quwwatli as well as official Syrian documents shed new light on Britain's efforts to weaken Egypt's foothold in Sudan in mid-1947 before the debate in the Security Council. Najib al-Armanazi, the Syrian ambassador to London, informed his superiors in Damascus that the British were willing to help King Faruq to establish his sovereignty over Libya on condition that he agree to the two following points:

the final settlement of the Sudan question and the recognition of Great Britain's privileged position in Tripolitania. Concluding an agreement on this matter is in the interest of Egypt itself from all points of view, for in this way Egypt would gain in the Sudan and in Libya something it could not even dream of. Also, the Arab point of view would gain considerably by suppressing the barrier imposed between the Arab countries and the countries of the Maghreb which remain under French influence and which we are wholly unable to liberate completely if they are not our neighbors.[38]

Referring to this proposal, Faruq told Quwwatli that the British machinations were intended to weaken Egypt's position as far as Sudan was concerned and to direct Egypt's wishes to other items. Moreover, stated Faruq, the British wanted to exploit our name and the crown at the same time to establish their sovereignty over Libya using Egypt "as a cover for their colonialist ambitions and that is what we absolutely refuse to countenance. Also, they would like us to work to light the fire in North Africa and to distance France. It is something we would like and which we shall all force ourselves to do, but in the interests of the Arabs and not in the interest of Great Britain which considers itself the guardian of the Arabs."[39]

On 14 September, shortly after the Egyptian failure in the UN, the vice governor-general of Sudan announced his government's plan to advance the Sudanization of the administration. The Sudan government, it was noted, would swiftly implement its plan to establish a legislative assembly and executive council.[40]

As expected, the Egyptians were furious with the British declaration. Most Sudanese newspapers were not pleased with its content, asserted *al-Ahram*, referring to the stand taken by a variety of political groups, starting with the secretary of the Graduates' General Congress, Muhammad al-Fadly, who declared that "under no circumstances we would deviate from our intention to see the end of the condominium and the realization of the unity of the Nile valley even at the cost of [government] violence directed at us." The newspaper *al-Sawt* wrote that because the Sudan government did not consult the Sudanese people before it published its intentions, the latter had the right to criticize its plan and even reject it. The Egyptian failure in the Security Council should have no effect on the desire to terminate the condominium. Sudanese political parties of all stripes, stressed *al-Sawt*, were determined to continue the jihad until their goals were achieved. The *New Sudan* newspaper took a similar approach.[41]

On 28 October 1947, the pro-Wafdist paper *al-Balagh*, in its prominent column "*Safhat Wadi al-Nil*" (Nile Valley Page), protested the Sudan government's ban on its publication in Sudan. *Al-Balagh* asserted that the British, who pretended to be democratic, banned *al-Balagh* because they concluded that the anti-imperialist paper, as the chief propagandist of the unity of the Nile valley, was sabotaging British separatist efforts.[42] *Al-Balagh* called upon the people of the Nile valley to launch a jihad against the British as the only way to stop their ugly democratic playacting in Sudan. The nationalist partisans of unification should take vigorous action to win the support of those Sudanese who allied themselves with British imperialism in the naive belief that the latter would grant them separate independence. The British misled and deceived the international community and some Sudanese by stating that their goal was to prepare the Sudanese people for self-government, using their Sudanization scheme to support their deceptive claim. However, the people of the Nile valley could no longer rely on support from the outside; rather they must take matters into their own hands.[43]

Al-Balagh expressed satisfaction with the decision made by *Hizb al-Ashiqqa'* (the Brothers Party) to dispatch a delegation to the United States and some European countries to advocate for the unity of the Nile valley. The paper urged members of the delegation to "open the eyes of world public opinion to the deviltry of imperialism in the Sudan."

The Egyptian government, which was tacitly cooperating with the Sudanization policy, should be inspired by al-Ashiqqa's move and do the same
by launching a public relations campaign worldwide to promote the legal
and historical rights of the peoples of the Nile valley to full sovereignty
over their land. The UN experience, remarked al-Balagh, clearly showed
the ignorance of countries worldwide to the complex issue of the Nile
valley. Moreover, the world should realize that the Sudan government as
well as major Sudanese institutions were totally dominated by British
officials who served London. The real purpose of the British was to
divide Sudan into two entities – North and South Sudan – shaped and
constructed in accordance with British interests.[44] The paper reported
that Sudanese who served in the public service complained that the
British were campaigning aggressively to root out their culture, including
the scorning of Islam – the common religion of the people of the valley.
The British took pains to disseminate their ideas and values by founding
and managing schools, through which they imposed the British educational system upon the people of the valley.[45]

In its column "Safhat Wadi al-Nil," al-Balagh placed greater emphasis
on the voices of unionists representing the educated class from within
Sudan. For instance, in December 1947, it closely monitored the interrogation of Muhammad Amin al-Husayni, a lawyer and editor of the paper
Sawt al-Sudan, by the Khartoum police, following an article he published
under the heading "The Head of the Beast" (Ra's al-Hayya). Husayni
was questioned, inter alia, by his interrogators:

Q: What was the meaning of the wording "by these Satans"?
Answer: Imperialism.

Q: Did you mean the English?
Answer: Yes.

Q: And what did you mean by using the wording "it would happen just by
means of proper Jihad"?
Answer: Resistance to imperialism by all possible means.

Q: When you wrote "Jihad" did you mean war?
Answer: Yes, if possible.

Q: What did you mean by saying "his satanic interests"?
Answer: The plundering of the liberties of groups of peoples and the military
and economic occupation of their land.

Q: What was your meaning by saying "those who bound themselves to the
imperialist wagon"?
Answer: The elements who call themselves "freedom fighters."

Q: What did you mean by saying "the methods employed by imperialism"?
Answer: Anti-Egyptian attacks through newspapers used by the British in
the Sudan.

Q: Don't you think this article may result in growing hatred directed at the Front struggling for independence?
Answer: The criticism is mutual ... I don't understand why the [Sudan] government made the efforts to protect that Front from criticism. People should understand what they want.

The purpose of the interrogation was clear: the British officials in Sudan, who took pains to advance Sudanization and subsequently separation, had a twofold tactic: first, to encourage separatist and anti-unionist trends in Sudan; and second, to discourage and intimidate unionists and pro-Egyptian elements, who acted against British interests.[46] *Al-Balagh* disputed the international legality of the legislation issued by the Sudan government in relation to the implementation of Sudanization. The 1899 treaty granted the governor-general the authority to administer Sudan, but not sovereign powers. Sudan was not a British colony. The Ottoman *firmans* (orders issued by the sultan), which had legal validity until the disintegration of the Ottoman Empire, were taken over by the Egyptian king. Therefore, any legislation in Sudan should be subject to the king's agreement. Accordingly, Egypt had the prerogative to introduce legal reforms.[47]

Egypt remonstrated that the process of Sudanization, particularly as implemented by Huddleston, was not intended to improve Sudanese welfare or to advance them toward self-government. Those Sudanese qualified to occupy administrative posts were usually given junior positions under full British control and supervision. Moreover, the senior jobs staffed by British were not included in the Sudanization plans. The Sudan government had an ulterior motive – cutting off Sudan from Egypt. The British employed a divide-and-rule method not only in the sphere of civil posts but also in the field of religion. They usurped the highest religious-judicial post, traditionally occupied by an Egyptian, and transferred it to a Sudanese proxy under the pretext of Sudanization.[48]

Nuqrashi too dwelled on this issue. He was very critical of the governor-general of Sudan for his constant effort to diminish Egypt's role in the condominium by replacing senior Egyptian officials with Sudanese and, by doing so, advancing British separatist policy. A case in point was the governor-general's decision not to renew the term of Sheikh Hasan Ma'mun, an Egyptian who served as the supreme justice in the Sudan government, beyond January 1947. Ma'mun was to be replaced by a Sudanese judge, Sheikh al-Tahir, who was depicted as "well-experienced in Sudanese Sharia courts." Tahir had served in the legal department of the Sudan government as a junior judge on sharia affairs; he excelled and was appointed in 1941 inspector general of the sharia courts all over Sudan. In 1942 he became the Sudan mufti, and in early 1947, in addition to his mufti duty, he acted as Ma'mun's deputy. In an effort to make the governor-general reconsider his decision, Nuqrashi held talks with the British ambassador to Cairo, during which he stressed the significance of that position in maintaining the strong and inseparable spiritual and religious bonds between Egypt and Sudan. These bonds were also related to the application of sharia law in Sudan. Egypt, emphasized Nuqrashi, had no intention to deprive the Sudanese of their right to hold senior positions, and therefore, his government was willing to pay the salary of the Egyptian supreme justice and also appoint a Sudanese judge to a senior position in the sharia courts in Sudan and thus increase the number of Sudanese serving in the courts. The British ambassador promised to bring Nuqrashi's proposal to the attention of the Foreign Office.[49]

Nevertheless, Nuqrashi's efforts were in vain. Persuaded by James Robertson, civil secretary to the Sudan government, who was determined to go ahead with the plan, London, which had, until then, wanted to avoid further strife with Egypt over Sudan, approved Tahir's nomination. In October 1947, the Sudan government announced that Sheikh Ahmad al-Tahir, the Sudan mufti, was to replace Ma'mun. The British Sudanization plan was gathering momentum.[50]

As early as 1948, the governor-general of Sudan enacted an ordinance setting up the legislative assembly and an executive council to advise the governor-general. The legislative assembly, which was elected directly and indirectly, was completely Sudanese (except for four British members), and the majority of the executive council was also Sudanese. Still, the governor-general enjoyed supreme authority, which allowed him to overrule decisions made by the two Sudanese institutions. In addition, the British reserved the most important posts for themselves – the civil, financial, and legal secretaryships. More importantly, not all Sudanese parties cooperated with the governor-general's program. The Khatmiyya, originally a Sufi order dominated by the Mirghani family that became an influential religious-political group during the condominium period and favored some form of association with Egypt, boycotted both institutions, thus creating a situation whereby the newly formed state authorities were not truly representative of the entire Sudanese political spectrum.[51] It was only in 1950 that the governor-general managed to appoint a commission of fourteen members drawn from all political parties including the Khatmiyya (the pro-unionist *Ashiqqa'* remained outside) to recommend amendments to the constitution.[52]

The advisory council for northern Sudan began its discussions in early March 1948, on the bill related to the formation of the legislative and the executive councils. When the issue of the relations between the Sudan government and the governments of Britain and Egypt was raised, the advisory council chairman remarked that the legislative council would be entitled to discuss these relations, yet would be prohibited from enacting laws that would affect them. Sudan was not a sovereign state and therefore could not ratify treaties with foreign countries. However, economic agreements should – according to the legal advisor – not require special legislation, and the council could approve them. Every bill discussed in the legislative council would still have to be presented to both the Egyptian and the British governments for ratification before becoming law. At the end of deliberations, the advisory council expressed its basic agreement to the formation of the new councils, yet called to make sure that at least half of its members would be Sudanese and that the executive council would include Sudanese ministers. The Sudan government was asked to implement the Executive and Legislative Councils bill as soon as possible, and the law took effect on 19 June 1948.[53] The new constitutional reform left the supreme authority in the hands of the governor-general. He could appoint or discharge ministers and approve or cancel laws promulgated by the legislative council. Moreover, he was the supreme commander of the armed forces. The new constitutional reform satisfied neither Sudanese nor Egyptians. An era of Sudanese social and political discontent had begun.

The Egyptian government refused to ratify the new constitutional reform in Sudan. It argued that the reform, introduced by the governor-general without asking its approval, contravened the condominium treaty, as the governor-general was subservient to both the Egyptian and the British crowns. The Egyptians therefore refused to participate in the executive council, which was to replace the governor-general's council. The bone of contention touched on two central issues: first, the Egyptians were offered two seats only – irrigation and economy. They wanted equal representation to the British (the executive council was to have twelve to fifteen members, at least half of them Sudanese). Second, the British wanted a twenty-five-year transitional period, during which Sudan would be administered in line with the 1899 treaty, whereas the Egyptians agreed to a transitional period of three years only, during which the Sudanese would be prepared by Egypt toward self-government and thereafter manage their own affairs within the framework of the unity of the Nile valley under the Egyptian crown.[54]

Neither the British government nor the governor-general paid particular attention to the Egyptian government's remonstration. The newly elected legislative council assembled for its first meeting on 16 December 1948. Most of Sudan's main political parties boycotted the elections. The pro-unionist parties launched an anti-government campaign, and leading figures such as Azhari were arrested. This was followed by social discontent manifested by waves of workers' strikes, which continued in 1950.[55]

Among the pro-unionists, who led the anti-British struggle in both Egypt and Sudan, was Tawfiq Ahmad al-Bakri, a preeminent poet and leading Sudanese intellectual, who had been educated in Egyptian institutions and was in close working relations with Taha Husayn and other renowned Egyptian intellectuals. Commenting on the recent developments in Sudan he condemned the anti-democratic actions taken by the British to punish large segments of Sudanese society, who boycotted the elections to the legislative council, as well as demonstrators and strikers. The elections were a failure since only nineteen percent of the Sudanese participated – proving the inadequacy of the new constitutional reform designed to perpetuate British rule over Sudan. The desire to see the unity of the Nile valley under the Egyptian crown was shared by most Sudanese people, who boycotted the elections and expressed willingness to have neither the current administration nor the new legislative council in Sudan. The world should know that the British had constantly diffused lies saying that the Sudanese were against union with Egypt. Political instability and social discontent would continue to prevail in that part of the world as long as the international community would not force the British to withdraw from the Nile valley.[56]

'Ali Mahir, a former prime minister and King Faruq's confidant, rejected offhandedly what he deemed as British Sudanization maneuvers, which were doomed to failure because the inhabitants of the Nile valley had a different agenda. He called upon both Egyptians and Sudanese to define first the common goals of the valley and then piece them together in "a covenant for the liberation of the valley." Egypt, he stated, did not wish to seize full control over Sudan but to share power with the Sudanese based on devotion and loyalty to a single homeland. Mahir's views were not exceptional and presented the Egyptian national consensus on the Sudan question:

If I were a Sudanese native, I would do everything in my power to be tied with Egypt regardless of my love for freedom and independence ... I believe that the Sudan can gain its freedom only through Egypt ... the future of Egypt and the Sudan is a unified government. When Egypt demands unity it calls for the liberation of the Sudan because the latter's land is part of the homeland – the Sudanese and Egyptians are one people – the people of the Nile valley ... Sudan and Egypt constitute the southern and northern regions of the valley. Sudanese and Egyptians are partners in power – there is no ruler-and-ruled relationship – their rights and duties are equal – they constitute one people whose loyalty is to one throne that is of King Faruq.[57]

The Egyptian government refused to take part in the executive council. Two positions previously occupied by Egyptians – controllers of education and economy in Sudan – remained unoccupied. *Al-Ahram* urged the government to appoint two worthy Egyptians to these important posts, otherwise Egypt's centrality and interests in Sudan would be harmed. Traditionally, the economic expert was responsible for fostering economic and commercial relations between Egypt and Sudan. In the field of education Egypt had played a pivotal role in nurturing and developing the Sudanese educational system and should not write off its achievements and let the British sabotage Egypt's interests by taking control of this "delicate and sensitive" field. Official Egyptians in Sudan should treat and regard Sudanese as brothers and be familiar with their social customs and integrate into their everyday life.[58]

One of the issues that caused confusion amongst pro-unionist Sudanese was the Egyptian law of citizenship and its application to Sudanese living in Egypt. A case in point was the candidacy of Sudanese to the Egyptian parliament in the coming elections (January 1950). In an article published in *al-Ahram* by Riyad al-Shams on the candidacy of Sudanese to the Egyptian parliament, he argued that they should first declare their Sudanese citizenship. This in fact ran counter to the Egyptian law of citizenship, which did not differentiate between Egyptian and Sudanese, granting both equal political and civil rights. 'Ali al-Barir, an advocate of the unity of the Nile valley and a member of the Sudanese delegation, condemned Shams for going too far with his statement – even the British did not dare to promulgate a Sudanese law of citizenship because they were restricted by the 1899 treaty. The distinction made by Shams between Sudanese and Egyptian citizenship was meaningless. The entrance of Sudanese candidates to the Egyptian parliaments would be vivid proof that the unity between the two sides of the valley was an eternal phenomenon – a hard blow to British imperialism, asserted Barir.[59]

By late 1951, the Egyptian Wafd government viewed the Sudanization project as a complete failure as far as the development and progress of Sudan were concerned. A pamphlet issued by the Nahhas government under the title *The Egyptian Question 1882–1951* was a severe indictment against the British long- and short-term policies toward Sudan. Under the camouflage of "protection" the British created divisions between the people of Sudan, asserted the Egyptian government. Moreover, after fifty years of "almost" exclusive British administration, the record of achievements in the field of education was poor – 95 percent remained illiterate. Industry was not developed at all, and there was no progress in the field of agriculture. The Sudan government created an educational system that would perpetuate the state of dependency of the Sudanese on their British masters. Very few were entitled to become bureaucrats or minor officials. British officials in Sudan took pains, by means of propaganda and other methods, to neutralize and root out large segments of Sudanese, who demanded the unity of the Nile valley: "In the mosques the traditional weekly prayer for the legitimate Sovereign was suppressed. Severe censorship has been established to ban all newspapers – whether Egyptian or Sudanese – if they expressed an opinion or supplied information not endorsed by the British administration of the Sudan."[60]

As part of their segregation policy, the Nahhas government asserted, the British raised obstacles to diminish and subsequently stop natural Egyptian immigration to Sudan. They prevented the development of modern means of communications between the northern and southern parts of the valley. The post of *qadi al-qudat* – a religious function that symbolized the spiritual bonds between Sudanese and Egyptians – was taken away by the British and was transferred to local Sudanese. Egypt's rights based on the 1899 and 1936 treaties were denied. Egyptian officials were not allowed to enter Sudan. Those Egyptians who used to occupy high positions in the Sudan administration were gradually removed. The British hindered the natural cultural relations between Egypt and Sudan, and opposed Egypt's efforts to develop the field of public health in Sudan. The British goal was to create a separate Sudanese nationality and encourage Sudan to secede from Egypt. The British also employed a policy of dividing the northern and southern parts of Sudan. Egypt, for its part, made no distinction between an Egyptian and a Sudanese. Thus, for instance, Sudanese could aspire to occupy the highest functions in Egypt including undersecretaries of state, distinguished civil servants, and high-ranking military officers.[61]

The allegations and assertions made by the Egyptian government were arguable. However, despite the fact that the British were the dominant party in the condominium rule, Egypt could not plead blamelessness since it also bore some responsibility for the general development of Sudan since the early nineteenth century. As future events were to demonstrate, the Sudanization program with all its faults was a catalytic agent in creating the required conditions for Sudanese independence. The following section discusses the politics of education within Sudan and its effect on the development of Sudanese territorial nationalist awareness.

Who Is a Better Educator? Anglo–Egyptian Rivalry and Sudanese Education

As we have seen, much scholarly attention has been lavished upon the relations between Great Britain and Egypt from the beginning of the condominium (1899) in Sudan up until the Suez Crisis (1956). Most of the studies have focused on the political aspects of this complex relationship, whereas the education system in Sudan has usually been mentioned marginally, in the broader context of British or Egyptian activity in Sudan. A relatively small number of studies have discussed more specifically the matter of the historical development of the education system in Sudan during this period, focusing on the changes in education policy in both the northern and the southern regions of Sudan.[62]

There have also been several studies of the influence of political, economic, and administrative developments on the progression of the education system in Sudan. Foremost among these is Mohamed Omer Beshir's comprehensive book *Educational Development in the Sudan, 1898–1956*.[63] Also noteworthy is Lilian Passmore Sanderson and Neville Sanderson's book *Education, Religion and Politics in Southern Sudan 1899–1964*,[64] which focuses primarily on the more underdeveloped southern Sudan, where the level of education was far inferior to that of the north, the location of the civil service. Its main focus is on administrative developments and, above all, studying the politics of education. Iris Seri-Hersch examines the restructuring of the relationships between Britain and its colonies and the profound impact it had for Sudanese politics and education during and after World War II. Her study focuses on the politics of literacy in the last decade of the condominium regime (1946–1956).[65] Heather Sharkey shows that the founding of Gordon Memorial College in 1902 was motivated primarily by politics rather than by financial considerations. True, the college served as a training ground for the bureaucracy, but more significantly, it served as "crucible for nationalism."[66] The graduates of Gordon College were the bearers of modern Sudanese nationalism and were groomed for government service.[67]

These studies, however, did not consider the development of the educational system in Sudan in the broader political context of the escalating rivalry between Britain and Egypt for influence in Sudan in the latter years of World War II and its immediate aftermath. The remaining part of the chapter aims to bridge the lacuna left by these previous studies and to contextualize the developments in Sudanese education between 1943 and 1953 as a facet of the Anglo–Egyptian political struggle over the determination of the future destiny of this region. At first the discussion focuses on the interplay between British educational policy and foreign policy in Sudan, relying mostly on primary British archival material unavailable to the mentioned studies. In this section we will see that British education policy in Sudan was partly driven by altruistic motivations and considerations of pertinent needs, but also, and primarily, by broader British interests in the Middle East and colonial Africa. The development of the Sudanese educational system was an integral part of the British policy of Sudanization, which was designed to neutralize Egyptian ambitions to unify the Nile valley. The last section of the chapter presents the Egyptian response to the British practices.

Sowing the Seeds of Sudanese Nationalism: Colonialist Politics of Education

The issue of "mass education" in African societies was addressed in a profound report by the Advisory Committee on Education in the Colonies on 31 December 1943. The committee's findings noted that investment in education should be directed to both adults and youth, estimating that it would be possible to "eradicate ignorance in the colonies" within twenty to thirty years with the proper institutional support.[68]

It is worth noting that this report did not constitute a reversal of longstanding educational policy in the colonies. Thus, for example, a pamphlet published by the Sudan government bearing the title *The Sudan: A Record of Progress, 1898–1947* noted that the British director of the education office in Sudan had already determined in 1900 the objectives of his office were as follows:

1. The provision of vernacular schools to diffuse elementary education among the masses to enable them to understand the elements of the system of government.
2. The creation of a technical school to train a small class of competent artisans.
3. The beginning of primary schools with classes for the training of schoolteachers and headmasters to produce a small administrative class for entry to the government service.[69]

Yet, there was considerable delay in the effort to realize these objectives, due to budgetary constraints in the various departments, as well as hindrances stemming from the particular character of the locals. As additional resources were eventually found, the local population's consciousness of the need for education on numerous levels advanced. Already in the 1930s, there was substantial progress in the building of the general education system in Sudan, as reflected in the gradual but systematic entrance of trained Sudanese into positions in the civil service. The objective and subjective difficulties engendered by World War II did not impinge on the development and progress of the education system.[70]

The report divided Sudan into two educational districts – the north and the south. In both districts non-governmental schools functioned prior to the arrival of the British, established and operated by foreign communities or by Sudanese initiatives, and constituted an important contribution to the education system in Sudan. Moreover, in the decade preceding the report, secondary schools were established upon Sudanese initiative; in 1947 there were estimated to be nine of these. In addition, two non-governmental Sudanese high schools were established. The report highly estimated the value of these schools, with the government assisting them by means of scholarships, advice, guidance, and supervisory staff.[71]

In the period preceding the arrival of the British in Sudan, there were numerous *kuttab* (*Khalwa* – Islamic elementary schools) in the villages, which taught Quran and offered a rather limited curriculum and inferior logistical infrastructure. Such schools were active in Sudan before the country was occupied by Muhammad 'Ali. However, the latter's educational policy was to encourage the continuity of such institutions as he gave grants to local schools and trained religious teachers (*fekis*). He also introduced the Sudanese to agricultural studies, and the Sudan government employed those who graduated from Egyptian institutions. Many Sudanese conducted their religious studies in al-Azhar with the Egyptian government subsidizing their studies. In 1853, Khedive Abbas (1848–1854) established the first modern primary school in Khartoum similar to those that existed in Egypt. However, the school was closed a year later.[72] Under Khedive Isma'il (1863–1879), the development of the education system in Sudan gathered momentum. More Sudanese were admitted to al-Azhar, and seven primary schools were established between 1863 and 1865, at Khartoum (124 students), Berber, Dongula, Kordufan, Kassala, Suakin, and Sennar (75 students in each). These schools were based on the Egyptian system and were supervised by the Egyptian department of education. In addition, two vocational training schools were established in 1870. Education in the field of agriculture also developed considerably. Khedive Tawfiq (1879–1892) continued to develop the educational system, and the highlight of his period was the foundation of the school of medicine and pharmacy.[73] Beshir concluded that the Turco–Egyptian rule laid the foundation for the development of modern education in Sudan.[74]

The first measure implemented by British authorities upon their arrival was an effort to improve these schools by giving simple methodology courses to teachers who showed promise and by providing direct supervision and monetary support. Later, in 1934, schools were established in the villages, which integrated some of the functions that the *kutab* had filled. They were funded and controlled by the district administrative authorities, who were subordinate to the state education system. In 1947 there were 239 of these schools, each with 50 pupils. This number would grow to 460 within a few years.[75]

One of the aims of the elementary schools was to provide a more balanced education to those children who did not want or were unable to continue their schooling to the secondary level. According to the education plan for the years 1947–1956, 56 percent of the children in the cities and 29 percent in rural areas would be integrated into the elementary school system. The number of elementary schools for girls also grew substantially in subsequent years, reaching 69 in 1947. In addition, three secondary schools were established, and a high school was in the process of being established. The first woman admitted to Gordon College in 1946 was a landmark for girls' education.[76]

As a rule, most of the secondary schools were not state-run, and the level of instruction at the beginning was inferior. In the elementary schools, here too there was a shortage of qualified teachers. After 1932 there was some improvement, and in 1947 there were already thirteen state secondary schools, and the outlook for further growth was promising.

Gordon College was named after Charles Gordon (1833–1885), a British general who was active in the Egyptian and British governments in Sudan.[77] The college opened in 1902 and included a vocational school, two elementary schools, and a small teacher training department. High school education began only in 1905 and constituted the main focus of the college from that point on. In 1946 another government school was opened in Hantub in the Blue Nile region, with 300 boarding students, and in 1949 another government high school was planned. It had been determined in 1938 that high school final examinations would follow the format of the Cambridge School Certificate Examination. In the first year the examinations were held, there was a substantial success, with 20 out of 22 students passing. In the first years of World War II the failures outnumbered the successes, but in the years following the war there was substantial improvement,[78] as Table 4.1 shows.

Table 4.1 *Student Enrollment and Graduation, 1938–1946*

	1938	1939	1940	1941	1942	1943	1944	1945	1946
Enrolled	22	70	81	57	61	99	101	113	123
Graduates	20	25	20	33	46	56	72	81	91

In terms of higher education, the Lord Kitchener Medical School was established in 1924, and selected teachers were sent for training at the American University of Beirut in that year as well. In subsequent years schools were established for the sciences, arts, engineering, veterinary medicine, agriculture, medicine, law, and education. The Earl De La Warr Commission,[79] which began operating in 1937, recommended making the Gordon College high school independent and turning the college into an institute of higher education, a sort of university. The college moved to a new campus in Wadi Sayedna, about 25 km from Khartoum, which included student dormitories. Due to wartime constraints the implementation of the commission's recommendations was deferred to the end of the war, and Gordon College in its new format was opened officially only in February 1945.

All these aims were achieved in the northern part of Sudan. In southern Sudan, however, the educational picture was decidedly bleak. There was real difficulty building and developing the system there, since the south was, in many respects, more backward than the north, and the multiplicity of languages and dialects there did not facilitate the task. Although aware of the need to develop education in the south, the government did not do enough to change the situation. The government, which was situated in the north, focused its attention mainly on the development of that region. To develop education in the south, the government required appropriate human and material resources; as these were not available, they made in the meantime use of Christian missionaries, some of whom were already active in the south. In 1925, the government appointed an educational supervisor to be based in the south for the purpose of advising and supervising the awarding of assistance grants for education. This measure brought substantial progress in the effort to build an education system in the south. Elementary schools were established, along with secondary schools and commerce schools. Those with relevant education were assigned to key positions, and teacher training facilities were improved. The increase in the number of supervisory staff enabled the government to tighten supervision of education. Thus, for example, an assistant to the government director of education was appointed in the southern district. The government also made efforts to improve the curricula as far as possible. Despite these efforts, a huge gap remained between the state of the education system in the south and that in the more developed north.[80]

On 11 February 1944, Christopher W. M. Cox, who was responsible for education in Sudan between 1937 and 1939, and who served as semi-private educational advisor to the colonial secretary, prepared a rather detailed report on the education system in Sudan. He submitted this report to Douglas Newbold, head of the civil secretary office, who forwarded it to Sir Hubert Huddleston, the British governor-general of Sudan.[81] Cox's comprehensive report opened with an expression of great appreciation for the Sudan government, which, even in difficult wartime circumstances, continued to advance and develop education – post-secondary schools, high schools, secondary schools, and education for girls, all this despite the shortage of trained professional man power and the lack of proper facilities.[82] The body of the report analyzed the state of education in Sudan. Although an eight-year education plan (1938–1946) had been prepared in 1938,[83] and the process of reorganization of the schools of higher learning was supposed to have begun in the first stages of the plan, in actuality, Cox noted, they began operating only in 1941.

Cox recommended that the British government compensate Sudan, even if only symbolically, for its contribution to the British war effort, by reopening Gordon College in the course of 1944. This important gesture should be accompanied by the extension of monetary scholarships similar to those awarded in British colonies, even though Sudan did not have the status of a colony. The success of a "higher college" as an academic institution awarding advanced degrees largely depended on the nature and effectiveness of the recommendations of the Asquith Committee[84] – the ability to build a professional teaching and research faculty separate from the University of London – and the effectiveness of their implementation in Sudan.

Cox also recommended appointing a person of appropriate abilities and virtues to direct the college and creating the additional function of a deputy – someone well-versed in the ins and outs of Sudan – rather than the then-current function of assistant director. Cox recommended unifying all the institutions for higher education under a single aegis – the Gordon Memorial Higher College, which would operate in the "Gordon College Building." The college should have an autonomous status free from government interference in its administration. This would enable the college to develop into one of the best institutions of higher learning in colonial Africa. He recommended applying the supervision procedures practiced in the Kitchener School of Medicine, as in other institutions of higher learning, involving annual audits by external, particularly British, professionals. These procedures had contributed greatly, in his estimation, to the development of the high standards and reputation of the school of medicine. As stated, in his view, the school of medicine ought to be integrated into a single college along with the schools of agriculture and engineering. Regarding the latter two, Cox considered their planning and reorganization to be among the most important achievements of the war period, along with the development of the technical schools.[85]

Gordon College: A Breeding Ground for
Sudanese Nationalism

Governor-General Huddleston was impressed by the Cox report and adopted its recommendations regarding Gordon College. In mid-June 1944, he sent a letter to the British ambassador in Cairo, Lord Killearn, requesting a grant of £1 million from the British government for the academic and logistical needs of the renewed Gordon College in Khartoum. The ambassador forwarded the request to Foreign Secretary Eden, adding his own support and providing two reasons to approve it. First, from a practical point of view, it would greatly aid the development of the education system in Sudan. Second, from the political point of view, it would contribute to the improvement of relations with local power centers and constitute a gesture of gratitude to Sudan for its contribution to the British war effort.[86]

Huddleston opened his letter with the observation that the political awareness of the Sudanese had advanced impressively in recent years. He credited this to the participation of the Sudanese in the war, as opposed to the Egyptians, who had been passive in the battles the British had fought in the region. This state of affairs highlighted the difference between British relations with the Egyptians and with the Sudanese. Egyptian ties to Sudan, Huddleston wrote, were based on similar language and religion, close commercial ties, and, no less important, mutual dependence on the water of the Nile. Economically capable Sudanese, mainly from among the educated classes, had visited Egypt frequently during the war and were in closer contact than ever before with Egyptian politics and society. While many of them were put off by the corruption and inefficiency of the Egyptian administration, there was no doubt, in Huddleston's view, that Egyptian political and religious propaganda in Sudan had a substantial degree of influence, and that Egyptian promises of aid, which had in the past met with Sudanese disregard, were being received with greater interest in recent times. Huddleston wrote that a separate Sudanese nationality was accepted as a fait accompli in Egypt, and noted the growing tendency to integrate Sudanese in various Egyptian frameworks on an equal basis. Moreover, Egypt even considered granting status of dominion to Sudan. Beyond this, the Egyptian offers of social services and material aid – such as the recent opening of the high school in Khartoum and the offer to establish a large Egyptian hospital in Sudan – as well as Egyptian promises to expand commerce with Sudan and increase the Sudanese share of profits in that commerce – all these could not but be attractive to a poorer country like Sudan. Despite this, Huddleston noted, most Sudanese looked suspiciously on Egyptian overtures in Sudan, except for a small but significant group interested in deepening the ties with Egypt out of profit and utilitarian motives.[87]

Despite this Egyptian initiative, argued Huddleston, the battle over Sudanese public opinion was not lost for Britain. Huddleston tried to persuade, by use of statistics, that the Sudanese contribution to the British war effort in terms of personnel and financial contributions was greater than that of any other territory in the Middle East (such as Egypt, Palestine, Syria, Iraq, and Iran), and was, therefore, worthy of notice and appreciation. Huddleston clarified that his request for economic assistance stemmed from political rather than financial considerations. In light of his estimation that Egypt would set the question of the future of Sudan at the top of its postwar agenda, compensating the Sudanese for their part in the war in material terms, to bolster the Sudan government's efforts to reduce and weaken Egyptian propaganda and claims regarding the future of Sudan, took on greater urgency.[88]

Huddleston recommended that the British government provide a £1 million grant to be dedicated to Gordon College, intended to be reopened in its new format, integrating all the schools of higher learning. Investment in higher education would be a worthy objective for several reasons: first, without higher education it would not be possible to achieve self-rule; second, it was very important to the Sudanese intelligentsia; and third, much attention was given by the Colonial Office to higher education in other African territories. The Sudanese, in his estimation, were alert to the importance of higher education and derived a great deal of encouragement from Cox's visit to Sudan in early 1944 and from his conclusions regarding this issue. Therefore, a £1 million grant, which would produce an annual dividend of 3 percent, i.e., £30,000, would be an important and constant financial contribution to the new college, thus achieving both objectives Huddleston had mentioned, i.e., a large and generous gesture by Britain to Sudan as a sign of gratitude for its part in the British war effort as well as a substantial material aid package that would help maintain and expand the education system throughout the country.[89]

Huddleston's request was greeted with enthusiasm by Foreign Secretary Eden, who accepted all the governor-general's arguments in support of extending the requested grant. Eden referred the request to the British Exchequer with a warm recommendation to approve the grant.[90] A letter sent by Sir Alexander Cadogan of the Foreign Office to Sir Richard Hopkins of the Exchequer stressed above all the political importance of the grant:

That the Sudan has deserved well of us in this war is not open to doubt. That we should continue to play the dominant role in guiding the Sudan to nationhood

I regard as an axiom based on a worthy tradition of some forty-five years and on our own wider interests in Africa. That our position is about to be challenged by Egypt is evident from all reports reaching us. Defensive tactics against Egypt are not enough – though they may soon have to be adopted. What is required at this moment is a gesture which will appeal to the imagination of the Sudanese and convince them that we remote beings in London are no less interested in their welfare than in that of the colonies, and no less interested than the King or the politicians in Egypt.[91]

The supporters of the grant were in for a great disappointment, however, when, several weeks later, the Exchequer denied the request due to the budget deficit. In his response to Cadogan, Hopkins explained that the British government was facing severe difficulties with any request for foreign aid funds. He also mentioned the difficulties of persuading the Americans of "the severity of our economic position if we continue dispensing moneys abroad as we were wont to do in the past."[92]

Douglas Newbold, the civil secretary in the Sudan government, expressed his frustration at the decision. In a letter to the British embassy in Cairo he suggested asking the Exchequer to reevaluate the issue of the grant. He felt that the denial of the grant was liable to harm British interests in Sudan and would disappoint the Sudanese, who would interpret it as ingratitude on Britain's part. Newbold derided the Exchequer's argument regarding the anticipated negative position of the United States, saying: "I thought the American thesis was that we [Britain] neglected and exploited our colonies."[93] The embassy in Cairo replied that it had recently received instructions from the Foreign Office to cut foreign expenditures as much as possible, except for vital projects. It would have to prove that denying the grant request would have a significant negative impact on the political situation in Sudan.[94]

Huddleston decided to take up the gauntlet and to try to prove that the grant was vital. In a letter to Killearn in Cairo on 7 December 1944 he vehemently reiterated the arguments he had raised in favor of the grant in his original request. He focused on the political aspects, i.e., the rivalry between British and Egyptian influence in Sudan. He reemphasized the sophisticated propaganda campaign Egypt was conducting in Sudan with the aim of gaining Sudanese support for Egypt's future maneuvers regarding the dispensation of Sudan. To the descriptions of Egyptian activity in Sudan in his previous letter, he added data underscoring the urgency of the matter. Thus, for example, he argued that the cost of the high school the Egyptians had opened in Khartoum was £250,000, and the planned hospital was in the same cost range. Egypt also allowed Sudanese to study at Egyptian universities at no expense, and in 1943,

158 Sudanese students were estimated to have studied in Egypt at the expense of the Egyptian government.

Most Sudanese, he noted, were not interested in being governed by Egypt and recalled with great revulsion the period of Egyptian rule, but there was a small minority with an Egyptian orientation. He supported his contention that denial of the grant request would cause much pain in Sudan with citations from the Sudanese press expressing cynicism regarding British promises. If the Sudanese concluded that the denial of the grant request reflected a weakened British interest in Sudan, they would look to Egypt for development aid. The Sudanese reaction to the denial of the grant would be exacerbated by daily press reports of British grants to various colonies in Africa, while the Sudanese were not entitled to similar grants because they were not officially a colony. It would create the perception that Britain considered them eligible to bear the full brunt of the war effort and send their men to the front, but not to receive the material aid others were receiving. In the war years they provided products to the British army and the British supply office in Sudan at the lowest prices in the Middle East, thus contributing to significant savings for the British taxpayer.

Huddleston concluded his letter with the warning that if the British government did not take advantage of this last opportunity and approve the grant, it would lose the battle for the hearts and minds of the Sudanese to the growing pressure of Egyptian propaganda. The British, by their denial, were liable to bring about the collapse of a forty-five-year project in which they had invested great effort and cause it to fall into the "corrupt and inefficient" hands of the Egyptians – as the Sudanese were not yet prepared to take their destiny into their own hands.[95]

Killearn agreed to Huddleston's request to ask the Exchequer to reconsider its denial of the grant application. In a letter to Foreign Secretary Eden, Killearn reiterated and reinforced Huddleston's arguments in favor of the grant. Killearn was of the opinion that Sudan's "odd" international status, jointly administered by two countries and not defined as a British colony, did not imply that Sudan's request for monetary aid for advancing higher education was less important than those of the colonies. He saw no reason to discriminate and deny the aid to Sudan because of its formal ineligibility for British aid.

Killearn added additional data not mentioned in Huddleston's letter regarding the activity, interest, and involvement of Egypt in Sudanese affairs. In Egypt, he explained, a serious proposal to establish a separate government ministry for Sudanese affairs, to be funded by the palace, was under consideration. He added that 'Ali Barir, a Sudanese who advocated unification, had recently been nominated for the Egyptian parliament. According to Killearn, the Egyptian press had recently been preoccupied with Sudanese affairs, infused with anti-British provocations and presenting a bleak picture of Britain's involvement in Sudan. The victor in recent elections to the Graduates' General Congress in Khartoum was the party known for its admiration of Egypt and favoring full unification between Sudan and Egypt. Although the Graduates' General Congress was not a representative body, Killearn stressed, the trend indicated by this election was worrying. In light of the above, Killearn requested that Eden undertake another and more serious consideration of the matter.[96]

Huddleston did not satisfy himself with these correspondences and felt he must preserve the momentum and not allow the matter to die out. He decided to appeal directly to the Exchequer, hoping that a personal approach might garner greater attention, even among the Exchequer bureaucrats with their reputation for intransigence. He directed his letter to John Anderson, the Chancellor of the Exchequer, whom he knew from their time together in government service in Calcutta, hoping personal contacts might also help.[97] Huddleston reiterated arguments made in his previous letters, and his concluding words focused on the strategic-political ramifications. From a realistic point of view, he reasoned, if Britain were not to provide the funding for higher education in Sudan, Egypt would be happy to do so, and this would likely impinge upon long-term British political and strategic interests: "if they [Sudanese] don't like us they have got Egypt next door to them, far more akin in language, culture and religion than we can ever be."[98]

The letter of response, which took a long time to arrive, was short and to the point. In his reply John Anderson wrote rather drily that all the former arguments for denying the grant request were still valid and to his great regret, with all good will, the decision could not be changed. He expanded a bit on the American connection, saying that the sum of money was not the primary problem, rather the way in which such a gesture would be understood in other places in the world, particularly in the United States: "Much as we would like to be independent of American opinion, in such matters we cannot afford to move without carrying the Americans with us."[99]

Anderson's explanation accurately reflected the shift in the power relations among the great powers. The United States emerged from the war as a rising power, while Britain, in its own self-estimation as well, was in a process of decline and was alert to its dependence on the new hegemonic power in the Western camp, a dependence that would express itself in the economic and political international arenas. Huddleston, a retired British general with a rich imperial background, was unsatisfied by Anderson's reply. What dismayed him more than anything else were Anderson's words regarding the United States: "I cannot imagine why we should have to pay such attention to American opinion," remonstrated Huddleston angrily.[100]

In the first weeks of 1945 a concerted effort was made to obtain the desired grant despite the hurdles, on the occasion of the celebration of the reopening of Gordon College, scheduled for 20 February. However, these efforts did not bear fruit, and the Exchequer remained consistent in its denial.[101]

The new college was intended to be a university including the schools of arts, sciences, engineering, agriculture, administration, and policing, while maintaining a close relationship with the Kitchener Medical School, which was meant eventually to become an integral part of the college. This development was clearly a highlight in the annals of higher education in Sudan.[102]

At the opening ceremony, held as planned on 20 February, Huddleston gave an emotional speech. He began with an encomium to the memory and intellectual heritage of Charles George Gordon, after which he spoke of the journey of the college from its foundation – its beginnings as an elementary school, then as a secondary school and high school, to the stage where it was to become a university in the near future. To achieve that aim it would need to achieve a level of instruction and research on a par with other enlightened countries. This would largely depend upon the will and determination of the Sudanese. They must aspire to fill most of the university's teaching and research positions, currently filled mostly by British and Egyptian faculty, with Sudanese graduates. Huddleston declared that from that moment on the college would become independent of the government and would be administered by a Sudan-based council and coordinating committee. Academic freedom, he stated, would be the guarantor of scientific success. Nevertheless, the Sudan government would continue to support the college in every way possible to advance it to the desired goal. The government would continue to develop and nurture education on its lower levels.

The student representative, Ibrahim Ahmad Ibrahim, extensively praised Britain and the Sudan government for their contribution to the development of education in Sudan and called on his fellows to make a supreme effort to achieve the level of higher learning and culture, which would enable the college to attain the status of university. The burden of its development and advancement would be primarily on its graduates and educated people, who would need to lead the reforms vital for the extension of the success of this process to all aspects of life, and stressed the dependence of success upon the full cooperation of the general public.[103]

The difficulties in the process of building the education system did not discourage the Sudan government, and the momentum of development was not weakened at all. To the contrary, in the latter half of 1945 the Sudan government, the British embassy in Cairo, and the Foreign Office could already present a record of proven success in the process of building, developing, and expanding the education system in Sudan. Another affirmation of this success was found in the positive assessment expressed in the Asquith Committee's report, published in June 1945,[104] which praised the plan to reopen Gordon College at the beginning of the year. This progress encouraged the advocates of the £1 million grant to renew their efforts in the hope that it could yet bear fruit. A campaign of persuasion, lobbying, and pressure on the Exchequer and the British government was redoubled by high-level British officials in Egypt, Sudan, and the Foreign Office in London. They reiterated the repercussions of the grant on the future development of education in Sudan and the moral and political considerations behind the need to award the grant. These efforts eventually did avail, and in 1946 the British government decided to award the sum of £2 million to Sudan, justifying this measure as a gesture of gratitude to the Sudanese people for their contribution to the British war effort. Half of the sum was transferred by the Sudan government to Gordon College for the purposes for which the grant had initially been requested.[105]

Picking Up the Gauntlet: Egyptian Countermeasures in the Sphere of Education

In the early years of the condominium, Egypt ran schools for children of its functionaries in addition to the few schools run by the Coptic community living mainly in northern Sudan. The Coptic community increased significantly following a wave of migration from north to south in the early nineteenth century as a result of the Egyptian occupation. At the time, the Coptic schools admitted a small number of Sudanese students. The situation for Sudanese students in government schools was no better, as there was a disproportional number of Egyptian students. Thus, for instance, in 1911, 108 out of 241 students in the Khartoum primary school were Egyptians. The state of the educational system in Sudan was wretched and backward, and until 1913, the Egyptian government granted the Sudan government a certain amount to cover the annual deficit that hindered further development of education in the country.[106]

Following the assassination of Lee Stack in 1924, the British expelled Egyptian functionaries from Sudan, among them many schoolteachers.

In addition, Sudanese were prohibited from joining non-governmental schools. However, the 1936 Anglo–Egyptian treaty marked the gradual return of Egyptian teachers to Sudan and more involvement in Sudanese educational affairs. Sudanese were again allowed to attend Egyptian schools. A report prepared by the Egyptian government in 1937 emphasized the urgent need to train Sudanese teachers in Arabic, particularly at the intermediate schools and Gordon College. Egypt was willing to provide the required quota of highly qualified teachers.[107]

The Egyptians were indeed very much involved in Sudanese educational affairs in the late 1930s and the World War II years. They took advantage of the fact that the Sudan government was reluctant to advance secondary education. The Egyptian plan to establish a new secondary school in Khartoum was coolly received by the Sudan government. The latter feared such a school would be used to advance Egypt's political goals. However, the British tactic of procrastination came to an end with the establishment of the King Faruq secondary school in the mid-1940s. By then the number of Sudanese attending Egyptian schools in Sudan was around 1,500. In addition, by 1946 the number of students in the Coptic schools had increased to 3,000, with 50 percent of them being Sudanese (compared to 20 percent Sudanese out of 1,737 students in 1936).[108]

In 1940 the Sudan government lifted its restrictions on Sudanese pursuing higher education in Egyptian institutions. The Egyptian government offered full scholarships, and in 1942 the GGC was involved in the selection of worthy students for these institutions. In 1943 the number of Sudanese studying in Egypt reached 594; 36 of them studied at university and 95 in secondary schools, while the majority attended al-Azhar. As part of its warm hospitality policy, the Egyptian government sponsored the Sudan House in Cairo – a hostel to accommodate Sudanese students. The Anglo–Egyptian rivalry over the development and direction of the Sudanese educational system intensified in the 1940s.[109]

It is noteworthy that in its first months in power, the Wafd government (1942–1944) was mainly preoccupied with consolidating its control domestically following the unpopular measures taken by the British to instate Mustafa al-Nahhas as prime minister. As mentioned, the immediate threat for Egypt, at the time, was the advancement of the Nazi and Fascist forces in the Western Desert. The Sudan issue did not occupy a central place on the government agenda, with one exception – the ministry of education. The latter was the only office to correspond officially with the Sudan Congress Committee in Cairo, discussing the advancement of two educational projects that are particularly noticeable: one of them was the creation of a Sudan chair or institute at Fu'ad I University. Seminal intellectuals such as Taha Husayn showed interest in the project, as well as Ali Ibrahim, the university's rector, and Prince Omar Toussoun ('Umar Tusun) . The second project was the opening of an Egyptian secondary school in Sudan. The government included for that purpose a sum of £8,700 in the 1943 budget, and arrangements to facilitate the realization of the project were slowly made.[110]

In September 1943, the Egyptian ministry of education announced that "entrance by Sudanese to Egyptian schools would henceforth be easier" and that there would be no restriction on the number of Sudanese students who could be admitted each year. The ministry also delegated Egyptian professors to give lectures at Khartoum before potential candidates. The British Sudan agent in Cairo concluded that Egypt's educational projects in Sudan were purely motivated by political interests and not by any desire to help the Sudanese.[111]

The Wafd government's long-term educational projects materialized in the postwar period. During a visit to Sudan in January 1946, Dr. 'Abd al-Razzaq Sanhuri, the minister of education, celebrated the launch of several new Egyptian schools in Sudan. On 8 January he opened the new Faruq School and met with Sudanese from all walks of life. The visit intended to tighten relations with educated Sudanese, to learn of Sudan's educational requirements, and to learn how Egypt could improve and deepen its involvement in and contribution to the development of Sudanese education on all levels. The minister's delegation realized that much work should be done in Sudan and that they had little knowledge about average Sudanese citizens and their basic needs. Egypt should nurture and tighten its cultural and economic relations with Sudan. The delegation concluded that the Sudanese people in both the northern and the southern regions were sympathetic toward Egypt. The opening of new schools by Egypt left a strong impression on Sudanese, commented a British report.[112]

The Egyptian ministry of education realized that more infrastructure work was essential to create conducive conditions to the deepening of Egypt's influence in Sudan. Solid cultural bonds were of the utmost importance in advancing the project of the unity of the Nile valley. Egyptians and Sudanese should get acquainted with each other's customs and cultures – they should believe in unification as a natural course of development. The minister probed the possibility of forming a high-ranking committee (with himself included) to organize exchange visits of cultural missions between the two countries. He also examined the possibility of reciprocal recognition of education certificates and the options of fostering cultural relations in general with Sudan.[113]

Table 4.2 *Figures of Pupils in Non-Government Schools, 1933–1946*

	Number of Boys	Number of Girls	Total Number	Number of Sudanese
1933	2,005	1,966	3,971	1,340
1935	2,793	2,288	5,081	1,579
1936	3,152	2,195	5,347	2,200
1937	3,732	2,478	6,210	2,092
1938	4,397	2,622	7,019	3,345
1946	8,707	3,560	12,267	8,700

The Sudanese educated class manipulated the Anglo–Egyptian rivalry to advance Sudanese education. After the conclusion of the treaty of 1936 both Britain and Egypt were praised for their contribution to the development of education, yet they both were asked to invest more material and spiritual/ideational resources. They knew that the treaty gave the Egyptians more room for maneuver in Sudanese affairs compared to the pre-1936 state of affairs, in which Egypt's steps in Sudan were restricted and closely monitored by Britain. Indeed, there was a marked increase in the involvement of the Egyptian authorities in Sudanese education. Table 4.2 shows that the number of Sudanese pupils attending non-government schools (in northern Sudan), run by the Egyptian government, Coptic community, Sudanese nationals, and others, increased tremendously.[114]

From Table 4.2, it follows that the number of Sudanese students increased markedly. In 1946 they constituted 71 percent of the overall students, compared to 1937 – about a year after the conclusion of the Anglo–Egyptian treaty – when they constituted only 34 percent. However, despite the significant increase in the number of non-government schools and students, these were still smaller than the number of schools run by the government. This situation was to change in favor of non-government education, as by 1954 the total number of non-government schools including Christian missionary and Egyptian schools increased and constituted 62 percent of the total of 117 intermediate and secondary schools. In other words, 14,150 out of a total of 22,048 students studied in non-government intermediate and secondary schools – boys and girls.[115] Egyptian education, concluded Beshir, "was fully accepted by 1946 as a valuable source for the education of the Sudanese."[116] In 1949, the number of Sudanese studying in Egyptian universities (Fu'ad, Faruq, and al-Azhar) was 764 – 60 percent of them in the prestigious religious institution.[117] Egypt's motives in the educational field were clear: to win the support of present and future educated Sudanese, many of whom played and would play an important role in the emerging Sudanese political scene and the rise of nationalism.

Britain was held accountable by many in Egypt for the backward state of the educational system in Sudan. Foaming with rage, the Muslim Brothers called for the broadening and deepening of Egyptian education in Sudan to gradually root out illiteracy among the young generation. Education could serve as an effective tool in the natural process of amalgamation of Sudanese and Egyptians into one entity.[118] The British, criticized *al-Balagh*, argued worldwide that they were a sound prop of democracy and the bearer of education and progress in Sudan. They argued that they spread and advanced education in Sudan, but in fact they corrupted the educational system in both Egypt and Sudan. They carried a fallacious message pretending to introduce a revolutionary order in the educational system, but their overall output was not impressive at all. They built only two high schools in the south and in the Sayedna valley, with no more than 600 pupils. As far as higher education was concerned, the British claimed that their Gordon College was in the scope of an Egyptian university, but in fact it was much smaller, with only 227 students, who studied law, engineering, and agriculture. The college employed a large number of British lecturers, with no proportion to the number of students. According to *al-Balagh*, in the college's constitution there was a section stating that the Sudan government would facilitate the ground for Arab students from neighboring countries, who preferred British education over Egyptian, to join Gordon College. The goal was clear – to diminish Egypt's regional centrality by encouraging anti-Egyptian sentiments among young educated Arabs.[119]

Egypt did more to develop and spread education in Sudan, argued *al-Balagh*. Despite all obstacles placed by the British, Egypt managed to build four elementary schools and two high schools in Sudan. Egypt spread education to all Sudanese including those who could not afford it by providing scholarships. Egypt also opened its educational institutions to any Sudanese who wanted to study in Egypt. For instance, at Fu'ad I University, the number of Sudanese students exceeded 320; in the higher institutes there were 25 Sudanese students, in the junior high schools 60 pupils, and in the high schools about 300. For most of these students, Egypt provided accommodation free of charge. To discourage Sudanese from taking their studies in Egyptian schools in Sudan, the Sudan government refused to allow graduates of such institutions to continue their studies in Sudanese educational institutions.[120]

Table 4.3 *Figures of Pupils in Government Schools*

	1944		1945	
	Schools	Pupils	Schools	Pupils
Secondary Schools	1	514	1	517
Junior Secondary Schools	2	86	2	107
Intermediate Schools	11	1,847	12	1,963
Boys' Elementary Schools	117	19,381	121	19,301
Teachers' Training College	1	149	1	171
Sub-grade School	165	12,738	222	15,462
Subsidized Khalwes	183	9,530	178	10,133
Technical School	2	221	2	249
Girls' Training Colleges	1	90	1	103
Girls' Secondary School	1	12	1	12
Girls' Intermediate School	1	114	1	128
Girls' Elementary Schools	62	6,681	64	6,538

The accusations made by *al-Balagh* against British educational policy in Sudan were based on data that can be supported by British official documents. For instance, in 1945 Gordon College comprised five higher schools, with a total of 168 students. However, it would be inaccurate to state that the British neglected education in Sudan. They took pains to improve Gordon College's academic standards. In December 1945, they linked the college with London University for degree purposes. The college's library was developed in both size and quality. The number of volumes increased from about 3,000 to 9,000. The Sudan government, under budgetary difficulties, undoubtedly planned to develop education in both northern and southern Sudan. Nevertheless, there was a tremendous gap between the northern and southern parts of Sudan in favor of the former. The spread of education, it was argued, would disperse unionist ideas and increase separatist nationalist orientations among Sudanese. Table 4.3 shows the number of pupils attending government schools in northern Sudan.[121]

The British assigned a significant place to Gordon College in their Sudanization project. They wanted the college to attract Sudanese who had hitherto opted to pursue their higher education in Egyptian universities. Until then, Sudanese students preferred the latter because Gordon College could not confer academic degrees, only diplomas. Robertson, the civil secretary, one of the architects of Sudanization, believed that the academic standards maintained by Gordon College were likely to be "much higher than those of Egyptian universities in view of the link with London University, and the idea of that university that our students should sit for London degrees." In his view, now that Gordon College could offer degrees, "the draw of the Egyptian universities will diminish." From Robertson's account it follows that Gordon College was not an autonomous institution under the direct control of an independent council, as it formally stated to be, but rather an academic institution that was utterly dominated by the Sudan government, which also provided most of its finance.[122]

A report submitted by the office of the civil secretary, on 16 November 1947, provided a comprehensive account of the educational progress in northern Sudan for the period 1945–1946. The period under review was depicted as "one of very great educational activity in the Northern Sudan." This period marked the end of Cox's eight-year plan of educational expansion and reforms. A new ambitious educational program was prepared for the period 1947–1956, "expressly designed to facilitate and accelerate the process of the Sudanization of the public service of the country, on the one hand by providing adequate numbers of highly-trained Sudanese, who will be well equipped to take over superior government posts, and on the other hand by raising the general level of culture in the countryside." A successful implementation of the program, it was noted, would require the recruitment of foreign educational experts. If the annual educational expenditure for 1946 was £412,314, it was to increase by 69 percent in the year 1951 to £698,800, and by 126 percent (compared to 1946) to £931,400 in 1956. Moreover, the Sudan government had decided to grant cost-of-living allowances for "all categories of its officials and employees," a step that would increase the annual cost of the new education program by nearly 20 percent, that is, to £1,100,000 by 1956. Also, the Sudan government allotted £1,290,000 to educational projects.[123]

Egypt was furious with the British project of Sudanization, generally, and its application in the educational system, particularly. As we have seen, Egypt was very active in developing and nurturing new schools in Sudan as a counterweight to the British enterprises in that field. Numerous propaganda activities were taking place in different parts of Sudan, which displeased the British authorities. Funding for propaganda purposes focused on three levels: public, private, and secret. As for public funding, money was given to the poor and indigent on public festivities such as the birthdays and accession days of King Faruq. Funds given on a private basis were drawn from the Egyptian army and distributed by arrangement with the Khartoum province. Some of these funds were contributed to education, mosques, etc. In addition, money was apparently given secretly to individual Sudanese who served Egyptian interests.[124]

Muhammad 'Abd al-Hadi, the controller of Egyptian education in Sudan, established a scheme enabling the reduction of student fees to the Coptic College, alleviating the burden from the parents, most of whom were Sudanese. *Abad al-Jil*, a monthly student magazine, praised al-Hadi in its May 1947 issue, for doing

great things which have had the greatest effect on the cultural progress of those engaged in education in the Sudan. It was he who had supervised the institution of the Faruq Secondary School and made it grow and made it a model of all schools in the Nile valley. He also supervised the institution of many schools in the Sudan ... where the students – boys and girls – enjoy the advantages of education, which had in the past been denied to them. Due to his efforts, education in the intermediate classes for boys and girls in the Khartoum Coptic College has become free and the school fees in the secondary section have been reduced.... [He] furnished the culture with many means of encouragement and reforms. For these reforms and for others, he has earned the confidence and affection of the people of the Sudan.[125]

'Abd al-Hadi was one of the chief advocates for unification by means of education. Egypt would never achieve its goals in Sudan without competing aggressively with Britain over hegemony in the field of education. On 26 June 1947 he published an article in *al-Musawwar* attacking the educational policy of the Sudan government, a proxy of the British government. The British were depicted by 'Abd al-Hadi as the cause for the backwardness of Sudanese education. The Sudan government did all it could to sabotage any Egyptian attempt to establish new schools in Sudan. It refused to increase the number of schools and limited the number of classrooms and pupils. Moreover, 'Abd al-Hadi accused the Sudan government of pursuing a discriminatory policy as far as the filling of vacancies in a variety of educational posts was concerned. British candidates were always favored even over more qualified Egyptian candidates.[126]

'Abd al-Hadi's article was condemned by British officials in both Sudan and the Foreign Office. It was portrayed as utterly falsified and spiteful – nothing in his allegations corresponded with the historical facts. As a result the acting governor-general of Sudan sent a letter to Nuqrashi Pasha, the Egyptian prime minister, requesting 'Abd al-Hadi's dismissal from his post.[127] Nuqrashi refused.[128]

The mounting tension in Anglo–Egyptian relations following the deliberations in the UN Security Council led to the prohibition of official Egyptian delegations to enter Sudan. A case in point was a delegation of Egyptian students and lecturers representing the ministry of education in September 1947. The governor-general explained that his move was intended to prevent further escalation in the current turbid political situation.[129] Indeed, this gloomy state of affairs had been reinforced since the launching of the Sudanization project and continued in the early 1950s. For instance, in June 1950 during a visit to Sudan by the retired Egyptian general Muhammad Salih Harb, he argued that "the Sudanese expect Egypt to provide them with schools, hospitals, mosques, and religious institutes." The Sudanese were yearning for education, and the British exploited their desire to provide them with their mode of education. Egypt should challenge the British and diffuse its modes and programs of education throughout Sudan. Egypt should cooperate with the progressive Graduates' General Congress, which raised the banner of educational awakening.[130] Harb opined that Egypt should take control of Islamic religious affairs and nurture Islamic education in Sudan. The Sudanese people, he emphasized, were mostly orthodox, and the fact that mosques were crumbling because of British neglect required Egypt to take the lead and reconstruct them as well as to build new mosques all over the country. Egypt should also found religious institutions for the purpose of developing and advancing religion and education – two fields that touched the hearts of many Sudanese.[131]

Harb also advised the Egyptian government to dispatch Islamic missionary delegations to southern Sudan as a counterweight to the Christian missionaries acting there on behalf of Britain. The latter, he asserted, fabricated the historical facts by inventing new narratives aimed at depicting the northern Arab Sudanese as traders who exploited the southerners for their benefit. The British goal was clear: the split of Sudan into two entities, the south and the Arab north. To sabotage the British plan the Egyptian missionary delegations should comprise senior religious scholars from al-Azhar. Their chief mission was to diffuse and bequeath the southerners with spiritual and material values that would strengthen the natural bonds between them and the northerners. The unity of the Nile valley could be materialized by a constant constructive educational campaign.[132]

Harb criticized the way Sudanese students were treated by Egyptians, both officials and members of the public, while pursuing their studies in Egyptian institutions. These students felt isolated, and Egyptians did not help their integration and assimilation within society. Moreover, they did not regard them as equal citizens. Consequently their experience in Egypt was bitter, and upon their return to Sudan they were not expressing sympathy to Egypt or acting as advocates of Egyptian–Sudanese unity despite the large amount of money the Egyptian government spent on their education and hospitality. Sudanese of all walks of life should feel that they were equals and that there was no distinction or discrimination between Sudanese and Egyptians: they were both people inhabiting the Nile valley.[133]

Ahmad Abu Bakr Ibrahim of *al-Risala* followed suit. In a comprehensive report he sent to the Egyptian ministry of education, he referred to an array of issues related to cultural and religious relations between the two parts of the valley. His main criticism focused on the ignorance of Egyptian pupils regarding Sudan. They knew nothing about the history, geography, political currents, or social life of contemporary Sudan. The education ministry should deepen and nurture cultural relations between the northern and the southern parts of the valley. Egyptian students should keep track of the developments in the south by means of reading Sudanese newspapers and other media. They should learn more about Sudanese poetry and poets that dealt with humanism, Arabism, and nationalism. The students' curriculum should be reformed to incorporate more subjects related to Sudan written by Egyptian and Sudanese scholars alike. The enrichment of knowledge of each other's society and day-to-day life would unify the people of the Nile valley culturally and politically within a single state.[134]

The Egyptians were right: the British were determined to develop and nurture the Sudanese educational system in the late 1940s and very early 1950s. The British goal was clear: to drive a wedge between educated Sudanese and the Egyptian nationalist vision of unification. However, based on the given facts, 'Abd al-Hadi's accusations as presented earlier were inaccurate. The Sudan government took pains to persuade the British government not to halt or cut its subsidy for Sudanese education. No wonder that Robertson, the civil secretary, remonstrated following the decision made by the British Council to cut down all its grants to Sudan institutions. By early 1951, there were no representatives of the British Council in Sudan, and all subsidies to Sudanese schools were halted. The expectations from the British Council were high when it had just started its activities in Sudan – it was believed that its cultural activity would enhance the British image in Sudan and thus counterbalance the Egyptian "cultural offensive." As a result of the closing down of the Council's activity, all its past and recent efforts would be wasted, warned Robertson.[135] The Foreign Office replied that the British Council faced a drastic cut in its annual budget for the period 1951–1952. However, the Foreign Office expressed its desire to see a renewal of the grant to the Sudan Cultural Centre at Khartoum and therefore exerted its pressure on the Council to alter its decision. The pressure yielded fruit, and it was decided to give Sudan half of its annual grant. The goal was to double it in the next fiscal year.[136]

The Egyptians remained committed to the development of Sudanese education during the transitional period of Sudanese self-government (1953–1956). In October 1955, a few months before the Sudanese elite opted for independence, Egypt agreed to finance the establishment of a branch of Cairo University, which was to reside in the premises of the Egyptian secondary school in Khartoum. It admitted 286 students. The admission criteria were lower than those of Gordon College or Cairo University, and it attracted mainly government officials, as the studies took place in the evenings, allowing them to work during daytimes.[137] Overall, it appeared that British diplomacy in Sudan had gained an important achievement in the extended struggle for the determination of Sudan's political future. From the British point of view, Britain provided the Sudanese with important assistance in the process of nation building and acted to create the necessary conditions for transferring control of the country to those they viewed as its rightful owners. Britain was, in effect, ever since the final stages of World War II, in a political and diplomatic confrontation with Egypt on an array of national issues, one of which was its plan to unify the Nile valley under the Egyptian crown. As future events were to demonstrate, in the struggle between Britain and Egypt a third party emerged victorious: the Sudanese people, who gained their independence in the mid-1950s.

Notes

1 The Earl of Cromer, *Modern Egypt* (New York: The Macmillan Company, 1909), pp. 114–115.
2 Ibid., p. 116. On Anglo–Egyptian relations during Cromer's period, see Afaf Lutfi Sayyid-Marsot, *Egypt and Cromer: A Study in Anglo-Egyptian Relations* (New York: Praeger, 1969).
3 Peter Woodward, *The Horn of Africa: Politics and International Relations* (London: I.B. Tauris, 2003), p. 18; Woodward, *Condominium and Sudanese Nationalism*, pp. 1–2; Woodward, "Sudan: Political transitions past and present," Sir William Luce Fellowship Paper No. 9, Durham Middle East Papers No. 83 (September 2008), p. 3.
4 Sharkey, *Living with Colonialism*, p. 73.
5 Ibid., pp. 74–76.
6 Ibid., pp, 76–80.
7 Ibid., pp, 80–85.
8 Beshir, *Educational Development in the Sudan*, p. 82.
9 Ibid., pp. 85–91.
10 "Memorandum on Anglo–Egyptian Relations for the Information of his Majesty's Representatives Abroad," 9 May 1947, J 2128/12/16, SA521/5/7–8.
11 Rizq, *Qadiyyat wahdat wadi al-nil*, pp. 89–90.
12 Sharkey, *Living with Colonialism*, p. 92.
13 Rizq, *Qadiyyat wahdat wadi al-nil*, pp. 12–13. See al-Azhari's biography in al-Hajj, *Mu'jam Shakhsiyyat Mu'tamar al-Khirrijin*, pp. 109–113.
14 *al-Ahram*, 10 September 1944.

15 See a report by the governor-general on the administration of Sudan for the year 1943, attached to Letter 1380/1/44, from British Embassy, Cairo, 6 October 1944, FO371/97051, J3562; memorandum on the future of Sudan, annexure to Dispatch 31 from Huddleston, Khartoum, to British Embassy, Cairo, 23 February 1946, FO141/1096. See also al-Rafi'i, *Fi a'qab al-thawra al-misriyya – Thawrat 1919*, Vol. 3, p. 127.

16 *al-Ahram*, 10 September 1944.

17 Dispatch 124 from Ronald Campbell, Cairo, 26 March 1946, FO141/1096.

18 Foreign Office memorandum, 23 March 1946, FO141/1096, 122/71A/46.

19 Letter No. 71 from Huddleston, Khartoum, to Campbell, Cairo, 6 April 1946, FO141/1096, 122/1/46G.

20 Collins, *A History of Modern Sudan*, p. 53. See also "Wahdat misr wa-al-sudan – hakadha yaraha al-injliz," *al-Balagh*, 31 July 1946.

21 See the record of a meeting between members of the Sudanese delegation and British officials in Cairo, 12 April 1946, and Foreign Office Minute, 13 April 1946, FO141/1096, 122/93/46.

22 al-Rafi'i, *Fi a'qab al-thawra al-misriyya – Thawrat 1919*, Vol. 3, p. 196.

23 Collins, *A History of Modern Sudan*, p. 53.

24 See note "on the Recommendations of the Sudan Administration Conference embodying the results of the Study made by the Royal Egyptian Government," 1947, Robertson Files, The Sudan Archive, Durham University Library, Archives and Special Collections, 518/2/13–17 (hereafter cited as SA with appropriate reference). See also "Tawsiyat mu'tamar idarat al-sudan," *al-Ahram*, 22 October 1947, pp. 2, 5.

25 Robertson Files, SA 518/2/13–17. See also, CS/SCR/1.A.9/6, 2 December 1947, SA 518/11/91-2.

26 Robertson Files, SA 518/2/8 and 518/11/87, a copy of a letter from the Egyptian Prime Minister regarding the above, to the Governor-General of the Sudan, 26 November 1947; Letter from the Egyptian Ambassador to London to the FO, November 1947, Robertson Files, SA 5/8/10–11; "Raghbat al-hukuma al-misriyya al-sadiqa fi tamkin al-sudaniyyina min hukm anfusihim," *al-Muqattam*, 8 November 1947, p. 2.

27 Letter from the Governor-General covering H. E.'s Aide Memoire to the Egyptian Government, 5 January 1948, Robertson Files, SA518/2/18–22.

28 For a record of the Juba Conference 1947, see Letter EP/SCR/1.A.5/1 from B. V. Marwood, Governor of Equatoria, 21 June 1947, to the Sudan Government, at www.gurtong.net/LinkClick.aspx?fileticket=OBZ%2B7v1SXis%3D&tabid=124 (accessed 21/3/2013).

29 Daly, *Imperial Sudan*, p. 242.

30 C. R. H. Tripp, "Sudan: State and Elite," *Africa*, 67:1 (1997), p. 166.

31 "Ihtijaj al-sudaniyyin 'ala al-muqtarahat al-baritaniyya," *al-Ahram*, 23 September 1946; "Wafd al-sudan yarfudu mashru' al-sawdana," *al-Balagh*, 14 October 1947, the Nile Valley Page.

32 Salih 'Ashmawi, "Diktaturiyyat al-injliz fi al-sudan," *al-Ikhwan al-Muslimun*, 21 June 1947, p. 3.

33 al-Sayyid Sabri, "Hawla ta'yin khalaf li-hakim al-sudan," *al-Ahram*, 17 March 1947, p. 3. The governor-general of Sudan was also severely criticized by

the pro-monarchial paper *al-Muqattam*. See "Qadiyyat al-sudan wa-haki-muha al-'amm," *al-Muqattam*, 10 December 1946, p. 1.

34 "Hawla ta'yin hakim jadid lil-sudan," *al-Ahram*, 17 March 1947, p. 2.

35 Ibid.

36 "Taghyir hakim al-sudan wa-atharuhu fi siyasat baritaniyya," *al-Ahram*, 18 March 1947, p. 2.

37 "al-Nuqrashi basha yaruddu 'ala al-mistar bifin," *al-Ahram*, 19 May 1947, p. 2.

38 Letter from Najib al-Armanazi, the Syrian ambassador to London, to President Shukri al-Quwwatli, Damascus, 15 May 1947, in Meir Zamir, *The Secret Anglo-French War in the Middle East: Intelligence and Decolonization, 1940–1948* (London: Routledge, 2014), document 384.

39 Letter from King Faruq to Shukri al-Quwwatli, the Syrian President, 23 May 1947, in ibid., document 387.

40 "Bayan na'ib al-hakim ila al-sudaniyyina," *al-Ahram*, 15 September 1947, p. 2.

41 "Bayan al-hakim wa-'id lil-sudaniyyina," *al-Ahram*, 16 September 1947, p. 2.

42 "al-Injliz al-dimuqratiyuna yakhnuquna al-huriyyat wa-yamna'una al-balagh min dukhul al-sudan," *al-Balagh*, 28 October 1947, The Nile Valley Page.

43 Muhammad Khalifa al-Jumla, "Tahrir wadi al-nil la tuhaqqiquhu al-asalib al-diblumasiyya," *al-Balagh*, 4 November 1947; al-Jumla, "al-Baritaniyyuna yuwasiluna khida' hadha al-wadi," *al-Balagh*, 24 November 1947, the Nile Valley Page.

44 'Ali 'Abd al-'Athim al-Muhami, "Madha fa'alna li-hadhihi al-haraka al-wataniyya al-mubaraka?" *al-Balagh*, 25 July 1948, p. 3; al-Muhami, "Ayyah maslaha li-misr wa-al-sudan fi qubul hadhihi al-sawdana alati tuhadidu wah-datahuma," *al-Balagh*, 5 June 1948.

45 "'Kull shay' sudani," *al-Balagh*, 24 November 1947, the Nile Valley Page.

46 "Hadhihi lughat al-huriyya!! fa-hal yafhamuha al-musta'miruna," *al-Balagh*, 1 December 1947, the Nile Valley Page. See also "Sudaniyyuna yatahad-dathuna," *al-Balagh*, 24 November 1947, the Nile Valley Page.

47 Muhammad Khalifa al-Jumla, "Ayna siyasatuna al-thabita lidaf' 'udwan al-injliz!?" *al-Balagh*, 1 December 1947, the Nile Valley Page.

48 "Siyasat fasl al-sudan 'an misr," *al-Ahram*, 17 September 1947, p. 3. On the British efforts to diminish Egypt's influence over the Sudanese educational system, see the second part of this chapter.

49 "Majlis al-nuwwab bi-jami' ahzabihi yu'ayyidu al-hukuma," *al-Ahram*, 1 January 1947, p. 3. See also Haykal, *Mudhakkirat*, Vol. III, p. 57.

50 "Ta'yin sudani qadiyyan lil-qudat," *al-Ahram*, 12 October 1947, p. 3.

51 For the Khatmiyya, see Voll and Voll, *The Sudan: Unity and Diversity*, pp. 18–19, 37–38, 45, 52–53. See also Ali Salih Karar, *The Sufi Brotherhoods in the Sudan* (London: Hurst, 1992).

52 Minute by Roger Allen, Foreign Office, 2 November 1951, FO371/90154, JE1052/89.

53 "Munaqashat mashru' al-sawdana," *al-Ahram*, 9 March 1948, p. 2.

54 "Mashru' al-sawdana bayna misr wa-baritaniyya wa-al-sudan," *al-Ahram*, 17 May 1948, p. 5; "al-Mudhakkira al-misriyya ila al-hukuma al-baritaniyya,"

174 The Struggle for Sudan

al-Ahram, 7 July 1948. See also "Madha tadammanat mudhakkirat al-hukuma al-misriyya 'an tanfidh mashru'at al-sawdana," al-Muqattam, 23 June 1948, p. 2; "Limadha lam tuwafiqu al-hukuma al-misriyya 'ala mashru' idarat al-sawdana," al-Muqattam, 6 July 1948.

55 "Iftitah al-jam'iyya al-tashri'iyya fi al-sudan," al-Ahram, 16 December 1948, p. 4.

56 Tawfiq Ahmad al-Bakri, "Hadhihi al-ahdath al-jariyya fi janub wadi al-nil," al-Ahram, 17 November 1948, p. 3. Hasan al-Tahir Zuruq, a member of the Sudan delegation of 1946, criticized in the pro-Wafdist al-Balagh the tepid response of the Nuqrashi government to the recent Sudan government's moves. See Hasan al-Tahir Zuruq, "Mashru' al-sawdana – wa-limadha yata'ajjalu al-jnjliz ibramahu," al-Balagh, 12 June 1948, p. 3.

57 "Mithaq tahrir al-wadi," al-Ahram, 30 March 1949.

58 "al-Watha'if al-misriyya fi al-sudan," al-Ahram, 21 September 1949, p 5.

59 'Ali al-Barir, "al-Sudaniyyuna wa-al-barlaman al-misri," al-Ahram, 14 December 1949.

60 See a pamphlet issued by the Egyptian government entitled The Egyptian Question 1882–1951, attached to Letter from British Embassy, Washington, 5 December 1951, FO953/1115, PG11637/102.

61 Ibid.

62 See, for instance, 'Abd al-'Aziz 'Abd al-Majid, al-Tarbiyya fi al-sudan min al-qarn al-sadis 'ashar ila nihayat al-qarn al-tasi' 'ashar (Cairo: al-Matba'a al-Amiriyya, 1949); V. L. Griffiths, An Experiment in Education: An Account of the Attempts to Improve the Lower Stages of Boy's Education in the Moslem Anglo–Egyptian Sudan, 1930–1950 (London: Longmans, 1953).

63 Beshir, Educational Development in the Sudan. The study makes use of a wide variety of previously unpublished primary sources.

64 Lilian Passmore Sanderson and Neville Sanderson, Education, Religion and Politics in Southern Sudan 1899–1964 (London: Ithaca Press, 1981).

65 Seri-Hersch, "Towards Social Progress and Post-Imperial Modernity," pp. 333–356.

66 Sharkey, Living with Colonialism, p. 7

67 Ibid., pp. 16–66.

68 See a report by the Colonial Office, the Advisory Committee on Education in the Colonies, Mass Education in African Societies, 31 December 1943, attached to Letter 12041/43 from Colonial Office, 12 January 1944, FO371/41320, J165/15/16.

69 See a booklet by the Sudan government, The Sudan: A Record of Progress, 1898–1947, attached to Letter L.O./MSF/1-A from R. C. Mayall, Sudan Government, London Office, 18 June 1947, FO371/63058, J2815/584/16.

70 Ibid.

71 Ibid.

72 Beshir, Educational Development in the Sudan, pp. 13–14

73 Beshir, Educational Development in the Sudan, pp. 15–16; Anthoni M. Galatoli, Egypt in Midpassage (Cairo: Urwand and Sons Press, 1950), p. 125.

74 Beshir, Educational Development in the Sudan, p. 22.

75 The Sudan: A Record of Progress, 1898–1947.

76 Ibid.
77 On Gordon's activities in Sudan, see Alise Moore-Harell, *Gordon and the Sudan: Prologue to the Mahdiyya, 1877–1880* (London: Routledge, 2001).
78 *The Sudan: A Record of Progress, 1898–1947.*
79 The committee was invited by the Sudan government to visit Sudan to examine the state of the education system. The committee was named after its chairman Earl De La Warr. The committee submitted to the Sudan government a comprehensive report that included applicable recommendations. For a detailed account of the committee and its reports, see Beshir, *Educational Development*, pp. 111–116.
80 *The Sudan: A Record of Progress, 1898–1947.* For details on the state of education in southern Sudan, see Passmore Sanderson and Sanderson, *Education, Religion and Politics*, pp. 233–255.
81 Letter L.O.805.1/19 from the office of the Sudan Government, London, to R. Scrivener, Foreign Office, 30 May 1944, FO371/41320, J2012/15/16.
82 A full copy of Cox's report is attached to Letter L.O.805.1/19.
83 For a detailed account of the consolidation of the plan and its content, see Beshir, *Educational Development*, pp. 131–148.
84 In August 1943, the British government appointed the Committee for Higher Education in the Colonies, headed by Sir Cyril Asquith, to assess the problems of higher education and to prepare a broad plan with the purpose of improving and advancing it. On the Asquith Committee, see letter 12041/8/43 from the Colonial Office to the Under Secretary of State, Foreign Office, 12 January 1944, J165/15/16. The committee's assessment was sent to the British Foreign Office by the British embassy in Cairo on 20 May 1944. See Telegram 605 from British Embassy, Cairo, 29 May 1944, FO371/41320, J1970/15/16.
85 Ibid., pp. 2–5.
86 Telegram 764 from Killearn, British Embassy, Cairo, 27 June 1944, FO371/41320, J2635/15/16; see also Letter CS/107.A.4 attached to Telegram 77 from Huddleston, Khartoum, to Killearn, Cairo, 10 June 1944, FO371/41320, J2655/15/16. On the reopening of Gordon College, see a detailed account in Ginat, "The Reopening of Gordon College," pp. 217–239 [Hebrew].
87 Telegram 77 from Huddleston to Killearn.
88 Ibid.
89 Ibid.
90 See two letters from the Foreign Office to the Treasury, 26 July 1944, FO371/41320, J2635/15/16.
91 Letter from Alexander Cadogan, Foreign Office, to Richard Hopkins, Treasury, 26 July 1944, FO371/45973, J1318/99/16.
92 Letter from Richard Hopkins to Cadogan, 10 August 1944, FO371/45973, J1318/99/16.
93 Letter CS/SCR/107.A.4 from Douglas Newbold, Civil Secretary's Office, Khartoum, to T. A. Shone, British Embassy, Cairo, 23 September 1944, FO141/960, 377/4/44G.
94 Letter CHJ/EP from Shone, British Embassy Cairo, to Newbold, 6 October 1944, FO141/960, 377/4/44G.

95 Letter 107.A.4 attached to Telegram 128 from H. J. Huddleston, Khartoum, to Killearn, Cairo, 7 December 1944, FO371/45973, J99/99/16.

96 Letter 377/25/44 attached to Telegram 1506 from Killearn to Eden, 22 December 1944, FO371/45973, J99/99/16.

97 The two knew each other ever since they served together in the Indian government. For more details, see Telegram 193 from Huddleston to Killearn, 26 January 1945, FO371/45973, J890/99/16.

98 Personal letter from Huddleston to Sir John Anderson, Treasury, London, 10 December 1944, FO371/45973, J890/99/16.

99 Personal letter from Anderson to Huddleston, 22 January 1945, FO371/45973, J890/99/16.

100 Telegram 192 from Huddleston to Killearn, 26 January 1945, FO371/45973, J890/99/16.

101 On these efforts, see, for instance, Letter from Orme G. Sargent to Richard Hopkins, 3 February 1945, FO371/45973, J1318/99/16; Letter from Hopkins to Sargent, 13 February 1945, ibid.

102 Telegram 482 from Killearn to Anthony Eden, 28 March 1945, FO371/45973, J1305/99/16.

103 On the inauguration ceremony and the speeches delivered by the three as well as by other Sudanese speakers in Arabic, see the attached file ("Inauguration of the Gordon Memorial College, Khartoum") to Telegram 442 from Killearn, Cairo, 22 March 1945, FO371/45973, J1186/99/16. See also Letter 17.A.11 from the office of the Governor-General, Khartoum, to British Embassy, Cairo, 19 February 1945, FO141/1041, 697/3/45.

104 On 8 December 1945 the College Council adopted the main recommendations of the Asquith Commission's report. See *The Gordon Memorial College at Khartoum, Reports and Accounts to 31st December 1945*, 1 April 1946, FO371/63095, J2775/2073/16.

105 On the grant, see *The Sudan: A Record of Progress 1898–1947*, pp. 23–24. See also SA 521/2/40, Letter L.O. 406.1/13 from R. C. Mayall, Sudan Government, London Office, to J. W. Robertson, Civil Secretary, Sudan Government, Khartoum, 7 January 1946.

106 Beshir, *Educational Development in the Sudan*, p. 36.

107 Daly, *Imperial Sudan*, p. 199; Beshir, pp. 117–118.

108 Daly, *Imperial Sudan*, pp. 199–200; Beshir, pp. 160–161.

109 Daly, *Imperial Sudan*, pp. 200–201.

110 See a copy of a note by the Sudan Agent in Cairo, attached to Dispatch 271 (840/1/43) from British Embassy, Cairo, 17 March 1943, in FO141/905.

111 Ibid.

112 See a note on the visit to Sudan of Dr. 'Abd al-Razzaq Sanhuri, Egyptian Minister of Education, January 1946, FO141/1092, 104/15/46.

113 Muhammad Zaki 'Abd al-Qadir, "al-Rawabit al-thaqafiyya bayna misr wa-al-sudan," *al-Ahram*, 21 January 1946, pp. 3–4. See also Dispatch 193 from British Embassy, Cairo, 22 February 1946, FO371/53381, J788/762/16.

114 Beshir, *Educational Development in the Sudan*, p. 162.

115 Ibid., p. 165.

116 Ibid., p. 162.

117 Ibid., p. 166.
118 See al-Mijnah Maqsus, "al-Madaris al-wataniyya shawka fi khalq al-isti'-mar," *al-Ikhwan al-Muslimun*, 7 December 1946, p. 7; Maqsus, "al-Lugha al-'arabiyya yuharibuha al-isti'mar," *al-Ikhwan al-Musliman*, 16 November 1946, p. 9.
119 "Ba'da 50 sana min isti'mar al-injliz lil-sudan (1)," *al-Balagh*, 23 December 1948, p. 3.
120 "Ba'da 50 sana min isti'mar al-injliz lil-sudan (2)," *al-Balagh*, 25 December 1948, p. 3.
121 See report by the Governor-General of Sudan on the Administration, Finance, and Conditions of Sudan in 1945, in FO371/53444, J5057/5057/16.
122 Letter CS/SCR/107-A-4, from J. W. Robertson, Civil Secretary, Sudan Government, to T. J. Bowker, British Embassy, Cairo, 27 April 1947, FO371/63095, J2095/2073/16.
123 See *Report on Educational Progress in the Northern Sudan for the period 1945–1946*, by the Education Department, 26 May 1946, attached to Letter CS/SCR/17.A.1-1, from G. E. R. Sandars, Acting Civil Secretary, Sudan Government, Khartoum, to Sudan Agent in London, 16 November 1947, FO371/63095, J5797/2073/16.
124 See Letter L.O./MSF/1 from Sudan Government Agency in London, to D. W. Lascelles, Foreign Office, 3 June 1947, FO371/63084, J2582/16. The Sudan Government Agency in London said that a reliable source obtained information on this subject "from local Egyptians who are closely associated with the leading Egyptians in Khartoum and particularly with the Economic Expert." See ibid.
125 Quoted from Ginat, "Egypt's Efforts," p. 202.
126 See *al-Musawwar*, 26 June 1947.
127 See Letter 52.A.1 from Kit Haselden, Sudan Agency, Cairo, to R. L. Speaight, British Embassy, 12 July 1947, Cairo, FO371/63084, J2582/16; Letter No. E. 17 from J. W. Robertson, Acting Governor-General of Sudan, Khartoum, to the President of the Council of Ministers, Cairo, 28 August 1947, FO371/63084, J2582/16.
128 "Siyasat fasl al-sudan 'an misr," *al-Ahram*, 17 September 1947, p. 3.
129 Ibid.
130 "Madha yuridu al-sudaniyyuna min misr," *al-Balagh*, 22 June 1950, p. 5.
131 Ibid.
132 Ibid.
133 Ibid.
134 Ahmad Abu Bakr Ibrahim, "Nasib al-sudan," *al-Risala*, No. 973, 25 February 1952, pp. 218–219.
135 Letter SCO/1/A/10 from Robertson to R. Allen, Foreign Office, 14 March 1951, FO924/935, CRL1161/2.
136 Letter from J. P. G. Finch, Foreign Office, to Robertson, Khartoum, 17 April 1951, FO924/935, CRL1161/2.
137 Beshir, *Educational Development in the Sudan*, pp. 186–187.

5   The Aftermath of the Security Council Hype
Whither the Unity of the Nile Valley?

Following Egypt's debacle at the UN Security Council, Anglo–Egyptian relations deteriorated rapidly. Nuqrashi Pasha, the Sa'dist prime minister (1946–1948) who was displeased and disappointed with his personal failure, began to consider other methods to advance Egypt's foreign affairs internationally. Yet, he soon found himself embroiled in the Palestine War of 1948, and his tragic death at the end of that year placed the Sudan question on a temporary hold. However, the return of the Wafd to power (1950–1952) witnessed a growing radicalization in Egypt's foreign policy, which took an anti-Western stand on issues related to the East–West conflict and caused a deterioration in Anglo–Egyptian relations, which reached their lowest ebb with the Egyptian government's unilateral abrogation of the 1936 treaty and the declaration of Faruq as King of Egypt and Sudan. This move, as we shall see, did not achieve its goal as the British refused to recognize it and continued with their policy of preparing Sudan for self-government and separation from Egypt. The latter part of the chapter shows that the Free Officers' revolution of July 1952 constituted a landmark for the future of Sudan. It explains why the new military regime abandoned the project of the unity of the Nile valley, relinquishing Egypt's claim to Sudan.

A Missed Opportunity? The Internal Political and Public Altercation

The month following the debate in the Security Council witnessed a mounting propaganda campaign between Britain and Egypt over the future of Sudan. Britain's long-term interests, which were revealed in a secret Foreign Office report, testified to their intentions to maintain direct control over Sudan, until the Sudanese were prepared for self-determination and self-government. Britain's desire remained constant, and the report underlined London's intentions to remain the external arbiter in Sudanese politics at the expense of Egypt. The British also sought to quell Egyptian influence in Sudan as a means to preserve their own special prerogatives and to dent public support for the potential unification of the Nile valley. Britain believed that the Egyptian failure at the Security Council would have a lasting impact on Sudanese public opinion and presented an opening for the British to expand their influence, seizing the initiative from Cairo. The emptiness of its case, the British report noted, "and the ineptitude of [its] methods had been widely recognized. Above all, [Egypt] failed, and the East has little respect for failure."[1] However, London's main worry about the Egyptian propaganda rhetoric was that it would continue further incitement within Sudan against Britain and the British-backed Sudan government.[2] The British assessment was not wrong.

The Egyptian sense of missed opportunity in the Security Council manifested itself in mounting criticism domestically. The Wafd, a firm supporter of the unity of the Nile valley under the Egyptian crown, and the Egyptian left, which held opposing views on this matter, both condemned Nuqrashi's performance and line of argument. For instance, the Marxist Tali'at al-'Ummal asserted that the strong language used by the prime minister in his speeches was the result of heavy pressure exerted upon him by the awakening national movement. Holding on to power was Nuqrashi's raison d'être, and for that reason he was willing to strike a deal with Britain and thus yield to British pressure and serve their interests.[3]

Among opposition groups, the radical right wing – the Muslim Brothers and Misr al-Fatat – held an entirely different standpoint. For them, on the balance, Nuqrashi's performance was a success story – his tenacity in presenting Egypt's national demands was commendable. Mahmud Shakir portrayed Egypt and Sudan as one nation that was struggling for justice in the face of British tyranny "that attacked their independence and occupied their land from the source of the Nile to its estuary." Cadogan's plea was based on lies and a distortion of history. If doing justice was one of the postulates of the Security Council, then Egypt would unconditionally have achieved its full rights. Egypt and Sudan, asserted Shakir, were an extraordinary model that would surprise British imperialism and its allies: "if the UN Security Council is a modern slave market founded by rival nations to sell and buy God's creation, then Egypt and the Sudan will teach it a new lesson which is not expected from a nation weakened by despotic British rule for sixty-five years. Egypt and the Sudan are a hardy nation taught by [British] despotism that rights could only be gained by employing bitter jihad, bloodshed and unshakable faith."[4]

Shakir, who often employed Islamic terminology, appealed to the mujahedin not to be afraid, because such a state of mind might cause damage to the jihad. They should take an example from Nuqrashi, who overcame his fear in the Security Council and compelled the British to rely on lies. The way to root out British and French imperialism from Arab lands was for other Arab leaders to follow Nuqrashi by displaying determination in safeguarding their positions and interests.[5] If it was impossible to defeat Britain militarily, then it might be possible to do so by creating regional instability and thus undermining Britain's major argument that a necessary condition to maintain stability in the region was for British forces to remain in the region:

The British interest is to maintain peace in the Near East, yet this is just a pretext to extend its staying in Egypt, the Sudan, Palestine and Iraq. We should seek ways to unmask this fake peace ... The Arab world knows that Egypt and the Sudan are its heart, and if this heart remains weak and bound to the chains of imperialism, then the Arab world will become powerless and fail to act for its awakening sons ... we should unite our ranks, not only in Egypt and the Sudan, but also in every other place in the Arab and Muslim world.[6]

Fathi Radwan, a member of the Nationalist Party (formerly a leader of *Misr al-Fatat*), followed suit. Radwan, whose former party represented the most radical nationalist standpoint on Sudan, complimented Nuqrashi, calling upon him to continue with his nationalist approach:

We should present our stances vis-à-vis the English in a clear manner and take the essential steps corresponding with our new position. The first step we may take is to recall our ambassador from London. The Egyptian government should totally boycott the British ... Egypt should foster relations with those countries that are hostile to Britain or hold similar views to ours. Egypt should consequently tighten relations with the USSR and Poland – both countries that helped us [at the Security Council] and therefore we should stand on their side internationally as a close friend ... Our national demands will be fulfilled only by conducting an overall jihad against the English and their supporters.[7]

Egypt's bitter experience in the Security Council was analyzed in a more profound way by the independent newspaper *al-Ahram,* which pointed at a triple failure – Egyptian, British, and international (UN). The tragedy of the Egyptian appeal before the Security Council came to an end, at least for a while. It came to a similar end as other tragedies – with the death of its heroes. Egypt, the complainant, presented arguments and evidence to support its incontestable rights, but it was incapable of overcoming opposing interests of other powers with greater advantages in the forum of the Security Council. Egypt's major demands – the complete and speedy withdrawal from and the termination of the condominium over Sudan – were not achieved. Although the Security Council accepted the Egyptian demand for a complete withdrawal, it nevertheless wanted it to be done through negotiation. Britain, the object of Egypt's complaints, asserted *al-Ahram*, was overly confident that it would easily remove the appeal from the Council's agenda, but failed to do so. Its efforts to advance various proposals not in Egypt's favor were also doomed to fail. However, the greatest failure was that of the UN Security Council, which showed indecisiveness throughout a month of deliberations. It did not honor the very foundations of the UN Charter – the developing of "friendly relations among nations based on respect for the principle of equal rights and self-determination of peoples." Overall, it deliberately failed to resolve the Anglo–Egyptian dispute. Egypt, concluded *al-Ahram*, was determined to continue its jihad until its goals were achieved.[8]

The national disappointment crossed political borders within Egypt – after all there was a broad consensus as far as the unity of the Nile valley was concerned. Following the UN fiasco, public opinion favored the idea of a comprehensive anti-British campaign from within the country. In mid-September 1947 an apolitical platform was formed to advance Egyptian–Sudanese unification. The group called itself the Committee for the Liberation of the Valley (*Lajnat Tahrir al-Wadi*), chaired by Sabri Abu al-Majid, who depicted the Committee as a movement for liberation seeking to transfer the leading positions to youth not embroiled in inter-party disputes.[9] *Lajnat Tahrir al-Wadi* published a manifesto in *al-Ahram* on 14 September, calling on the government to announce the unilateral abrogation of the 1936 and 1899 treaties and subsequently warning the British that they should evacuate the Nile valley immediately and speedily. It also urged the country's leaders, youth, institutions, and political parties to form a united front to face the British. Those Egyptians who collaborated with the British forces – contractors, workers, importers, etc. – were called upon to halt their activities. The movement opened branches in various places in Egypt and Sudan.[10]

'Abd al-Majid Salih Pasha, the Egyptian irrigation minister, told *al-Ahram* that Egypt's jihad would not stop. The struggle against Britain had not come to an end. The Sudan question was not a simple one. Egyptians regarded the Sudanese

as brothers, who should share with us moments of ease and moments of calamity ... The Egyptian acts to liberate the Sudan and fights for its independence and happiness. He would not abandon the Sudanese as prey in the hands of foreign and oppressive imperialism. This was the Egyptian stance, and there is no doubt that the vast majority of educated and senior Sudanese knew that. However, some Sudanese were led astray by British statements pretending to portray themselves as champions and defenders of Sudanese independence ... behind such words of self-determination there is a hidden imperialist fang aiming at tearing apart the unity of the Nile valley after it cut off the northern from the southern part of the Sudan in order to annex the Sudan in its entirety to the British Empire.[11]

The major opposition party, the Wafd, took advantage of Nuqrashi's failure at the UN. In a letter addressed to Nuqrashi, the people of the Nile valley, and the British ambassador to Cairo, Mustafa al-Nahhas, the party's uncontested leader, who styled himself the chief spokesman of both Egyptians and Sudanese, presented an uncompromising approach – the struggle for the unity of the Nile valley would continue. He blamed Nuqrashi for groveling and for abandoning the nationalist consensus regarding Sudan. The prime minister was asked to transfer the issue to the people, the sovereign, who would handle it responsibly. Time did not work in Egypt's favor – the British were safely fulfilling their separatist plans, warned Nahhas. Nuqrashi's government was held responsible for Egypt's failure to defend the integrity of the Nile valley and the refusal of the British to evacuate it.[12]

The letter to the British ambassador was presented in a firm but fair manner. Nahhas reviewed, historically, Egypt's struggle to attain its national rights ever since the British occupation. Constant British efforts to aggressively break the spirit of the Egyptian nation and its respective leaders were doomed to failure. Sudan was reoccupied in the very late nineteenth century by the Egyptian army with insignificant support from British troops. During World War II Egypt sided with Britain and the democratic camp, yet with the war's conclusion Britain refused to respect Egypt's rights as derived from the UN Charter. It agreed to evacuate Syria, Lebanon, India, and other countries and granted them independence, but refused to do so in the case of Egypt. Egypt was furious, stressed Nahhas, over the Sudan government's separatist maneuvers, as expressed by its leaders since the conclusion of the deliberations in the Security Council. The British, warned Nahhas, should not take Egypt's failure at the UN as the last word. Speaking in the name of the Egyptian people, he suggested that if the British would respect Egypt's just rights to independence and full sovereignty over its territory by withdrawing from the Nile valley, they would then gain the sound friendship of the people of the Nile valley, but failure to do so would incur the hatred of this people, hostilities, and God knows what.[13]

In his demagogic appeal to the people of the Nile valley, Nahhas presented Nuqrashi's government as weak and submissive. It could not stand up to Britain's imperialist oppressive measures domestically and deceptive maneuvers internationally. Under Nuqrashi and his predecessor, Isma'il Sidqi, "our rights were lost, our wills were paralyzed, the body of the nation torn limb from limb." Nahhas's line of argument was riddled with inaccuracies. His political rivalry with Nuqrashi and his desire to replace the latter led him to distort the historical facts. Nuqrashi was blamed for supporting the Bevin–Sidqi draft agreement and his readiness to sign it with the British on 1 December 1946. He did not follow Egypt's top legal advisors, who recommended a unilateral abrogation of the 1936 treaty before presenting Egypt's case in the Security Council – such a move would have strengthened Egypt's arguments, which were in line with the UN Charter. Nahhas, who addressed his letter to the people of the Nile valley, depicted the state of affairs at the time as an emergency and called on the people to gird up loins and be prepared to defend the interests of the nation. To quote him: "get organized, resist your enemy and risk your life to defend your rights ... Jihad is not aggression but rather an action for your homeland; the warrior should not ask for wages unless he is a mercenary. By acting you serve your homeland, honor your martyrs and therefore you will be respected worldwide."[14]

A tail wind of support for Nuqrashi was blowing from the direction of Azhari and the Sudanese delegation. According to them, despite the fact that Egypt failed to persuade the Security Council to call for British withdrawal, the presentation of the issue of the Nile valley, internationally, achieved two tremendous gains: political and moral. Politically, the Sudan issue, against British opposition, was internationalized. From now on Britain would have to listen to the international community that disregarded its request to remove the Egyptian demand from the Security Council agenda. The Council's member states formally recognized the links bonding the two sides of the Nile valley – the north and the south.[15]

Prior to this statement, Azhari was criticized by *Ruz al-Yusuf* for not doing enough to advance the anti-British struggle in Sudan. For Ikhsan 'Abd al-Quddus, the Sudanese advocates of the unity of the Nile valley were to take the lead in the struggle and act as the vanguard because only the Sudanese could undermine the foundations of British colonialism in the Nile valley. In his view, the Egyptian nationalist politicians were useless.[16]

The severe criticism directed against Nuqrashi from the Egyptian opposition did not dampen the triumphal reception on his return from New York on 20 September 1947. For his supporters and the silent majority it was not his fault that his mission was not successful as anticipated. The prevailing belief was that he did his best for his country and that Egypt emerged in a better posture than Britain. Its dispute with Britain was brought to the fore of the international arena, and many states showed sympathy with its nationalist demands.[17]

The bitter experience in the Security Council resulted in Nuqrashi's decision to reconsider Egypt's stance on international affairs. In late 1947 he declared that Egypt "would consider the possibility of neutrality in the international arena and that Egypt would seek the support of other powers in its struggle against Britain."[18] A few months later, in February 1948, he sent a military mission to purchase arms in Czechoslovakia, and a month later Egypt signed a large barter agreement with the Soviet Union for the first time.[19] Nuqrashi's overtures in the Eastern bloc were short-lived. Several months after the outbreak of the war in Palestine, a student member of the Muslim Brothers assassinated him on 28 December 1948. Ironically, that murderer came from within a movement that had strongly supported Nuqrashi's politics on the issue of the Nile valley. However, on the issue of Palestine the Muslim Brothers opposed Nuqrashi's position and led the street demonstrations and violent riots following the Arab military and political debacle. His subsequent decision to outlaw the movement triggered his assassination.[20] The internationalization of the Sudan question and its placement in the fore of Egypt's foreign and domestic policies should be attributed to Nuqrashi's leadership and determination. His successors Ibrahim 'Abd al-Hadi of the Sa'dist Party (December 1948–July 1949) and Husain Sirri (July 1949–January 1950), an independent anti-Wafdist and "a competent and pro-British administrator,"[21] did not advance the issue of the unity of the Nile valley – the standstill caused by Anglo-Egyptian gloomy relations remained the chief obstacle. As noted earlier, at that historical junction the British were heavily embroiled in advancing their long-term project of Sudanization that was to pave the way for Sudan's independence.

The Future of the Unity of the Nile Valley in Light of Escalating Anglo–Egyptian Relations

In the early 1950s, the Sudanese champions of the unity of the Nile valley remained persistent in their stance. With the return of the Wafd to power in January 1950 these Sudanese cherished hopes that the new government would be more determined and persistent to advance the national consensus on the unity of the Nile valley. The Nahhas government was nevertheless divided into two main factions – the right and the left. The former was led by the mighty minister of interior, Fu'ad Siraj al-Din, who represented the old-guard conservative Wafd; the latter was led by the highly dynamic foreign minister, Muhammad Salah al-Din, who represented the young generation dominated by left-wing orientations. As we will later see, the rivalry between the two factions manifested itself in the strategy to be employed on the question of the future of Sudan.

On 3 March Siraj al-Din held a meeting with Isma'il al-Azhari, during which he reassured his Sudanese guest that his government would take the required measures to advance unification because the Sudanese and the Egyptians shared similar interests.[22]

The unionist groups including the National Bloc in Sudan – the Nile Valley Party, the Federalists (al-Itihadiyyin), and the Liberal Federalists (al-Ittihadiyyin al-Ahrar) – issued a communiqué calling for the formation of a democratic government in Sudan united with Egypt under the Egyptian crown. Azhari, the head of the Sudanese delegation, who spoke on behalf of the National Bloc, stated that the Sudanese delegation that represented the vast majority of the Sudanese people remained consistent in its adherence to the formation of the Nile Valley State, united under the Egyptian crown with one army and a single foreign policy. In this framework, Sudan would enjoy a domestic democratic government.[23] In late March, Azhari gave an interview to al-Balagh, during which he criticized his Sudanese political adversary, 'Abd al-Rahman al-Mahdi, a leader of al-Ansar, for holding the view that the Nile water should not be the reason for unity with Egypt. On the contrary, stated Azhari, the Nile water constituted one of the main elements in the natural need for unification.[24] Later on, while visiting Cairo in September 1951, Azhari criticized Mahdi's anti-unionist standpoint, stating that only unification with Egypt would guarantee the Sudanese short- and long-term interests. The Sudanese people would rule themselves under the protection of the Egyptian crown. Egypt was "our older sister," and it invested enormous efforts and resources to advance the Sudanese people in the fields of education and the building and developing of Sudan's infrastructures.[25]

On 20 March 1950, General Salah Harb, the Egyptian minister of defense, started his visit to Sudan after years of prohibition by the Sudan government. Harb confirmed that his visit was designed to enhance the bonds and strengthen the dialogue with "our Sudanese brothers." The solution to the Sudan problem could be achieved

if our brothers in the Sudan, whether in favor or disfavor of unification, would comprehend that spiritual and religious bonds are not the only factors to connect between us. Our common interests, our existence, our entity and future, created the strongest bonds between us that no human power can shatter. Economically, neither the Sudan nor Egypt can live separately. Egypt does not think, at all, that its relations with the Sudan are founded on its sovereignty over that country, or that the Sudan is Egypt's slave. Egypt and the Sudan are one land and one people, who have a single sovereignty that derives its power from the crown represented by Faruq. [Egypt and the Sudan] are united behind one military and represented internationally as one entity.[26]

On his return from Sudan Salah Harb argued that every Egyptian had the right to visit or live in Sudan according to the 1899 and 1936 treaties. The sons of the Nile valley could move freely along the valley without any interruption because they held a single citizenship.[27]

In late 1950, Britain and Egypt held another round of fruitless talks aimed at settling their ongoing dispute – the Sudan issue featured prominently. The core differences between the two countries were already revealed during two meetings between Mahmud Zaki al-Tawwil, the Egyptian deputy minister of Sudanese affairs, and 'Izz al-Din, the Sudan government chargé d'affaires in Cairo, which took place in Cairo in November 1950. According to 'Izz al-Din, the British government did not plan to separate Sudan from Egypt, yet it was not willing to yield to Egypt's demand to unite the Nile valley. The British continued with Sudanization, that is, to prepare the Sudanese for self-government. On his part, Tawwil asserted that no one in Egypt intended ruling Sudan. On the contrary, Egypt wished to see the Sudanese managing their own affairs, yet this should be under the Egyptian crown. Tawwil acknowledged that his office was preparing a plan to dispatch Egyptian experts in the fields of education, irrigation, military, and economy on long-term missions. 'Izz al-Din said that the Sudan government was interested in increasing Sudan's Nile water quota to expand the agricultural land following the growth of the Sudanese population. The two also discussed the participation of Sudan in the construction of the Tana Dam at the Blue Nile. Tawwil promised that Egypt would do everything possible to improve the welfare of Sudanese.[28]

In his speech marking the festive opening of the winter session of the parliament, King Faruq restated the national consensus on Sudan employing Wafdist hard-line terminology. Britain should respect the Egyptian people's twofold and inseparable demands: a full withdrawal of its troops from the Nile valley and the unity of the Nile valley. The 1936 treaty, he declared, could no longer constitute a basis for Anglo–Egyptian relations. There was no other way but to declare its abrogation, which should be followed by the promulgation of new laws reinforcing the foundations of the unification of Egypt and Sudan under the Egyptian crown.[29]

Indeed, at the close of its first year in power, the Wafd government conducted intensive talks aiming at settling the dispute with Britain. The talks took place in December 1950 between Muhammad Salah al-Din, the Egyptian foreign minister, and his British counterpart, Ernest Bevin. Salah al-Din refused to discuss further the Western plan of defending the Middle East within the context of the Cold War as long as Britain was not willing to pull out its troops from Egypt and Sudan and accept Egypt's

plan to unite the Nile valley under the Egyptian crown.[30] Bevin's refusal
to accept Egypt's demands received tail wind from the direction of the
Sudan government – two of its senior ministers, education and health,
spurned the idea of the unity of the Nile valley under the Egyptian crown,
urging the British government to declare immediately the separation of
Sudan from Egypt.[31]

In early February 1951, Sir Ralph Stevenson, the British ambassador
to Cairo, proposed to the Foreign Office to approach the Egyptian
government with the following formula for the solution of the Sudan
problem. First, since both Egypt and Sudan were mutually dependent on
the water of the Nile River, "it is agreed that the closest and friendliest ties must always unite them." Second, Egypt and Britain were in
consensus that the Sudanese people would be granted the right to self-
government as soon as possible, and in due course could decide independently the mode of their future relationship with Egypt. Third, since
the people of Sudan lacked homogeneity in many aspects – culture, race,
religion, political awareness – both Egypt and Britain should closely
cooperate in preparing them for "full and adequate self-government."[32]
The Sudan government in Khartoum thought the proposal required
some amendments. Stevenson, it was stressed critically, failed to point
out that the vast majority of Sudanese sought full independence with no
links to Egypt. Also, regarding the Nile water issue, it might be advisable
to set up an international technical authority "to control all matters
affecting irrigation of the waters." Such a solution, it was estimated,
would safeguard "Egypt's resultant requirements in the event of the
Sudanese opting for independence" and would protect Sudanese rights
too. The authority would also fairly monitor the technical plans for
increasing water supply by both Egypt and Sudan.[33]

Stevenson did not remain indifferent to such criticism. My proposal,
he asserted defensively, was based on the fact that

our responsibility to the Sudanese cannot absolve us from our responsibility to
Egypt which is implicit in the 1899 Agreement and the 1936 Treaty. Our aim
should therefore surely be to promote the closest and friendliest relations
between the inhabitants of the Nile Valley rather than to favour separatism ...
I do not see how in view of that responsibility [toward Egypt] Britain can possibly
suggest Sudanese independence. The Sudanese themselves may be able to
establish it in the long run but we surely cannot go further than to say that we
would welcome any system of relationship with Egypt which the Sudanese might
choose to fulfil the needs of the independence between Egypt and the Sudan.

Stevenson offhandedly ruled out the idea of an international controlling
authority for the Nile water – Egypt, he determined, would never agree
to it.[34] The Sudan government remained adamant in its viewpoint:

the Sudanese people would never agree to any Egyptian involvement in their country, and most of them wanted full independence.[35]

The state of relations within the British–Egyptian–Sudanese triangle was well depicted in a letter sent by J. W. Robertson, the civil secretary, to R. J. Bowker, the undersecretary of state at the Foreign Office. He urged the Foreign Office not to negotiate with the Egyptian government behind the back of the Sudanese, because such a move would lead to fermentation and troubles all over the country: "the Sudanese of all political views, and the tribal leaders, and the southern representatives are completely united on this: they are determined that they themselves will, at some time or other, decide their own future." The civil secretary excluded the Ashiqqa' group – a firm supporter of the unity of the Nile valley under the Egyptian crown. Robertson argued that the Egyptians heavily subsidized that group so that the voices of unity continued to be heard. However, the situation was that among the politically conscious Sudanese a real feeling of nationalism prevailed. The Egyptians intensified their propaganda in Sudan, spending a large amount of money, particularly on education. The Egyptian state radio had an evening *Sudan Programme* presenting "in a most tendentious way every little item of news which is damaging to the Sudan Government and to our Ministers – half-truths not outright lies, but everything is twisted with malicious ingenuity." There was a spate of Egyptian students visiting Sudan acting as propagators and stirring up a lot of feeling by stressing that Egyptian grants were given to charities and religious foundations including the building of new mosques. Thus, for instance, a grant of £60,000 was paid by Egypt to victims of flood damage that occurred in 1950. In addition, the Egyptian controller of education continued to visit Egyptian schools in Sudan, encouraging Sudanese pupils to study in these schools and in Egypt, ignoring the educational authorities in Sudan.[36]

The Foreign Office position, however, appeared to endorse Stevenson's outline: "Stevenson's suggestions seem helpful and Khartoum's comments a little parochial, though the Department fully recognizes the strength of nationalist and anti-Egyptian feeling in the Sudan." However, the assumption was that Egypt would not be satisfied by any concession the British could make on the Sudan issue. Egypt, it was noted, was talking of "federation" in a vague manner or "dominion status" for Sudan under Faruq's crown. That is, Faruq would become King of Egypt and Sudan, and there should be a common currency for the two countries, a customs union, and common foreign and defense policies. The Foreign Office opined that such a formula would not be accepted by the Sudanese, and Britain could not impose it on them.[37]

The anti-British struggle, which gathered momentum following the formation of Nahhas's government, aggravated markedly during 1951. The reviling rhetoric employed by Wafd ministers was a cause for worry among British diplomats in both Egypt and Sudan. For instance, shortly after Ahmad Hamza, the Egyptian minister of supply, concluded his visit to Sudan, he was quoted by *al-Misri* as saying that the Sudan government was to be held accountable for "gross negligence regarding malaria and cerebro-spinal meningitis epidemics." The chief goals of the British were to create "a spirit of hatred" between Sudanese and Egyptians and to turn the former into a weak and servile people. The British segregated northern Sudan from the southern part, and northerners were not allowed to travel south without a special permit.[38]

British and Egyptian senior officials held utterly contradictory perceptions as to the Sudanese people's political aspirations. The Foreign Office drew a comparison between the British and the Egyptian governments' stands on this issue. The former was committed to the principle that the Sudanese people would be allowed to choose their own future including independence, whereas the latter "are equally committed to retaining some degree of Egyptian sovereignty over the Sudan though they may in the last resort be prepared to concede to the Sudanese a large measure of self-government." The Foreign Office appeared to be resolute that no Egyptian government "in the foreseeable future" would agree to less than the Sidqi–Bevin protocol of 1946. The gap between the two governments regarding the Sudan question, concluded the Foreign Office, was therefore wide.[39]

In a conversation between Ibrahim Faraj Pasha, the minister for Sudanese affairs, and British diplomats in Alexandria on 27 July 1951, the former belittled the effect and essentialness of the British-made legislative assembly, saying disparagingly that it was supported by only 2 percent of the Sudanese. The British strongly disagreed, saying conversely that "at least 70% of the Sudanese were solidly behind it, and that as a result of its success great interest was taken in it by everyone." Faraj was advised by his interlocutors not to believe everything he was told by those Sudanese "who were in Egyptian pay" as they would tell him anything he wanted to hear. They represented hardly anybody and had no influence. Faraj on his part pondered that if that was the case, how come they had won all the elections for local governments.[40] The British disagreed with him, saying that they won only in a few places. Still, if that was the case, it indicated that they had more than insignificant influence in Sudan. The verity, as future events were to demonstrate, lay somewhere in between these two assertions.

The pressure on the Wafd government to take unilateral steps to achieve the twofold national goal – evacuation and unification – came from all directions. Ihsan 'Abd al-Quddus, editor-in-chief of the influential independent weekly *Ruz al-Yusuf*, was particularly critical in his editorial. Thirty years of negotiations with the British were fruitless for a simple reason: the British had no intention to agree to Egypt's national demands. The Egyptian government, he wrote sarcastically, "believes in half evacuation and half unification hoping that Britain would grant it two halves." The Wafd government deceived the people by issuing statements and diffusing slogans that it would achieve both evacuation and unification. Instead it approached the British from a compromising and frail standpoint, thus repeating similar policies employed by its predecessors, who regarded the British as the superior power and Egypt as the inferior element in the Anglo–Egyptian equation of relative strength. Even Sa'd Zaghlul held a similar viewpoint, and in one of his speeches in parliament he referred to Egypt's inability to regain Sudan, asking members of parliament: "do you have an expeditionary force" to expel the British from Sudan? Qudus concluded that only the people, the real sovereign, could force the government to change its weak position or face its downfall.[41]

In a conversation between Salah al-Din and the British ambassador to Cairo on 13 July 1951, the former outlined his scheme for the future of Sudan, saying that unlike the British who wanted to separate Sudan from Egypt and then to control that country through its proxy, the Sudan government, the Egyptians were willing to grant the Sudanese full self-government, which would be based on well-defined natural links to be agreed upon by the majority of Egyptians and Sudanese. That is, two entities unified under one crown, with a common foreign policy, army, and currency. In Salah al-Din's view, his plan for future self-rule of Sudan was so far the most comprehensive and generous, compared to any other proposals made by the British or the Sudan government.[42] On 26 July the two continued their talks, and Salah al-Din asked his interlocutor if Britain would agree to a "free plebiscite in order to ascertain how serious you [the British] were in proposing the consultation of the Sudanese and I [Salah al-Din] made it clear that this freedom cannot be achieved unless your administration and forces are withdrawn." Do you accept this condition? asked Salah al-Din. The British ambassador replied gingerly that "a premature withdrawal would cause breakdown of the Sudan administration." Salah al-Din concluded that the British aim was therefore to continue the status quo in Sudan so that the British could safeguard their interests there under the pretext of being the guardians of "the will of the Sudanese."[43]

By late 1951, prominent figures within the Sudanese political elite presented confidently their own views concerning the doctrine of the unity of the Nile valley and the future of Sudan. In a conversation between Fu'ad Siraj al-Din, the minister of interior, and Muhammad Salih Shingeiti, the speaker of the Sudanese legislative assembly, in September, the latter took pains to communicate to Siraj al-Din the general sentiments of the Sudanese concerning Egypt, generally, and the Egyptian crown, particularly. The Sudanese way of life was entirely different from that of Egypt: "there were no rich men, no large land-owners and no governing class. The Sudanese feared that unity with Egypt would upset this and introduce into the Sudan elements which they wished to keep out." Shingeiti expressed his opinion that Egypt's main concerns for the future were the supply of Nile water and its development to the utmost, as well as Egypt's growing population and the option of settling part of the surplus population – particularly hundreds of thousands of fellahin – in Sudan. Siraj al-Din, like Salah al-Din before, reiterated Egypt's government policy, that is, it supported self-government for Sudan in two years "with certain reserved subjects." He nevertheless argued that his government "had no intention of unifying the Sudan defense force with the Egyptian army. The Sudan would continue to have her own troops but the military policy of the two countries would be under the direction of Egypt." Shingeiti responded that Sudan was reluctant to be controlled by Egypt and wanted to advance its development toward complete self-government and to determine freely its future relationship with Egypt. Overall, he disfavored the idea of Sudan becoming a monarchy.[44]

Egyptian protagonists of the unity of the Nile valley such as El-Barawy argued conversely that the majority of Sudanese favored unification with Egypt. To justify his contention, Barawy relied on Anthony Galatoli's "neutral" study *Egypt in Midpassage*s (1950). To quote him:

In view of the fact that the majority of Sudanese favour dominion status under the Egyptian Crown, Britain may well assist in carrying out the difficult constitutional scheme ... The programme of the Blood Brothers [*Ashiqqa'*] based on Sudanese administrative autonomy and allegiance to the Egyptian Crown is sound in that it satisfies the Egyptian aspiration for the unity of the Nile Valley and allays Sudanese apprehensions of an Egyptian predominance in Sudanese domestic matters.[45]

However, Galatoli's analysis was based on the political credo of the *Ashiqqa'* Party, whose pro-unionist views were not endorsed by the entire Sudanese society. In fact, the issue of the unity of the Nile valley under the Egyptian crown was more of a divisive factor among Sudanese, which Britain did indeed encourage.

Unilateral Abrogation and Its Repercussions

The Anglo–Egyptian talks reached an impasse, and 1951 witnessed a further deterioration in Anglo–Egyptian relations and growing anti-Western sentiments followed by a process of rapid rapprochement with the Soviet bloc. The Egyptian government was split with regard to the unilateral abrogation of the 1936 treaty. Salah al-Din was enthusiastic to materialize annulment, whereas his chief rival within the government, Fu'ad Siraj al-Din, struggled to prevent such a decision. In this power struggle Salah al-Din prevailed – his stand was supported by the press, the public, and opposition parties.[46] King Faruq, who disfavored such a move, admitted that he could not do anything to prevent it: "I cannot set myself in opposition to the whole country and in this instance the whole country is of the same mind as the government." Salah al-Din, blamed the king, "was young and impulsive and also has other drawbacks," and was to be held accountable for the abrogation and the severe deterioration in Anglo–Egyptian relations.[47]

The deadlock in the Anglo–Egyptian talks led the Wafd government to act unilaterally. On 8 October 1951, Nahhas declared before parliament that his government decided to abrogate the 1936 treaty and announced Faruq as King of Egypt and Sudan. The government also declared the condominium treaty of 1899 to be null and void. Concessions and facilitations hitherto given to British forces in Egypt were abolished. The government decisions were to come into effect immediately.[48]

The repeal of the treaties with Britain was warmly received by the Egyptian people, who took to the streets to express their satisfaction with this popular move that was endorsed by all political parties including the opposition. The crowds chanted slogans such as "Long live the King of Egypt and the Sudan" and "Long live al-Nahhas, the hero of independence," as well as anti-British slogans such as "Get out of our country."[49]

The Egyptian government decision was followed by the announcement of several unilateral steps, the most prominent of which were the dismissal of the governor-general of Sudan and his administration, and the implementation of the unity of the Nile valley. In a meeting with Isma'il al-Azhari, Ibrahim Faraj, the minister for Sudanese affairs, spurned the announcement made by the governor-general, stressing that his legal authority was derived from the treaty of 1899, which the British government continued to honor. According to Faraj, the governor-general was appointed to his post by the king of Egypt, and since the abolition of the 1899 treaty put an end to the condominium, the governor-general was no longer the representative of the British government but a high-ranking official subordinate to the authority of the

Egyptian government.[50] The Egyptian government insisted from that stage on that all credentials of foreign and Egyptian diplomats should be addressed to and from Faruq, the King of Egypt and Sudan.[51]

The unilateral abrogation was warmly welcomed by the majority of the Egyptian political currents. Ahmad Hasan al-Zayyat, a founder, owner, and editor of the Islamist-oriented al-Risala, noted complacently that it had taken official Egypt nearly fifteen years of insult and humiliation to realize that its past treaties with Britain were based on false imperialist terminology. Zayyat drew a distinction between the nationalist Egyptians and those Egyptians holding official posts. The former, he stressed, had already comprehended what the latter naively failed to foresee: that the 1899 and 1936 treaties were designed to split the Nile valley – thus serving the long-term goals of imperialist Britain.[52]

Al-Balagh covered comprehensively the demonstrations of Egyptian and Sudanese students that took place in Paris before the UN General Assembly session in December 1951. The students, narrated al-Balagh, wanted to reveal to the world the truth behind the issue of the Nile valley and the exploitative and ruthless nature of British imperialism. They distributed pamphlets to journalists explaining key issues related to the Nile valley and paid special attention to the fact that the 1936 treaty was a violation of the sovereignty of both Egypt and Sudan. The 1936 treaty was in contradiction to other international treaties and particularly to the UN Charter. British rule over Sudan was nothing but a military regime in the full sense of the word.[53]

The governor-general of Sudan made it clear that he would not recognize the abrogation of the 1899 condominium treaty and that "he intends to continue to administer the Sudan in accordance with that agreement and to continue the present policy of accelerating the attainment of self-government by the Sudanese."[54] The abrogation was warmly received by "all politically minded parties," who had waited for a long time to see the end of the condominium as well as the end to the protracted Anglo–Egyptian disputes over Sudan. Britain, he asserted, should react accordingly to this development, and if it declined to do so, "it may weaken the very genuine gratitude felt for the British stand against the Egyptian attempt at domination."[55]

The British government endorsed the governor-general's statement. It announced that the unilateral repudiation of the agreements and treaties and the announcement of unilateral measures in Sudan "have placed the Governor General of the Sudan in a position in which he can no longer act as representative of HMG and the Egyptian government, or fully carry out his responsibilities towards the people of the Sudan." Britain would continue to advance its ongoing program for self-government in

Sudan, intending to bring it to conclusion by the end of 1952. This would lead to the formation of a constituent assembly representing the views and desires of the Sudanese people and would eventually determine the final status of Sudan before 18 October 1954. The British government therefore decided to take unilateral steps in this direction "after consultation with representatives of the great majority of the Sudanese." Sudan would be placed under British trusteeship "to be administered by a High Commissioner in whom shall be vested the supreme civil and military authority in the Sudan. The period of this trusteeship shall last for three years from October 18 1951." The British government invited the governments of the United States, Australia, Egypt, Ethiopia, and India to become members of an international commission stationed in Sudan to observe the transitional period, advise the high commissioner if necessary, or make direct recommendations to the British government. The British government acknowledged the interests "common to Egypt and the Sudan in the control and distribution of Nile waters and other matters." To mitigate its unpleasant steps, which were designed to shatter the Egyptian national vision of the unity of the Nile valley under the Egyptian crown, the British government announced that it would "accept and support any decision the Sudanese make for the future status of their country and for the nature of their relationship with the Egyptian crown."[56]

On 16 November, in a speech before the UN Assembly, Muhammad Salah al-Din decided to test Britain's commitment to enable the Sudanese to decide their political future by means of general referendum under the auspice of the United Nations. He called upon both Britain and Egypt to pull out their personnel and armed forces from Sudan so that the Sudanese would be able to vote freely and without foreign interference. He sneered at the British delegates, casting doubt whether their government would be brave enough to go ahead with such a daring move.[57] Two weeks later, on 30 November, in a meeting in Paris with pro-unionist Sudanese, Salah al-Din declared that Egypt "does not recognize any official title of Britain in the Sudan, and no one in the Sudan claims that there are ties that bind Britain to the Sudan."[58]

The British refused to play according to the new Egyptian rules. They refused to allow the Egyptian government to dictate the pace of progress toward self-government in Sudan. G. D. Lampen, the deputy Sudan agent in London, depicted the British dilemma in the wake of the abrogation as follows:

We all agree that union with Egypt would be disastrous for the Sudan ... it would be morally wrong to hand over the Sudan to a corrupt power like Egypt dominated by self-seeking plutocracy. This possibility must be fought by every means ... Although we all agree to self-determination for the Sudan, I believe that every thoughtful person must have very grave doubts of its future if it becomes a completely independent isolated state. It has probably not got the manpower, finance and ability to survive. Whatever form of constitution it might adopt, there would be no guarantee of stability and permanence ... Connection with the British Commonwealth seems to be really the only hope for the Sudan, if it is to get through its adolescent stage, without being extinguished by Egypt or going to the dogs on its own.[59]

Just before the abrogation announcement, most Sudanese political parties favored an orderly development toward self-government, that is, a fully representative legislative assembly along with an entirely Sudanese government. They firmly believed that only the Sudanese people should decide their future status. The *Ashiqqa'* was an exception – it favored complete fusion with Egypt and boycotted the present Sudanese constitution. The majority parties wanted to see the end of the condominium rule but were willing to follow a gradual process toward self-government. The parties welcomed the abrogation of the 1936 treaty, but repudiated the imposition of the Egyptian crown and the manner of imposing a constitution on Sudan unilaterally. In this regard, there was a consensus between two of the main rival groups – Khatmiyya and Ansar. The general feeling was that following the abrogation, the condominium rule ended.[60] The possibility that the Sudanese parties, even those who looked more favorably toward some sort of unification with Egypt (except for the *Ashiqqa'*), would agree to symbolic Egyptian sovereignty in line with the Bevin–Sidqi protocol of 1946 was now null.[61]

The *Ashiqqa'* continued to support Egypt's moves following the abrogation. The abrogation had far-reaching consequences, since the presence of British troops in the Suez Canal area was considered illegal by many Egyptians, as well as by the *Aahiqqa'* that supported the anti-British guerilla warfare conducted by Egyptian fighters along the Suez Canal in late 1951–early 1952. The harsh retaliatory actions of the British forces, which included the occupation of the Suez Canal zone, were severely criticized by Azhari and his Sudanese followers. They regarded these British imperialist actions as directed against all the people of the Nile valley.[62] In a meeting with Nahhas in Cairo on 4 February 1952, Azhari expressed satisfaction and agreement with Nahhas's linkage between complete British evacuation and the unity of the Nile valley. Azhari praised the Egyptian leader for his courageous anti-imperialist policy and for placing both the Sudan question and Egypt's liberation in one basket – two inseparable issues.[63]

The presence of British troops in the Suez Canal zone after the unilateral abrogation was perceived by opposition groups as illegal. The Egyptian government overlooked the guerrilla activities carried out by radical groups against British troops, which led to violent clashes for several months until the downfall of the Wafd government on 27 January 1952. The Egyptian press representing the opposition as well as the government expressed sympathy with the Egyptian insurgents, whom Salah al-Din described as "Egyptian patriots."[64] His party mouthpiece, al-Misri, urged the police to resist British aggression with arms. The Wafdist paper also ridiculed ideas that the Nahhas government would be so unpatriotic as to suppress terrorism in the Suez Canal zone.[65] Oppositional figures and anti-government press attacked the government for trying to come to terms with the British and not stirring up hatred of the British.[66]

The Military Regime and the Sudan Question

Shortly after the downfall of the Wafd government (January 1952), the new prime minister, 'Ali Mahir (January 1952–March 1952), made a statement of his intention to grant Sudan autonomy. He called on the Sudanese people to remain united on all crucial issues even if that meant to be united against Egypt for the sake of their country. Any future solution to Sudan should first and foremost serve the interests of the Sudanese.[67] The next government, of Ahmad Najib al-Hilali (March 1952–July 1952), conducted talks with Sudanese key figures, among them 'Abd al-Rahman al-Mahdi, the moderate leader of al-Ansar, looking for a solution that would satisfy both pro- and anti-unionist Sudanese. According to al-Ahram, Mahdi showed no objection to Faruq using the title of King of Egypt and Sudan.[68] Nevertheless, Mahdi remained consistent in his demand for Sudanese independence. The Ansar group was depicted in 1951 by C. W. M. Cox (education adviser to the secretary of state for the colonies, 1940–1970) as politically linked with the various "independence" groups, republican or otherwise, which favored self-government for Sudan with or without the British connection.[69]

Mahdi was among the first to greet the Free Officers on their successful take-over in July 1952. He wrote to Muhammad Najib, ostensibly the true leader of the revolution, that the Sudanese people were satisfied by the rise of the military movement and the overthrow of the old regime.[70] Yet, Mahdi's general view on the future of Sudan remained unshakable, as he revealed about a year later in a conversation with the British minister of state. Mahdi did not hide his national aspirations: an independent Sudan with continuous cooperation with the British.[71]

However, the revolution of 1952 also marked a turning point in Egypt's policy toward the future of Sudan. In fact, as an Egyptian diplomat who was closely involved in Anglo–Egyptian negotiations since the mid-1940s put it, the only workable and realistic solution to the Sudan case was the one achieved by Isma'il Sidqi in 1946. Since then Egypt's grip on Sudan had been gradually weakened. The unilateral abrogation of the 1936 treaty was a show-off move that was not recognized internationally. As we shall see, ever since the military took power, Egypt relinquished its uncompromising nationalist demand to unite the Nile valley under its hegemony. In fact, since the demise of the monarchial regime, the slogan "the unity of the Nile valley: one Nile, one people, one king" was no longer valid. Pragmatism and realpolitik were the chief features in the Free Officers' foreign policy – the Sudan question was an integral part thereof. In a way, the old political parties such as the Wafd and the Nationalist Party (al-Hizb al-Watani) misread the new development and upheld the pre-revolution paradigm of the unity of the Nile valley.[72]

Signs of the forthcoming shift in the Free Officers' policy toward the future of Sudan became already discernible shortly after the military revolution. On 30 August, al-Ahram reported that Sudanese politicians representing a wide spectrum of political parties gathered in Egypt under the auspices of their Egyptian hosts to discuss the next steps. They agreed that there was a need to establish solid relations between the northern and southern parts of the valley, calling upon the "northerners" to respect the right of their southern neighbors to self-determination. Sudan would enter into a transitional period during which its affairs would be managed by a "council as a governor-general" comprising Egyptian, Sudanese, and British members. At the same time, a Sudanese coalition government representing all political parties would be formed – a government led by a neutral figure. The provisional government would then form a committee to draft a constitution and election law. Free elections would then be held, and a parliament representing all Sudanese people was to be elected; a constitutional committee would thereafter be formed and together with the parliament decide Sudan's political future: independence or unification with Egypt.[73]

In late October 1952, Muhammad Najib's cabinet held talks with representatives of the Sudanese Umma Party and the Independent Front. The Sudanese delegation included 'Abd al-Rahman al-Mahdi and 'Abdallah al-Fadl, and the Egyptian delegation was advised legally by 'Abd al-Razzaq al-Sanhuri. The latter was against the idea of granting Sudan self-government. On 30 October, an agreement was reached between the parties according to which Egypt accepted the Sudanese demand for self-government based on their right to self-determination.

The Sudanese people would be the only factor to determine the future of Sudan: full independence or any other form of political structure. Egypt now appeared to be the champion of Sudanese rights, taking the lead from Britain, which was bewildered by and unprepared for Najib's move.[74]

On 2 November 1952, the military regime signed an agreement with the Sudanese parties (including al-Umma and the Independent Front). The agreement was a major breakthrough in Egypt's policy toward Sudan. This was the first time Egypt acknowledged and agreed to leave the future of Sudan to be determined by the Sudanese people. Egypt would respect their decision and cooperate with them in the political, economic, and social fields. A transitional period would lay the foundations for Sudanese self-rule, during which they would enjoy the free, neutral, and conducive atmosphere they needed to define their form of self-determination.

Nevertheless, in reality, the British were still deep in the game, although the omnipotent governor-general was to relinquish much of his authority on domestic policies and to act as the representative of the supreme constitutional ruler. He would be advised by a committee comprising an Egyptian, a British, and an Indian or a Pakistani member, all appointed by their respective governments, as well as two Sudanese elected by the Sudanese parliament. Another committee including a British, an Egyptian, an American, and an Indian or a Pakistani member, appointed by their respective governments, in addition to three Sudanese appointed by the governor-general, would be formed to monitor the forthcoming elections.[75]

'Abd al-Salam Fahmi Jum'a, a former Wafd minister, defended Muhammad Najib's agreement with the Sudanese. Egypt, he noted, wanted its Sudanese brothers to have their right to self-determination and subsequent independence. The main goal was to drive British imperialism out of the Nile valley in the shortest possible time. "Egypt and the Sudan are sisters – they both have the common goal – to get rid of British imperialism even at the price of an independent Sudan and its separation from Egypt ... We did not seek unification in order to exploit the Sudan for imperialist goals, we rather wanted unification because we requested for the Sudan what we requested for ourselves."[76]

About half a year after the Free Officers' cabal marked the demise of Egypt's monarchy, the country's new rulers announced the end of the nation's sweet dream of the unity of the Nile valley. The agreement between the governments of Egypt and the United Kingdom of 12 February 1953 determined that it was "a fundamental principle of their common policy to maintain the unity of the Sudan as a single territory."

Article 9 of the treaty stipulated that "the two contracting governments undertake to bring the transitional period to an end as soon as possible. In any case this period shall not exceed three years." Article 11 could be perceived by Egyptians as the beginning of the end of British imperialism in the Nile valley. For Sudanese it meant the end of an epoch of dual imperialism – British and Egyptian: "Egyptian and British military forces shall withdraw from the Sudan immediately upon the Sudanese Parliament adopting a resolution expressing its desire that arrangements for self-determination be put in motion. The two Contracting Governments undertake to complete the withdrawal of their forces from the Sudan within a period not exceeding three months."[77]

On 12 February 1953, Anthony Eden, the foreign secretary, stated in the British parliament that the Anglo–Egyptian agreement:

expressly recognises the right of the Sudanese people to self-determination and the effective exercise thereof at the appropriate time and with the necessary safe-guards. It also provides that, in order to enable them to exercise self-determination in a free and neutral atmosphere, there shall be a transitional period not exceeding three years which shall provide full self-government for the Sudanese and which shall begin after the Sudanese Parliament has been elected.[78]

Egypt's transition from monarchy to republic following the military coup emptied the nationalist consensual paradigm of the unity of the Nile valley under the Egyptian crown of its content. The drastic change in the Free Officers' position toward the future of Sudan was well expressed by Major Salah Salim, who negotiated with the Sudanese prior to the conclusion of the 12 February treaty. Salim did not hide his anti-unionist approach deriving from the Sudanese desire for self-rule. A few months before the conclusion of the agreement, he made his views clear. In an interview he gave *al-Ahram* upon his return from a visit to Sudan, Salim revealed that his meetings with representatives of the political elite showed that there was a solid consensus in Sudan behind the Egyptian memorandum concerning the future of Sudan (which was submitted to the British government on 2 November). In this memorandum, Salim emphasized, the Egyptian government was determined to grant the Sudanese their right to self-government and self-determination in a united and indivisible Sudan.[79]

Later, on 2 February 1953, Salim challenged in *Ruz al-Yusuf* the hitherto prevailing nationalist consensus regarding the unity of the Nile valley. He attacked the old political guard who endeavored for many years to achieve the impossible and constantly deceived the Egyptian people by claiming that unification was not realized because of British imperialism. These past leaders presented Egypt as an aggressor who aimed at enslaving the Sudanese people. No wonder, opined Salim, that they wanted to get rid of us and deemed unification as national enslavement and humiliation. Salim's article reflected the downfall of the paradigm of the unity of the Nile valley and its replacement by the Sudanese right to self-determination. Only the Sudanese would determine their political future – unification or separation. Egypt should show goodwill and support and respect their decision. Moreover, it would struggle along with the Sudanese to remove the British from Sudan because the two countries had a common nationalist goal: to get rid of British imperialism.[80]

Several months later Salim did not hide his belief that mutual interests would bring Egypt and Sudan together in the near future: "The Nile Valley could become self-sufficient more easily than any other areas in the world except America. Egypt would benefit from offering her money and experience to the Sudanese regardless of what kind of government they might have. All that mattered was that there should be a free Sudan, with no foreign or British influence. Once the nightmare of imperialism was removed the Sudanese would realize that their interests lay with Egypt."[81]

Muhammad Najib made it clear that the 12 February agreement gave the Sudanese only two options to choose from – either unification with Egypt or full independence without any foreign presence or intervention. Najib called on the Sudanese to remain united throughout the three-year transitional period. Egypt, he promised, would do all it could to protect them. The agreement meant freedom and the end of British imperialism.[82]

The *Ashiqqa'* Party, which favored unification with Egypt, found itself in an ideological void following the treaty of February 1953. Khidr 'Umar, its secretary general, gave an interview to the party's organ *al-Sudani* on 27 May 1953, during which he expressed his party's political labyrinth. Nobody, he asserted, was able to define accurately the present Egyptian policy toward Sudan "as General Najib's behavior does not permit us to infer that he believes in Sudanese national unity or in union between Egypt and the Sudan. On the contrary, the Egyptian prime minister endeavors to break off links between the two countries." Egypt's new regime had hitherto pursued an unclear and confusing policy regarding Sudan. Egypt wanted to achieve something for Sudan with the intent to gather the Sudanese around a common objective. Its leaders tried to unify the policies of the various Sudanese groups and in doing so unintentionally destroyed that very objective. Khidr drew special attention to contradictory statements made by the Free Officers ever since the conclusion of the February agreement:

They have been telling the Egyptian people that what they have done for the Sudan will ultimately lead to union between it and Egypt. On another occasion they say that their only aim is Sudan's independence while at the same time they speak of the Nile valley, Nile valley freedom and Nile valley people ... General Najib sends agents to the Sudan to produce evidence that the Sudan and Egypt are one and the same thing. However, pro-independence elements in the Sudan immediately renounce such behavior ... and reaffirm their desire to secure unity of action among the Sudanese, which cannot be done so long as the final political aim is self-contradictory.

Khidr advised his fellow Sudanese to refrain from wishful thinking and faith in the British. Only hard work and strong belief in themselves would pave their way to national liberation.[83]

Daly and Hogan opined that most Sudanese who supported the unity of the Nile valley were tactically employing a calculative yet pragmatic approach. Unification was a means to weaken those Sudanese separatists who supported independence under the auspices of British imperialism. Moreover, they saw "Egypt as the lever with which to winkle the British out of the country ... [the unity of the Nile valley] was a strategy for independence, and one more likely of success than the 'Sudan for the Sudanese', whose adherents seemed all too willing to accept continued British rule as a means of keeping out the Egyptians."[84]

However, as we have seen, pronouncements and statements made in real time clearly showed that Azhari and his Sudanese fellows, who vehemently supported the doctrine of the unity of the Nile valley, had good reasons to feel betrayed by the Egyptian Free Officers regime. Shortly after their takeover they negotiated with Azhari's anti-unionist political adversaries and subsequently came to terms with them. However, he who laughs loudest, laughs last: surprisingly Azhari was chosen by the Sudanese people as their first prime minister for the transitional period stipulated by the February treaty.

The political estrangement between Azhari and the Egyptian ruling elite manifested itself throughout the transitional period (1953–1956). Clashes between south and north were inevitable following the abandonment of the British "Southern Policy," which safeguarded the southerners' interests and its replacement with the policy of Sudanese self-determination in a united Sudan led by the dominant north. The revolt of the south in August 1955 (Anyanya Rebellion) was manipulated by Egypt to postpone Azhari's intended realization of self-determination and independence. To quote Daly: "the fate of the south was that common to peripheral regions, determined in part by geography, reinforced by colonial economic priorities and mismanagement, overlain by a legacy of slavery and consequent spectre of exploitation, and enforced by religious and racial aspects of Northern Sudanese Nationalism. Stirring this witch's brew was Egypt's last act in the drama of Condominium."[85] Egypt exploited the created opportunities to drive a wedge between the belligerent parties by backing the southerners and promising them security in return for their support for federation with it. The irony of fate was that Azhari – hitherto Britain's bitter enemy – was given support by those British officials who had supported his rivals and by those British administrators who had sought to perpetuate the condominium; whereas Egypt, Azhari's previous partner, was now employing manipulative tactics to postpone the demise of the condominium.[86]

However, Egypt's and Britain's final imperialist maneuvers in Sudan were doomed. By the end of the transitional period, Azhari had no commitments to his former Egyptian allies: he became the champion of Sudanese independence. The unity of the Nile valley – the prevailing Egyptian doctrine during the first half of the twentieth century – became a shattered dream.[87] To quote Collins, "Just as the British Empire was in disarray, so too was that of the decadent rulers of Egypt. Of course, the British were there with the stiff upper lip of neutrality, but every Sudanese of whatever persuasion knows that they were not about to become an Egyptian colony."[88]

Notes

1 Top Secret Report No. 97.H.6, "Egyptian Propaganda in the Sudan," 30 September 1947, FO371/63084, J4680/16. Indeed, the Sudanese supporters and adherents of the unity of the Nile valley suffered a domestic setback following Egypt's failure at the UN. For details, see Daly, *Imperial Sudan*, pp. 265–266.
2 Top Secret Report No. 97.H.6, "Egyptian Propaganda in the Sudan."
3 "Misr fi majlis al-amn," *Kifah al-Sha'b*, Vol. 12, 25 September 1947; M. A., "Inna al-sha'b la yuridukum," *al-Jamahir*, 5 May 1947; M. A., "Inna al-sha'b la yuridukum," *al-Jamahir*, 5 May 1947. On the reaction of the Egyptian left to Nuqrashi's speech, see Chapter 6.
4 Mahmud Muhammad Shakir, "'Ibar liman ya'tabiru," *al-Risala*, No. 738, 25 August 1947, pp. 915–916. On the debate in the Egyptian press on Egypt's experience in the Security Council, see also Telegrams 110, 112, and 115, from British Embassy, Cairo, 20 August 1947, 27 August 1947, and 3 September 1947, FO953/51, PME 1619/627/916.
5 Shakir, "'Ibar liman ya'tabiru."
6 Mahmud Muhammad Shakir, "Mu'tamar al-mustad'afina," *al-Risala*, No. 742, 22 September 1947, p. 1,030.

7 "Ma yajib an yaf'alahu ra'is al-hukuma," *al-Ikhwan al-Muslimun*, 27 September 1947, p. 5.
8 "Fashl muthallath – Bayna misr wa-injiltra wa-majlis al-amn," *al-Ahram*, 12 September 1947, p. 3.
9 "Lajnat tahrir al-wadi," *al-Ahram*, 15 September 1947, p. 5.
10 "Lajnat tahrir al-wadi," *al-Ahram*, 14 September 1947, p. 2.
11 "Madha ba'da qarar majlis al-amn," *al-Ahram*, 19 September 1947, p. 1.
12 Mustafa al-Nahhas, "Min al-wafd al-misri ila abna' al-wadi wa-ra'is al-hukuma wa-al-safir al-baritani," *al-Ahram*, 21 September 1947, p. 3.
13 Ibid.
14 Ibid.
15 "Wafd al-sudan wa-qadiyat al-wadi," *al-Ahram*, 28 September 1947, p. 2.
16 Ihsan 'Abd al-Quddus, "Madha nastati'?!," *Ruz al-Yusuf*, No. 1045, 21 June 1948.
17 Telegram 129 from British Embassy, Cairo, 24 September 1947, FO953/51, PME 1619/627/916.
18 Ginat, *The Soviet Union and Egypt*, p. 76.
19 Ibid., pp. 84–85.
20 On Nuqrashi's biography, see Rami Ginat, "Nuqrashi, Mahmud Fahmi al-," in Emmanuel K. Akyeampong and Henry Louis Gates (eds.), *Dictionary of African Biography*, Vol. 4 (Oxford and New York: Oxford University Press, 2012), pp. 508–509.
21 See Sirri's biography in James Jankowski, "Sirri, Husayn," in Akyeampong and Gates (eds.), *Dictionary of African Biography*, Vol. 5, pp. 395–396.
22 "al-Bahth fi amr al-ittisalat bi-kibar al-sudaniyyina," *al-Balagh*, 4 March 1950, p. 5.
23 "Hukuma dimuqratiyya muttahida ma'a misr tahta al-taj al-misri," *al-Balagh*, 13 March 1950, p. 4.
24 "Limadha la yatlubu al-mahdi basha jala' al-injliz?" *al-Balagh*, 30 March 1950, p. 5.
25 "al-Injiliz alghu al-mu'ahadah fa-limadha la nulghiha?" *al-Balagh*, 5 September 1951, p. 1.
26 "al-Ijtima' bi-zu'ama' al-sudan lil-tashawur," *al-Ahram*, 21 March 1950, p. 5.
27 Tawfiq Ahmad al-Bakri, "Ziyarat al-misriyyina lil-sudan," *al-Ahram*, 3 April 1950.
28 "Baritaniya la tufakkiru fi tasl al-sudan 'an misr," *al-Ahram*, 5 November 1950.
29 "Khutut al-siyasa al-misriyya li-tahqiq al-matalib al-wataniyya," *al-Ahram*, 18 November 1950.
30 "al-Ijtima' al-thani bayna bifin wa-salah al-din," *al-Ahram*, 8 December 1950, p. 1; "Bifin lam yay'as min al-ittifaq 'ala hall 'adil," *al-Ahram*, 9 December 1950.
31 "Misr tu'akhkhiru bahth al-hukm al-dhati bi-al-jam'iyya al-tashri'iyya," *al-Ahram*, 11 December 1950. See also a record of conversation of the talks in Sud/50/5, FO800/505, pp. 122–127.
32 Telegram 106 from R. Stevenson, British Embassy, Cairo, 6 February 1958, FO371/90152, JE1052/2.

33 Telegram 20 from Governor-General, Khartoum, 16 February 1951, FO371/ 90152, JE1052/5.

34 Telegram 130 from Stevenson, Cairo, 19 February 1951, FO371/90152, JE1052/6.

35 Telegram 23 from Governor-General, Khartoum, 24 February 1951, FO371/ 90152, JE1052/4.

36 Letter from Robertson to Bowker, 22 January 1951, FO371/90152, JE1052/9.

37 Minute by Roger Allen, Foreign Office, 5 March 1951, FO371/90152, JE1052/14.

38 al-Misri, 17 April 1951.

39 Telegram 338 from Foreign Office, London, to British Embassy, Cairo, 12 April 1951, FO141/1435.

40 See a record of conversation in FO371/90153, p. 2.

41 Ihsan 'Abd al-Quddus, "Nisf jala' wa-nisf wahda!!" Ruz al-Yusuf, No. 1191, 10 April 1951, pp. 3–4.

42 "Landan tatabi'u siyasat al-amr al-waqi' fi al-sudan," al-Ahram, 21 October 1951, p. 6.

43 See a record of conversation between the two in FO371/90153, pp. 1–10.

44 Dispatch 319 from British Embassy, Cairo, 26 September 1951, FO371/ 90153, JE1052/43.

45 Quoted from Galatoli, Egypt in Midpassage, p. 141, in El-Barawy, Egypt, Britain and the Sudan, p.19.

46 Letter from G. W. Bell, Sudan Agency, Cairo, to E. H. Nightingale, Civil Secretary's Office, Khartoum, 15 August 1951, Robertson Files, SA524/5/ 51–52. On the power struggle within the Nahhas Cabinet, see Ginat, The Soviet Union and Egypt, pp. 121–122. On the failure of the July 1951 talks between Salah al-Din and Ralph Stevenson, see "Qat' al-mubahathat li-ya'siha min al-tafahum ma'a al-injliz," al-Balagh, 28 July 1951, p. 1. In late August 1951, Nahhas Pasha warned that Egypt was considering the possibility of abrogating the 1936 treaty with Britain. For the content of his speech at the annual Sa'd Zaghlul memorial rally, see "Misr lan tusaqa ba'da al-yawm ila ghayr ma turidu," al-Balagh, 25 August 1951.

47 Ginat, The Soviet Union and Egypt, p. 122.

48 "al-Hukuma tu'linu fi al-barlaman ilgha' al-mu'ahada wa-ittifaqiyyatay al-sudan," al-Ahram, 9 October 1951; "Min ajil misr wuqi'at mu'ahadat 1936 wa-min ajliha utalibukum bi-ilgha'iha," al-Balagh, 9 October 1951. See also Ministère Royal des Affaires Etrangères, Exposé De S.E. Moustapha El Nahas Pacha Président du Conseil des Ministres Fait au Parlement le 8 Octobre 1951 (Cairo: Département de la Presse), in FO953/1113; Riyad Zahir, al-Sudan al-Mu'asir: mundhu al-fath al-misri hatta al-istiqlal 1821–1953 (Cairo: Maktabat al-Anjlu al-Misriyya, 1966), pp. 276–277.

49 "Ibtihaj al-bilad bi-ilgha' al-mu'ahadah wa-ittifaqiyyatay al-sudan," al-Ahram, 10 October 1951, p. 4.

50 "al-Hakim al-'amm lil-sudan yakhruju 'ala ta'at misr," al-Ahram, 15 October 1951, p. 4. See also Salah al-Din's press conference of 26 October 1951, in "al-Hall al-silmi huwa jala' al-quwwat al-baritaniyya," al-Ahram, 27 October 1951.

51 "Awraq al-diblumasiyyina bi'ism malik misr wa-al-sudan," *al-Ahram*, 30 October 1951.
52 Ahmad Hasan al-Zayyat, "Nihayat ma'sah," *al-Risala*, No. 956, 29 October 1951.
53 "Talabat misr wa-al-sudan fi baris yafdahuna al-isti'mar," *al-Balagh*, 18 December 1951.
54 See Foreign Office Minutes, 27 and 28 October 1951, FO371/90154, JE1052/45.
55 Telegram 149 from Khartoum, 30 October 1951, FO371/90154, JE1052/69.
56 Statement by His Majesty's Government, Robertson Files, SA524/5/78–79.
57 "Misr tatahadda injiltra an taqbala istifta' hurran fi al-sudan," *al-Ahram*, 17 November 1951, p. 1. Salah al-Din reiterated his proposal to Britain on 28 December, during his visit to Rome. See "al-Matalib al-misriyya kama yu'linuha salah al-din basha," *al-Muqattam*, 28 December 1951, p. 1.
58 "Inha' mahammat hakim al-sudan li-tajawuzihi sulutatahu," *al-Ahram*, 1 December 1951, p. 2. Among these Sudanese was Ibrahim al-Mufti, whose loyalty to the unity of the Nile valley would soon be questionable. See, for instance, Hassan Amhad Ibrahim, *Sayyid 'Abd al-Rahman al-Mahdi: A Study of Neo-Mahdism in the Sudan, 1899–1956* (Leiden: Brill, 2004), p. 220.
59 Note by G. D. Lampen, Deputy Sudan Agent in London, 11 January 1952, SA 523/1/22.
60 Telegram 131 from the Governor-General, Khartoum, 17 October 1951, FO371/90154, JE1052/55.
61 Letter SCO/97.H.1 from Sir Robert Howe, Governor-General of Sudan, 26 November 1951, FO371/90154, JE1057/81.
62 "Zu'ama' al-sudan sahamu fi khuttat hukumat al-wafd," *al-Balagh*, 4 February 1952, p. 2.
63 "al-Jala' wa-al-wahda shatrani li-matlab wahid," *al-Balagh*, 5 February 1952, p. 2.
64 Ginat, *The Soviet Union and Egypt*, p. 129.
65 *al-Misri*, 30 November and 2 December 1951.
66 *al-Ahram*, 5 December 1951; *al-Jumhur al-misri*, 26 November 1951.
67 "Inni utalibu bi-al-istiqlal al-dhati lil-mudiriyyat," *Ruz al-Yusuf*, No. 1237, 25 February 1952, p. 6.
68 "Ba'that al-mahdi aqarrat bi-al-rida laqab al-faruq," *al-Ahram*, 2 July 1952, p. 4.
69 C. W. M., Cox, "The Growth of Nationalism in the Sudan," *The Times*, 1951, in C. W. M. Cox Files, SA 676/3/15.
70 "al-Qa'id al-'amm yataqabbalu tahani wufud al-sha'b," *al-Ahram*, 29 July 1952, p. 4.
71 See a record of conversation between al-Mahdi and the British Minister of State, London, 18 June 1953, FO371/102757, JE1051/574.
72 "I'adat al-nathar fi barnamaj al-hizb al-watani lil-'ahd al-jadid," *al-Ahram*, 3 August 1952, p. 8; "Misr wa-al-sudan balad wahid wataniyyan wa-suyasiyyan," *al-Ahram*, 14 August 1952, p. 9.
73 "Mashru' jadid li-taswiyat mas'alat al-sudan," *al-Ahram*, 30 August 1952, p. 1.

74 Mahjub 'Umar Bashiri, *Ma'alim al-haraka al-wataniyya fi al-sudan* (Beirut: Maktabat al-Thaqafa, 1996), pp. 367–368.
75 "al-Thamra al-ula li-ittifaq misr wa-al-sudan," *al-Ahram*, 2 November 1952, p. 6; "al-Siyada 'ala al-sudan li-ahlihi ila an yuqarriru masirihim," *al-Ahram*, 1 November 1952, pp. 1, 11. See also "Ittifaq misr wa-al-sudan bayna misr wa-al-ahzab al-istiqlaliyya," *al-Muqattam*, 30 October 1952, p. 2; "Intiha' al-muhadathat ma'a al-istiqlaliyyina wa-taqarub wujhat al-nathar," *al-Balagh*, 25 October 1952, p. 2; "Ba'da muddah aqsaha 3 sanawat yuqarriru al-sudan masirihi fi huriyya," *al-Balagh*, 25 June 1952, p. 2.
76 "Ittifaqiyyat al-sudan hall 'amali muwaffaq," *al-Ahram*, 3 November 1952, p. 6; "al-Ittifaq bayna misr wa-al-sudan khutwa ula nahw al-jala' 'an al-sudan," *Ruz al-Yusuf*, 3 November 1952, p. 4; "al-Liwa' najib yuhaqqiqu 'misr al-kubra' bi-ittifaqihi ma'a mumaththili ahzab al-sudan," *al-Muqattam*, 28 October 1952, p. 1.
77 "Agreement between the Egyptian Government and the Government of the United Kingdom of Great Britain and Northern Ireland Concerning Self-Government and Self-Determination for the Sudan Signed at Cairo, on 12 February 1953," in SA 520/1/68; Zahir, *al-Sudan al-mu'asir*, pp. 279–281; Fabunmi, *The Sudan in Anglo–Egyptian Relations*, pp. 297–302.
78 See the full text of his speech in HC Deb 12 February 1953, Vol. 511 cc602–12, at http://hansard.millbanksystems.com/commons/1953/feb/12/ sudan-anglo-egyptian-agreement (accessed 18 February 2016). See also "al-Ra'is yadhi'u bushra al-ittifaq 'ala al-sha'b," *al-Ahram*, 13 February 1953, p. 1.
79 "al-Hukuma al-misriyya tatalaqqa radd baritaniyya al-niha'i yawm al-ithnayni," *al-Ahram*, 22 November 1952, p. 1. On the change of the Free Officers' approach to the future of Sudan, see also Voll, "US Policy toward the Unity," pp. 102–103.
80 Salah Salim, "Lastum mamnu'ina min al-radd ayyuha al-zu'ama'," *Ruz al-Yusuf*, No. 1286, 2 February 1953, p. 4; Salim, "Nahnu natahadda al-injliz min ajlikum," *Ruz al-Yusuf*, No. 1294, 30 March 1953, p. 4. Ihsan 'Abd al-Quddus opined that the agreement was bilateral between Egypt and Sudan, and that Britain had nothing to do with it and therefore had no right to alter its content or approve or disapprove it. Ihsan 'Abd al-Quddus, "'Ala al-sudan an yadfa'u thaman taqrir masirihi," *Ruz al-Yusuf*, No. 1294, 30 March 1953, p. 3. The Egyptian memorandum was endorsed by a wide spectrum of Sudanese political parties (the *Umma*, the Republican and Socialist Party, the United National Party, and the National Party) on 14 January 1953, following their meeting with Salim in Cairo. "Nass wathiqat ittifaq khartum al-jadid," *al-Ahram*, 14 January 1953, p. 6.
81 Telegram 169, British Foreign Office, FO371/102757, JE1051/586.
82 "La duminyun wa-la kumunwalth bal istiqlal tamm aw ittihad ma'a misr," *al-Ahram*, 17 February 1953, p. 1. Warburg noticed that Husayn Dhu al-Faqar Sabri (Hussein Zulfakar Sabry), an Egyptian military officer who was stationed in 1949 in Sudan (during the transitional period, 1953–1956, he was a member of the governor-general's commission there), had played a significant role in persuading the Free Officers to support the idea of

self-determination for Sudan. His meetings and talks with key Sudanese figures – politicians and religious leaders – led him to conclude that the vast majority of Sudanese did not support unification with Egypt. He developed close relations with the Free Officers, who were persuaded by his analysis of the situation in Sudan. See Warburg, *Islam, Sectarianism and Politics*, pp. 132–134. See also Sabri's detailed account in Hussein Zulfakar Sabry, *Sovereignty for Sudan* (London: Ithaca Press, 1982), pp. 24–75. Sabri recommended "genuine Self-Determination ... which would ensure the dismantling of British influence." Egypt should insist "on the establishment of a free and neutral atmosphere prior to Self-Determination." Ibid., p. 73. For Sabri, the most important goal was to remove the British from Sudan. He took pains to persuade Salah Salim and members of the Revolutionary Command Council to accept his paradigm, warning: "We cannot just stand by and throw the Sudan up! What would you do if the British were to shut the Nile waters off!" Ibid., p. 68.

83 See Khidr 'Umar's interview in *al-Sudani*, 27 May 1953, quoted from FO371/102757, JE1051/564.

84 M. W. Daly and Jane R. Hogan, *Images of Empire: Photographic Sources for the British in the Sudan* (Leiden: Brill, 2005), p.45. See also Voll, "Unity of the Nile Valley."

85 Daly, *Imperial Sudan*, p. 381

86 Gabriel Warburg, "The Condominium Revisited: The Anglo-Egyptian Sudan 1934–1956: A Review Article," *Bulletin of the School of Oriental and African Studies*, 56:1 (February 1993), pp. 8–9.

87 On the relations between Egypt and independent Sudan, see Muhammad 'Abd al-Fattah Abu al-Fadl, *Judhur al-'alaqat al-misriyya al-sudaniyya ba'da istiqlal al-sudan* (Cairo: al-Hay'a al-Misriyya al-'Amma lil-Kitab, 2005); Filib Raflah and Farid 'Izz al-Din, *al-'Alaqat al-ta'rikhiyya wa-al-iqtisadiyya bayna al-jumhuriyya al-'arabiyya al-muttahida wa-al-sudan* (Cairo: Maktabat al-Anjlu al-Misriyya, 1965).

88 Collins's book review of Warburg's *Historical Discord*, p. 800.

6   Social Movements and the Sudan Question
A Case Study in the Divergence of National
Liberation Movements

The post–World War II years witnessed a significant growth in the power and influence of social movements representing the two sides of the Egyptian political spectrum – left and right. The 1940s saw an upsurge in popularity for the Egyptian communists, who formed an important voice in the public discourse on issues of national liberation. Like their right-wing nationalist and Islamist rivals, represented by Young Egypt (*Misr al-Fatat*) and the Muslim Brothers, the Egyptian communists also sought to free Egypt from the grasp of British imperialism. Yet the two sides of the political spectrum took decidedly different views when it came to the issue of the unity of the Nile valley. This chapter will demonstrate that the groups on the right were not only part of the broad national consensus, which called for the unification of the Nile valley under the Egyptian crown, but also pursued the most extreme position on this issue, objecting vehemently to any compromise on the matter. In contrast, the communist left, as we shall see, went against the national mainstream, staking out an unabashedly dissident position calling for the independence of the Nile valley from British colonial rule in Egypt and from British and Egyptian rule in Sudan, granting self-determination to the Sudanese people, including the right to determine their destiny. This unpopular approach, rejected out of hand by the establishment and most of the political spectrum, damaged the legitimacy and prestige of the communist organizations. And yet, a number of years later, the leaders of the July 1952 revolution adopted the principles of the communist formula for the resolution of the Sudan issue, while denying their origin and continuing the brutal struggle to eradicate organized communism in Egypt.

Historical Narratives: The Egyptian Right and the Struggle for Sudan

The Muslim Brothers (MB) were founded in Egypt in 1928 by Hasan al-Banna as a modern religious protest movement and quickly turned into an international Islamic movement, whose influence on the development of modern Islam can be seen to this day. The MB adopted a radical and paternalistic nationalist agenda regarding the special historical connection between Egypt and Sudan, assuming that Sudan was actually an integral part of the Egyptian homeland. Their ideological mouthpiece held fast to the Egyptian national historic narrative, stressing that it is the hand of Allah that drives the engine of unification and guides it to a safe harbor despite the maleficent efforts of British imperialism to undermine the unity of the valley. In fact, argued *al-Ikhwan al-Muslimun*, the southern Nile valley,

whose history is unforgettable and must not be removed from [people's] minds and hearts, is part of the body of the homeland. No matter how many organs there are in this body, the English imperialist policy tries to tear them apart ... the hand of Allah organizes this unity and the flow of the mighty river supports it ... Muhammad 'Ali and Isma'il founded huge villages so that the Nile valley, from its source to its estuary, would constitute a single "political entity." The history, language, unity of hopes and suffering, all these came together to strengthen and intensify the connection. The English saw this and it disturbed them. They limited the rule of Muhammad 'Ali to the Nile valley. Later they besieged [Khedive] Isma'il until they stopped his conquests southward. With regard to anything connected with the Nile sources, they grabbed strategic positions and established military bases there.[1]

As far as the MB were concerned, it was the British, acting out of imperialist interests, devoid of morals and justice, who created the Mahdi movement encouraging fragmentation and separatism in the Nile valley. Thus, for example, when the movement was established, adopting an Islamic guise and championing the struggle for the liberation of Sudan from British rule, the British imperialist regime in Sudan waged all-out war against this movement, exploiting the circumstances to demand the withdrawal of Egypt from Sudan in 1882. From then on, Britain used all available means to separate Sudan from Egypt. The British planted the "seeds of hatred and rivalry between the northerners and the southerners. They closed the gates of the south to the northerners in order to separate them from one another and prevent them from meeting and developing familiarity ... they managed to postpone the [discussion] of the issue of the Sudan in every negotiation ... the supporters of separatism [in the Sudan] are the disease of the east."[2] In the view of the MB, activism in support of unification should be driven by the Egyptians, and the opinion of the Sudanese made no difference. So, for example, Salih 'Ashmawi, Hasan al-Banna's deputy and the first commander of the MB's "Special Organization," who was one of the representatives of the most extreme faction, announced in August 1944, "Egypt and the

Sudan are a single nation, and we will not permit the Sudan to secede from us any more than we would permit Alexandria and Aswan to secede from us, [even if they should wish to]."[3]

'Abd al-'Aziz Kamil, one of the senior Muslim Brothers and one of the heads of the Special Organization, urged the members of the Sudanese delegation that came to Egypt in April of 1946[4] not to fall into the trap that British imperialism had laid for the unified nation. He addressed the delegates directly from the pages of the MB's paper, al-Ikhwan al-Muslimun: "It pained me to hear about the recurring calls to strike an alliance with the enemy. I thought perhaps it was the influence of imperialism which caused you to lose your faith even in your brothers ... I do not want you to silence these voices or to fight these ideas, because the greatest ill in the east is the eradication of liberty, the liberty of the nations and the liberty of thought."[5] Kamil does not take issue with each person expressing his thoughts. In the second half of his article he changes to second person plural and describes his experience during his most recent journey to Sudan:

As I traversed Egypt and reached Aswan, I found the signs of life rising gradually to the south, and the yearning drove me to go there. But then a [British] foreigner stopped me and said to me, "Stop! This is the Sudan!" So I said, "They are my family and my brothers! Why do you stop me here? Did the Sudanese or the Egyptians agree to this?" So I went into myself and considered what stands and separates between brothers in an era of coalescence. I felt sadness when I recalled that a group of your sons [southerners] want this foreigner as an ally.

Kamil declared that the only remedy to the presence of Britain in Egypt and Sudan was withdrawal. In his view, Britain was a tiresome guest "who sucked the blood of life, and poisoned the thoughts of the sons." It created an artificial border between parts of the Nile valley and prohibited mutual visits and even cooperation among the sons of the valley. "My brother, do you think that what Britain wants is good for me and for you? That they are concerned for your welfare and mine?" asked Kamil. The answer to the question is as clear as day: the British are the exploiters and we are the ones who have the rights. The only way to reach a mutual understanding is by restoring the rights of the exploited, concluded Kamil.[6]

As we have seen earlier, Egyptian historians and geographers consistently argued that the unity of the Nile valley was not a modern phenomenon but a historical one whose roots were planted deep in the soil of the valley. The radical nationalist Young Egypt also saw the effort to realize the unification as an Egyptian issue from start to finish, demonstratively ignoring any role that the other side, i.e., the Sudanese, could play.

Their leader, Ahmad Husayn, set out the position of Young Egypt in a letter to King Faruq in August 1945, entitled "National demands (*al-matlib al-qawmiyya*) and the means to achieve them." In the letter he wrote, inter alia, "The Egyptian parliament must resolve that the king [Faruq] is the king of Egypt and the Sudan. The Sudanese are Egyptians and enjoy fully equal rights. This is the solution of the Sudanese question, and should England object to this, it will be perceived as an exploiter, and we will drag it to arbitration in the international courts and institutions."[7]

The communists rejected Husayn's demands scornfully. Ahmad Sadiq Sa'd published a scathing critique of Husayn in the Marxist magazine *al-Fajr al-Jadid* (this was also the name of a Marxist organization, whose leaders were central contributors to the journal). Sa'd wrote that Husayn's position on the Sudanese question reeked of colonialism. Husayn argued that the increasing population of Egypt required the annexation of Sudan and an opening of the borders so that the inhabitants of Egypt would not die of starvation. Sa'd rejected this, arguing that starvation and poverty in Egypt were the result of class issues. The Egyptian demand for British withdrawal from Sudan should be based on defense considerations, not exploitative colonialist intentions; British withdrawal from the Nile valley would improve the ability of Egypt and Sudan to defend themselves against imperialism. Husayn called on the Egyptian parliament to pass a resolution calling for the integration of Sudan into the Egyptian kingdom, without consulting with the people of Sudan, who emphasized, through their institutions and political parties, that they were not interested in being liberated from British colonialism, only to fall into the hands of Egyptian colonialism. Husayn, Sa'd remonstrated, was not at all interested in the will of the Sudanese people.

Sa'd noted that Young Egypt's memorandum was published in the journal *al-Wafd al-Misri* and claimed that this was the continuation of a dangerous alliance that began with the elections of 1945, in which the Wafd (which boycotted the elections) supported candidates of "Egyptian Fascism." This odd coupling, claimed Sa'd, "contradicts the hostility which reigns between the two movements" and is also contrary to the Wafd's own policy and interests. Worse yet, it is dangerous to the people because it could lead to the victory of the forces of colonialism and reaction in Egypt.[8]

As mentioned, the two dissident rightist movements, Young Egypt and the MB, presented the most extreme right-wing position in the spectrum of the national consensus. Along with both establishment and anti-establishment historians and geographers, they emphasized the geographical foundations that united the two regions of the Nile valley and determined paternalistically that the geographical boundaries of Egypt included Sudan. As World War II was winding down, the MB announced in the pages of *al-Ikhwan al-Muslimun* that the Nile Valley was "a symbol of rootedness and unity" and that it had "a wonderful enchantment." The unified borders included all of the demographic elements of the valley from the source of the Nile to the Delta. This unity ensured the movement of merchandise and industry to the southern Nile region and abetted the organization of the administration there, similarly to that in the north, and aided in maintaining security. It was the British occupation that led to the Egyptian withdrawal from Sudan in 1884, but in 1896 it was reconquered. *Al-Ikhwan al-Muslimun* cited the saying attributed to Sharif Pasha, "[even] if we were to leave the Sudan, the Sudan would not leave us."[9]

Young Egypt, which adopted fascist symbols and even made occasional use of Nazi terminology in its propaganda, chose to view the resolution of the question of the unity of the Nile valley in the context of the Egyptian need for *lebensraum*. Young Egypt went beyond Egyptian–Sudanese unification to a more expansionist conception (*al-mafhum al-tawassu'i*), which exceeded the recognized geographical boundaries of the two peoples. One of their leaders, Muhammad Sabih, expressed this in a lecture at a branch meeting in Mansura in January 1940. In his view, the Nile valley "spreads from the lakes of the equator in the south to the Mediterranean Sea in the north; from the upper part of Ethiopia and the Red Sea and the border of the Sinai in the east to the contemporary western borders of Egypt and the Sudan. Thus, the equatorial region, including the equatorial lakes, which Egypt took over during the reign of Isma'il, was part of Egypt's living space." Sabih even bothered to add to "Egypt's living space" an important water source – Lake Tana, the major reservoir of the Blue Nile – "the important source of the Nile, which ought properly to be under Egyptian supervision."[10]

The position of the MB was similar to that of Young Egypt, but focused on the religious ties inextricably connecting the two regions of the valley.[11] So, for example, Hasan al-Banna, their general guide, announced on 13 August 1945 that

this country wishes its natural boundaries to be recognized and not to be displaced by others from its land. When Egypt demands unification with the Sudan and the end of British rule and cessation of British intervention in the affairs of the inhabitants of the valley, this is not in order to exploit the Sudan for imperialistic aims or to take over a nation and pillage its land, rather in order to liberate its southern half, which is tied to it by the Nile in an unbreakable bond ... The Sudan is not a colony that Egypt wishes to colonize, but the southern region of Egypt, which must unify with its northern sister so the Nile valley will be unified.[12]

The MB, like Young Egypt, championed expansion further south. So, for example, in September 1945, Hasan al-Banna declared that

it is our desire to defend our southern frontier and preserve our rights in Eritrea, Zeila, Massawa, Harar, and the Upper Nile – the regions, with whose soil the blood of the Egyptian conqueror mixed, which were given life by Egyptian hands, and in whose skies the Egyptian flag flew. Later they were stolen from the body of the homeland by foreign aggression. There is no international agreement or legal statute granting the right to them, to anyone but Egypt. It is our duty to return to our history and see the price we have paid, in money as well as in human life, for securing our borders, not out of imperialist ambitions or for the sake of geographical profit, but rather out of a vital need, which cannot be denied. Now there is an appropriate opportunity for Egypt to demand the return of what was taken from it by exploiting the distraction and forfeiture of [previous Egyptian] governments.[13]

Salah 'Abd al-Hafiz, a lawyer by profession and a member of the MB's General Guidance Office, warned "his Sudanese brothers" against entering an alliance with British imperialism.

As for us, we live as slaves in the guise of free men ... As regards the sources of the Nile and the rights of the people of the valley from the south to the north, their lives and livelihoods are dependent upon this great river. It is their right that its sources not be in the hands of foreign exploiters, and to control their Nile from its source to its estuary ... Our word to the Sudanese is based on the economic, social, linguistic and geographic unity between Egyptians and Sudanese ... The traditional and well-known role of imperialism is to create a wedge between peoples and nations ... We must demand of our Sudanese brothers to cleave to Egypt and to be devoted to the Egyptian administration so long as there is no Egyptian governor in the Sudan who can demand satisfaction for the Sudanese or the Egyptians.[14]

It enraged 'Abd al-Hafiz that the Egyptian negotiators did not include Sudan in the Anglo–Egyptian treaty of 1936. He called on the students representing the younger generation and on the Egyptian people not to be deterred and to endanger their own lives and fortunes to achieve liberation and full independence throughout the Nile valley from its upper to its lower ends. It is up to the younger generation, declared 'Abd al-Hafiz, to always remember the words of their young leader Mustafa Kamil.[15]

Ahmad Hasan al-Zayyat, the owner, manager, and editor in chief of the Egyptian periodical *al-Risala*, who represented an emphatically reformist Islamic message, wrote a position paper on the unity of the Nile valley, addressed to "Our dear brothers in the upper *wadi*" (valley), and called upon them to unite with the Egyptian people, for "We and you are a single people, and this is no exaggeration." Zayyat referred to a "handful" of Sudanese who rejected unification as intending "to cut off what Allah commanded them ... Allah created us all from this blessed river ... He arranged that the character and facial characteristics should be similar, even the color. He gave us this earthly paradise ... How can this small handful of people help the 'red beast' [i.e., the British] to incite you to foster enmity ... The British beast is not made of the clay of the Sudan and Egypt ... This beast has misled this handful of people." Zayyat stressed the common destiny of the two peoples, saying, "The sovereign over the heavens and the earth bound our destiny to yours ... Cairo and Khartoum are twin Arab cities, dwelling as neighbors in a single country, drinking the same water."[16]

Young Egypt presented a similar line in its journals. The British, declared Young Egypt, were not interested in the advancement of the Sudanese; they rather viewed them as "docile subjects," whereas the Egyptians viewed them as brothers.[17] Their leader Husayn declared that "The Sudan is part of Egypt, and the Sudanese people belongs to the Egyptian people – they speak our language, share our faith, drink what we drink, and eat what we eat, and they are of the same Egyptian race."[18] Fathi Radwan, one of the leaders, emphasized that "The Sudanese are a component of Egypt, who live in southern Egypt."[19]

From the left, the communists rejected the ethnic argument for unity:

The Sudanese consist of several peoples or tribes, some of which are Negroes and some Arabs ... each tribe speaks its own special dialect and is not connected with the other tribes. In fact the man from the north of the Sudan is quite cut off from the south, and so on, all of which shows that the Sudan is behind the times, and the circumstances in it are not such that we can speak of the existence of one nation there. More correctly we can say that the Sudanese are a people, which is still in the stage of being formed and that the elements of its growth have not become complete, such elements being economic circumstances, one language, similar tradition, etc.[20]

Crossing the Nationalist Consensus: The Left's Stance on Sudan

Organized communism emerged in Egypt in the late 1910s, and as far as the Sudan question was concerned, the communists adhered to the national consensus that Sudan and Egypt were one entity. This view was clearly stated by the first Egyptian Communist Party (ECP), which joined the Comintern in December 1922. In January 1923 it presented its political manifesto, which displayed a radical anti-British orientation and called, inter alia, "for the nationalization of the Suez Canal, the liberation and unification of Egypt and the Sudan."[21] In February 1924 the ECP issued its political credo stating, inter alia, that the party would struggle for the independence of the Nile valley – politically, economically, and socially.[22]

As for the national question, including the Sudanese question, the party objected to the "English presence" in Egypt and Sudan and demanded action to bring the two peoples together to secure their common interests in terms of utilization of the natural resources of both countries. The party staked a position opposing those who exploited the rights of both peoples, whether foreigner or Egyptian nationalist.

The first time the communists strayed from the national mainstream on the Sudanese question was in the platform the party published toward the end of 1931. This did not yet constitute a significant deviation from the consensus, focusing primarily on the expulsion of colonialism from the Nile valley and the achievement of full unconditional economic and political independence for Egypt and Sudan. The novelty of the platform lay in the party's recognition of the right to self-determination of the Sudanese and the Egyptian nations, a recognition that was at odds with the Egyptian consensus that viewed Sudan as an Egyptian prerogative since the days of Muhammad 'Ali. The platform demanded "a complete guarantee of the right of the Sudan to self-determination (*al-daman al-kamil lihaq al-sudan fi taqrir masirihi*). The platform also included a demand to enter into an alliance with the Soviet Union in a campaign to expel the colonialists. It also called for the separation of religion and state. The social planks called for the nationalization of assets and the cancellation of debts and taxes for the peasants.[23] The paradigm shift, at this stage, had no influence on Egyptian politics, given that the communist movement was persecuted by the authorities and operated clandestinely. Its influence during the time of Isma'il Sidqi's dictatorial regime was practically non-existent.[24]

The decisive paradigm shift from the unity of the Nile valley to the Sudanese right to self-determination occurred at the very outset of the 1940s. The communists of the 1940s went against the national mainstream with regard to the Sudan question, presenting a provocatively different approach: a concerted Sudanese–Egyptian struggle to expel British imperialism from the Nile valley and the recognition of the Sudanese's right to determine for themselves whether to opt for unification with Egypt or independence. Sudan was not the only question on which the communists went against the mainstream; by 1947 they had already adopted the Soviet line on Palestine, which supported partition, and were paying a heavy political price for this position.[25] This begs the question: was the communist dissenting approach due to the fact that they liaised closely with Sudanese communists and thereby became more aware of Sudanese aspirations? Or was it because Egyptian communists sensed the imperialist undertones of the standard Egyptian position? Sudanese communists did work closely with their Egyptian counterparts, who supported, sponsored, and encouraged them. Nevertheless, as we shall see, the new paradigm on the future of Sudan was originally formulated and advocated by the Egyptian Movement for National Liberation (al-Haraka al-Misriyya lil-taharrur al-Watani – Hametu) and its leader Henri Curiel. Egyptian communists who were anti-colonialist rejected both British and Egyptian colonialism. They were firm believers in the rights of all peoples to self-determination, and in this regard Sudan and Sudanese were no exception.

During World War II, the British made every effort to join forces with anti-fascist elements in Egyptian society and tried to collaborate with the communists, but the latter declined. They championed a new slogan demanding the broadest possible front against fascism, at the same time condemning British occupation: "Against Fascism ... but not with the English (Didda al-fashiyya ... wa-lakinna laisa ma'a al-ingiliz). Another difference between the communists and the other political forces was the consensual paradigm, expressed in the slogan: "The Unity of the Nile Valley – One Nile – One People – One King" (wahdat wadi al-nil – nil wahid – sha'b wahid – malik wahid). The communists adopted an alternative slogan: "Political and economic independence, and a common struggle with the Sudanese people and their right to self-determination" (al-istiqlal al-siyasiyya wa-al-iqtisadi wa-al-kifah al-mushtarak ma'a al-sha'b al-Sudani wahaqhu fi taqrir masirihi). The communists were also opposed to negotiations with the occupiers, raising the banner of "armed struggle" – representing a new political direction that began to take form in the early 1950s.[26]

New communist organizations emerged in the early 1940s. The most prominent of these were Hametu, founded by Henri Curiel, and Iskra (al-Sharara), founded by Hillel Schwartz. Other prominent groups were al-Fajr al-Jadid (the New Dawn), founded by Ahmad Sa'd Sadiq, Yusuf Darwish, Raymond Duwayk, and Salih Rushdi, and Munazzamat Tahrir al-Sha'b – the Organization of the People's Liberation.

Among these new organizations, it was Curiel's group, Hametu, that most prominently advocated the Sudanese right to self-determination. Curiel actively recruited Sudanese and Nubians to his organization alongside Egyptian workers. The communists in Hametu played a leading role in Sudanese unions, publishing Huriyyat al-Shu'ub (1941) and Umdurman, starting in 1945, periodical forums in which the movement's ideas on the Sudanese question were advocated. The communists successfully promoted the slogan, "The common struggle against the common enemy" (*al-kifah al-mushtarak didda al-'adu al-mushtarak*) as a counter-slogan to what they viewed as the slogan of the nationalist bourgeoisie: "One Nile – One People – One King." The most important fruit of this endeavor was a group of Sudanese activists, who later established the Sudanese Movement for National Liberation (*al-haraka al-sudaniyya lil-taharrur al-watani - Hasetu*).[27] *Hametu* was also active among the Nubian minority and assisted in the establishment of Nubian cells. The movement objected to the proposal of the British and *al-Umma* party, who called for separating Nubia from Egypt and annexing it to Sudan.[28] In mid-1947 *Iskra*, *Hametu*, Marcel Israel, and most of the members of his organization, People's Liberation, merged to form the Democratic Movement for National Liberation (*al-haraka al-dimuqratiyya lil-taharrur al-watani – Hadetu*), which became the largest communist group, number-wise, and the most active in the Egyptian political and social arenas. The new movement maintained a similar line to *Hametu* on the Sudan question, i.e., the Sudanese people should determine their own future.[29]

Al-Jamahir served as an important conceptual forum at first for the *Iskra* activists, later for *Hadetu* activists as well, who gave less weight to the Sudan question. *Iskra*, which was very active among the students, called for the establishment of a "united front for liberty and democracy." After merging with *Hametu* in mid-1947, they accepted Curiel's approach. The *al-Fajr al-Jadid* group, in its eponymous house organ, toed a similar line to Curiel's, but less focused on the Sudan question.[30]

Of all the communist newspapers, it was *Umdurman* that became the main voice opposing the Egyptian consensus on the Sudan question. Thus, for example, 'Abd al-Majid Abu Hasabu wrote that "the questions of the peoples do not arise on the basis of sentiment, but on the basis of the struggle, the national (*qawmi*) struggle for justice. The young people of Egypt must study the issue of the Sudan and the actions of the colonialist policy in the country, rather than approaching the issue from the sentimental standpoint, as the Egyptian government does in its efforts to mislead the public." He argued that the capitalist interests in Egypt calling for unification were no less dangerous than those in Sudan calling for separation. In his view, the first group comprised Egyptian capitalists seeking new markets, while the second group comprised Sudanese capitalists seeking a monopoly on Sudan's economic resources. The conflicts between the two groups, noted Abu Hasabu, were merely conflicts between personal interests. In his words, the peoples of the valley shared language, religion, and common interests, but above all they shared the anguish of colonialism. Both peoples must cooperate in the struggle for liberation against the common enemy – British imperialism. They must first of all rid themselves of colonialism, and the two peoples will resolve the details of what will happen afterward of their own free will.[31]

Umdurman stressed that the slogans of the struggle should be: "The Nile Valley for its Inhabitants" (*wadi al-nil li-ahlihi*), "Complete Withdrawal from the Nile Valley" (*al-jala' al-tam 'an wadi al-nil*), "Stay away from Egypt and the Sudan," and "Liberation, then Self-Determination."[32] The calls of students in Egypt and Sudan for "Withdrawal and Unification of the Nile Valley" (*al-jala' wa-wahdat wadi al-nil*) were heartfelt and pure in intention, but the content was mistaken, stated *Umdurman*: "We need to be demanding 'Complete withdrawal from the Nile Valley' (*al-jala' 'an wadi al-nil bi-akmalihi*), because what was the point of withdrawal from Egypt without withdrawal from the Sudan? Our call must be focused and our objective clear. We are currently facing a single problem, the expulsion of colonialism which is exploiting and exhausting us."[33]

Several days before the fall of the first Nuqrashi government (1945–1946) *Umdurman* launched a frontal attack on him and his government for their inability to deal with the British presence in the Nile valley. Nuqrashi argued that silence was the most effective policy. He could justify such an approach because for him the question of the Nile valley was the private domain of himself and his partners. He needed a reminder, however, that the question of the Nile valley was the concern of all of its inhabitants. "No, oh prime minister! Egypt for the Egyptians, and the Sudan for the Sudanese. You have no right to speak or be silent, except what the people permits and directs you!" Nuqrashi's idea to meet with religious leaders in Sudan to learn their positions was no different than the Sudanese government's program to turn to the Sudanese delegates in the advisory council and province councils to clarify their intentions. Was there, then, "a conspiracy on the part of the government of the Sudan and the government of Egypt to turn the Sudan into a colony? We are perplexed on this point. The Sudan will not accept any referendum while colonialism is in control here. First we must rid ourselves of colonialism and expel it, and only then the people will speak out of their own free will and determine what sort of regime they desire."[34]

Umdurman made it clear that there could be no discussion of the independence of Egypt as long as the occupation of Sudan continued, or of the independence of Sudan as long as the occupation of Egypt continued. The freedom fighters thus saw their primary obligation in the common struggle of the two peoples for the expulsion of foreign colonialism and the achievement of liberty and independence. However, the

Egyptian negotiators generally ignored this position, enabling British colonialism to exploit the best resources of the Nile valley over the course of generations, in exchange for which the British requited the inhabitants with poverty, ignorance, and disease. Judging by the inferior and ingratiating way the Egyptian government managed the negotiations with the British on the future of the Nile valley, the Sudanese people might have been expected to give up hope, but this did not occur, as remnants of faith and national and political awareness remained.[35]

Was the slogan "Unity of the Nile Valley" uniting or dividing the struggle of the Egyptian and the Sudanese people? asked 'Amir Hamadi al-Sudani, a Sudanese by origin, in *al-Fajr al-Jadid*. In his view there was no doubt that the answer was that it was dividing them. In Sudan flourished a nationalism, which began to sense its independence and resisted "being swallowed up by any other nationalism, and views anyone interested in swallowing it as an enemy to rise up and fight against." The nascent and developing economy in Sudan, stressed Sudani, completely resisted being swallowed up by the Egyptian or British economies. He contemptuously dismissed the demands of Egyptian leaders and politicians "to eradicate and ignore Sudanese nationalism." Such a demand, he declared, "constitutes a betrayal of the Egyptian people struggling for their liberty and rights, and a betrayal of the Sudanese people."[36]

Within *Umdurman* were also voices expressing more moderate approaches to the future of Sudan. So, for example, Muhammad Amin Husayn wrote that there was no one among the Sudanese who was in favor of separatism. However, there was a disagreement regarding the manner and details of unification. There was no need at this stage to determine the details of such a unification, so as not to appear divided on the direction and intentions and not to intensify the division. At this historical stage there was a need to unify all efforts and focus all thoughts and actions of the people of the Nile valley. Slogans such as "Sudan for the Sudanese" (*al-sudan-lil-sudaniyyun*) or "Sudan First" (*al-sudan awwalan*) were not to be understood as calls for separating the two parts of the Nile or for division. Egypt and Sudan had "a common problem" (*qadiyya mushtaraka*) and "common interests" (*musalih mushtaraka*), which must not be compromised.[37]

In April 1945, the Graduates' General Congress adopted a resolution on "the formation of a democratic Sudanese government, united with Egypt under the Egyptian crown" (*qiyam hukuma sudaniyya dimuqratiyya fi ittihad ma'a misr taht al-taj al-misri*).[38] This resolution aroused controversy in the communist community. Muhammad Amin Husayn wrote in *Umdurman* that the resolution was adopted by a majority of the congress and was subsequently confirmed by the provincial committees, so everyone was obligated to uphold it. The Sudanese opposition claimed that the discussion of the issue was rushed and the resolution should be reexamined, as it would bind future generations. Husayn, for his part, defended the resolution and claimed that it was reached in a democratic manner.[39] He further argued that the resolution was preceded by numerous discussions in caucuses, conferences, and meetings, so that it could not be claimed to have been rushed. The inhabitants of the Nile valley in general and of Egypt in particular "must understand that this was the greatest and most important resolution in the modern history of the Sudan." Husayn further argued that the days when the issues of nations were decided without consultation with the people were over:

We always said that the issues of the liberties of nations suffering from various kinds of exploitation and colonialism were a single issue the world over. We always said that the interests of these nations was a single interest – liberation. We said that any weakening of the powers ruling over the exploited nations anywhere in the world would benefit the nations in general ... On this basis, the interests of the inhabitants of the Nile valley are a single interest, their anguish is a common anguish, and their cooperation toward the achievement of their interests and the breaking of their chains is inescapable ... The first part of the resolution, regarding the establishment of a democratic Sudanese government, is a matter on which there is no argument among the Sudanese of all parties, including parties active outside of the Graduates Congress, including al-Umma party whose slogan is "Sudan for the Sudanese."[40]

Husayn addressed "our Egyptian brothers" and argued that there was no intent of separatism. He noted that it was the natural right of the Sudanese to manage their own affairs and that there was no contradiction between this and the principle of cooperation between the two parts of the Nile valley, citing the example of the United States, the Soviet Union, and Switzerland. Egypt, wrote Husayn, is a constitutional monarchy, and unification with Egypt must be on the basis of a constitutional and monarchical Egypt, so that "under the Egyptian crown" must be part of the resolutions of the Graduates' General Congress.[41]

The treaty of 1936 triggered a national awakening in Sudan, wrote Umdurman. This became first evident in the appearance of the Graduates' General Congress,

a fighting organization which began to rise up against British colonialism by every legal and illegal means in order to return to the Sudanese people the rights usurped from them and their right to liberty and a life of dignity. The congress could not have been conceived if not for the treaty of 1936 – a treaty ratified by a cabal of bourgeois leaders – collaborators with colonialism who suckled [colonialism] with their mothers' milk. This treaty condemned the Nile valley to continued occupation and colonialism. What could the Sudanese people expect from an Egyptian leader, who could not serve his own people and does not realize their objectives, demands and aspirations? This sin is ascribable not to the Egyptian people but to the defeatism of these leaders who have betrayed their national concerns since 1923. History repeats itself in the present as well. The leaders of Egypt – collaborators with colonialism – mislead the Egyptian people when they tell them that they will realize their national aims and yearnings. In actuality they sold the remnants of the motherland in order to satisfy their own greed and personal ambitions.[42]

According to *Umdurman*, such leaders can never be expected to change their mode of operation, since their interests coincide with the interests of colonialism. The Egyptian and the Sudanese peoples must realize that the time for miracles has past and their issues will be resolved only if they take them back from the politicians and leaders and deal with them according to their own will and interests.

There is no need to prove the defeatism of the governments and leaders, since the latest Egyptian memorandum is in front of our eyes, in which they plead for independence like beggars and in addition, haggle over sacrosanct rights. [The Egyptian government] took the treaty of occupation and turned it into a basis for negotiations and bargaining, despite the fact that the treaty is inoperative and incompatible with current developments and world events.[43]

The Root of All Evil: The 1936 Treaty and British Colonialism

The MB as well as the communists had consistently and vociferously called for the abolition of the 1936 treaty since the end of World War II. For example, *al-Ikhwan al-Muslimun* announced on 9 February 1946 that the 1936 treaty affirmed the separation of Sudan from Egypt and was the cause for the jihad being carried out against Britain.[44] About a month later the movement's ideological mouthpiece published a sharp attack on the Egyptian government for its powerlessness to protect the national interests of Egypt. "The Muslim Brothers, who are the largest popular body, saw that the country is devoid of independence because of British involvement, its liberty is chained by the treaty [of 1936] and, the unity of the Nile valley is torn to shreds because of these chains. Moreover, the national economy is controlled by monopoly and exploitation."[45] As far as the MB were concerned, the treaty of 1936 could no longer serve as a basis for British–Egyptian relations, and the international circumstances created as the result of World War II compelled its nullification, since the League of Nations – the body that gave the treaty its international legal standing – no longer existed.

Table 6.1 *Survey among Students and Faculty of Fu'ad I University*

	Lecturers		Students	
Question	Yes	No	Yes	No
Is it right that the Egyptian national issue is dealt with bilaterally between us and the British?	18%	82%	19%	81%
Do you believe that independence can be achieved by means of negotiation?	79%	21%	31%	69%
Are you optimistic concerning our political future?	62%	38%	42%	58%
Do you believe that Egypt is an independent state?	8%	92%	1%	99%
Do you believe/trust any of the parties' leaders?	8%	92%	24%	76%
Are you satisfied with your life?	74%	26%	57%	43%

Moreover, Egypt's signature on the UN Charter and its UN membership created a reality that gave Egypt more room for maneuver in its relations with Britain, including the abolition of the treaty of 1936.[46]

In January 1946 the MB conducted a survey among students and faculty of Fu'ad I University on central national questions, including the future of Sudan.[47] Among the questions were those included in Table 6.1. The journal drew the following conclusions from the survey: First, there was partial agreement that the Egyptian issue should be dealt with at the international level; this should be given serious thought, and it is a patriotic duty to bring this to the attention of the leadership. Second, the older generation still places its trust in negotiations, which led to our downfall, whereas the younger generation is not particularly enthused by negotiations and even express a clearly negative view. This generation gap can also be seen with regard to Egypt's political future. Even so, both faculty as well as students expressed negative positions regarding their trust of the political echelon and the degree of Egypt's current independence. There was also widespread dissatisfaction with their life in Egypt.[48]

As the negotiations between Egypt and Britain were about to open in April 1946, Hasan al-Banna sent a letter to the Sidqi government in which he wrote:

The realization of the nation's basic demand is the complete withdrawal from the Nile valley and the preservation of its unity, a unity which will make its inhabitants the children of a single homeland, who will share rights and obligations ... if you [the government] succeed in achieving this objective, good for you. If not, then you must reveal this to the nation (who have the right to the final word) immediately and raise the issue before the Security Council before the end of its session. Rest assured that the nation will not demur in jihad and is ready for confrontation.[49]

Banna expressly demanded that the negotiation not last long. The general guide of the MB concluded

that we will not miss the opportunity to present our problem to the Security Council, in which we are represented ... How fine it would be if the negotiation would be completed before the coronation festival on 6 May, when Egypt will celebrate two festivals at once – the festival of [King] al-Faruq and the festival of the victory or the jihad. It would be good if you would state clearly to the British negotiator that the nation intends to achieve its rights or to die without them, and will not return to the path of negotiations – either success or struggle."[50]

Salih 'Ashmawi praised the heroism of the Egyptian students during the events of 21 February 1946. On that day the students set out toward the king's palace to submit a memorandum calling for the nullification of the treaty of 1936. They were attacked aggressively by the British, aided by the Egyptian police. Their brutality reached its peak when the 'Abbas Bridge was deliberately opened while the demonstrators tried to cross it, resulting in many of them falling into the river and drowning. The British did this, said 'Ashmawi, because they wanted "to paralyze the nerve of the nation which had risen up against them, in an effort to buy time." In his words, after months of negotiations, when the talks appeared to have reached a dead end, pessimism on the Egyptian side grew, and disappointment along with it. The Egyptians lost their trust in the sincerity of British intentions. 'Ashmawi called on the Egyptian people to unite in this difficult hour, "to stand as a single bloc, and struggle for your rights, waging jihad for liberty and independence."[51]

The communists, for their part, vociferously demanded the nullification of the treaty as well, though for different reasons. In their view only the nullification of the treaty would enable Egypt to negotiate with Britain on an equal footing rather than from the inferior position established in the treaty of 1936. Egypt would achieve independence only if three fundamental conditions were met: British withdrawal from land, sea, and air; Egypt's withdrawal from any alliance with Britain; and the denial of any special status to Britain.[52] *Al-Fajr al-Jadid* declared that both the Nuqrashi and the Sidqi governments agreed to negotiate with the British on the basis of the 1936 treaty, and reiterated its position that any negotiation on the basis of the status quo would end in failure. Despite its announcement that it was entering negotiations free of all restraints, the government was in fact restrained by the borders determined in 1936. The current situation, stressed Ahmad Sadiq Sa'd, was that "Egypt is a member of the UN whose Charter overrides any treaties that contradict the principles of the organization, including the Anglo–Egyptian Treaty of Alliance, because the treaty puts Egypt in the status of an indentured country while, as a UN member, it is a state with full sovereignty and equal to other states including Britain." In light of this new reality, declared Sa'd, Egypt is entitled to unilaterally nullify the treaty of 1936.

According to him, Britain grossly violated the treaty when, despite the clause declaring the end of the military occupation of Egypt, the British military not only continued, but even expanded its presence in Egypt. The 1936 treaty also included the aspiration to immediately wind down British presence in the security establishment, even though it allowed for the possibility of a five-year transition period. This clause, stressed Sa'd, was not fulfilled. He also sharply criticized paragraph 5 of the 1936 treaty, which subjugated Egyptian foreign policy to the interests of imperialism. This paragraph declared that the parties committed themselves not to implement positions in their foreign relations that contradicted the treaty. In practice, however, this prevented Egypt from ratifying treaties without British approval. Britain also got preference in supplying external experts for Egyptian needs and was also guaranteed exclusivity in supplying equipment to the Egyptian military. Sa'd concluded that the paradigm of "negotiations" that served only to perpetuate the status quo must be abandoned.[53]

A few days before the establishment of *Hadetu*, *al-Jamahir*, the mouthpiece of *Iskra*, launched a frontal attack on Nuqrashi. Mahmud al-Nabawiy sharply criticized Nuqrashi's procrastination in raising the Egyptian issue in the Security Council. He claimed that there were rumors of secret negotiations between Nuqrashi and the British on the issue of Sudan. According to Nabawiy, Nuqrashi hoped to avoid having to raise the issue in the Security Council and was prepared to negotiate with British imperialism on the basis of a procedural amendment in the Sudan Protocol, while all other matters, including military, economic, and political restraints that imperialism wished to impose on Egypt in the framework of an overall agreement, were not included in these talks and were dealt with in the framework of a mutual understanding (between Nuqrashi and the British).[54] Nabawiy referred to Bevin's declaration that the parties would reach an initialed summation on the issue of withdrawal and that on the issue of Sudan there remained disagreements on the interpretation of the Sudan Protocol. He claimed that the Egyptian government agreed, in essence, to the continued occupation of the country for three more years, agreed to a military alliance with imperialists, and agreed to the establishment of a joint security council. "The significance of this is that all the restraints the two of them wish to impose on the Nile valley and all the chains with which they wish to shackle [the Nile valley] have been agreed upon [between the two parties] and all that remains is the 'interpretation' of the 'Sudan Protocol.'" Nuqrashi sent a public statement on the matter to the press. According to Nabawiy, he did not demand the abolition of the 1936 treaty as the people wanted, or of the 1899 treaty, but in essence ratified the treaties by agreeing to the appointment of the British governor-general Robert Howe. Neither did Nuqrashi reject the proposed Bevin–Sidqi draft agreement, which he had enthusiastically endorsed in the parliament in the past. From these facts Nabawiy concluded that Nuqrashi's public statement was merely an attempt to distract the people from their primary objective, the complete withdrawal from the Nile valley, and to present the talks as concerning a minor disagreement on the Sudan Protocol. "Our struggle against Imperialism is not a struggle over the 'Sudan Protocol,' but a struggle for the liberty and independence of the Nile valley," declared Nabawiy.

Our struggle against Imperialism is not over 'the Sudan,' as Bevin and Nuqrashi are trying to paint it. Moreover, it is beyond that and deeper than that. It includes all aspects of our economic, political and military lives. This is a struggle for the liberation of Egypt and the Sudan. This struggle will not be resolved by an arrangement between Bevin and Nuqrashi, but by the struggle of the people of the Nile valley united in a single front against Imperialism and its collaborators.[55]

Mahmud Hammadi (pseudonym of Shuhdi 'Atiyya), too, asserted that the Bevin–Sidqi draft agreement, which "Nuqrashi's government endorsed," was the main weakness in the presentation of the problem to the Security Council. Regarding the issue of Sudan Hammadi wrote:

The demand for the unification of the Nile valley without a demand for complete withdrawal from the Nile valley and simultaneous recognition of the right of self-determination of the Sudan . . . and without clearly warning of the danger that the continued presence of the British in the Sudan poses to the independence of Egypt and to the freedom and welfare of the Sudan, and without drawing attention to the danger of separation in the shadow of Imperialism, [the presentation] of the issue before the Security Council] can only be described as a service to Imperialism and a severe weakening of the issue of the Nile valley.[56]

The left wing within the Wafd, which had cooperated in many matters with the Tali'at al-'Ummal group, was also categorically opposed to making compromises with Britain and called for the abrogation of the 1936 treaty. However, unlike Tali'at al-'Ummal, it supported Egyptian–Sudanese unification. At a conference in the village of Awlaila in early 1947, for example, the Wafd Youth wing, which represented students and workers, called for linking the issue of the Nile valley to the people's will. They harshly attacked the current leadership that "insists on our servitude" and demonstrated its incompetence in both domestic and foreign policy. They further accused the government of "relegating the issue of the homeland to the shelf" and of taking a cynical view of the bloodshed inflicted by the Sudanese government on the nationalists in Sudan, and called for struggle against imperialism and its offshoots. They declared that as students and workers who constitute the young backbone of Egypt, they were aware that all eyes were on them; that they were "ready to spill their blood to liberate the valley, to evict the English from the land, to defend liberty and democracy, to support the rights that were stolen from the people and to protect the workers and peasants"; and that they were fulfilling the program under the direction of their commander and leader Mustafa al-Nahhas, the opposition leader at the time.[57]

Within the MB, further nuances regarding the demand for Egyptian unification can be discerned. For example, 'Abd al-Hafiz al-Sayfi, the founder of the department of foreign relations in the Muslim world in the period of Hasan al-Banna, tried to ease somewhat the tension between the Sudanese, who objected to unification, and the Egyptian and Sudanese supporters of unification. To begin, he did not reject the possibility of the establishment of a separate Sudanese entity, if such a possibility should present itself:

It would be a mistake to imagine that this view is only held by those who are calling for it. We wish to reassure those who support this view, that we Egyptians are true partners in this purpose and will be truly pleased, if this precious and desired aspiration would be embraced by all Egyptians and Sudanese equally. Any Egyptian, who does not want Sudan to be for the Sudanese, is thus not a true nationalist, who wishes for the good of his homeland. We believe that the day the Sudan will be [self-sufficient], the true happiness of all the people of the Nile valley will be realized. We want to assure our southern brethren, that we wish them all the best as we wish for ourselves, and that we will act together with them toward the realization of our common aspirations, and we will stand by their side in achieving our rights that have been usurped by the imperialist foe, who has driven a wedge between us and the realization of our aspirations ... Oh, people of the south, we are your partners in everything you do and everything you struggle for ... Regarding the claims often made that behind these people [who call for separation] stands the foreign occupier, who is interested in dividing a single land and a single people to make it easier for him to conquer smaller parts of the valley, we declare clearly that there is no way the Egyptian and Sudanese brothers would enable the imperialist exploiter to drive the people, who hold this view, and achieve the result he desires. We have positive views of our brothers in the south. We support them in the realization of a common cause and the expulsion of a common foe.[58]

Although Sayfi ostensibly supported the slogan "Sudan for the Sudanese," he argued that achieving this aim would require a joint Sudanese–Egyptian effort against the common enemy – Britain. He turned "to his Sudanese brothers," exposing the malicious British scheme to take over Sudan. His assumption was that before the right of the Sudanese to self-determination and the possibility of deciding their own future could be discussed, they still needed Egypt's help in the complete liberation of the Nile valley. The two peoples must buckle down and struggle together to achieve the desired liberation. He called on the Sudanese and Egyptians to establish a strong joint government "to stand up to the exploiting foe and for a free parliament based on the true will of the people." Sayfi noted the recent parliamentary elections (January 1945), in which 'Ali al-Barir (a native Sudanese, perceived as "the popular Sudanese ambassador to Egypt and the sponsor of the Sudanese students, who came to study in Egypt") ran in one of the districts – a move that, according to Sayfi, was well-received in Egypt and that demonstrated "an Egyptian willingness to involve their Sudanese brothers equally in the political system."[59]

Sayfi, who did not wish to appear as diverging from the official position of the MB, concluded with the words of the general guide, Hasan al-Banna, in favor of unity:

Have our Sudanese brothers not heard the statement of the general guide of the Muslim Brothers at the celebration in honor of their leaders at the General Center in Cairo: We are in a time of consolidation, when various peoples are taking advantage of the opportunity and are looking for simple matters that bring them together. All the more so when the earthly and heavenly powers unite the people of the Nile valley. Does this people not have the right to unite, particularly in the era of the Arab League, to be followed by the Islamic League?[60]

As we have seen, even before the first significant round of talks between Egypt and Britain began in May 1946, a Sudanese delegation, including representatives of the main Sudanese political currents, arrived in the Egyptian capital at the beginning of April with the objective of presenting a united position, which they had formulated on 19 March 1946. This position included the following points:

1. Egypt and Britain must make a joint declaration recognizing the existence of a democratic Sudanese government in union with Egypt.
2. The Sudanese government will determine the nature of the union with Egypt.
3. The free and democratic government of Sudan will enter into an alliance with Britain reflecting the nature of its union with Egypt.

On 7 April the Sudanese delegation published a declaration expressing its reliance on the government of Egypt to support its demands, since both countries were struggling for liberation from imperialism.[61] British withdrawal from the Nile valley, it declared, must be total – political, military, and economic – and to achieve this aim the Sudanese and the Egyptian people must unite. A separate solution for Egypt and Sudan must be rejected out of hand. Only following full British withdrawal could Egypt and Sudan reach an agreement on "the internal organization of the Nile valley."[62]

The visit of the Sudanese delegation and its demands aroused widespread controversy within and among the political currents in Egypt. For example, the editorial staff of *al-Fajr al-Jadid* conducted an internal debate on the Sudanese demands. They reached the conclusion that there is a Sudanese nationalist movement led by a developing and progressive "national capitalist class" struggling against colonialism and playing an important historic role – the establishment of a democratic regime. Egyptian progressive forces must join the developing Sudanese nationalism and its revolutionary leadership and open a united struggle against the common enemy – British colonialism. "We need to understand that the Sudanese nationalist movement is the most significant player and the central power, and our interest is that it become stronger and join us in the common struggle against colonialism."[63]

The editorial staff of *al-Fajr al-Jadid* assessed the Sudanese nationalist movement as being unified and free in its direction, as evinced by the interparty agreement and the coalition established on that basis. Addressing the calls for separatism within Sudan, the members of *al-Fajr al-Jadid* argued that those came from a tiny segment of the colonialist-oriented Sudanese parties. Dividing the political forces within Sudan before the completion of the British withdrawal meant throwing Sudan into the maw of British colonialism, which aspires to determine the type of regime in Sudan before withdrawal, thereby separating Sudan. On the other hand, they stressed, "the Egyptian reactionaries" also aim to define the type of regime in Sudan, namely its program for full merger of Sudan and Egypt. The significance of this was that both British colonialism and Egyptian reaction set their primary goal as determining the form of the regime in Sudan, whereas the Sudanese nationalist movement viewed the liberation from colonialism as its primary objective. It was no surprise, then, they wrote, that British colonialism and Egyptian reaction were fighting the Sudanese nationalist movement, since it posed a threat to their interests by aspiring to achieve liberation from colonialism and the establishment of a democratic Sudanese regime, resisting foreign – particularly British and Egyptian – exploitation of Sudan.

The editorial staff of the Marxist journal called for unification of the Sudanese and the Egyptian nationalist forces in light of the bourgeoisie's betrayal of its national mission. Unification of the nationalist forces in both countries should be unification in the struggle against colonialism, whereas the position of the bourgeois leadership was the reverse. It held on to general slogans such as "The Unity of the Nile Valley," "Unity of Blood," etc., without explicating the substance of these slogans. The editorial staff of *al-Fajr al-Jadid* criticized what it considered to be corrupt methods employed by Egyptian politicians toward the Sudanese delegation, including intimidation and threats such as, "either the delegation first declares their allegiance to the unification of the Nile valley, which means accepts the determination [by Egyptian political leaders] of the character of the regime in the Sudan, or the examination of the Sudan question will be postponed pending an agreement between the north and the south of Sudan."

The editorial staff noted that the Egyptian people supported the Sudanese demands and their slogan, "A united struggle against a common enemy" (*Kifah mushtarak didda 'adu mushtarak*), and called on the Sudanese nationalists to address the Egyptian people and ally themselves with "its aware leadership." It also called on the Egyptian nationalists to fight against any colonialist calls for "separatism" or "unification" and to support the Sudanese nationalist movement. "Loyal nationalists" in Egypt and Sudan must turn their attention first and foremost to resistance to the occupation. Their first objective should be the liberation of Egypt and Sudan from British colonialism. It concluded with the call: "Long live Egypt and the Sudan as two independent democracies."[64]

In contrast, the response of the MB to the visit of the Sudanese delegation and its declared common points was highly critical. They rejected the Sudanese demand for self-determination and freedom to determine the future of the unification with Egypt democratically. The unity of the Nile valley was unquestionable because the peoples of the valley, on both sides, were united in their language, religion, origin, traditions, customs, hopes, and torments, as well as in their commercial and economic bonds. Materially, the Sudanese and the Egyptian economies would be inextricably linked after the expulsion of British imperialism. Separation would entail severe economic crisis in both sister countries.[65]

Referring to the Sudanese delegation's demands, Hasan al-Banna, the general guide of the MB, wrote in *al-Ahram* a message to Isma'il al-Azhari, the head of the delegation. First, reasoned Banna, the desire of the delegation to participate in the Anglo–Egyptian talks as a third party was used as a pretext by the British to evade discussion of the Sudanese problem, and Egypt's right to speak on behalf of Sudan was denied. This might jeopardize the advancement of the national question, of which Sudan was an integral part. Second, the delegation's mission did not correspond with the hopes and desires of the people of the valley – the unity of Egypt and Sudan. The mission should change its declared aims to the following:

1. To call for the evacuation of British troops from the entire Nile valley, thus ensuring its complete independence, as already declared by the delegation.
2. For the Sudanese representatives to come to terms with the Egyptian government on the future links between the southern and the northern parts of the valley.
3. To authorize some members of the delegation to negotiate as representatives of the south within the Egyptian delegation, to display solidarity and unity of goals vis-à-vis the British.[66]

Banna, who represented a mass movement with deep roots in the Nile valley, reminded the Sudanese delegation of his movement's stand on the solution for the Sudan question:

[The MB] believe that we are one nation and want to see a full unity between the Egyptians and Sudanese as the sons of one people, with one homeland, identical rights and duties, with one nationality and one constitution. This means that the elections would be held and conducted in the Sudan similarly to Egypt. The Sudanese would enjoy a proportional representation in the parliament. They would also have ministers and heads of governments, and there would be no objection to changing the name of the united country from "the Egyptian Kingdom" to "the Kingdom of the Nile Valley." The high and junior administrative posts within Sudan would be for the Sudanese, as they know better the affairs of the country. Such steps would dispel the argument that the unity of the Sudan and Egypt would give the latter on account of its culture, wealth and large number of educated residents, a monopoly of the South's posts. On the contrary [stressed Banna], talented Sudanese would be able to hold positions and serve in a variety of jobs in the northern part of the valley.[67]

Banna concluded by making an appeal to the delegation to reconsider its demands. He promised that the MB would be happy to maintain close contacts and cooperate with the representative of the Sudanese to learn their problems and to reach a rational and optimal solution.[68]

The journal *al-Ikhwan al-Muslimun* conducted a study with the aim to prove that Egypt and Sudan were bound together not only in political, religious, and cultural terms but also in economic and commercial aspects. The study's target audience were all parties involved in the negotiations between Egypt and Britain. The study related to the Sudanese delegation as follows:

Recently a Sudanese delegation arrived in Cairo to participate indirectly in the Egyptian–British negotiations and take a close look at them ... We are taking this opportunity to examine the economic situation in the Sudan in order to demonstrate to the negotiators that the unity of the two parts of the Nile valley is not determined only by ethnicity, language, religion, tradition, customs, aspirations and sufferings; rather, the two parts of the valley are bound as well by economic and commercial ties. The Sudan completely depends on Egypt for the marketing of its primary products in the event that the imperialist British market is cut off. If the Sudan is separated from Egypt, this will cause economic crises in both sister states, as neither one can manage without the other.[69]

In other words, the position of the MB remained firm: the Egyptian course for the solution of the unity of the Nile valley was an incontrovertible axiom.

Like the communists, yet for opposite reasons, the MB were active within Sudan in the latter part of the 1940s to advance their vision of the unity of the Nile valley. In addition, Sudanese students in both Egypt and Sudan were affiliated with the Egyptian movement already in the late 1940s. Unlike *Hametu*, which supported, sponsored, and encouraged the formation of its Sudanese counterpart *Hasetu*, a Sudanese branch of the MB was established officially by Sudanese activists only in August 1954. At that historical phase, the doctrine of the unity of the Nile valley was no longer an Egyptian nationalist consensus – it was rather in a terminal phase. Al-Rashid al-Tahir, who became the leader of the Sudanese branch, was on good terms with the Free Officers, particularly with Salih Salim. However, following Nasser's assassination attempt in October 1954, relations severely deteriorated. Consequently, the Sudanese MB joined forces with the anti-unionist Sudanese forces. In independent Sudan, they, unlike their Egyptian counterpart, were initially pragmatic and cooperated with local political organizations, including communist.[70]

Right and Left on the Egyptian Failure in the Security Council and Its Consequences

Opposition pressure on the various Egyptian governments between 1945 and 1947 not to reach an agreement with Britain that would include concessions on core national issues bore fruit. While the Nuqrashi (1945–1946) and Sidqi (1946) governments tried to resolve the disagreements with Britain by negotiations (and even, in the case of the Sidqi government, the formulation of a draft agreement including concessions on the issue of Sudan), the second Nuqrashi government (1946–1948) embarked on a different policy. It decided to bring the dispute with Britain for deliberation in the UN Security Council. Egypt hoped that it would have the upper hand in this arena, since the two new superpowers, the USSR and the United States, were expected to support Egypt's national demands. In a speech on 5August 1947 before the Security Council, Nuqrashi declared that the unity of the Nile valley was an undisputed fact. The border between Egypt and Sudan was an artificial boundary created by Britain. He emphasized that the economic unity between the two countries was based on common agricultural, industrial, and commercial interests – and influenced by their complete dependence on the Nile. The process of Egyptian penetration into Sudan that began in the early nineteenth century was peaceful and natural, based on common language and culture. Nuqrashi accused Britain of being responsible for all the ills and difficulties faced by Sudan and stated that the future of the Nile valley was an internal Egyptian–Sudanese matter that would be resolved between the two nations only after the complete British withdrawal from the valley. Nuqrashi's patronizing speech left no room for doubt: Sudan was Egyptian property, and only Egypt knew what was good for the Sudanese and how to advance Sudan politically.[71] However, Egyptian hopes of persuading the members of the Security Council of the justice of their demands were frustrated.[72]

The Egyptian failure in the Security Council led to sharp criticism at home. *Tali'at al-'Ummal* (*al-Fajr al-Jadid* group) argued that Nuqrashi's aggressive language in the Security Council stemmed from the heavy pressure from the awakening nationalist movement. The international reality was such that British imperialism was on the retreat in the face of growing national liberation movements, and Egypt, in this sense, was no different than the others. Nuqrashi's talk of imminent British withdrawal was hollow, since it was clear to him and the upper classes associated with him that Britain was prepared to withdraw, and what remained to be determined was the price of the withdrawal. The major landholders and monopolists wanted the withdrawal to take place in a manner that would ensure the perpetuation of "reactionary rule in Egypt." The communists viewed the Bevin–Sidqi draft agreement as proof of this. The Nuqrashi government, in their view, worked to achieve the same objective by colla-boration with the allies of imperialist Britain. They went further, stating that this government was planning to promulgate "a law of mandatory recruitment, acquisition of American ordnance and American training of the Egyptian military when the treaty with Britain is finalized ... Putting this plan into action makes it necessary that the reactionary government remain in power."[73] The communists accused the MB of collaborating with Nuqrashi in the implementation of the scheme by organizing mass demonstrations with empty slogans calling for British withdrawal and protesting the UN Security Council, actions intended in actuality to distract the public from the substance of the national problem.[74]

As far as the *Tali'at al-'Ummal* members were concerned, the Nuqrashi government was responsible for the failure in the Security Council, and the primary reason for this was that the government was not democratic and its relations with the common classes were hostile. *Tali'at al-'Ummal* objected to any future agreement with imperialism and called for complete British withdrawal from the Nile valley and for the fall of the government.[75] Nuqrashi's presentation of the Egyptian cause before the Security Council constituted the greatest retreat of Egyptian reaction in the face of the pressure of the democratic nationalist movement – pressure that led to the fall of the Sidqi government, the rejection of the Sidqi–Bevin program, and the cessation of the Anglo–Egyptian negotiations. Still, the Egyptian reaction used the period of calm following the presentation at the Security Council to increase the pressure on the common classes, particularly the proletariat. The forces of Egyptian reaction implemented measures intended to shore up its rule: increased subjection of the government to the palace and conveyance of the message that "our country is for Anglo-American imperialism." Britain was in a state of retreat due to the circumstances in Europe and the world over and not interested "in losing more of its bases, so they established central military bases in Kenya and Central Africa, and they talk of the right to self-determination for the Sudanese so that the Sudan will become formally independent but subject in actuality to British rule." *Tali'at al-'Ummal* called vociferously to refrain from any kind of bilateral talks with Britain, whose sole objective was the advancement of its imperialist aims.[76]

The members of the Democratic Movement for National Liberation (*Hadetu*), the largest communist movement, also claimed that Nuqrashi's decision to go to the Security Council stemmed from public pressure: "The government senses the people's rage and is engaging in deception and terror. At one moment they try to claim that the withdrawal is near, and at another they try to show how firmly they are standing up to the English when in fact they are best buddies. At yet another moment they are trying to claim that putting off the presentation of the issue serves the interests of Egypt and not of the English."[77] *Hadetu* announced that behind the presentation of the Egyptian national demand was the intention to create an alliance between local reaction and imperialism – to ensure the continued rule of the Egyptian reactionaries and safeguard imperialist interests. Nuqrashi's demands in the Security Council were the result of popular pressure and were primarily intended for "local consumption in Egypt." The speech was, in effect, "the nail in the coffin of the national aspirations." The Nuqrashi government accepted, in effect, the principles of the Sidqi–Bevin draft agreement, including the establishment of a Joint Defense Council with Britain and a three-year timetable for withdrawal.[78]

In an article on the Sudan issue published in *al-Jamahir*, the ideological mouthpiece of *Hadetu*, Nuqrashi and his advisors were attacked for ignoring the right of the Sudanese people for freedom and the call for the abolition of the 1899 treaty, and for settling instead for the demand to "alter the status quo in the administration of the Sudan." This formulation ensured the continuation of the British imperialist regime in a new guise, whereas our demand was always the complete expulsion of imperialism from Sudan and not just the introduction of a merely procedural change in the administrative system.[79] *Hadetu* claimed that the spirit in which the matter was presented in the Security Council was liable to lead in a perilous direction, removing this issue of great national import from the Council's political agenda and transferring it to a course of legal-constitutional discussions. Such a situation would only increase the likelihood of the establishment of international commissions of inquiry on Sudan that would not necessarily serve the interests of the people of the Nile valley. The deliberations on the burning national issues would continue to be fruitless, and certain questions would not be resolved, such as whether the 1899 treaty was or was not imposed upon Egypt; whether the 1936 treaty achieved its objectives; whether the English were really encouraging separatist movements that sowed the seeds of division in the Nile valley; and whether England could rule Sudan without Egypt. All of this legal sidetracking could be prevented if Egypt had a popular government committed to the abolition of the treaties of 1936 and 1899. Such a government would make clear to the world the gravity of the danger in the continued occupation of the Nile valley – an occupation that threatened the peace of the Middle East because of the strategic location and importance of the valley – and would also emphasize the importance of the integrity of the valley and the welfare of its peoples.[80]

In spite of this, *Hadetu* saw a few points of light in the list of demands that Nuqrashi intended to present to the Security Council: first, the demand for the complete withdrawal from the Nile valley and the abolition of the current administrative regime over Sudan; and second, the presentation of the roots and characteristics of the Anglo–Egyptian conflict. The document also included, however, "dangerous loopholes":

1. The lack of a clear rejection of the Sidqi–Bevin draft agreement.
2. The lack of a demand to abolish the treaty of 1899.

3. Settling for complete withdrawal from the Nile valley without mentioning other areas of imperialist rule in the region.
4. Ignoring the popular demand that the withdrawal be without an alliance or treaty with imperialism.[81]

Nuqrashi paid no attention to the liberation of the Sudanese people and settled for the demand for "changing the current system of administering the Sudan." This formulation, basically similar to the Sidqi–Bevin draft, would ensure the continued rule of British imperialism in a new guise, whereas the people's demand was to expel imperialism from Sudan and not merely change the administrative system.

These perilous loopholes were liable to open the door to the renewal of negotiations with the British. The only way to prevent a retreat in Nuqrashi's positions and the continuation of the negotiations with Britain was to continue the popular struggle, based on the following slogans:

1. "Imperialism must fall."
2. "The Sidqi–Bevin program must fall."
3. "The 1936 and 1899 treaties must fall."
4. "No to a treaty or alliance with imperialism."
5. "Complete withdrawal from the Nile valley with no treaty or alliance."[82]

In a public statement published by *Hadetu* on 21 July 1947, the organization declared its commitment to the citizens to continue to struggle until the Nile valley achieved full independence. The statement praised the people, whose struggle and consciousness brought down the "tyrant" Sidqi, forced his successor, Nuqrashi, to cease the negotiations, and forced his government to lodge a protest at the Security Council after much foot-dragging. *Hadetu* called on the people to take the initiative into their own hands and raise their voice before the world and emphasize their demands:

1. Complete, immediate, and unconditional withdrawal from the Nile valley without any alliance with imperialism.
2. Complete rejection of the Sidqi–Bevin plan.
3. Insistence on the abolition of the treaty of 1936 and the agreements of 1899.[83]

In an additional public statement released on 4 August 1947, *Hadetu* claimed that Sudan was suffering under a slave regime in the south and a semi-feudal regime in the north, and its citizens were living in dire, inhumane conditions, in the shadow of a military regime lasting fifty years. Therefore, argued *Hadetu*, "our fundamental demand is full, immediate, unconditional withdrawal from the Nile valley with no treaty or alliance. This is a right guaranteed to us by the UN Charter." *Hadetu* declared that the unity of the Egyptian–Sudanese struggle stemmed from the unity of objectives and the common economic and cultural interests of both nations, and from the historic ties that connected Egypt and Sudan in their common struggle for the complete liberation of the Nile valley. *Hadetu* stressed, as well, the right to self-determination for Sudan, while asserting the need for a transition period, in which Egypt would be the warden for Sudan under UN supervision. Egypt would be responsible "for the progress of the Sudan and for the development of its culture and national economy, and its full liberation from every remnant of imperialism, in order to create the necessary conditions to allow the Sudanese to implement their democratic right to self-determination, [and enable them] to determine the kind of relations they wish to maintain with Egypt following this period [of wardenship], be it autonomy or unification or full independence."[84]

Hadetu argued that Egypt should emphasize to the Security Council that it would not deny the Sudanese their right to self-determination and that it was the British who prevented and continued to prevent them from realizing this right, creating a climate of terror in Sudan. Just as bad was their prevention of economic progress and of the development of the national culture and a free press. *Hadetu* rejected the notion of full Egyptian sovereignty over Sudan and the premise that Sudan was "a large portion of our land," as Nuqrashi declared. "Full Egyptian sovereignty over the Sudan," argued *Hadetu*, would open a loophole for the imperialists to point to a denial of basic principles of the UN, which include the right of peoples to self-determination. All this would increase the threat of Sudanese separatism. *Hadetu* also rejected the idea of a referendum following the withdrawal, as proposed by Nuqrashi: "Neither the Egyptians nor the Sudanese have an interest in such since the current imperialist and enslaving administration, which has lasted fifty years, is tainted with bribery, bankruptcy and deception, which have permeated to the heads of the tribes who control a large portion of the Sudanese." Therefore, in *Hadetu*'s view, a referendum in Sudan immediately following withdrawal would not necessarily represent the true view of the Sudanese. In light of contemporary circumstances, the idea of wardenship as part of the process realizing the Sudanese right to self-determination was the best practical option, according to *Hadetu*.[85]

The wardenship proposed by *Hadetu*, which was a slight deviation from the movement's original trajectory, was the butt of sharp criticism from the rival communist group *Tali'at al-'Ummal*, which expressed its support for the Sudanese national movement as long as it was struggling against imperialism and working to throw off its yoke. The Sudanese national movement, it stressed, should continue to fight against the feudalism inherent in the alliance with imperialism and to destroy the enslavement regime that imperialism wished to leave in place in Sudan. *Tali'at al-'Ummal* declared that

the position of the opportunist group [*Hadetu*] appropriated the idea of the right to self-determination for the Sudanese people, while calling for the imposition of a protectorate. This movement [*Hadetu*] takes no account of the Sudanese national movement, nor of the interests of the Sudanese people and supports the most reactionary Egyptian bourgeois elements ... Wardenship will lead the feudal Sudanese reactionaries to create a bloc with the Egyptian reactionaries at the expense of the burgeoning Sudanese bourgeoisie; Egypt will thus be taking the place of Britain as occupiers and imperialists. Moreover, this solution constitutes support of the call for Sudanese separatism which leads to the continuation of the British occupation of the Sudan.[86]

Tali'at al-'Ummal also attacked *Hadetu* for its readiness to exonerate the Socialist Party, formerly known as *Misr al-Fatat*,[87] for its past and to focus on its current positions (1951). *Misr al-Fatat* was painted as a fascist organization in every sense of the word. Even if the most recent declarations of the party leaders had a socialist character and spoke of the defense of liberties and a constitution, in actuality this was not a significant departure from its policy and methods, since the class makeup had not changed. *Misr al-Fatat* belonged to the Second International of the type of Bevin, Atlee, and the rest of the Western European countries. Worse yet, this party continued to call enthusiastically for the colonialization of Sudan and Egyptian migration to Sudan. Its leader, Ahmad Husayn, still supported the regime of King Ibn Sa'ud in Saudi Arabia.[88]

Nuanced differences among the various communist groups regarding the future of Sudan were insignificant in subsequent years as well. The paradigmatic line shaped by *Hametu* (and later *Hadetu*) remained dominant in the communist camp until the decision of the Free Officers' regime to sign an agreement along those lines in 1953. The platform of the Egyptian Communist Party established in 1949 (known as *al-Raya*) also called for independence and the liberation of the Nile valley from "English and American" foreign colonialism and for the withdrawal of British forces from Egypt and Sudan. *Al-Raya*'s platform emphasized the freedom of the Sudanese people and their right to self-determination, expressing absolute support for their struggle for full liberation and for full withdrawal of "British and Egyptian colonial forces" from their land.[89]

Fu'ad Mursi, a founder of *al-Raya*, sharply and openly denounced rival communist organizations, calling them "leftist" and "rightist" opportunists. As far as the future of Sudan was concerned, he argued unpersuasively and inaccurately, *al-Raya* was the first and only Egyptian political organization to fervently call for the right of the Sudanese people to self-determination. Mursi argued that his party condemned both British and Egyptian imperialism, calling upon the two to evacuate Sudan at once.[90]

Although *al-Raya's* program embraced the general communist line on the Sudan question, it nevertheless added some new ideas regarding a possible solution. *Al-Raya* committed itself to battle "against all policies propagated by the Egyptian ruling class which do not respect the Sudanese right to self-determination." It also promised to see that the slogan of Sudanese self-determination would not be manipulated by the British to strengthen and consolidate its imperialist basis in Sudan.[91] *Al-Raya* recommended a federal union between Egypt and Sudan on the basis of equality between the two peoples, after British evacuation of the entire Nile valley. A federal union was not a compulsory solution, however, but an option. It would be made clear to the Sudanese people that their right to self-determination was guaranteed. In other words, they themselves would determine their future – and the option of secession would also be granted and guaranteed.[92]

Al-Raya's program drew a distinction between its solution to the problem of Sudan and that favored by the Egyptian bourgeoisie. The latter wanted to see "the unification of the Nile valley under the Egyptian crown. But it is strange that they never mention a single word about the future of the Sudanese people and their right of secession. Not only does the Egyptian bourgeoisie impose unity with Egypt upon the Sudan, but it enslaves the Sudan in the expression 'under the Egyptian crown.' In other words, it will become an Egyptian colony governed by the same regime as Egypt."[93] In contrast, *al-Raya* stressed that it represented the approach of "the Egyptian proletariat," which aimed at defending Sudan and liberating it from tyranny. In addition to the earlier insistence on unity as a free choice for the Sudanese people, the communists opted for economic, geographic, and political unity after "the abolition of British rule in the Sudan and the abolition of the legislative assembly. We want a Sudanese national government elected by the people. We want the immediate withdrawal of the British army and the handing over of all administrative posts to the Sudanese. We want the evacuation of Egyptian troops and the recall of Egyptians occupying administrative posts" from Sudan.[94]

In early 1952, on the background of the anti-British guerrilla activity in the vicinity of the Suez Canal following the unilateral abolition of the 1936 treaty, *Tali'at al-'Ummal* disseminated the "National Committees" program in the Azhar neighborhood. The program called, inter alia, for organizing the nation in national committees as a condition for the success of the armed popular uprising against imperialism, and for tying the popular struggle in Egypt to the struggle in Sudan and declaring the right of self-determination for the Sudanese following the withdrawal of the imperialist forces from Sudan. In other words, there continued to be uniformity on the matter of self-determination for the Sudanese people in the divided communist camp even on the eve of the revolution of July 1952.[95]

The position of the Egyptian right on the deliberations in the Security Council and its results was different than that of the communists. Nuqrashi was praised for his firm stance in presenting the Egyptian demands. Mahmud Muhammad Shakir, a senior writer for *al-Risala*, characterized Egypt and Sudan as a single nation struggling for justice against British tyranny "which assaulted their independence and occupied their land from the source of the Nile to its delta." According to him, Nuqrashi exposed Britain's aggressive imperialist policy since 1882 and its exploitation of the people and the injustice caused to them. Nuqrashi's statement concerning the Egyptian–Sudanese issue forced the British delegate in the Security Council to hurriedly present before the members of the Council a false and partial history of "British aggression."[96] If the Security Council were founded on the execution of justice, argued Shakir, Egypt would unconditionally have achieved its full rights from those who exploit it. Egypt and Sudan were an outstanding model that would surprise British imperialism and its supporters:

If the Security Council is a modern slave market established by the rival nations in order to buy and sell Allah's creation, then Egypt and the Sudan will teach the Security Council a new lesson it is not expecting from a nation weakened by the tyrannical British rule for over 65 years. Egypt and the Sudan are a strong nation that [British] tyranny has taught that rights are achieved by bitter jihad, bloodletting and unshakeable faith.[97]

Shakir, who made frequent use of Islamic terminology, declared that it would be well "that the *Mujahaddin* guard themselves against fear" because fear impairs jihad. They must take an example from Nuqrashi, who overcame fear when appearing before the Security Council and forcing the British to take refuge in falsehoods. Shakir also had a message for the other Arab leaders: "If the Arab politicians would be unwavering in their stance on every issue and every agreement, French and British imperialism would not have struck roots in our lands to this day."[98]

Shakir believed that if Britain could not be defeated by force, it could be defeated by shaking up the stability of the region, because Britain, in his view, excuses its continued presence in Egypt and Sudan on the pretext that it is the one keeping stability there:

Britain's interest is to keep the peace in this region of the Near East. This is a pretext for it to remain in Egypt, the Sudan, Palestine and Iraq. We must seek a way to expose this counterfeit peace ... The entire Arab world knows that Egypt and the Sudan are its very heart, and if this heart remains weak and chained in the chains of imperialism, the Arab world will not have the power to do something for the arousal which is stirring in the breasts of its sons ... We must unite, not only in Egypt and the Sudan, but throughout the Arab world and every region in the Muslim world.[99]

Fathi Radwan, now a member of the Nationalist Party and a representative of the most nationalist point of view on the matter of Sudan, praised Nuqrashi and called upon him to continue to take a nationalist line, because this was what he needed to do:

We must present clear positions vis-à-vis the English and take steps compatible with our new position with respect to them. Perhaps the first step we must take would be to recall the Egyptian ambassador from London. The Egyptian administration must boycott them completely: every English official must leave the government, the [Egyptian] delegations must be recalled from England, doors must be closed to English companies; and the government must deny any easements concerning the English. Next the government must strengthen its ties with any country hostile to England or maintaining a position similar to ours. It should increase cooperation with Russia and Poland, who helped us in our problem, and stand with them as friends in every matter. These are some first steps Nuqrashi should take. There should be coordination between his position in the Security Council and his position following the presentation of the issue. He must clearly point out the sole means that will bring the realization of our demands, jihad in every field against the English and their helpers.[100]

The mouthpiece of the MB took a more critical approach to the results of Nuqrashi's embassy to the Security Council about a year later on the background of increasing tension in the relations between the MB and the Nuqrashi government. Nuqrashi Pasha stood up in the Security Council and fought, while the Nile valley watched his position "so the world would see and history take note." Upon his return from the United States he announced that he would continue his struggle until the complete liberation of the Nile valley. In practice, however, he did nothing. The MB gave him gentle advice by memoranda and articles addressing public opinion. They tried to push Nuqrashi into action but to no avail.

Instead, in the vacuum that arose "the germs of evil and corruption incubated." And now Nuqrashi's government, which trembled in fear before the external struggle, was waging an intense internal struggle against those who challenged it. "Oh Nuqrashi government, these internal crises are the afflictions brought on by this vacuum, and some of the ministers are liable to clash with their colleagues because they cannot find anything to do ... Save us from this vacuum," concluded *al-Ikhwan al-Muslimun*.[101]

Indeed, as we have seen, the Egyptian failure in the Security Council led Nuqrashi to reconsider his foreign policy. In the latter months of his rule he embraced a policy of pragmatic neutralism in international affairs. This shift of foreign orientation was reinforced under the last Wafd government (1950–1952). Prime Minister Mustafa al-Nahhas concluded that the inter-bloc rivalry could be manipulated by Egypt for the advancement of its national objectives. It was Nahhas who formulated and implemented the doctrine of "Calculative/Pragmatic Nationalist Neutralism," which led in October 1951 to the unilateral abolition of the 1936 treaty and declaration of Faruq as king of Egypt and Sudan. Relations with the Soviet bloc improved significantly, and, respectively, relations with the West deteriorated. The armed struggle against British targets in the Suez Canal area by Egyptian guerrilla fighters brought Anglo–Egyptian relations to their lowest ebb.[102]

British military activity in the Suez Canal zone against Egyptian guerrilla groups led to increased and sharper criticism against Britain and the West. Sayyid Qutb was particularly unrestrained in his criticism. Qutb was a Wafd member until his visit to the United States in 1951. The "culture shock" he experienced there caused him to become extreme in his views toward the West and the way of life there, and from there the path to the MB was short. At this point he had not yet developed his radical Islamic outlook against Egyptian "*Jahili* society," and he was clearly at an early stage in the forging of his radical ideas. In his articles in the months leading up to the July 1952 revolution he did not discuss Egyptian society as "apostate" and still had faith in its ability to expel the British and bring change to Egypt. The arrows of his criticism were aimed at imperialism. Between the lines there were hints of the possibility that the Egyptian government might be siding with the imperialist state's position, but he still was not taking the government to task on that score. Qutb was adamantly opposed to an alliance with the British enemy or its allies. In the wake of the killing of Egyptian guerilla fighters by the British military on Egyptian soil he declared that the only response to the despicable British actions was a bloody struggle. "Today the die was cast; the blood that has been spilled destroyed any dam and any bridge.

Oh God, after today no whisper or sound can be heard regarding friend-ship or alliance. Oh God, no man or half a man of this valley who speaks from the corner of his mouth of a Western front. The words are made of blood and fire . . ."[103]

According to Qutb, "the wheels of time have turned and put an end to any opportunity for the servants of the English and of the West in general. Any attempt to bind us to the Western camp is gone and will never return. There is no room for anything but bullets and blood . . . for holy revenge . . . for jihad and struggle." According to Qutb, whoever wants to return to the negotiating table, to appeasement and alliance, must seek another country and not "this land," must seek another nation and not "this nation," must seek another homeland and not "this home-land." He challenged Britain and its "friends" and called upon them to leave Egypt immediately:

After today there is no friendship with the English. Let the friends of the English also know this. After today there is no cease-fire with Imperialism. Talk of a cease-fire between us and the English is a crime. The attempt to extinguish the fire burning between us and them is sticking a knife in the back of those who imperil their lives (*fida'iyyin*) and the innocent martyrs (*shuhada'*). Let the English leave our land. Let all who think to tie between us and the English leave this homeland . . . Let no one think he is stronger, greater or higher than this people . . .[104]

Qutb believed that British imperialism could no longer bear the burden of ruling the Nile valley because of its many weaknesses: "No matter the conditions and circumstances, it is the beginning of the end of Western Imperialism everywhere, particularly in the Arab and Islamic world, which is confronting imperialism today on a variety of fronts . . . in Egypt, in Tunisia, in Morocco, in Iran, in Iraq, in Syria, Algeria and Yemen. They all point to the inevitable end [of imperialism] despite the circumstances." He addressed not only imperialist Britain but also France: "France clashed with the Tunisian people and subdued them with steel and fire; at the same time that England clashed with the people of the Nile valley and subdued them with steel and fire. The same means, the same objectives, and the same mentality: the mentality of imperialism."[105]

Qutb believed that the liberation movements drew their strength from the people and not from lone individuals, and therefore "a setback here or a setback there" would not destroy them. He noted:

Imperialism always turns to the institutions which dominate the countries under imperialism in order to help them subject their peoples. But these institutions cannot stand up to the movement of the nations . . . We see this in Egypt and

Tunisia. In Egypt the move to abolish the treaty [of 1936] was a direct result of pressure from the people. The government was replaced and the new prime minister followed the line set by the people.

Another phenomenon Qutb pointed out among the liberation movements was that sometimes they suffer from ennui and impatience, and this is an opening for weakness to creep in. He argued that Britain and France were in a state of fiscal deficit and military weakness, indicating the beginning of the end for them. They therefore could not withstand a prolonged struggle with the nations, who could not be wiped out, so they wanted to hit the liberation movements. The people must not give up what they already achieved, because "the movement of the people is the movement of the times, and the times do not go backward."[106]

Abu al-Futuh 'Atifah, one of the founders of the Wafd, also believed that Egypt could oust Britain. In a comprehensive article he wrote for the Islamic journal *al-Risala*, 'Atifah declared that all revolutions have a single objective and that is the liberation of the East from the rule of the West:

Egypt is fighting for her freedom, for her independence and for the unity of her valley. Her sons have sworn not to rest and not to skimp on blood and sacrifice until they achieve for their homeland their legitimate objectives. England refuses to grant Egypt its legal rights; in fact the English have come out against all humanistic principles and ethical laws and committed horrendous crimes. They have assaulted the weak and the old during prayer; they have assaulted women and children and chased people out of their homes into the street under a rain of bullets ... Even the houses of Allah, the mosques and the churches, even the cemeteries were not spared the aggression and crimes [of the English].[107]

'Atifah mentioned "the Iranian revolt against the English pirates," referring to the British Petroleum company, which made huge profits in Iran, particularly in 1950, until Iran decided to nationalize the oil in its territory and expelled the British from their houses. Later, in February 1952, Iran directed Britain to close its consulate in Iran. According to 'Atifah, the British influence in Iran thus expired and would not return. He also lashed out at the American conscience, which invested great efforts to find out whether the American nun in Isma'ilia was killed by British or Egyptian bullets, but when Britain killed and expelled thousands of innocents the American conscience was quiet. 'Atifah also noted the Tunisian struggle for independence from the French occupier, presenting France in a negative light and the Tunisians as victims. He concluded by emphasizing that "This is how the West conspires against the East and its freedom. Britain and France are the main obstacles to the hopes of the peoples of the East ..."[108]

Anti-British sentiments in Egypt intensified following the July 1952 Revolution. The Free Officers made Egypt's complete liberation of British imperialism their primary goal. However, as we have seen, their commitment to the unity of the Nile Valley was shaky right from the start. Egypt's military leaders invested great efforts in the resolution of the dispute with Britain and were prepared to sacrifice the vision of the unity of the Nile valley on the altar of a separate agreement with Britain for the withdrawal of its forces from Egypt proper. Practically speaking, they adopted central elements of the communist formulation for the resolution of the issue of the Nile valley.

To conclude, the right- and left-wing radical movements operated in dissident sociopolitical milieus. These movements strove to generate revolutionary change in Egyptian society and state. Their polar views on the issue of the unity of the Nile valley highlighted the differences in their worldviews. Whereas the right-wing movements presented radical and uncompromising nationalist positions regarding the inseparable bond between Egypt and Sudan and complete rejection of particularistic Sudanese nationalism, the communists viewed the Sudanese and the Egyptians as two different peoples with a common historical heritage. They were determined to advance the idea of the right to self-determination for the Sudanese, including their right to determine their political future. The communists viewed the British as the common enemy of both peoples and called on Sudanese and Egyptians to conduct a common struggle to eradicate British imperialism in the Nile valley. At the same time, they also rejected out of hand Egyptian imperialist tendencies regarding Sudan – tendencies well represented by their right-wing rivals, the MB and Young Egypt.

The patterns of political and intellectual activism of the Egyptian leftist social movements were compatible with the definition of the role of the intellectual set out by Edgar Morin and J. P. Nettl, according to which the intellectual is "a qualitative dissenter," someone who works in extra-establishment dissident frameworks and has a universal consciousness. The intellectual creates and disseminates ideas whose realization will benefit society as a whole.[109] Indeed, the communists worked in dissident organizational frameworks, which demanded radical socioeconomic change in Egypt and Sudan. They came out against imperialism wherever it may have been and raised the banner of the lofty value of the right to self-determination of all peoples. They did not hesitate "to speak the truth to power," to employ Edward Said's phrase,[110] and chose to go against the national mainstream even when they understood that this impaired their popular image. The Egyptian right also worked in extra-establishment dissident frameworks and toiled indefatigably to advance its ideas. Nevertheless, the right did not fit into Nettl and Morin's model because their universal mission was only partial: their struggle against imperialism may have qualified as universal, while their position on the Sudanese right to self-determination was clearly nationalist/colonialist, and in that sense not universal. In the ideological and political battle over the future of Sudan between the right and the left in Egypt the latter had the upper hand.

Notes

1 Anwar, "Likay la nansa," *al-Ikhwan al-Muslimun*, 14 December 1946, p. 8.
2 Ibid.
3 Rizq, *Qadiyyat wahdat wadi al-nil*, p. 169.
4 On the visit of the delegation, see in detail Chapter 3.
5 'Abd al-'Aziz Kamil, "Khitab maftuh min shimal al-wadi ila janubihi," *al-Ikhwan al-Muslimun*, 23 April 1946, pp. 6, 22.
6 Ibid.
7 Rizq, *Qadiyyat wahdat wadi al-nil*, p. 167.
8 Ahmad Sadiq Sa'd, "Wahadha sawt misr al-fatat," *al-Fajr al-Jadid*, 16 September 1945.
9 Muhammad Mahmud Jalal, "al-Sudan," *al-Ikhwan al-Muslimun*, 4 October 1945, pp. 8–10.
10 Rizq, *Qadiyyat wahdat wadi al-nil*, 168. It is noteworthy that 86 percent of the water irrigating Egypt comes from Ethiopia's Nile sources, mainly from the Blue Nile, which begins in Lake Tana. "It is there and then that the lifeblood of Egypt is created," declared Haggai Erlich. See his *The Cross and the River: Ethiopia, Egypt and the Nile* (Boulder, CO: Lynne Rienner Publishers, 2002), p. 1.
11 See Hasan al-Banna's view on this subject in *al-Ikhwan al-Muslimun*, 26 January 1946.
12 Hasan al-Banna is quoted from Rizq, *Qadiyyat wahdat wadi al-nil*, p. 169.
13 *al-Ikhwan al-Muslimun*, 20 September 1945 and 27 September 1945.
14 Salah 'Abd al-Hafiz, "Kalimat thalath ...," *al-Ikhwan al-Muslimun*, 5 January 1946, pp. 17–18.
15 Ibid.
16 Ahmad Hasan al-Zayyat, "Ila ikhwatina fi a'ali al-wadi," *al-Risala*, No. 706, 13 January1947.
17 *Misr al-Fatat*, 14 July 1938.
18 *Misr al-Fatat*, 11 August 1938.
19 *Misr al-Fatat*, 1 September 1938.
20 For the full text of the article, see Letter DS(E) 200/128 from R. M. Shields, Security Service Representative (SSR), Cairo, to T. C. Ravensdale, British Embassy, Cairo, 9 August 1947, FP141/1158, 66/72/47.
21 Tareq Y. Ismael and Rif'at al-Sa'id, *The Communist Movement in Egypt, 1920–1988* (New York: Syracuse University Press, 1990), p. 21; Selma Botman, *The Rise of Egyptian Communism, 1939–1970* (Syracuse: Syracuse

University Press, 1988), p. 3; Suliman Bashear, *Communism in the Arab East 1918–1928* (London: Ithaca Press, 1980), pp. 29–33. For further details on the ECP's social and political program, see ibid., pp. 54–57; M. S. Agwani, *Communism in the Arab East* (Bombay and London: Asia Publishing House, 1969), pp. 4–5. On the first wave of organized socialism and communism, see Rif'at al-Sa'id, *Ta'rikh al-haraka al-ishtirakiyya fi misr 1900–1925*, 5th ed. (Cairo: Dar al-Thaqafa al-Jadida, 1981), pp. 170–296.

22 "Misr wa-al-shuyu'iyya," *al-Ahram* (Cairo), 14 February 1924.

23 'Asim Disuqi, "al-Mashru' al-watani wa-al-ijtima'i fi barnamaj al-hizb al-shuyu'iy al-misri fi al-'ishriniyyat wa-al-thalathiniyyat," *Qadaya Fikriyya*, July 1996, pp. 38–45. See a program of action of the ECP in Document 3148/6/2.4.32, 11 February 1932, RGASPI, Fond 495, OP 85, D-93, L186. See also Khalil Hasan Khalil, "al-Tawajjuhat al-iqtisadiyya lil-haraka al-yasariyya fi misr," *Qadaya Fikriyya*, July 1996.

24 Ginat, *A History of Egyptian Communism*, pp. 304–307.

25 On the various communist groups and their ideological differences, including their positions on the Nile valley, see Ginat, *A History of Egyptian Communism*, pp. 217–219, 301–372.

26 Rif'at al-Sa'id, *Ta'rikh al-munazzamat al-yasariyya al-misriyya, 1940–1950* (Cairo: Dar al-Thaqafa al-Jadida, 1976), pp. 94–95.

27 On the development of communism in Sudan and the students' involvement therein, see Salah El Din El Zein El Tayeb, *The Students' Movement in the Sudan* (Khartoum: Khartoum University Press, 1971), pp. 39–43.

28 Al-Sa'id, *Ta'rikh al-munazzamat al-yasariyya*, pp. 94–95, 195–196. For an interview with Abdu Dhahab Hasanayn (of Sudanese origin), see Rif'at al-Sa'id, *al-Yasar al-misri, 1925–1940* (Beirut: Dar al-Tali'a lil-Taba'a wa-al-Nashr, 1972), pp. 291–293. See also Henri Curiel, *Pages Autobiographiques Une Contribution à l'Histoire de la Naissance du Parti Communiste Egyptien – de 1940 à 1950*, File 402, ECE, IISH (International Institute of Social History), Amsterdam; Curiel, *Min ajil salam 'adil fi al-sharq al-awsat* (Cairo: Dar al-Thaqafa al-Jadida, 1999), pp. 6–7; Letter 284(170/9/46) from British Embassy, Cairo, 25 February 1946, FO371/53250, J1031/24/16; biographical details of "Henri Curiel" in FO141/1020, file 127; Muhammad Yusuf al-Jindi, "21 Fibrayir: dawr bariz lil-shuyu'iyyin al-misriyyin fi al-haraka al-wataniyya al-misriyya," *Qadaya Fikriyya*, July 1992, pp. 236–241.

29 Ra'uf 'Abbas, *Awraq henri curiel wa-al-haraka al-shuyu'iyya al-misriyya* (Cairo: Sina lil-Nashr, 1988), p. 41.

30 See Rif'at al-Sa'id, *Ta'rikh al-munazzamat al-yasariyya al-misriyya, 1940–1950* (Cairo: Dar al-Thaqafa al-Jadida, 1976), pp. 264, 305–307, 323. Sa'id remarked that the position of *al-Fajr al-Jadid* toward Sudan was signaled by the term *unity*, as opposed to the *Hametu* position, which championed the right of the Sudanese to self-determination. Notably, Sa'id's claim was not reflected in the publications by members of *al-Fajr al-Jadid*, who expressed a position similar to *Hametu*'s. The People's Liberation organization established by Marcel Israel did not specifically address the Sudan issue either, effectively adopting Curiel's position when it merged with *Hametu* and *Iskra* in 1947.

31 'Abd al-Majid Abu Hasabu, "al-Kifah al-mushtarak," *Umdurman*, 1 January 1946.
32 Balal, "al-Sha'b al-sudani," *Umdurman*, 15 March 1946.
33 "al-Shayu' bial-shayi' yudhkar," *Umdurman*, 16 February 1946.
34 Ibid.
35 "al-Mudhakara al-misriyya aqwa' min al-mawt," *Umdurman*, 16 February 1946.
36 'Amir Hamadi al-Sudani, "Kifah mushtarak didda 'adu mushtarak," *al-Fajr al-Jadid*, 7 May 1946.
37 Muhammad Amin Husayn, "Kalimat umdurman," *Umdurman*, 31 March 1945.
38 Muhammad Amin Husayn, "Kalimat umdurman," *Umdurman*, 21 June 1945; Husayn, "Hawla qarar al-mu'tamar," *Umdurman*, 5 July 1945.
39 Husayn, "Kalimat," 21 June 1945; Husayn, "Hawla qarar."
40 Muhammad Amin Husayn, "Hawla qarar al-mu'tamar," *Umdurman*, 21 July 1945.
41 Ibid.; "Walimadha ayadna al-mu'tamar," *Umdurman*, 21 July 1945.
42 "al-Mudhakara al-misriyya aqwa' min al-mawt."
43 Ibid.
44 "Bayan min al-ikhwan al-muslimin ila sha'b wadi al-nil," *al-Ikhwan al-Muslimun*, 9 February 1946, p. 5. See also Rami Ginat, "Zramim dissidentim mitsriyyim miyamin umismol veshe'elat ahdut 'emeq hanilus," *Hamizrah Hehadash*, 51 (2012), pp. 36–37.
45 "Bayan min al-ikhwan al-muslimina ila sha'b wadi al-nil," *al-Ikhwan al-Muslimun*, 12 March 1946, p. 3.
46 "Bayan min al-ikhwan al-muslimina ila sha'b wadi al-nil," *al-Ikhwan al-Muslimun*, 9 February 1946, p. 4.
47 "Madha yaqulu al-jil al-jadid?!" *al-Ikhwan al-Muslimun*, 5 January 1946, p. 19.
48 Ibid.
49 Hasan al-Banna, "al-Ikhwan al-muslimun wa-al-mufawadat," *al-Ikhwan al-Muslimun*, 23 April 1946.
50 Ibid.
51 Salih 'Ashmawi, "Laysa ba'da fashl al-mufawadat illa al-jihad," *al-Ikhwan al-Muslimun*, 3 August 1946, p. 3. On the events of 21 February, see a communist version in Marsil Shirazi, *Awraq munadil 'itali fi misr* (Cairo: Dar al-'Alam al-Thalith, 2002), pp. 113–114.
52 Khiyyal, "Qadiyyatuna wa-majlis al-amn."
53 Ahmad Sa'id (pseudonym of Ahmad Sadiq Sa'd), "Mu'ahadat 1936 limadha nunadi bi-ilgha'iha," *al-Fajr al-Jadid*, 27 March 1946, p. 10.
54 Mahmud al-Nabawiy, "Kalimat *al-jamahir*," *al-Jamahir*, 12 May 1947.
55 Mahmud al-Nabawiy, "al-Qadiyya al-wataniyya," *al-Jamahir*, 26 May 1947.
56 Mahmud Hammadi, "al-'Ahd al-hadir huwa nuqtat al-du'f al-ra'isiyya fi al-qadiyya al-misriyya," *al-Jamahir*, 26 May 1947.
57 "al-Mu'tamar, 1947," File 90, Collection of Tali'at al-'Ummal (*al-Fajr al-Jadid*), International Institute of Social History, Amsterdam.

58 'Abd al-Hafiz al-Sayfi, "Ajal: al-sudan lil-sudaniyyin," *al-Ikhwan al-Muslimun*, 20 September 1945, p. 15.
59 Ibid.
60 Ibid.
61 "Kifah mushtarak didda 'adu mushtarak," *al-Fajr al-Jadid*, 1 May 1946. For further details regarding disagreements among members of the united Sudanese mission on the issue of unification, see Warburg, *Islam, Nationalism and Communism*, pp. 69–72.
62 "Kifah mushtarak"; Balal, "al-Sha'b al-sudani"; Balal, "Hawla al-qadiyya al-sudaniyya," *Umdurman*, 1 July 1946.
63 "Kifah mushtarak."
64 Ibid.
65 Husayn Thabit, "Tijarat al-sudan al-kharijiyya," *al-Ikhwan al-Muslimun*, 2 April 1946, pp. 8–9.
66 "Ila al-wafd al-sudani – min al-ikhwan al-muslimina," *al-Ahram*, 8 April 1946. See also Hasan al-Banna, "al-Ikhwan al-muslimun wa-al-mufawadat," *al-Ikhwan al-Muslimun*, 23 April 1946, p. 3.
67 Hasan al-Banna, "Ila al-wafd al-sudani – min al-ikhwan al-muslimina," *al-Ahram*, 8 April 1946.
68 Ibid.
69 Thabit, "Tijarat al-sudan al-kharijiyya." The reader's attention is directed to two issues: First, the study relies solely on Sudanese statistics carried out by the Sudanese, effectively British, government. Second, there are likely to be contradictions between the Sudanese and Egyptian statistics.
70 Gabriel Warburg, "The Muslim Brotherhood in Sudan: From Reforms to Radicalism," Project for the Research of Islamist Movements (PRISM), Global Research in International Affairs(Gloria) Center, August 2006, pp. 1–2, at www.scribd.com/document/27714409/The-Muslim-Brotherhood-in-Sudan-From-Reforms-to-Radicalism-Prof-Gabriel-R-Warburg (accessed 16 October 2016). See also Daphna Ephrat, Copti Atallah, and Meir Hatina, *Introduction to the History of Islam*, Vol. IV (Raanana: Open University of Israel, 2008), pp. 226–227 [Hebrew].
71 For the content of Nuqrashi's speeches, see Note No. 95, FO407/226, J7828/24/16; "Khutbat al-nuqrashi pasha," *al-Ahram*, 12 August 1947, pp. 1–3. See also, Ginat "Zramim dissidentim mitsriyyim," pp. 44–45
72 See on this subject Chapter 3.
73 "Misr fi majlis al-amn," *Kifah al-Sha'b*, Vol. 12, 25 September 1947.
74 Ginat, "Zramim dissidentim mitsriyyim," p. 46.
75 Ibid.
76 An inside document of *Tali'at al-'Ummal*, 11 January 1948, File 22, T\U, IISH.
77 M. A., "Inna al-sha'b la yuridukum," *al-Jamahir*, 5 May 1947.
78 "al-Nuqrashi yatlubu min majlis al-amn isti'naf al-mufawadat," *al-Jamahir*, 14 July 1947.
79 "Nuridu tahrir al-sudan wa-yuridun taghyir al-nizam al-hadir," *al-Jamahir*, 21 July 1947.
80 "al-Nuqrashi yatlubu."

81 "Thughra khatira ... wa-lakuna hunaka makasibu lil-sha'b," *al-Jamahir*, 21 July 1947.
82 Ibid.
83 "Bayan wa-nada'a min al-haraka al-dimuqratiyya liltaharrur al-watani," *al-Jamahir*, 21 July 1947.
84 "Ila majlis al-amn," *al-Jamahir*, 4 August 1947.
85 Sh., "al-Qadiyya al-sudaniyya adiq naqatahu fi mutalibina amam majlis al-amn," *al-Jamahir*, 11 August 1947.
86 "Jabahatna: nadalha – siyasatiha – maqifiha min al-antahaziyya," 6 November 1947, in File 8, Collection of *Tali'at al-'Ummal* (*al-Fajr al-Jadid*), International Institute of Social History, Amsterdam.
87 Young Egypt changed its name after World War II to the Socialist Party.
88 An inside document of *Tali'at al-'Ummal*, August 1951, File 53, T\U, IIHS.
89 Da'ud 'Aziz, "al-Barnamaj al-thawri – ta'liq 'ala al-barnamaj al-thawri lil-hizb al-shuyu'iy al-misri (al-raya)," *Qadaya Fikriyya*, July 1996.
90 Fu'ad Mursi, *Tatawwur al-ra'smaliyya wa-kifah al-tabaqat fi-misr* (Cairo: al-Maktaba al-Ishtirakiyya, 1992), pp. 45–48, 85–86. The book was first published in 1949 in Alexandria.
91 See a draft program of the Egyptian Communist Party, undated, File 27, ECE, IISH.
92 Ginat, *A History of Egyptian Communism*, pp. 322–323. The full text of the draft of the program of the Egyptian Communist Party is attached to Dispatch 583 (66/129/49), 12 November 1949, FO371/73476, J9217/10118/16G.
93 Ginat, *A History of Egyptian Communism*, p. 323. The full text of the second draft of the program of the Egyptian Communist Party is attached to Letter 1014/3/50, 9 January 1950, FO371/80354, JE1041/1G. See also Mursi, *Tatawwur*, p. 113.
94 Ginat, ibid.
95 "Barnamaj al-lajna al-wataniyya bi-hayy al-azhar," January 1952, File 50, T\U.
96 Shakir, "'Ibar liman ya'tabiru," p. 915.
97 Ibid., pp. 915–916.
98 Ibid.
99 Shakir, "Mu'tamar al-mustad'afina."
100 Radwan is quoted in "Ma yajib an yaf'alahu ra'is al-hukuma," *al-Ikhwan al-Muslimun*, 27 September 1947, p. 5.
101 Muhammad Fathi 'Uthman, "Hadhihi 'aqibat al-futur," *al-Ikhwan al-Muslimun*, 30 October 1948, p. 7.
102 Ginat, *Syria and the Doctrine of Neutralism*, pp. 13–16.
103 Sayyid Qutb, "Nar wa-dam," *al-Risala*, No. 968, 21 January 1952, p. 69.
104 Ibid., pp. 70–71.
105 Sayyid Qutb, "Bidayat al-nihaya," *al-Risala*, No. 970, 4 February 1952, p. 125.
106 Ibid., pp. 125–126.
107 Abu al-Futuh 'Atifah, "Thawrat al-sharq," *al-Risala*, No. 971, 11 February 1952, p. 162.
108 Ibid., pp. 162–163.

109 J. P. Nettl, "Ideas, Intellectuals and Structures of Dissent," in P. Rieff (ed.), *On Intellectuals: Theoretical Studies, Case Studies* (New York: Doubleday, 1969), pp. 53–122.

110 Edward W. Said, *Representations of the Intellectual: The 1993 Reith Lectures* (New York: Vintage Books, A Division of Random House, 1996), p. 97, at www.mohamedrabeea.com/books/book1_10178.pdf (accessed 18 October 2016).

Conclusion

As we have seen, the national consensus in Egypt regarding the unity of the Nile valley crossed party and ideological lines. The Egyptian political elite was determined not to let the process of de-colonialization following World War II pass by the valley, and official Egypt made extensive international diplomatic efforts to persuade the international community of the validity of its claims regarding an inextricable historical connection between the populations inhabiting the valley.

As part of the struggle for international public opinion the Egyptian political establishment recruited intellectuals, theoreticians, academics, and journalists who worked indefatigably and out of deep conviction to help achieve this primary national objective. Given that they chose to act in the service of the political elite, they may well have fit in with what Bourdieu described as the "dominated fraction of the dominant class," that is, as intellectuals they were socially perceived as both privileged and subordinate.[1] Their mission was clear: to formulate and disseminate the doctrine of the unity of the Nile valley.

The material produced by these varied sources, which was sent, inter alia, to many member states of the United Nations to garner support, asserted that the Egyptian demand for unification was based on shared historical foundations: physical-geographical, economic, cultural, and ethnographic.

The Egyptian press – whether independent such as *al-Ahram* or politically oriented – served the national cause. As we have seen, from the early 1940s the communist movement was the only social/political movement to swim against the nationalist current. The communists wanted to see the Sudanese people exercising independently their right to self-determination. The communists foresaw the postcolonial new order and the decline of the traditional empires, particularly Britain.

For better comprehension of the role played by right- and left-wing opposition groups some aspects of social movements theory may be useful. Social movement as defined by Zald and McCarthy is "a set of opinions and beliefs in a population, which represents preferences for changing some elements of the social structure and/or reward distribution of a society."[2] The Egyptian right- and left-wing opposition movements were social/political movements that may be portrayed as "decisive agents of historical transformation," to employ Boggs's phrase.[3] In his view, "It is by studying social movements that one becomes able to construct a new image of society."[4] Indeed, the communists and the Muslim Brothers as well as other opposition groups radicalized the political and social spheres to advance their radical platforms – each wanted to reshape and reconstruct society like clay in the hands of the potter. Radicalization as defined by Wilner and Dubouloz is "a personal process in which individuals adopt extreme political, social, and/or religious ideals and aspirations, and where the attainment of particular goals justifies the use of indiscriminate violence."[5] Although physical violence did not play a role in these movements' struggle to advance their platforms on the issue of the unity of the Nile valley, they did employ verbal violence in their publications, directed particularly against British imperialism. After the Egyptian unilateral abrogation of the 1936 treaty in October 1951, they shifted temporarily to physical violence in the form of an armed struggle against British targets in the Suez Canal zone (November 1951–January 1952).

In the monarchial era (1922–1952), Egyptians of all political stripes unquestioningly accepted the doctrine of the unity of the Nile valley as an axiom. Successive Egyptian governments incorporated that doctrine as a central item of their political platforms. The only prime minister in the pre-revolution period who was more realistic and was willing to make some compromise over the Sudan issue was Isma'il Sidqi (February 1946–December 1946). The draft agreement (October 1946) that he reached with Ernest Bevin, according to which Britain agreed to recognize symbolic Egyptian sovereignty over Sudan, was the best Egypt could get from the British. However, the wide harsh and demagogic criticism voiced by his political opponents and the Wafd-led opposition contributed to Sidqi's downfall and to the political burial of the agreement.

The British hardened their position on Sudan following Nuqrashi's appeal to the UN Security Council (July 1947–August 1947). They now argued that Britain was in favor of eventual self-government for the Sudanese, and only the Sudanese should decide on their future, whether they wanted independence, some form of association with Egypt, or even complete union with Egypt. Therefore, the British rejected Nuqrashi's complaint about a British policy of "inciting the Sudanese to secede from Egypt."

Although Nuqrashi (1946–1948) and his successors agreed to prepare Sudan, jointly with Britain, for self-government and self-determination, they insisted that such a development would be within the framework of the unity between Egypt and Sudan under the common crown. Nuqrashi's failure to harness the international community in Egypt's favor and to force the British to evacuate the Nile valley brought the Sudan question to a standstill. His successors refused to come to terms with Britain on any future agreements in which Sudan would be separated from Egypt. Britain, for its part, took all possible measures to split the two countries – it had its own reasons for and interests in such an outcome.

British policy toward and interests in Egypt and Sudan were derived from Britain's broader economic, political, and strategic interests in the Middle East and colonial Africa. Before the disintegration of the British Empire, Egypt (the Suez Canal) and Sudan were an essential link in a long chain of territories that the British controlled directly or indirectly to protect their interests in India, the "jewel in the crown." In the post–World War II period the emphasis changed, however. With the outbreak of the Cold War, the desire to contain future Soviet expansionist plans into the Middle East and Africa reinforced the strategic vitality of the Nile valley. In the case of Egypt, the British could temporarily rely on their 1936 treaty, which allowed Britain to deploy military forces along the Suez Canal for twenty years. Egypt was an independent country, whereas Sudan was practically speaking ruled by the British. The geographic location of Sudan could be a strategic advantage given that the Nile, Egypt's main artery, passed through the country. British control of Sudan meant control of the Egyptian nerve center. The British assumption was that in future Anglo–Egyptian disputes, Egyptian governments would have to consider their positions cautiously vis-à-vis Britain. The British were wrong. The Nahhas government (1950–1952) adopted a neutralist policy in the inter-bloc conflict and even abrogated the 1936 treaty in pursuit of an independent foreign policy.

Efficient control of the Nile valley, the British believed, required the establishment of a proxy Sudanese political administration, and for that reason it was essential to promote and develop Sudanese self-government, which "in itself will militate against Egyptian re-entry into the Sudan," as the British put it.[6] Until the Sudanese would be able to rule themselves, it was essential to keep the condominium arrangements intact. Therefore Britain made sure that it remained the dominant party and that the Egyptians stayed away from power centers, by diminishing their influence, culturally, economically, politically, and socially.

In brief, the goal was to drive a wedge between Egyptians and Sudanese by championing Sudanese self-government and enhancing their separate national identity, so that in the long term, they would favor Britain over Egypt as their senior partner. The British developed and enhanced Sudanese collective identity and encouraged anti-Egyptian separatist trends. One of the means to achieve that goal was the development of separatist Sudanese nationalism. Therefore the British had to concentrate on the development and nurturing of the Sudanese educational system, which would serve as a hotbed for the emergence of a new generation of political and social elites with a clear vision toward the building of a nation-state independent from foreign control. Sudanization of as many posts as possible in all administrative fields and in the military became Britain's official doctrine in the post–World War II period. As future events were to demonstrate, British endeavors were successful – Sudanese nationalism did emerge.

How did the Egyptian elite perceive Sudanese and Sudan? Although they spoke of them as "equal brothers" who shared a common land, it was noticeable throughout that they held a patronizing approach in their dealing with Sudan and Sudanese. They believed that Sudanese would prefer to tie their future to Egypt as a more advanced and sophisticated country. Egypt could fulfill their needs and requirements and protect them from future adversaries. Egypt was the savior of Sudan: it saved the Sudanese from the fate "of almost all other African peoples, who have been suffering from European exploitation ever since the partition of the Dark Continent," as 'Ammar put it.[7] For Egyptians of all political currents (except for communists), it was taken for granted that the Sudanese desired unification and were not seeking any alternatives. Moreover, they posited point-blank that it was in the "interests of the Sudan in general, and the people of its southern regions in particular that this part of the Upper Nile should be converted to Islam."[8]

British political streams of all stripes disputed Egyptian allegations that Sudan was an integral part of Egypt. The new labor government that took power in 1945 continued its conservative predecessor's policy toward Sudan and even hardened its objection to Egypt's demand for the unity of the Nile valley. The Fabian society, which was associated with the Labor Party, published a pamphlet on Sudan, ruling categorically that the Sudanese were not Egyptians. Except for the north of Sudan during the era of the Pharaohs, Sudan was never controlled by Egypt. The first Egyptian leader to occupy the entire Sudan was Muhammad 'Ali. The Egyptians regarded the Sudanese "as barbarians," and throughout the period of Egyptian suzerainty,

they plundered the country rather than governed it . . . the Sudan has never been a united country. It has been rather a part of Africa where for hundreds of years encroaching Arabs gradually pushed out the original inhabitants, a land of vague African kingdoms where inter-tribal war was constant and where no strong unifying government ever existed. Its frontiers were not the present frontiers but rather the frontiers between Arab and black, a frontier which a man or woman crossed to the North only as slave.[9]

Egyptian scholars ridiculed such allegations, particularly that the Egyptians encroached Sudanese territories and drove out the indigenous populations. They opined that if that were true, then "one would have expected rigid racial barriers, with distinct ethnic regions – a feature totally absent from the Sudan."[10]

Egyptians argued that Sudan was an integral part of Egypt from ancient time. Was it correct historically? As we have seen, such assertions were disputable, and there were deep and extended historical hiatuses in Egypt's presence in Sudanese lands. There was a consensus, however, between the British and the Egyptians that Sudan was annexed by Egypt in the early nineteenth century following its occupation by Muhammad 'Ali – an occupation that was purely based on imperialist calculations and motivations. Tellingly, Egypt did not promote the development of Sudan and in fact exploited the country economically for decades until the Mahdi uprising in the 1880s. Sudan experienced more significant development under the condominium administration.

However, both imperialist masters – Britain and Egypt – failed to equally develop and nurture the south of Sudan, which continued to be neglected in all fields, particularly education. In fact, there were no rational or substantial reasons, other than imperialist ones, to link between the more developed north and the underdeveloped south. The inhabitants of the Nile valley were not all of the "same race, language and religion" as Egyptians often argued. Although Arabs constituted the largest ethnic group in northern Sudan, and Islam was the dominant religion there, Sudan in its entirety comprised many ethnic/linguistic groups of a variety of origins, which were divergent culturally and religiously. True, for hundreds of years, parts of Sudan were directly and indirectly ruled by Egyptian dynasties in pre-Islamic and Islamic eras, yet it would be utterly incorrect to speak of the inhabitants of the Nile valley as one people, as Egyptian politicians, intellectuals, scholars, journalists, and other advocates of the unity of the Nile valley argued vehemently.[11]

The doctrine of the unity of the Nile valley was invented and constructed in monarchial Egypt – from the inarticulate and inconsistent conceptions of the interwar period to the detailed and systematic formulations of the post–World War II years. It was an "imaginary" community rather than an "imagined" one, to employ Benedict Anderson's concept. An "imagined community" functions because people living in the same administrative unit, usually a state, share similar life experiences, i.e., their daily lives are shaped by a similar economic, political, and social reality. Anderson's concept is based on the assumption that the majority of the people living within a territory share that collective identity.[12] Conversely, the reality shaping daily-life experience in Egypt and Sudan was rather diverse, and most people living in Sudan did not share the Egyptian vision of a unified Nile valley under the Egyptian crown.

It would not have been impossible for Egyptian protagonists of the unity of the Nile valley to create a mirage of one Egyptian–Sudanese people who shared a common language, history, and land from ancient time. A united Egypt–Sudan could have become a state that was no different than many other existing political entities worldwide that were built on diversity. There were many cases in history in which countries with a multiplicity of languages, traditions, cultures, and ethnic origins managed to pursue a policy of integration that united them under the umbrella of one nation (France, Germany, and the United States, to name just a few). The doctrine of the unity of the Nile valley failed because it was colonialist in its nature and as such was rejected by the British – the stronger imperialist power that dominated Sudan – and the newly born Sudanese nationalist movement that emerged in the postcolonial epoch. The Egyptian architects of the unity of the Nile valley never offered the Sudanese a Sudanese–Egyptian entity based on full partnership, equality, and "unity in diversity," to employ the Volls' phrase.[13]

In fact, pre-2011 Sudan had experienced constant waves of various imperialisms. It started with Muhammad 'Ali's occupation of the early nineteenth century and continued with the dual Anglo–Egyptian imperialist rule from 1899 until 1953. Independent Sudan was divided into two entities, north and south, while the latter was subordinated to the north, which employed imperialist methods in its handling of the south. However, years of civil war and constant struggle for self-determination led eventually to the partition of Sudan and the formation of the new state of South Sudan.

Why did revolutionary Egypt decide to abandon the doctrine of the unity of the Nile valley? As we have seen, Egypt's decision to refrain from further insisting on the unity of the Nile valley was made soon after the downfall of the monarchy. However, several weeks before the overthrow of King Faruq there appeared to be fissures in the Egyptian consensus regarding the unity of the Nile valley. The change occurred following the objection of Sudanese parties to Egypt's unilateral abrogation of the 1936 treaty and their refusal to recognize Britain's authority under the circumstances. The abolition of the condominium by Egypt, they argued, created a power vacuum in Sudan. The short-lived Egyptian government, led by Najib al-Hilali, was the first that nearly came to an agreement with Sudanese nationalists on the future of their country.

The military regime that took the reins of power following the 23 July Revolution was determined to reach an agreement with those Sudanese nationalists. The pragmatic and realistic approach that the Free Officers exercised during their talks with their Sudanese counterparts led to the abandonment of the doctrine of the unity of the Nile valley.

The doctrine of the unity of the Nile valley was historically associated with the Muhammad 'Ali dynasty and moreover with the hated, deposed King Faruq. As they explicitly declared, the Free Officers wanted to eradicate all symbols and traces of the monarchy – one of which was the unity of the Nile valley under the Egyptian crown. They realized that to gain international support for their demand for the withdrawal of British troops from Egypt, substantial concessions in Sudan were required. Whereas they displayed a rigid and uncompromising line throughout the Anglo–Egyptian talks on the liberation of Egypt – insisting on a full and speedy withdrawal of British troops from Egypt with no conditions attached – they showed a willingness to relinquish their demands over Sudan, a moderate and realpolitik stand that soon paved the way to an Anglo–Egyptian agreement over Sudan in February 1953. This was preceded by an agreement concluded on 19 October 1952 between the Egyptian government, led by General Muhammad Najib, and representatives of the *Umma* Party and the other Sudanese parties that favored independence. It was then that Egypt recognized for the first time the Sudanese right to self-determination and self-government – the condominium rule was to be abolished.

The revolutionary regime and Nasser as the strongest figure behind the scenes believed that the Sudan issue should be approached differently – not from a patronizing position but rather from one based on equality and mutual respect. They thus came to terms with the Sudanese because they appreciated that the overthrow of King Faruq (who was against an agreement with the Sudanese) and their willingness to grant the Sudanese people the right to self-determination would in turn improve the chances that the Sudanese would eventually favor unity with Egypt. Their assessment was soon to be proven wrong. Isma'il al-Azhari, the newly elected Sudanese leader (1954–1956) and the former champion of the unity of the Nile valley, responded pragmatically to the changing reality and opted for independent Sudan. The British, who had been active in sabotaging the Egyptian plan to annex Sudan under its crown, did indeed succeed. However, their gain was short-lived. Years of British imperialist manipulations and maneuvers in the Nile valley also came to an end with the declaration of Sudan's independence in 1956.

The game was over for both of the competing imperialist powers, the regional one and the global one. In the case of Britain, this was an integral part of the process of the disintegration of a worldwide empire.

In the Egyptian case, this was the shattering of a dream that had been kept in the hearts of Egyptians for decades. For those who had continued to dream of the unity of the Nile valley, the Sadat–Numayri convergence,[14] which led the two leaders to announce the Integration Charter in 1974 that was officially signed only in 1981, was a dream come true. The two countries were supposed to cooperate closely in a wide range of areas, which would eventually lead to full unity. However, this unity dream was shattered too following the downfall of Numayri's regime in 1985.[15]

Notes

1 Pierre Bourdieu, "The Intellectual Field: A World Apart," in Bourdieu, *In Other Words: Essays towards a Reflexive Sociology*, tr. Mathew Adamson (Stanford: Stanford University Press, 1990), p. 145. On intellectuals active within the framework of the regime, see also Eisenstadt, "Intellectuals and Tradition"; Shils, "Intellectuals."
2 M. Zald and J. McCarthy, *Social Movements in an Organizational Society* (New Brunswick, NJ: Transaction Books, 1987), p. 2.
3 Boggs, *Social Movements and Political Power*, p. 4.
4 Ibid., p. 14.
5 Alex Wilner and C J Dubouloz, "Homegrown Terrorism and Transformative Learning: An Interdisciplinary Approach to Understanding Radicalization," *Global Change Peace and Security*, 22:1 (2010), p. 38.
6 See minutes of Foreign Office officials, 8 January 1945, 18 January 1945, 21 January 1945, and 22 January 1945, in FO141/939, 31/76/44.
7 'Ammar, "The Transformation of Egypt and the Sudan," p. 60.
8 *The Unity of the Nile Valley*, p. 71.
9 Report to the Fabian Colonial Bureau, *The Sudan: The Road Ahead* (London: Fabian Publications, 1945), p. 9.
10 "The Physical, Ethnographic, Cultural and Economic Bases of the Unity," in *The Unity of the Nile Valley*, p. 17.
11 Husayn Sabry, an Egyptian military officer who served in Sudan from 1949 until the February 1953 agreement, challenged the paradigm of the unity of the Nile valley, saying that "historical Egypt had always stood off, separate and self-contained: a rigorously circumscribed society." See Sabry, *Sovereignty for Sudan*, p. 2. See also Chapter 5, Footnote 82.
12 Anderson, *Imagined Communities*.
13 Voll and Voll, *The Sudan: Unity and Diversity*, p. 1.
14 Anwar al-Sadat was the Egyptian president (1970–1981), and Ja'far Muhammad Numayri was the Sudanese president (1969–1985).
15 Warburg, "The Condominium Revisited: The Anglo-Egyptian Sudan 1934–1956: A Review Article," p. 1.

Bibliography

ARCHIVES AND PRIVATE COLLECTIONS

EGYPT

Al-Dawriyyat: majmu'at al-suhuf wa-al-majallat al-yawmiyya wa-al-ajnabiyya.
Dar al-Kutub al-Misriyya (Cairo: The Egyptian National Library).

GREAT BRITAIN

The National Archives (Public Record Office), London.
FO141 – Embassy and Consular Archives, Egypt: Correspondence. Foreign
  Office.
FO371 – Political Correspondence of the Foreign Office. Foreign Office.
FO800 – Foreign Office, Private Offices: Various Ministers' and Officials'
  Papers. Foreign Office.
FO407 – Confidential Print, Egypt and the Sudan. Foreign Office.
FO953 – Information Policy Department and Regional Information
  Departments: Registered Files. Foreign Office.
FO924 – Cultural Relations Department: Correspondence and Papers.
  Foreign Office.
Sudan Archive (SA), Archives and Special Collections, University of Durham
Files of: C. W. M Cox (1937–1970), J. S. R. Duncan (1942–1956),
  K. D. D. Henderson (1926–1953), D. M. H. Evans (1930–1935),
  W. G. Piper (1927–1953), J. W. Robertson (1922–1953); S. R. Simpson
  files (1926–1953), F. R. Wingate files (1861–1953).
Middle East Centre Archive, St. Antony's College, Oxford
Private Collections Egypt and Sudan: Farouk, King of Egypt (1920–1965);
  Keown-Boyd, Sir Alexander William (1884–1954); Lampson, Sir Miles
  Wedderburn, 1st Baron Killearn (1880–1964); Wingate, Sir Ronald Evelyn
  Leslie, 2nd Baronet (1889–1978).
Sudan Conferences, GB165-0356, Boxes 1–6.

INDIA

National Archives of India (NAI), Janpath, New Delhi, Ministry of External Affairs,
  1946–1955.

THE NETHERLANDS

Collection of Tali'at al-'Ummal (*Al-Fajr al-Jadid*). International Institute of
Social History, Amsterdam.
Egyptian Communists in Exile (Rome Group) Archives. International Institute
of Social History, Amsterdam.

RUSSIAN FEDERATION (FORMER SOVIET UNION)

Fond (Collection) 495, Ispolkom Kominterna (Comintern's Executive), Opis'
(Inventory) 85. Rossiiskii gosudarstvennyi arkhiv sotsial'no-politichskoi
istorii [Russian Governmental Archive of Social-Political History, RGASPI],
Moscow.

UNITED STATES

General Records of the Department of State, Record Group 59, The National
Archives and Record Administration, College Park, MD.

EGYPTIAN OFFICIAL PUBLICATIONS

Documents on the Sudan, 1899–1953 (Cairo: Egyptian Society of International
Law, 1953).
Egyptian Kingdom, Presidency of Council of Ministers, *Egypt Sudan* (Cairo:
Government Press, 1947).
  *The Unity of the Nile Valley, Its Geographical Bases and Its Manifestations in
  History* (Cairo: Government Press, 1947).
Egyptian Government, Committee of Experts, *Status of the Sudan* (Cairo:
Government Press, 1947).
Ghurbal, M. Shafiq, 'Ammar M. 'Abbas, Ahmad Badawi, Zaki 'Abd al-Rahman,
and Ibrahim Nashi, *Wahdat Wadi al-Nil: Ususuha al- Jughrafiyya
wa-mazahiruha fi al-ta'rikh* (Cairo: al-Matba'a al-Amiriyya, 1947).
Hay'at al-Mustasharin, *Qadiyyat al-sudan* (Cairo: al-Matba'a al-Amiriyya, 1947).
Ri'asat Majlis al-Wuzara', *Qadiyyat al-Sudan* (Cairo: al-Matba'a al-Amiriyya,
1947).
Nuqrashi, Mahmud Fahami al-, *Qadiyyat wadi al-nil* (Cairo: al-Matba'a
al-Amiriyya, 1947).
Presidence du Conseil des Ministres, Comite des Experts, *La Cause du Soudan*
(Cairo: Imprimerie Nationale, 1947).
Presidence du Conseil des Ministres, *Note sur les pouvoirs du gouvernement
Egyptien en matière législative au Soudan* (Cairo: Imprimerie Nationale,
1947).
Sanhuri, Ahmad 'Abd al-Razzaq, *Qadiyyat wadi al-nil, Misr wa-al-Sudan*
(Cairo: al-Matba'a al-Amiriyya, 1949).
Wizarat al-Kharijiyya, *Mu'ahadat tahaluf bayna Misr wa-Baritaniyya al-'uzma'*
(Cairo: al-Matba'a al-Amiriyya, 1936).

NEWSPAPERS AND PERIODICALS

al-Ahram, al-'Alam al-'Arabi, al-Asas, al-Balagh, al-Balagh al-Usbu'i, al-Bashir, al-Damir, Egyptian Gazette, al-Fajr al-Jadid, al-Hilal, al-Jamahir, al-Ikhwan al-Muslimun, al-Jihad, al-Jumhur al-misri, al-Katib al-Misri, Kifah al-Sha'b, Kifah al-Umma, al-Majalla al-Jadida, Misr al-Fatat, al-Misri, al-Muqattam, al-Musawwar, al-Nadhir, Qadaya Fikriyya, al-Risala, Ruz al-Yusuf, Sawt al-Umma, al-Siyasa, al-Siyasa al-Usbu'iyya, al-Sudani, Umdurman, Wadi al-Nil, Al-Wafd al-Misri.

PRIMARY AND SECONDARY PUBLISHED SOURCES

[anonymous] An Egyptian publicist, "Egypt's Claim to the Sudan," *Current History*, 21:5 (1925), pp. 721–727.

[anonymous] Anwar, "Likay la nansa," *al-Ikhwan al-Muslimun*, 14 December 1946, p. 8.

[anonymous] M. A., "Inna al-sha'b la yuridukum," *al-Jamahir*, 5 May 1947.

[anonymous] Sh., "al-Qadiyya al-sudaniyya adiq naqatahu fi mutalibina amam majlis al-amn," *al-Jamahir*, 11 August 1947.

Abbas, Mekki, *The Sudan Question: The Dispute over the Anglo-Egyptian Condominium 1884–1951* (London: Faber and Faber, 1952).

'Abbas, Ra'uf, *Awraq henri curiel wa-al-haraka al-shuyu'iyya al-misriyya* (Cairo: Sina lil-Nashr, 1988).

'Abd al-Hafiz, Salah, "Kalimat thalath . . . ," *al-Ikhwan al-Muslimun*, 5 January 1946, pp. 17–18.

'Abd al-Majid, 'Abd al-'Aziz, *al-Tarbiyya fi al-sudan min al-qarn al-sadis 'ashar ila nihayat al-qarn al-tasi' 'ashar* (Cairo: al-Matba'a al-Amiriya, 1949).

'Abd al-Qadir, Hasanain, *Ta'rikh al-sihafa fi al-sudan 1899–1919*, Vol. 1 (Cairo: Dar al-Nahda al-'Arabiyya, 1967).

'Abd al-Qadir, Muhammad Zaki, "al-Rawabit al-thaqafiyya bayna misr wa-al-sudan," *al-Ahram*, 21 January 1946, pp. 3–4.

'Abd al-Quddus, Ihsan, "'Ala al-sudan an yadfa'u thaman taqrir masirihi," *Ruz al-Yusuf*, No. 1294, 30 March 1953.

"Lahum al-sudan wa-lana al-kalam," *Ruz al-Yusuf*, No. 929, 4 April 1946.

"Madha nastati'?!," *Ruz al-Yusuf*, No. 1045, 21 June 1948.

"Nisf jala' wa-nisf wahda!!," *Ruz al-Yusuf*, No. 1191, 10 April 1951.

'Abdallah, Sayyid 'Abdallah al-Raziq Yusuf, *Mahmud Fahmi al-Nuqrashi – wa-dawrihi fi al-siyasa al-misriyya wa-hall jama'at al-ikhwan al-muslimin 1888–1948* (Cairo: al-Madbuli Library, 1995).

'Abdel Rahim, Muddathir, *Imperialism and Nationalism in the Sudan* (Khartoum: Khartoum University Press, 1986).

Abu al-Sa'ud, 'Abd al-Hafiz, "Isba' al-injliz fi al-nuba," *al-Risala*, No. 788, 9 August 1948, pp. 894–896.

Abu Hasabu, 'Abd al-Majid, "al-Kifah al-mushtarak," *Umdurman*, 1 January 1946.

Agwani, M. S., *Communism in the Arab East* (Bombay and London: Asia Publishing House, 1969).

Akyeampong, Emmanuel K., and Henry Louis Gates (eds.), *Dictionary of African Biography*, Vols. 4 and 5 (Oxford and New York: Oxford University Press, 2012).

'Ammar, 'Abbas, "The Physical, Ethnographical, Cultural and Economic Bases of the Unity," in *The Unity of the Nile Valley*, pp. 9–33.

"The Transformation of Egypt and the Sudan into a Muslim Arabic Speaking Country," in *The Unity of the Nile Valley*, pp. 58–60.

Anderson, Benedict, *Imagined Communities: Reflections on the Origin and Spread of Nationalism* (London and New York: Verso, 2006).

'Ashmawi, Salih, "Diktaturiyyat al-injliz fi al-sudan," *al-Ikhwan al-Muslimun*, 21 June 1947, p. 3.

"Laysa ba'da fashl al-mufawadat illa al-jihad," *al-Ikhwan al-Muslimun*, 3 August 1946, p. 3.

"Mawqif hasim fi ta'rikh al-da'wah," *al-Ikhwan al-Muslimun*, 25 August 1946, p. 3.

'Atifah, Abu al-Futuh, "Thawrat al-sharq," *al-Risala*, No. 971, 11 February 1952, pp. 162–163.

Azhari, Isma'il al-, *Difa' 'an wahdat wadi al-nil* (Beirut: Matabi' al-Kashshaf, n.d.).

'Aziz, Da'ud, "al-Barnamaj al-thawri – ta'liq 'ala al-barnamaj al-thawri lil-hizb al-shuyu'iy al-misri (al-raya)," *Qadaya Fikriyya*, July 1996, pp. 279–288.

'Azzam, Jamil 'Arif 'Abd al-Rahman, *Safahat min al-mudhakkirat al-sirriyya li-awwal amin 'amm lil-jami'a al-'arabiyya* (Cairo: al-Maktab al-Misri al-Hadith, 1977).

Baddour, Abd El Fattah Ibrahim El-Sayed, *Sudanese–Egyptian Relations: A Chronological and Analytical Study* (The Hague: Nijhoff, 1960).

Baker, Samuel, *Ismailia*, 2 vols. (London: Macmillan and Co., 1874).

Bakri, Tawfiq Ahmad al-, "Hadhihi al-ahdath al-jariyya fi janub wadi al-nil," *al-Ahram*, 17 November 1948.

"Ziyarat al-misriyyina lil-sudan," *al-Ahram*, 3 April 1950.

Balal, "al-Sha'b al-sudani," *Umdurman*, 15 March 1946.

"Hawla al-qadiyya al-sudaniyya," *Umdurman*, 1 July 1946.

Banna, Hasan al-, "al-Ikhwan al-muslimun wa-al-mufawadat," *al-Ikhwan al-Muslimun*, 23 April 1946, p. 3.

"Ila al-wafd al-sudani – min al-ikhwan al-muslimina," *al-Ahram*, 8 April 1946.

Barakat, Da'ud, *al-Sudan al-misri wa-matami' al-siyasa al-baritaniyya* (Cairo: al-Matba'a al-Salafiyya bi-Misr, 1924).

Barawy, Rashed El-, *Egypt, Britain and the Sudan* (Cairo: Renaissance Bookshop, 1952).

Barir, 'Ali al-, "al-Sudaniyyuna wa-al-barlaman al-misri," *al-Ahram*, 14 December 1949.

Bashear, Suliman, *Communism in the Arab East 1918–1928* (London: Ithaca Press, 1980).

Bashiri, Mahjub 'Umar, *Ma'alim al-haraka al-wataniyya fi al-sudan* (Beirut: Maktabat al-Thaqafa, 1996).

Beinin, Joel, and Zackary Lockman, *Workers on the Nile: Nationalism, Communism, Islam, and the Egyptian Working Class, 1882–1954* (Princeton, NJ: Princeton University Press, 1987).

Bell, Morag, Robin Butlin, and Michael Heffernan (eds.), *Geography and Imperialism, 1820–1840* (Manchester: Manchester University Press, 1995).

Berlin, Isaiah, *Against the Current: Essays in the History of Ideas* (London: Hogarth Press, 1979).

Beshir, Mohamed Omer, *Educational Development in the Sudan, 1898–1956* (London: Oxford University Press, 1969).

Beswick, Stephanie, *Sudan's Blood Memory: The Legacy of War, Ethnicity and Slavery in South Sudan* (Rochester, NY: University of Rochester Press, 2004).

Bishri, Tariq al-, *al-Haraka al-siyasiyya fi misr, 1945–1952* (Cairo: al-Hay'a al-'Amma lil-Kitab, 1972).

Boggs, Carl, *Social Movements and Political Power: Emerging Forms of Radicalism in the West* (Philadelphia: Temple University Press, 1986).

Botman, Selma, *The Rise of Egyptian Communism 1939–1970* (New York: Syracuse University Press, 1988).

Bourdieu, Pierre, "The Intellectual Field: A World Apart," in Bourdieu, *In Other Words: Essays towards a Reflexive Sociology*, tr. Mathew Adamson (Stanford: Stanford University Press, 1990), pp. 140–149.

Budd, Adrian, "Nation and Empire: Labour's Foreign Policy 1945–51," *International Socialism*, 62 (Spring 1994), at http://pubs.socialistreviewindex .org.uk/isj62/budd.htm (accessed 18 October 2016).

Churchill, Winston, *The River War: An Historical Account of the Reconquest of the Soudan* (London: Longmans, Green and Co., 1902).

Cliff, T., and D. Gluckstein, *The Labour Party: A Marxist History* (London: Bookmarks, 1988).

Cohen, Benjamin J., *The Question of Imperialism: The Political Economy of Dominance and Dependence* (New York: Basic Books, 1973).

Collins, Robert O., *A History of Modern Sudan* (Cambridge: Cambridge University Press, 2008).

"Historical Discord in the Nile Valley by Gabriel R. Warburg," *The International History Review*, 16:4 (November 1994), pp. 799–801.

Collins, Robert O., and Robert L. Tignor, *Egypt and the Sudan* (Englewood Cliffs, NJ: Prentice-Hall, 1967).

Cromer, The Earl of, *Modern Egypt* (New York: The Macmillan Company, 1909).

Curiel, Henri, *Min ajil salam 'adil fi al-sharq al-awsat* (Cairo: Dar al-Thaqafa al-Jadida, 1999).

Daly, M. W., and Jane R. Hogan, *Images of Empire: Photographic Sources for the British in the Sudan* (Leiden: Brill, 2005).

Daly, M. W., *Imperial Sudan: The Anglo–Egyptian Condominium 1934–1956* (Cambridge and New York: Cambridge University Press, 1991).

Di-Capua, Yoav, *Gatekeepers of the Arab Past: Historian and History Writing in Twentieth-Century Egypt* (Berkeley: University of California Press, 2009).

Dirar, Dirar Salih, *Hijrat al-qaba'il al-'arabiyya ila wadi al-nil misr wa-al-sudan* (Riyad: Maktabat al-Tawba, 1997).

Ta'rikh al-sudan al-hadith, (Beirut: Dar Maktabat al-Hayat, 1965).

Disuqi, 'Asim, "al-Mashru' al-watani wa-al-ijtima'i fi barnamaj al-hizb al-shuyu'iy al-misri fi al-'ishriniyyat wa-al-thalathiniyyat," *Qadaya Fikriyya*, July 1996, pp. 38–45.

Doran, Michael, *Pan-Arabism before Nasser* (New York and Oxford: Oxford University Press, 1999).

Eisenstadt, S. N., "Intellectuals and Tradition," in Eisenstadt and S. R. Graubard (eds.), *Intellectuals and Tradition* (New York: Humanities Press, 1973), pp. 1–19.

El Madani, Khalil Abdalla, "On the Epistemology of Ethnicity – A Critical Review of the Theories on Ethnic Formation," in Sayyid H. Hurreiz and Elfatih A. Abdel Salam (eds.), *Ethnicity, Conflict and National Integration in the Sudan* (Khartoum: University of Khartoum Printing Press, 1989), pp. 1–28.

Ephrat, Daphna, Copti Atallah, and Meir Hatina, *Introduction to the History of Islam*, Vol. IV (Raanana: Open University of Israel, 2008) [Hebrew].

Erlich, Haggai, *The Cross and the River: Ethiopia, Egypt and the Nile* (Boulder, CO: Lynne Rienner Publishers, 2002).

Egypt: The Older Sister (Tel Aviv: Open University Press, 2003) [Hebrew].

Students and University in 20th Century Egyptian Politics (London: Frank Cass, 1989).

Erlich, Haggai, and Israel Gershoni (eds.), *The Nile: Histories, Cultures, Myths* (Boulder, CO: Lynne Rienner, 2000).

Etheredge, Laura S. (ed.), *Middle East Region in Transition, Egypt* (New York: Britannica Educational Publishing, 2011).

Fabunmi, L. A., *The Sudan in Anglo–Egyptian Relations: A Case Study in Power Politics 1800–1956* (London: Longmans, 1960).

Fadl, Muhammad 'Abd al-Fattah Abu al-, *Judhur al-'alaqat al-misriyya al-sudaniyya ba 'da istiqlal al-sudan* (Cairo: al-Hay'a al-Misriyya al-'Amma lil-Kitab, 2005).

Fadlalla, Mohamed H., *Short History of Sudan* (Lincoln, NE: iUniverse, 2004).

Falola, Toyin, and Daniel Jean-Jackues (eds.), *Africa: An Encyclopedia of Culture and Society*, Vol. 3 (Santa Barbara, CA: ABC-CLIO, 2016).

Farman, Gha'ib Tu'mah, "Ya ikhwanina fi wadi al-nil!" *al-Risala*, No. 717, 31 March 1947, pp. 366–367.

Fawzy-Rossano, Didar, *Le Soudan en question* (Paris: LA Table Ronde, 2002).

Galatoli, Anthony M., *Egypt in Midpassage* (Cairo: Urwand and Sons Press, 1950).

Gershoni, Israel, "Geographers and Nationalism in Egypt: Huzayyin and the Unity of the Nile Valley, 1945–1948," in Erlich and Gershoni (eds.), *The Nile*, pp. 199–215.

Light in the Shade: Egypt and Fascism, 1922–1937 (Tel Aviv: Am Oved, 1999) [Hebrew].

"The Theory of Crisis and the Crisis in a Theory: Intellectual History in Twentieth-Century Middle Eastern Studies," in Israel Gershoni, Amy Singer, and Hakan Erdem (eds.), *Middle East Historiographies: Narrating the Twentieth Century* (Seattle, WA: University of Washington Press, 2006), pp. 131–182.

Gershoni, Israel, and James P. Jankowski, *Egypt, Islam and the Arabs* (Oxford: Oxford University Press, 1987).

Redefining Egyptian Nation, 1930–1945 (Cambridge: Cambridge University Press, 1995).

Gershoni, Israel, and Meir Hatina (eds.), *Narrating the Nile* (Boulder, CO: Lynne Rienner, 2008).

Ghurbal, M. Shafiq, "The Building-up of a Single Egyptian–Sudanese Fatherland in the 19th Century," in *The Unity of the Nile Valley*, pp. 61–75.

Gifford, Jayne. "Extracting the Best Deal for Britain: The Assassination of Sir Lee Stack in November 1924 and the Revision of Britain's Nile Valley Policy," *Canadian Journal of History*, 48:1, pp. 87–114.

Ginat, Rami, "British Concoction or Bilateral Decision? Revisiting the Genesis of Soviet–Egyptian Diplomatic Relations," *International Journal of Middle Eastern Studies*, 31 (1999), pp. 39–60.

"Egypt's Efforts to Unite the Nile Valley: Diplomacy and Propaganda, 1945–1947," *Middle Eastern Studies*, 43:2 (2007), pp. 193–222.

A History of Egyptian Communism: Jews and their Compatriots in Quest of Revolution (Boulder, CO: Lynne Rienner, 2011).

"India and the Palestine Question: The Emergence of the Asio-Arab Bloc and India's Quest for Hegemony in the Post-Colonial Third World," *Middle Eastern Studies*, 40/6 (November 2004), pp. 187–216.

"The Reopening of Gordon College: A Layer in the Anglo-Egyptian Struggle for Hegemony over the Building of the Sudanese Educational System, 1943–1946," in Ami Ayalon and David Wasserstein (eds.), *Madrasa: Education, State and Religion in the Middle East* (Tel Aviv: Dayan Center, 2005), pp. 217–239 [Hebrew].

The Soviet Union and Egypt, 1945–1955 (London: Frank Cass, 1993).

"Swimming against the Nationalist Current: The Egyptian Communists and the Unity of the Nile Valley", in Gershoni and Hatina (eds.), *Narrating the Nile*, pp. 67–90.

Syria and the Doctrine of Arab Neutralism (Brighton: Sussex Academic Press, 2005).

"Zramim dissidentim mitsriyyim miyamin umismol veshehelat ahdut 'emeq hanilus," *Hamizrah Hehadash*, 51 (2012), pp. 23–51.

Goldschmidt, Arthur Jr., *Modern Egypt, the Formation of a Nation State* (Boulder, CO: Westview Press, 2004).

Gordon, Joel, *Nasser's Blessed Movement* (New York and Oxford: Oxford University Press, 1992).

Griffiths, V. L., *An Experiment in Education: An Account of the Attempts to Improve the Lower Stages of Boy's Education in the Moslem Anglo–Egyptian Sudan, 1930–1950* (London: Longmans, 1953).

Hail, J. A., *Britain's Foreign Policy in Egypt and Sudan, 1947–1956* (Reading: Ithaca Press, 1996).

Hajj, al-Mu'tasim Ahmad al-, *Mu'jam shakhsiyyat mu'tamar al-khirrijin* (Umm Durman: Markaz Muhammad 'Umar Bashir lil-Dirasat al-Sudaniyya, 2009).

Hammadi, Mahmud, "al-'Ahd al-hadir huwa nuqtat al-du'f al-ra'isiyya fi al-qadiyya al-misriyya," *al-Jamahir*, 26 May 1947.

Hanes, William Travis, *Imperial Diplomacy in the Era of Decolonization: The Sudan and Anglo–Egyptian Relations, 1945–1956* (Westport, CT: Greenwood Press, 1995).

Hannawi, Muhammad 'Abd al-Hamid Ahmad, *Ma'rakat al-jala' wa-wahdat wadi al-nil, 1945–1954* (Cairo: al-Hay'a al-Misriyya al-'Amma lil-Kitab, 1998).

Hasan, Salim, "5000 Years of Unity," in *Egypt Sudan*, pp. 14–17.

Haykal, Muhammad Husayn, "Misr wa-matalibuha al-qawmiyya," *al-Ahram*, 4 January 1946.

Mudhakkirat fi al-siyasa al-misriyya, Part 3 (Cairo: Dar al-Ma'arif, 1990).

"No Basic Reason for Disagreement on the Sudan," in *Egypt Sudan*, p. 13.

Higham, John, "American Intellectual History: A Critical Appraisal," *American Quarterly*, 13/ 2 (Summer 1961), pp. 219–233.

"Intellectual History and its Neighbors," *Journal of the History of Ideas*, 15 (1954), pp. 339–347.

Holt, P. M., *A Modern History of the Sudan* (London: Weidenfeld and Nicolson, 1961).

Holt, P. M., and M. W. Daly, *A History of the Sudan from the Coming of Islam to the Present Day*, 6th ed. (London and New York: Routledge, 2011).

Hourani, Albert, *A History of the Arab Peoples* (Cambridge, MA: Harvard University Press, 1991).

Hurreiz, Sayed Hamid A., and Elfatih A. Abdel Salam (eds.), *Ethnicity, Conflict and National Integration in the Sudan* (Khartoum: Institute of Asian and African Studies, University of Khartoum, 1989).

Husayn, 'Abdallah, *al-Sudan min al-ta'rikh al-qadim 'ila' rihlat al-ba'tha al-misriyya*, 3 vols. (Cairo: al-Matba'a al-Rahmaniyya bi-Misr, 1935).

Husayn, Muhammad Amin, "Hawla qarar al-mu'tamar," *Umdurman*, 5 July 1945 and 21 July 1945.

"Kalimat umdurman," *Umdurman*, 31 March 1945 and 21 June 1945.

Huzayyin, Sulayman, "Rabitat al-jins wa-al-thaqafa fi wadi al-nil," *al-Katib al-Misri*, 6:21 (June 1947), pp. 228–242.

Ibrahim, Ahmad Abu Bakr, "Nasib al-sudan," *al-Risala*, No. 973, 25 February 1952, pp. 218–219.

Ibrahim, Hassan Ahmad, *Sayyid 'Abd al-Rahman al-Mahdi: A Study of Neo-Mahdism in the Sudan, 1899–1956* (Leiden: Brill, 2004).

Ismael, Tareq Y., and Rif'at al-Sa'id, *The Communist Movement in Egypt, 1920–1988* (New York: Syracuse University Press, 1990).

'Izz al-Din, Ahmad, *Mudhakkirat Mustafa al-nahhas: rub' qarn min al-siyasa fi Misr, 1927–1952* (Cairo: al-'Usur al-Jadida, 2000).

Jalal, Muhammad Mahmud, "al-Sudan," *al-Ikhwan al-Muslimun*, 4 October 1945, pp. 8–10.

Jawdat, al-Sayyid, "Wadi al-nil la yatajaza'u," *al-Ahram*, 27 October 1946.

Jaziri, Muhammad Ibrahim al-, *Athar al-za'im sa'd zaghlul and wizarat al-sha'b* (Cairo: Maktabat Madbuli, 1991).

Jindi, Muhammad Yusuf al-, "21 Fibrayir: dawr bariz lil-shuyu'iyyin al-misriyyin fi al-haraka al-wataniyya al-misriyya," *Qadaya Fikriyya*, July 1992, pp. 236–241.

Jumla, Muhammad Khalifa al-, "Ayna siyasatuna al-thabita lidaf' 'udwan al-injliz!?," *al-Balagh*, 1 December 1947, the Nile Valley Page.

"al-Baritaniyyuna yuwasiluna khida' hadha al-wadi," *al-Balagh*, 24 November 1947, the Nile Valley Page.

"Tahrir wadi al-nil la tuhaqqiquhu al-asalib al-diblumasiyya," *al-Balagh*, 4 November 1947.

Kamel, Mahmoud, "Documented Study on the Unity of the Nile Valley," *La Bourse Egyptienne*, 6 September 1948.

Kamil, 'Abd al-'Aziz, "Khitab maftuh min shimal al-wadi ila janubihi," *al-Ikhwan al-Muslimun*, 23 April 1946, pp. 6, 22.

Karar, Ali Salih, *The Sufi Brotherhoods in the Sudan* (London: Hurst, 1992).

Kedourie, Elie, *Politics in the Middle East* (Oxford and New York: Oxford University Press, 1992).

"The Transition from a British to an American Era in the Middle East," in Haim Shaked and Itamar Rabinovich (eds.), *The Middle East and the United States* (New Brunswick and London: Transactions Books, 1980), pp. 3–9.

Keita, Maghan, *Race and the Writing of History Riddling the Sphinx* (Oxford and New York: Oxford University Press, 2000).

Khalil, Khalil Hasan, "al-Tawajjuhat al-iqtisadiyya lil-haraka al-yasariyya fi misr," *Qadaya Fikriyya*, July 1996.

Khalil, Muhammad, *The Arab States and the Arab League: A Documentary Record* (Beirut: Khayats, 1962).

Khayr, Ahmad, *Kifah Jil: ta'rikh harakat al-Khirrijin wa-tatawwuriha fi al-Sudan* (Khartoum: al-Dar al-Sudaniyya lil-kutub, 2002).

Khiyyal, Sa'id, "Ila majlis al-amn," *al-Fajr al-Jadid*, No. 19, 30 January 1946, p. 11.

"Qadiyyatuna wa-majlis al-amn," *al-Fajr al-Jadid*, No. 27, 27 March 1946, p. 8.

Kimenyi, Mwangi S., and John Mukum Mkabu, "Turbulence in the Nile: Toward a consensual and sustainable allocation of the Nile River waters," the Brookings Institution (August 2010), at www.brookings.edu/~/media/research/files/reports/2010/8/nile%20river%20basin%20kimenyi/08_nile_river_basin_kimenyi.pdf (accessed 26 September 2013).

Lanfranchi, Sania Sharawi, *Casting off the Veil: The Life of Huda Shaarawi, Egypt's First Feminist* (London: I.B. Tauris, 2015).

Lawson, Fred H., "Reassessing Egypt's Foreign Policy during the 1920s and 1930s," in Arthur Goldschmidt, Amy J. Johnson, and Barak A. Salmoni (eds.), *Re-Envisioning Egypt 1919–1952* (Cairo: The American University in Cairo Press, 2005), pp. 46–67.

Lerman, Eran, "A Revolution Prefigured: Foreign Policy Orientations in the Postwar Years," in Shimon Shamir (ed.), *Egypt from Monarchy to Republic* (Boulder, CO: Westview Press, 1995), pp. 283–308.

Logan, Rayford Whittingham, "The Anglo–Egyptian Sudan: A Problem in International Relations," *The Journal of Negro History*, 16:4 (1931), pp. 371–381.

Macdonald, Robert W., *The League of Arab States* (Princeton, NJ: Princeton University Press, 1965).

MacMichael, A. H., *A History of the Arabs in the Sudan and Some Account of the People Who Preceded Them and of the Tribes Inhabiting Darfur*, 2 vols. (Cambridge: the University Press Publication, 1922).

Mahjub, 'Umar Bashari, *Ma'alim al-haraka al-wataniyya fi al-sudan* (Beirut: al-Maktaba al-Thaqafiyya, 1996).

Maqsus, al-Mijnah, "al-Lugha al-'arabiyya yuharibuha al-isti'mar," *al-Ikhwan al-Musliman*, 16 November 1946, p. 9.

"al-Madaris al-wataniyya shawka fi khalq al-isti'mar," *al-Ikhwan al-Muslimun*, 7 December 1946, p. 7.

Marlowe, John, *A History of Modern Egypt and Anglo–Egyptian Relations, 1800–1956*, 2nd ed. (Hamden, CT: Archon Books, 1965).

Marsot, Afaf Lutfi al-Sayyid, *Egypt's Liberal Experiment: 1922–1936* (Berkeley: University of California Press, 1977).

Marsot, Afaf Lutfi Sayyid, *Egypt and Cromer: A Study in Anglo–Egyptian Relations* (New York: Praeger, 1969).

Melucci, Alberto, *Nomads of the Present: Social Movements and Individual Needs in Contemporary Society*, ed. by John Keane and Paul Mier (London: Hutchinson, 1989).

Mills, David E., *Dividing the Nile: Egypt's Economic Nationalists in the Sudan 1918–1956* (Cairo and New York: the American University in Cairo Press, 2014).

Moore-Harell, Alise, *Gordon and the Sudan: Prologue to the Mahdiyya, 1877–1880* (London: Routledge, 2001).

Morgenthau, Hans J., *Politics among Nations*, Vol. 1 (Tel Aviv: Yachdav, 1968) [in Hebrew].

Mubarak, Ibrahim al-, "Mu'ahada 'arabiyya sudaniyya," *al-Risala*, No. 633, 30 August 1945, pp. 900–901.

Muhami, 'Ali 'Abd al-'Athim al-, "Ayyah maslaha li-misr wa-al-sudan fi qubul hadhihi al-sawdana alati tuhadidu wahdatahuma," *al-Balagh*, 5 June 1948.

"Madha fa'alna li-hadhihi al-haraka al-wataniyya al-mubaraka?," *al-Balagh*, 25 July 1948.

Mursi, Fu'ad, *Tatawwur al-ra'smaliyya wa-kifah al-tabaqat fi-misr* (Cairo: al-Maktaba al-Ishtirakiyya, 1992).

Nabawiy, Mahmud al-, "Kalimat *al-jamahir*," *al-Jamahir*, 12 May 1947.

"al-Qadiyya al-wataniyya," *al-Jamahir*, 26 May 1947.

Nahhas, Mustafa al-, "Min al-wafd al-misri ila abna' al-wadi wa-ra'is al-hukuma wa-al-safir al-baritani," *al-Ahram*, 21 September 1947.

Nazli, Salih Ahmad, *al-Dimuqratiyya wa-al-tarbiyya* (Cairo: Maktabat al-Anjlu al-Misriyya, 1979).

Neguib, Mohammed, *Egypt's Destiny* (London: Gollancz, 1955).

Nettl, J. P., "Ideas, Intellectuals and Structures of Dissent," in Philip Rieff (ed.), *On Intellectuals: Theoretical Studies, Case Studies* (Garden City, NY: Doubleday, 1969), pp. 53–122.

Okoth-Owiro, Arthur, "The Nile Treaty, State Succession and International Treaty Commitments: A Case Study of the Nile Water Treaties," *Occasional Papers, East Africa*, Konrad Adenauer Foundation, Nairobi, Kenia, 2004, at www.kas.de/wf/doc/kas_6306-544-1-30.pdf (accessed 26 September 2013).

Passmore Sanderson, Lilian, and Neville Sanderson, *Education, Religion and Politics in Southern Sudan 1899–1964* (London: Ithaca Press, 1981).

Porath, Yehoshua, *In Search of Arab Unity, 1930–1945* (London: Frank Cass, 1986).

Qasbi, Hamid al-, "al-Dhahab al-abyad – bughyat al-injliz min al-sudan," *al-Balagh*, 23 June 1951.

Qutb, Sayyid, "Bidayat al-nihaya," *al-Risala*, No. 970, 4 February 1952, pp. 125–126.

"Nar wa-dam," *al-Risala*, No. 968, 21 January 1952, pp. 69–71.

Ra'fat, Wahid, "Misr wa-al-sudan – Yajib an yattafiqa abna' wadi al-nil fima baynahum awalan," *al-Ahram*, 21 April 1946, pp. 3, 5.

Rafi'i, 'Abd al-Rahman al-, *Fi a'qab al-thawra al-misriyya – Thawrat 1919*, 3 vols. (Cairo: Dar al-Ma'arif, 1989).

Misr wa-al-sudan fi awa'il 'ahd al-ihtilal (Cairo: Sharikat Maktabat wa-Matba'at Mustafa al-Babi al-Halabi wa-Awladihi bi-Misr, 1942).

Raflah, Filib and Farid 'Izz al-Din, *Al-'Alaqat al-ta'rikhiyya wa-al-iqtisadiyya bayna al-jumhuriyya al-'arabiyya al-muttahida wa-al-sudan* (Cairo: Maktabat al-Anjlu al-Misriyya, 1965).

Ramadan, 'Abd al-'Azim Muhammad Ibrahim, *Misr wa al-harb al-'alamiyya al-thaniyya: Ma'rakat tajnibu misr wa-yalat al-harb* (Cairo: al-Hay'a al-Misriyya al-'Amma lil-Kitab, 1998).

Tatawwur al-haraka al-wataniyya fi misr min 1918 ila 1936 (Cairo: Maktabat al-Madbuli, 1983).

Tatawwur al-haraka al-wataniyya fi misr min sanat 1937 ila sana 1948, 2 vols. (Beirut: al-Watan al-'Arabi, 1973).

Thawrat 1919 fi daw' mudhakkirat sa'd zaghlul (Cairo: al-Hay'a al-Misriyya al-'Amma lil-Kitab, 2002).

Ramzi, Ahmad, "'Urubat mamlakat wadi al-nil," *al-'Alam al-'Arabi*, 10 March 1948, pp. 27–35.

Reid, Donald M., *Cairo University and the Making of Modern Egypt* (Cambridge: Cambridge University Press, 1990).

Rif'at, Muhammad, and Ahmad Muhammad Hasuna, *Ma'alim ta'rikh al-'usur al-wusta* (Cairo: Dar al-Ma'arif, 1947).

Rif'at, Muhammad, "Misr wa-al-sudan," *al-Katib al-Misri*, 6:21 (June 1947), pp. 22–36.

Rizq, Yunan Labib, *Qadiyyat wahdat wadi al-nil bayna al-mu'ahada wa taghyir al-waqi' al-isti'mari, 1936–1946* (Cairo: Jami'at al-Duwal al-'Arabiyya, 1975).

Sa'd, Ahmad Sadiq, "Wahadha sawt misr al-fatat," *al-Fajr al-Jadid*, 16 September 1945.

"Mu'ahadat 1936 limadha nunadi bi-ilgha'iha," *al-Fajr al-Jadid*, 27 March 1946.

Sa'id, Rif'at al-, *al-Yasar al-misri, 1925–1940* (Beirut: Dar al-Tali'a lil-Taba'a wa-al-Nashr, 1972).

Ta'arikh al-haraka al-ishtirakiyya fi misr 1900–1925, 5th ed. (Cairo: Dar al-Thaqafa al-Jadida, 1981).

Ta'rikh al-munazzamat al-yasariyya al-misriyya, 1940–1950 (Cairo: Dar al-Thaqafa al-Jadida, 1976).

Sabri, al-Sayyid, "Hawla ta'yin khalaf li-hakim al-sudan," *al-Ahram*, 17 March 1947.

Sabry, Hussein Zulfakar, *Sovereignty for Sudan* (London: Ithaca Press, 1982).

Said, Edward W., *Culture and Imperialism* (London: Wingate Books, 1994).

Representations of the Intellectual: The 1993 Reith Lectures (New York: Vintage Books, A Division of Random House, 1996), at www.mohamedrabeea.com/books/book1_10178.pdf (accessed 18 October 2016).

Salih, Mahjub Muhammad, *al-Sihafa al-sudaniyya fi nisf qarn 1903–1953*, Vol. 1 (Khartoum: Jami'at al-Khartum, 1971).

Salim, Salah, "Lastum mamnu'ina min al-radd ayyuha al-zu'ama'," *Ruz al-Yusuf*, No. 1286, 2 February 1953.

"Nahnu natahadda al-injliz min ajlikum," *Ruz al-Yusuf*, No. 1294, 30 March 1953.

Saville, J., *The Politics of Continuity: British Foreign Policy and the Labour Government 1945–51* (London: Verso, 1993).

Sayfi, 'Abd al-Hafiz al-, "Ajal: al-sudan lil-sudaniyyin," *al-Ikhwan al-Muslimun*, 20 September 1945, p. 15.

Sayyid-Marsot, Afaf Lutfi, *Egypt and Cromer: A Study in Anglo-Egyptian Relations* (New York: Praeger, 1969).

Egypt in the Reign of Muhammad Ali (Cambridge: Cambridge University Press, 1994).

Seligman, C. G., "Some Aspects of the Hamitic Problem in the Anglo-Egyptian Sudan," *The Journal of the Royal Anthropological Institute of Great Britain and Ireland*, 43 (1913), pp. 593–705.

Seligman, C. G., and B. Z. Seligman, *Pagan Tribes of the Nilotic Sudan* (London: George Routledge and Sons, 1932).

Seligman, C. G., *Races of Africa* (London: Home University Library, 1939).

Seri-Hersch, Iris, "Towards social progress and post-imperial modernity? Colonial politics of literacy in the Anglo-Egyptian Sudan, 1946–1956," *History of Education*, 40:3 (2011), pp. 333–356.

Shah, Tushaar, *Taming the Anarchy: Groundwater Governance in South Asia* (Washington DC: Resources for the Future, 2009).

Shakir, Mahmud Muhammad, "Hadhihi biladuna," *al-Risala*, No. 732, 14 July 1947, pp. 777–779.

"'Ibar liman ya'tabiru," *al-Risala*, No. 738, 25 August 1947, pp. 915–916.

"Innahu jihad la siyasa!," *al-Risala*, No. 714, 10 March 1947, pp. 271–273.

"al-Khiyana al-'uthma … !," *al-Risala*, No. 714, 24 March 1947, pp. 327–330.

"La tudabiru ayyuha al-rijal," *al-Risala*, No. 712, 24 February 1947, pp. 318–320.

"Misr hiya al-sudan," *al-Risala*, No. 708, 27 January 1947, pp. 104–106.

"Mu'tamar al-mustad'afina," *al-Risala*, No. 742, 22 September 1947, p. 1028–1030.

"Sha'b wahid, wa-qadiyya wahida!," *al-Risala*, No. 730, 30 June 1947, pp. 722–725.

Shami, Salah al-Din al-, *al-Mawani al-sudaniyya: dirasa fi al-jughrafiyya al-ta'rikhiyya* (Cairo: Maktabat Misr, 1961).

Sharkey, Heather J., *Living with Colonialism: Nationalism and Culture in the Anglo-Egyptian Sudan* (Berkeley: University of California Press, 2003).

Shils, Edward, "Intellectuals," in David L. Sills (ed.), *International Encyclopedia of the Social Sciences*, Vol. 7 (New York: Macmillan Company, 1968), pp. 399–415.

Shirazi, Marsil, *Awraq munadil 'itali fi misr* (Cairo: Dar al-'Alam al-Thalith, 2002)

Shukri, Muhammad Fu'ad, *al-Hukm al-misri fi al-sudan 1820–1885* (Cairo: Dar al-Fikr al-'Arabi, 1947).

Misr wa-al-siyada 'ala al-sudan: al-wad' al-ta'rikhi lil-mas'ala (Cairo: Dar al-Fikr al-'Arabi, 1946).

Misr wa-al-sudan: ta'rikh wahdat wadi al-nil al-siyasiyya fi al-qarn al-tasi' 'ashir, 3rd ed. (Cairo: Dar al-Ma'arif bi-Misr, 1963).

Sidqi, Isma'il, *Mudhakkirati* (Cairo: Dar al-Hilal, 1950).

Skinner, Quentin, "Meaning and Understanding in the History of Ideas," *History and Theory*, 8 (1969), pp. 3–53.

Smith, Charles D., "The Intellectual and Modernization: Definitions and Reconsiderations, the Egyptian Experience," *Comparative Studies in Society and History*, 22 (1980), pp. 513–533.

Snailham, Richard, "Europeans on the Blue Nile," *The Anglo-Ethiopian Society* (1992), at www.anglo-ethiopian.org/publications/articles.php?type=O&reference=publications/occasionalpapers/papers/europeansbluenile.php (accessed 15 January 2016).

Sudani, 'Amir Hamadi al-, "Kifah mushtarak didda 'adu mushtarak," *al-Fajr al-Jadid*, 7 May 1946.

Tayeb, Salah El Din El Zein El, *The Students' Movement in the Sudan* (Khartoum: Khartoum University Press, 1971).

Thabit, Husayn, "Tijarat al-sudan al-kharijiyya," *al-Ikhwan al-Muslimun*, 2 April 1946, pp 8–9.

Tignor, Robert, *Egypt: A Short History* (Princeton, NJ.: Princeton University Press, 2011).

Tripp, C. R. H., "Sudan: State and Elite," *Africa* 67:1 (1977), p. 159–173.

Troutt Powell, Eve, "Brothers along the Nile: Egyptian Concepts of Race and Ethnicity, 1895–1910," in Erlich and Gershoni (eds.), *The Nile*, pp. 171–182.

A Different Shade of Colonialism: Egypt, Great Britain, and the Mastery of the Sudan (Berkeley: University of California Press, 2003).

Tusun, 'Umar, *Misr wa-al-sudan* (al-Iskandariyya: Matba'at al-'Adl, n.d.).

'Uthman, Muhammad Fathi, "Hadhihi 'aqibat al-futur," *al-Ikhwan al-Muslimun*, 30 October 1948, p. 7.

'Uthman, Taha Sa'd, "al-Amana al-qawmiyya," *al-Damir*, No. 272, 3 October 1945.

Vatikiotis, P. J., *The History of Modern Egypt from Muhammad Ali to Mubarak* (London: Weidenfeld and Nicolson, 1991).

Voll, John O., "Unity of the Nile Valley: Identity and Regional Integration," *Journal of African Studies*, 3:2 (Summer 1976), pp. 205–228.

"US Policy toward the Unity of the Nile Valley, 1945–1952," in Gershoni and Hatina (eds.), *Narrating the Nile*, pp. 91–112.

Voll, John O., and Sarah P. Voll, *The Sudan: Unity and Diversity in a Multicultural State* (Boulder, CO: Westview Press, 1985).

Warburg, Gabriel, "The Condominium Revisited: The Anglo-Egyptian Sudan 1934–1956: A Review Article," *Bulletin of the School of Oriental and African Studies*, 56/1 (February 1993), pp. 1–12.

Historical Discord in the Nile Valley (Evanston, IL: Northwestern University Press, 1992).

Islam, Nationalism and Communism in a Traditional Society: The Case of Sudan (London: Frank Cass, 1978).

Islam, Sectarianism and Politics in Sudan since the Mahdiyya (London: Hurst & Co., 2003).

Waterbury, John, *Hydropolitics of the Nile Valley* (New York: Syracuse University Press, 1979).

Welter, Rush, "The History of Ideas in America: An Essay in Redefinition," in Robert Meredith (ed.), *American Studies: Essays on Theory and Methods* (Columbus, OH: Charles E. Merrill, 1968), pp. 236–253.

Wichhart, Stefanie Katharine, "Intervention: Britain, Egypt and Iraq during World War II" (PhD Dissertation, University of Texas at Austin, 2007).

Wilner, Alex, and C J Dubouloz, "Homegrown Terrorism and Transformative Learning: An Interdisciplinary Approach to Understanding Radicalization," *Global Change Peace and Security* 22:1 (2010), pp. 33–51.

Wittfogel, Karl, *Oriental Despotism: A Critical Study of Total Power* (Oxford: Oxford University Press, 1957).

Woodward, Peter, *Condominium and Sudanese Nationalism* (London: Rex Collings, 1979).

The Horn of Africa: Politics and International Relations (London: I.B. Tauris, 2003).

"Sudan: Political Transitions Past and Present," Sir William Luce Fellowship Paper No. 9, Durham Middle East Papers No. 83 (September 2008), pp. 1–14.

Wright, Gordon, "Contemporary History in the Contemporary Age," in Charles F. Delzell (ed.), *The Future of History* (Nashville: Vanderbilt University Press, 1977), pp. 219–230.

Zahir, Riyad, *al-Sudan al-mu'asir: mundhu al-fath al-misri hatta al-istiqlal 1821–1953* (Cairo: Maktabat al-Anjlu al-Misriyya, 1966).

Zald, M., and J. McCarthy, *Social Movements in an Organizational Society* (New Brunswick, NJ: Transaction Books, 1987).

Zamir, Meir, *The Secret Anglo-French War in the Middle East: Intelligence and Decolonization, 1940–1948* (London: Routledge, 2014).

Zayyat, Ahmad Hasan al-, "Ila ikhwatina fi a'ali al-wadi," *al-Risala*, No. 706, 13 January1947.

"Nihayat ma'sah," *al-Risala*, No. 956, 29 October 1951, p. 1.

Zuruq, Hasan al-Tahir, "Mashru' al-sawdana – wa-limadha yata'ajjalu al-jnjliz ibramahu," *al-Balagh*, 12 June 1948.

Index